The Right Kind of History

SMYTHE LIBRARY

Stamp this label with the date for return.
Contact the Librarian if you wish to renew this book.

- 1 MAR 2012		

D0300473

The Right Kind of History
Teaching the Past in Twentieth-Century England

David Cannadine
Dodge Professor of History, Princeton University, USA

Jenny Keating
Research Fellow, Institute of Historical Research, University of London, UK

Nicola Sheldon
Research Fellow, Institute of Historical Research, University of London, UK

palgrave
macmillan

First published 2011 by
PALGRAVE MACMILLAN

Palgrave Macmillan in the UK is an imprint of Macmillan Publishers Limited, registered in England, company number 785998, of Houndmills, Basingstoke, Hampshire RG21 6XS.

Palgrave Macmillan in the US is a division of St Martin's Press LLC, 175 Fifth Avenue, New York, NY 10010.

Palgrave Macmillan is the global academic imprint of the above companies and has companies and representatives throughout the world.

Palgrave® and Macmillan® are registered trademarks in the United States, the United Kingdom, Europe and other countries

ISBN-13: 978-0-230-30086-6   hardback
ISBN-13: 978-0-230-30087-3   paperback

This book is printed on paper suitable for recycling and made from fully managed and sustained forest sources. Logging, pulping and manufacturing processes are expected to conform to the environmental regulations of the country of origin.

A catalogue record for this book is available from the British Library.

A catalog record for this book is available from the Library of Congress.

10 9 8 7 6 5 4 3 2 1
20 19 18 17 16 15 14 13 12 11

Printed and bound in Great Britain by
CPI Antony Rowe, Chippenham and Eastbourne

907
N 68L00P

To history teachers:
past, present – and future

A comprehensive survey of the place of history in ... education is a necessary thing, and its publication when completed is essential to secure the progress required, but these are ends to aim at, not points to start from.

(The National Archives: ED 24/1680: C.H. Firth to H.A.L. Fisher, 15 June 1919.)

Courses of study are inflicted by one generation, not on itself but on its successors, and it is only fair to wait till the victims have come in their turn to speak. They have a disagreeable way of siding with their grandparents.

(M. Sadler, 'National Education and Social Ideals', in R.D. Roberts (ed.), *Education in the Nineteenth Century* (London, 1901), p. 214.)

Contents

List of Illustrations   ix
Acknowledgements   xi

Introduction: Themes and Problems   1
  Nation and Schools   3
  Teachers and Teaching   7
  Pupils and Numbers   11
  Curriculum – and Qualifications   15

1. History Goes to School, 1900–18   18
    The Government Suggests and Recommends   20
    First Thoughts on Teaching History   30
    Teachers and Resources for History   40
    History in the Classroom   47
    History Goes to War   55

2. History in Peace and War, 1918–44   61
    The State and the Schools   63
    Prescribing History for Peacetime   70
    History Teaching in Theory and in Practice   77
    History Inspected, Remembered and Examined   85
    History Goes to War – Again   97

3. History and the Welfare State, 1944–64   102
    The Butler Act and Beyond   104
    History Justified, Encouraged and Examined   111
    More Teachers and More Technology   117
    History Assessed and Recollected   125
    School History at Empire's End   137

4. History for a Nation 'In Decline', 1964–79 140
   The Comprehensive Revolution 142
   History for the Comprehensive Classroom 148
   New Teaching for New Schools 156
   History Remembered and Examined 166
   Towards a National Curriculum? 178

5. History in the National Curriculum, 1979–2010 181
   A Counter-Revolution in Education? 184
   The GCSE and the National Curriculum 192
   Classroom History across Two Millennia 202
   History is Now and is England 215

Conclusion: Perspectives and Suggestions 219
   Government, Politics, Education and History 221
   Continuity and Change in History Teaching 227
   History, the Curriculum and the Classroom Future 232

Appendixes: 239
   A. Names of Interviewees 240
   B. Names of Lenders and Donors 243
   C. School Certificate Examinations in History in 1923 244
   D. History Syllabuses from the 1970s Onwards 246
   E. History Examination Candidates and Results, 1919–2010 251
   F. Principal Education Ministers, 1900–2010 255
   G. The History in Education Website 257

List of Abbreviations 258
A Note on Sources 259
Notes 260
Index 295

List of Illustrations

1. Infants class, Lavender Hill School, SW London c1925
   or 1926 (courtesy of John Geddes who is standing on
   far left)   84
2. Time chart in exercise book from Bermondsey Central
   Technical School, c1935 (courtesy of Norman Roper)   91
3. Exercise book showing use of illustrative material
   including cigarette cards, Westborough Senior Girls'
   School, Southend, c1935 (courtesy of Irene Eaton)   92
4. Revision list from exercise book, Raine's Foundation
   School for Boys, East London c1939 (courtesy of
   Kenneth Kelsey)   93
5. Empire Day at Mauldeth Road Primary School,
   Manchester, c1938 or 1939 (courtesy of Enid Deeble
   who is 'England' second from the left)   96
6. Exercise book showing topics studied in the early 1950s;
   some grammar schools did topic work in the first and
   second year, Minchinden Grammar School, North
   London, c1950 (courtesy of Monica Wafford)   114
7. A first-year grammar school pupil's notes on
   'Alfred the Great', Morecambe Grammar School, 1961
   (courtesy of Ian Colwill)   133
8. The dismantling of the British Empire coincided with an
   increase in the teaching of the nineteenth century and
   emphasis on such episodes as the 'Scramble for Africa',
   Littlehampton Comprehensive School, 1977 (courtesy of
   Julie Johnson)   153
9. A 'Timeline of Me', from third-year history at
   Islington Green School, 1979, shows the influence
   of 'child-centred' history teaching – in contrast to the
   1930s time chart in Fig. 2 (courtesy of Charlotte Crow)   158

10. The vivid experience of a history trip to Warwick
    Castle in 1977, as recorded in a seven-year-old pupil's
    exercise book (courtesy of Jillian Andrews)   167
11. The results of a pupil's 'investigation' into the burial
    mounds at Sutton Hoo, showing how Anglo-Saxon
    kingship was taught via 'new history' methods, in
    contrast to the traditional treatment in Fig. 7, Islington
    Green School, 1980 (courtesy of Charlotte Crow)   174
12. A pupil's work on the French Revolution, taught in Year 8
    of the National Curriculum, from a comprehensive
    school in the north-east of England, 1996 (courtesy of
    anonymous donor)   207

Acknowledgements

This book is the result of a two-and-a-half-year research project, entitled History in Education, investigating the teaching of history in English state schools from the early twentieth century to the present day, and our first and most grateful thanks are to the Linbury Trust, which generously funded two research fellows and also made possible the establishment of an extensive oral history archive. Throughout its existence, the project has been based at the Institute of Historical Research at the University of London, and we are deeply grateful to its Director, Miles Taylor, for his constant support and encouragement; to Martin Steer, who has worked so hard to establish our website; to Jane Winters for unfailing assistance and advice; to Elaine Walters, who has dealt patiently with our many queries; and to Hardip Syan Singh, who photocopied numerous documents for us. We are much indebted to the Friends of the IHR who provided funding for the recording equipment for the oral history interviews, and also for the set-up and continuing costs of the website which will offer online access to the project's interviews, source materials and background papers at: http://www.history.ac.uk/history-in-education.

Throughout our researches, we made continual use of the libraries and archives at the University of London Senate House and at the Institute of Education, and we are most grateful to their staff for all their help. We would also like to thank the staff at the London Metropolitan Archives, the National Archives, the Bodleian Library, the British Library, Birmingham City Library and Archives, the BBC Written Archives Centre, the Historical Association (both its Kennington headquarters and the University of Nottingham Manuscript and Special Collections which holds its archives), the Mass Observation Archive at the University of Sussex, Cambridge Assessment Archives, the AQA (Assessment and Qualifications Alliance) archives at the University of Surrey, the Geffrye Museum, the University of Reading

Archive of British Publishing and Printing, the East Sussex Record Office, the British Schools Museum, Hitchin, the History of Education Project Outdated Textbook Collection, Durham and the Brotherton Library Special Collections and Museum of the History of Education, both at the University of Leeds.

Formal records of history teaching were for the most part sparse, especially when we wanted to discover what happened at the level of individual classrooms, and we have been greatly helped in our search for them by many people currently involved in the teaching and support of history in schools. We would like to mention in particular the assistance given by Rebecca Sullivan of the Historical Association, and by Michael Riley of the Schools History Project, both of whom provided us with materials, linked us up to key individuals, and welcomed us at their conferences to publicize our work in its early stages. We would also like to thank the members of HTEN (History Teacher Education Network), HEIRNet (History Educators International Research Network), the Midlands History Forum and the History of Education Society (UK) whose gatherings gave us additional opportunities to present some preliminary findings, and we are grateful for the many helpful comments and suggestions that we received on these occasions.

We are also indebted to many people who shared their expertise with us and helped to broaden our knowledge and understanding of history teaching in the past: Richard Aldrich, Jim Belben, Patrick Brindle, Hester Barron, Gordon Batho, Andy Beer, Ray Barker, Paul Bracey, Ruth Bromley, Arthur Chapman, Anna Claydon, Ian Colwill, Tina Corri, Peter Cunningham, Adrian Elliott, John Elliott, Ian Fell, Stuart Foster, Jerome Freeman, Phil Gardner, Ian Grosvenor, Robert Guyver, Val Gwynn, Tristram Hunt, Chris Husbands, Terry Haydn, Fiona Kisby, Alison Kitson, Christine Lalumia, Sean Lang, Helen McCarthy, Amira Mekaouar, Kate Moorse, Rob Perks, Veronica Persey, Alice Prochaska, Richard Race, John Robottom, Richard Roberts, Ron Rooney, Jean Seaton, John T. Smith, Mary Stewart, Barbara Taylor, Pat Thane, Ben Walsh, Simon Woolley, Brian Wright and Bridget Yates. Nicola Sheldon and Jenny Keating both attended oral history training courses led by Anna Davin and Michael Kandiah at the Institute of Historical Research, which helped to develop their perceptions of the issues and skills involved in interviewing for historical research.

The creation of an oral history archive presented challenges, for how would we find potential interviewees? The conferences where history teachers gathered were a useful source, and the Historical Association circulated its members widely. We are also grateful to the editors of *Veterans News* (J. Sainsbury plc), to *Saga Magazine*, and to the *Daily Mail*, who gave us space on their pages to describe our project and elicit public response, as a result of which we received 335 completed survey forms, many of them very detailed and full of reminiscences about school history in the past, and we would like to thank those who took the time and trouble to fill them in. Some people also sent us their old history exercise books, which we were able to photograph and which will be reproduced on the website, and some former teachers gave us materials which were very useful for our research. We would also like to thank all those who agreed to be interviewed, whose names are listed in Appendix A, and those who provided us with information, directly, or via informal discussions, or by pointing us to others who might help.

The writing of this book has been a collaborative effort, but with clear boundaries of responsibility. Jenny Keating researched and wrote up all the material for the period 1900–65 and Nicola Sheldon did the same for the years 1965–2010. Both were involved in devising the survey forms for pupils and teachers, in evaluating the responses, and in carrying out the recorded interviews. As director of the project, David Cannadine was in overall charge of formulating the questions and setting the research strategy, and he has written this book. We are deeply grateful to our publishers Palgrave Macmillan, especially Ruth Ireland for co-ordinating the whole process, and to Ray Addicott for seeing the book through the press. Naturally the views expressed on these pages and on our website are our own, and none of those who offered help and information are responsible for any of our opinions or conclusions. With this project now completed, we offer this book as both a pioneering account of how history has been taught in English schools across the past one hundred years, and also in the belief that it will make an important contribution to the current debates about the place of history in the school curriculum, and thus in our national life.

David Cannadine
Jenny Keating
Nicola Sheldon

Introduction: Themes and Problems

There is so much that is peculiar to the teaching of history.
(James Bryce, *On The Teaching of History in Schools*
(Historical Association, leaflet no. 4, London, 1907), p. 2.)

In 2010, urged on by Vladimir Putin, the Kremlin authorities instructed a group of academics to draw up a new school textbook to present an approved version of Russian history. Putin wanted them to play down the excesses of the Communist regime, and to stress the heroic achievements of the Russian people in defeating Hitler, with the intention of building a new national identity on the basis of a selective, uplifting national narrative. As one party functionary explained, 'we understand that school is a unique social institution that forms all citizens', which meant it was essential they should be taught history, and especially what was deemed by the authorities to be the right kind of history. 'We need a united society', the apparatchik went on, and to achieve that end, 'we need a united [history] textbook'.[1] This was not the first time that such an enterprise had been undertaken at the behest of Soviet Moscow: in 1934, Joseph Stalin had convened an earlier meeting of historians to discuss the same issue, namely the correct teaching of Russian history in Russian schools. He disapproved of the conventional accounts then available, which were strongly influenced by Marxist theories and doctrines, and which traced the development of Russia from feudalism to capitalism and beyond. 'These textbooks', Stalin thundered, 'aren't good for anything. It's all epochs and no facts, no events, no people, no concrete information.' 'History', he concluded, 'must be history', by which he meant a triumphant cavalcade of national heroes, which would appeal more broadly to the Russian people than the arid and arcane abstractions of class analysis and social structure.[2]

Such disagreements about what constitutes the national past, and what version of it should be taught in the nation's schools, are not confined to dictatorships. In the 1990s, the Australian Prime Minister,

1

John Howard, deplored the 'black-armband' version of his country's history, stressing the genocide of the aborigines and the expropriation of their lands, which had become popular in recent years, and which seemed to conservatives like him to be too negative and guilt-ridden, and to neglect the heroic, creative and admirable aspects of Australia's past. The resulting furore, drawing in academics, politicians and the media, was known as Australia's 'history wars', and it showed how much disagreement there was about the national past, and the version of it that should be taught in schools.[3] In the United States, a similar controversy erupted early in 2010 among the members of the Texas Board of Education. Conservative activists wanted a drastic rewriting of what they regarded as the unpatriotic and mistaken history syllabus taught in state schools, so as to stress instead that the founding fathers of the United States, and the authors of its constitution, intended America to be a Christian nation, rather than one upholding the principle of the separation of the church and state. They were equally determined that greater attention should be given to Ronald Reagan, as the architect of the national revival and the victor of the Cold War, and to such key organizations as the Heritage Foundation and the National Rifle Association. And they sought to change the history textbooks as well as the history syllabus, by applying direct pressure on publishing companies, for whom Texas was an important market.[4]

In democracies as well as dictatorships, there has been, and still is, serious disagreement about the right kind of history to be taught in schools. When one authoritarian ruler is replaced by another, the national history is rewritten and updated, by taking some subjects out, and putting others in. When a dictatorial regime is overthrown, and is superseded by democracy, the national narrative is again reworked and redirected: in the case of Argentina, after the fall of the military, away from heroic and martial patriotism, towards the successful battle for freedom; and in the case of South Africa, once apartheid was vanquished, away from a celebration of Afrikaner nationalism, towards a more inclusive and multi-racial account of the national past.[5] But as the examples of Australia and Texas suggest, even in countries with (in recent times) settled constitutions, but with vexed and contentious histories, there can be deep divisions about the national past, which make it extremely difficult to come up with any agreed national narrative – or agreed history syllabus. Since the 1980s, the history of India has become a bitter battle-ground between

Hindu fundamentalists, who present it as an essentially nationalist, exclusionary and religious narrative, and those who urge that India's history is one of tolerance, inclusivity and peaceful co-existence between creeds, as embodied in the country's secular constitution.[6] And in such nations as France and Germany, Belgium and the Netherlands, Canada and Japan, there have been deep and bitter disagreements about the nature of the national narrative, the role of dissenting voices, the barely-acknowledged histories of wartime, the existence of a national canon, and so forth.[7]

These often wrenching disagreements may seem a long way from the less contested and more tranquil trajectory of our own past, which by comparison seems a model of ordered continuity and stable and consensual progress. Since 1688, there have been no revolutions and no dictators, no foreign invasions and no civil wars; and since 1782 there have been no military defeats that have threatened our national security let alone our national survival. The searing traumas that have characterized the histories of so many countries during the last 300 years seem to have been mercifully absent, as our nation has gradually and uninterruptedly evolved towards constitutional monarchy, stable democracy and full adult suffrage. Yet from the beginning of the twentieth century, when history first became a significant part of the curriculum in our state schools, there has been almost continuous controversy: about why history should be taught, about what sort of history should be taught, about how much history should be taught, about to whom history should be taught, about how history should be taught, and about how well history was being taught. Today's debates, then, are merely the latest instalment in a century-long dispute that is as old as the teaching of history itself. Our study breaks new ground by exploring history as taught and as experienced in the classroom since the early 1900s, and the controversies that have so often accompanied it. In so doing, we shall place today's disagreements in a broader context and longer perspective, and we will show that many arguments recently put forward, as if new and original insights, are but the latest iteration of long-held positions and entrenched viewpoints.

Nation and Schools

Our aim is to give history in the twentieth-century classroom the sort of many-layered, multi-dimensional treatment that does full justice to its 'elaborate, intricate involvement with the rest of society, and notes its shifting functions, meanings and purposes'.[8] In geographical and governmental terms, our concern is with *England* – because England is a sufficient area and complex unit of administration, and to extend our study to the whole of the British Isles (before 1922), and the United Kingdom of Great Britain and Northern Ireland (thereafter), would make it unwieldy and unmanageable. Such a larger-scale inquiry needs to be undertaken; but until work has been done on each of the 'four nations', the time is not yet ripe for a pan-British study; and by dealing in detail with England, we hope to encourage and provoke others to launch equivalent inquiries for Wales, Scotland and (Northern) Ireland, which would form the building blocks for a larger survey.[9] A second reason for focusing on England is that history teaching has always differed across the constituent nations of the United Kingdom. Wales was joined to twentieth-century England until devolution in 1997, but schooling and teaching were organized differently and examined locally.[10] Once the Scottish Office was established in 1885, education was separately administered north of the border, and the same was true after the Act of Union of 1801 for both pre- and post-partition Ireland. And once Northern Ireland was created, the divisions between Catholic and Protestant schools resulted in the teaching of very different versions of the Irish past, in a divisive, antagonistic and confrontational manner that (happily) has no equivalent in the twentieth-century English experience.[11]

The essential starting point for our inquiry, as for any subject taught in English schools, is the structure of power and control, funding and accountability at central and local levels of government. In 1900, the Board of Education was established as the body responsible for overseeing schooling (as well as universities) in England, and the politician in charge was designated President; in 1944, the Board was upgraded into the Ministry of Education, in recognition of its enhanced importance under R.A. Butler; and 20 years later it was expanded and re-branded as the Department of Education and Science. Since then, it has undergone many changes in its name and remit: as the Department for Education (1992–95), the Department for Education and Employment (1995–2001), the Department for Education and Skills (2001–07), the Department for Children, Schools and Families (2007–10), and (again) the Department for Education (since 2010). Across the period from 1900 to 2010, there have been

55 changes at the very top, as presidents, ministers and secretaries of state have come and gone on average at two-yearly intervals. Some of them, who were in power for even shorter periods, were minor figures of deserved obscurity; a few occupied the office for substantially more than two years, which increased (but did not guarantee) their chances of making an impact; and one of their number went on to become very famous, namely Margaret Thatcher who, as Minister of Education during Edward Heath's government of 1970–74, obtained her only experience of high office there before later becoming Prime Minister.

Since most ministers have only been briefly in charge of education, and since their remit has included primary, secondary and (until 2007) further and higher education, the time they have been able to give to the teaching of history (or any other subject) in schools has been extremely limited; and the same has been true of the senior civil servants on whom ministers rely, especially their permanent secretaries. Like their political masters, they have had many other things to do in addition to being concerned about history in primary and secondary schools. But they usually served for longer terms than presidents, ministers, or secretaries of state; there have been only 19 of them since 1900, which means an average tenure of more than five years; some of them spent the whole of their lives in the same department; and one or two were extremely influential. Working for these successively named government departments have been His (or Her) Majesty's Inspectors of Schools (hereafter HMIs), who until the 1980s were the main point of contact between the politicians and civil servants in Westminster and Whitehall, and the primary and secondary schools across England; and their reports on how history was taught in the classroom provide one of our major sources.[12] Until the early 1980s, the official records as they relate to ministers, mandarins and inspectors are abundant and available; and for the subsequent period, when the documents are closed, we have conducted interviews with former ministers, civil servants and school inspectors, whose recollections go back to the 1980s and before.[13]

The influence of Westminster and Whitehall on the organization, administration and funding of English schools (and on the history taught in them) is undeniable; and measures such as the Balfour Education Act of 1902, the Butler Education Act of 1944, and the Education Reform Act of 1988 fundamentally changed state schools and state schooling. But between these relatively infrequent interventions from the centre, education was generally left in the hands of local authorities (who built and funded the schools), and heads and teachers (who decided what was to be taught). In education as in health and policing, a careful balance was struck between central and local power; and with schools as with hospitals and county constabularies, most important decisions were taken locally, and every effort was made to shield them from centralized political interference. Before the 1980s, no government claimed the right to prescribe a national curriculum – for history or for anything else. These were decentralized matters, which meant that for much of the time (and indeed still today), there was a significant gap between what the politicians and the civil servants wished schools to teach, and what they were actually doing. Ministers could suggest; permanent officials could outline; Inspectors could report: but their power to influence what went on in particular localities, specific schools and individual classrooms was rarely all that great. So decentralized was educational power by European standards that before the 1980s, ministers of education could scarcely have implemented a national 'educational policy' even if they had wanted to do so.[14]

Our concern is with the teaching of history in those English schools over which both central and local government exercised some degree of control, and which have been wholly or partially funded by the state. We do not deal with long-established preparatory or public schools (such as Eton and Harrow), nor those that have come into being during the twentieth century (such as Stowe, Bryanston and Benenden). These private, independent, self-governing schools have always stood outside the state-funded system; and they have only ever educated a small minority of those of school age. Across the twentieth century, the proportion of English boys and girls educated in private schools has fluctuated at between 5 per cent and 10 per cent, which means that the overwhelming majority of England's boys and girls have always received their education in the state sector.[15] It is tempting to describe state education in England as a 'system' or a 'sector'; but it has always been so varied and differentiated that such words scarcely apply, and we shall be looking at pupils of all ages, and at the history they were taught in schools of all types: in what were termed 'voluntary' and 'maintained' schools; in elementary and primary schools in villages, towns and cities, and in London itself; and in the case of secondary schools, we shall not only be dealing with grammar schools, but also with central and non-selective secondary schools in the inter-war years, and technical, secondary modern and comprehensive schools in the post-war era.[16]

The astonishing diversity of educational experience across the length and breadth of England constantly defies easy generalization, in history as (no doubt) in other subjects, too. It differed in elementary and secondary schools, and within them, at the lower, intermediate and higher levels. Teaching history in a country primary school in the early 1950s, where numbers were relatively small, which was the focus of community life and identity, and with history visibly in evidence all around, but doing so in a dilapidated and insanitary building, might be one thing; teaching history in a large comprehensive school, on a newly built housing estate, where there was little sense of community, identity or history, but where there were many modern amenities, might be something very different. In grammar schools, concerned with academic achievement, history might be deemed an important subject; in commercial or technical schools, more geared to vocational training, it might be less significant or worthwhile; in secondary modern schools, it might occupy a different place again; and in comprehensive schools it is taught across a very wide range of ability. Moreover, across the twentieth century, some schools have been relatively well supplied with teachers, classrooms and amenities, while others have had far less money to spend. In 1951, there were just above 25,000 primary and secondary state schools in England, where almost 200,000 teachers in all subjects educated 5.3 million children.[17] In so many institutions, with so many different styles of pedagogy and levels of attainment, history was taught in many and varied ways, and with many and varied levels of expertise, commitment and success.

Teachers and Teaching

This explains why history teachers are one of our central areas of interest. Harold Wilson may not have been expressing a universal view when he observed that 'coming from my kind of background, teachers were the most important adults in your life'.[18] But they were formative influences, and it was the teachers who significantly determined what kind of history their pupils learned, whether they enjoyed learning it, whether they remembered any of it, and what impact (if any) it had on their subsequent adult lives. In 1906, the Historical Association was founded to support history teachers, especially those involved in secondary education; and for more than a century, it has helped give them a sense of shared mission and collective identity, as well as providing them, through its journals and conferences, with a forum for discussing history and debating teaching methods.[19] We have drawn extensively on the Association's archives and publications, and also on its recent surveys of history teaching. In addition, we have created our own archive, by undertaking a series of interviews with teachers of history of all ages, across the length and breadth of England, and from all levels and types of state school. Like most oral history projects, the testimonies recorded and transcribed constitute a random and impressionistic source, and we found no history teacher whose recollections of the classroom went back to the Second World War or before. But for the period since the late 1940s, we have assembled a significant amount of new material, and these interviews provide vivid and abundant evidence of what it was like to teach history in English schools, and also of the backgrounds, presumptions, attitudes, training and experiences of successive generations of history teachers.

Like their forbears, many teachers we interviewed spent their time teaching about the English past, but they were also living through the most recent stages of their nation's history, as the twentieth century unfolded, and as they lived out their professional lives. Those teachers who began in the classroom during the 1900s grew up in the era of the Golden and Diamond Jubilees of Queen Victoria and of the Boer War. For the next generation, the First World War and the League of Nations-inspired internationalism were their most resonant experiences, while for their successors the great depression and the Second World War were the defining episodes of their early lives. By contrast, the sixties generation grew up in the liberal climate and unprecedented affluence of the welfare state, while the British Empire gradually disappeared; and those termed 'Thatcher's children' came to maturity in a nation that was downsized and diminished, decolonized and de-Victorianized, post-imperial and multi-ethnic, socially liberal and increasingly secular. How far did these very different experiences, generation by generation, influence the kind of English history that teachers imparted in the classroom, and the ways in which they taught it? These are easy questions to pose, but difficult to answer, especially since teachers' careers might span 40 years and more, meaning that as they approached retirement, the nation whose history they might be teaching was very different from that in which they had grown up.

During the first decades of the twentieth century, down to the Butler Education Act of 1944, most of the history that was taught in English schools was at an elementary rather than secondary level; and most of those who taught it had received no formal training or academic instruction in the subject beyond that which they would have picked up when they were in elementary or secondary school. To be sure, by the mid 1920s the majority of recently-recruited teachers had attended teacher-training colleges, and after the Second World War these institutions were expanded and eventually re-branded as colleges of education. But very often, they were more concerned with teaching the students about educational theory and practice, rather than giving them a sustained and substantial grounding in any particular subject. This meant that until the 1950s, teachers with university degrees in history were a tiny minority, almost exclusively confined to the grammar schools; and it was only with the expansion of higher education during the next decade, culminating in the government's commitment to make higher education available to half the population of 18 year olds in the 1990s, that most history teachers in secondary schools had gained a degree in the subject.

But even though history graduates were a minority of history teachers across state schools for much of the twentieth century, their approach to teaching their subject was significantly (and increasingly) influenced by changing academic fashions. Those few teachers who graduated before and after the First World War were fed a diet of constitutional, political and diplomatic history, built around the nation state; during the 1960s and 1970s, their successors spent more time on economic, social and labour history, which owed less to any organizing national framework; and those who studied during the closing decades of the century encountered women's history, cultural history and world history, which often stressed multiple perspectives rather than single narratives.[20] During the same period, history outside the academy also changed, evolved and developed: from the costumed pageants, the local antiquarians and the big red volumes of the *Victoria County Histories* that were so marked a feature of the 1900s, to the wide appeal of television history, heritage and conservation, and family history by the 1990s. These changes in academic and popular history also help explain a broader shift in perceptions of the national past.

During the first half of the twentieth century, English history was widely regarded as an exemplary narrative of achievement, heroism and sacrifice, as evidenced in the statues put up to great men and in the war memorials commemorating the 'glorious dead' who gave their lives that the nation might live. But more recently, the national narrative has been re-cast in many people's eyes as a succession of regrettable (rather than heroic) acts, which most people endured as victims rather than determined as victors. Hence the prevailing fashion for memorials to those 'who had no choice', and for apologies by politicians for past historic 'wrongs'.[21]

Teachers of history have not only been influenced in their professional activities by the time and circumstances in which they grew up, and by the types of history (if any) they themselves studied, but have also been increasingly influenced across the twentieth century by significant (and disputatious) developments in theories of education and of child and adolescent psychology. Educational practitioners have often been divided between those who think the prime purpose of school is to discipline and instruct, so as to limit young people's natural inclination to misbehave, and those who think the main point of education is to nurture and encourage so as to cater to children's innate curiosity, and to bring out the best in them. Across the centuries, the balance between these two approaches, of the stick and the carrot, has shifted back and forth, and from the 1900s, the general trend has been away from repression and towards encouragement.[22] There has also been a growing awareness by educational psychologists of the importance of childhood, youth and adolescence, as separate and autonomous phases in individual development, which must be recognized and treated as such: hence the rise of the notion of what is termed 'child-centred' education, and of the 'child-centred' school.[23] As a result, there has been a constant tension in English classrooms between 'traditional' and 'progressive' history teaching methods: the former stressing dates, chronology and narrative; the latter empathy, experience and imagination.

This diversity of pedagogic practice has been further varied by the extra resources that have increasingly (but unevenly) become available for use in the classroom. For much of the twentieth century, in many secondary schools, textbooks were the only resource beyond the history teachers and the blackboard, and they have clearly evolved from the Edwardian national narratives illustrated with a few badly-printed images, to the vividly illustrated books now published, which often devote much space to original sources, and present a range of viewpoints and interpretations rather than tell a simple linear story. That much is clear; but it is less certain how these books were used by history teachers in school; how much their availability varied from school to school and class to class; how many pupils had access to them and actually read them; and what impact their content made.[24] From the beginning of the twentieth century, maps and wall charts and pictures were becoming increasingly important, and so were visits to museums, galleries and historic sites; but the same uncertainties and variations have always applied. How widely have visual aids been used? How frequent were school trips? What was the balance between education and recreation? This diversity of experience has been even more marked as technology has been increasingly imported into the history classroom: the wireless, film, the television, duplicating machines, videos, computers and ICT. Their impact has been to transform history teaching since the 1920s, bringing the subject alive, and making it visible, immediate, colourful, thrilling and accessible in ways that were unknown and unimaginable at the beginning of the twentieth century.

Pupils and Numbers

The national framework and local government, the range and variety of schools, the experiences, training, qualifications, aims and methods of teachers, and the classroom resources and technology available: all have profoundly influenced how history has been taught, and also how that teaching has varied, changed and evolved over time. Together they constitute what economists call the supply-side, but it is essential to balance the picture by attending to the demand side: the boys and girls who were learning history in the classroom. Yet despite their essential importance, as the object, purpose and justification of the whole enterprise, it is remarkable how little we know, and how difficult it is to find out about, the experiences of school pupils, or how they remember them in later life.[25] There are so many of them, they are of such diverse ages, genders, classes and (more recently) ethnicities, they inhabit such varied parts of the country, they belong to so many generations, and they have left behind such limited accounts of their school days, that it is exceptionally difficult to depict, or to generalize about, any single, collective 'pupil experience' of what it was like, and what it meant, to have been taught history in the classroom.

One defining aspect of this experience has always been the age to which school attendance was deemed compulsory. Only from 1880 did it become obligatory for all children to go to school until the age of ten; in 1893, the minimum leaving age was raised to eleven, and in 1899 it was advanced to twelve.[26] But such requirements were not easily enforced: until the First World War, truancy remained a serious problem, and since many children worked part time during their last years at school, their classroom attendance was decidedly irregular. After the First World War, the leaving age was raised to 14, but despite occasional efforts to increase it, it remained there for a generation. The result was that during the first half of the twentieth century, the majority of schoolchildren learned their history in elementary schools rather than secondary schools; it was not until 1947 that the school leaving age was raised to 15, and not until 1973 that it was increased to 16, where it remains today. Only during the second half of the twentieth century has secondary schooling been a significant part of the educational experience of most pupils, when they might be taught history beyond the elementary and primary level. But not necessarily all that much: for although the school leaving age has progressively risen, history has never been compulsory above the age of 14, which means only a minority of children beyond that age have ever studied it.

In a sense, history has always been beleaguered in the classroom – as, indeed, have many other subjects. In elementary and primary schools, the chief aim has been to teach all young children the crucial skills of reading, writing and arithmetic: all other subjects, including history, have been subordinated and peripheral to this over-riding enterprise. Even when required at secondary level, history has usually been allocated less time than English or mathematics; and once pupils reached the age where they were free to chose, history has been merely one of many competing subjects – and it has not always seemed well placed to compete. During the first half of the twentieth century, it was regarded in some quarters as inferior to the classics and English literature, which were deemed the pre-eminent subjects of humanistic study. Since the Second World War, the sciences have become much more assertive and vigorous than the humanities, and this has had an adverse impact on the appeal of history. And although the attraction of the classics has markedly diminished in recent decades, history has increasingly been competing with 'new' subjects introduced into the curriculum, such as sociology, economics, business studies, politics, environmental science, media studies and psychology. As more subjects are studied at school, and as more subjects can be taken at GCSE and A level, the competition for space in the timetable, and for the attention and interest of pupils, has become more intense, with the result that 'older' subjects like history seem to be in 'decline'. Yet any such 'decline' is a complex phenomenon, which has to be carefully measured, evaluated and assessed, because history has always been one subject among many, and nowadays is one subject among many more than there used to be.

What then, within these constraints, limitations and changing parameters, was it like to be taught history in a primary or secondary school during the twentieth century? In truth, no one knows very much about this. There are records and evaluations of the history teaching in the classroom by generations of HMIs; but although of great value, they are official accounts of teaching as pedagogy, and do not get close to the experience of being a pupil in the classroom, taking history in (or not taking it in) at the receiving end. Moreover, few of these millions of one-time English schoolchildren have left behind their recollections of the sort of history they were taught, of the ways in which they were taught it, of how well and/or badly they were instructed, of what the history they learned meant to them at the time, and of what if anything it has meant to them since. For the first third of the twentieth century, this is an evidential gap that it is virtually impossible to fill, although there is some relevant material from an earlier oral history project conducted by Paul Thompson and Thea Vigne at the University of Essex.[27] But for the later period, and increasingly so towards our own times, we have created a new evidential source, by surveying 335 and interviewing 68 people, of varied ages, backgrounds and locations, who have given their recollections of being taught history in the classroom. These filled-in questionnaires and transcribed interviews are a small and self-selected sample; but they enable us to learn from the pupils themselves, and this new and original material from those who were the objects and beneficiaries (and sometimes, the victims) of a history education, is of the first importance for our inquiry.

It also helps us to address a further question: what is the relation between the history taught and learned in school, the history pursued by boys and girls outside the classroom, and the history they engaged with in later life? Some pupils have enjoyed and delighted in the history they encountered through school, but others have done so outside the classroom, via field trips to museums and churches, or to stately homes and heritage sites, or through watching television and film, or by connecting to the internet. Alternatively, school history and extra-curricular history might reinforce each other in an appealing and resonant combination, or it might be that neither inside the classroom nor outside did history offer any appeal or make any impact. Among those former pupils whom we have interviewed are to be found examples of all these responses; and there is a similar variety of experience concerning the connections between history as education in school, and history as part of an adult's mental equipment. Some of our respondents had been excited and captivated by history in school, and have remained enthralled by it ever since. Others found being taught history deeply depressing, and only discovered its pleasures later in life, almost by accident, and in defiance of their earlier dismal recollections. And others again hated history in school so deeply that they never felt the slightest wish to engage with it later in life. Once again, generalization is hazardous: the connection between being taught history in school, and maintaining an interest in it later in life, is neither clear nor straightforward.

This suggests that there is no simple answer to another question: how far has the teaching of history helped promote a shared sense of national identity? It has long been recognized that schooling can help reinforce the established order, by inculcating deferential attitudes, or subvert that order by encouraging dissent and discord. This is especially the case with history teaching, since so much of it has been concerned with English history (just as French history has been taught in French schools, German history in German schools, and Russian history in Russian schools).[28] Yet even during the first half of the twentieth century, when history was so often conceived in political and biographical terms, and when two world wars were fought to save the British Empire, Whitehall did not urge that the subject should be taught to inculcate national pride, most teachers did not teach history with that aim, and most pupils did not learn about it for that purpose. Being able to recite the dates of the reigns of successive kings and queens does not of itself promote a collective feeling of national belonging: to many schoolchildren, they were (and are) simply (and often meaninglessly) names and dates. And insofar as the youth of the Edwardian era did feel a shared sense of patriotic pride, it was more likely to have been as a result of participating in such after-school and extra-curricular activities as the Boys' Brigade, the Boy Scouts or the cult of Empire Day.[29]

Curriculum – and Qualifications

So much for the supply of and the demand for history: but what of the substance of the history actually taught? There has always (and increasingly) been a bewildering variety of options, in terms of what to teach and how to teach it. History in the classroom can be concerned with England, or Britain, or the British Empire and/or Commonwealth, or Europe, or the United States, or Russia, or China, or Africa, or Latin America, or Australasia, or the whole world. It can be ancient history, or medieval history, or early modern history, or modern history, or contemporary history. It can be political history, or constitutional history, or diplomatic history, or religious history, or economic history, or social history, or cultural history, or gender history, or world history. It can be concerned with long periods of time, which convey some sense of the length of the past, or it can be concerned with shorter periods, which can be studied in greater depth. It can be about chronology and narrative and events and dates, or it can be about themes and topics, analysis and structure and slow time and the *longue durée*. It can be about acquiring information and mastering detail, or it can be about empathy and imagination.

There has always been a lot of history that could be taught, and for most of the twentieth century, the decisions determining what history was taught at elementary and secondary level were taken by and in the schools. Until the 1980s, neither central nor local government thought it appropriate to interfere, and it was left to the teachers to decide what history they should teach. Most of them would probably have agreed that the ideal curriculum would be connected and cumulative across all years, building up a coherent and extended picture of the past, and becoming intellectually more challenging along the way. But that ideal was constrained by the interests and expertise (and limitations) of the staff, by the age and content of the textbooks, and by the additional resources (if any) that were available. These have often been powerful forces making for pedagogic inertia, which means that changing the school history curriculum has often been a momentous and thus reluctant decision: brought about by the arrival of a new head, or new staff with new ideas; or by the need to replace outdated and disintegrating textbooks; or in response to a damning report from HMIs; or by the allure of changing fashions and expectations; or by the irresistible influence of new technology; or by the threat of growing competition from other, new (and easier?) subjects. Such have been the challenges and constraints faced by teachers across the country as they have pondered the history that they do teach – or might prefer to teach.

But for the minority of pupils who stayed on into the fifth and sixth forms, there was an additional consideration, namely the subjects and the periods covered in the papers set by the external examining boards. As with so many aspects of the subject, the history of public examinations is complex and varied. Before the First World War, the examining bodies and the exams they set were largely unregulated, and few people took them; the inter-war years were the heyday of the School Certificate and Higher School Certificate, although they were still taken by a tiny minority; they were superseded by O Levels and A Levels, and the number of people sitting both began to rise significantly in the 1960s; and the same has been true since then of the CSE and subsequently the GCSE. Across the twentieth century, more and more people sat history exams, on a wider variety of subjects, and with more varied questions, and this significantly influenced the history that was taught in schools. But as a result, there have been long-running controversies about the purpose of history examinations and the standards of examining, and there has always been a tension between the idea of examinations as ends in themselves, and the view that they are in fact incidental (or detrimental) to the more important task of awakening pupils' interest in the past. There have also been protracted disagreements about whether the exam questions were getting harder or easier, and about whether the marking was becoming more lenient or more severe.

These are the viewpoints from which we approach our inquiry into how history has been taught, and into how history has been learned, in English state schools from the 1900s until the early twenty-first century, and our perspectives very properly range from the global to the local, and from the panoramic to the particular. The only generalization on this subject that is truly safe is that few, if any, generalizations on this subject are ever safe. But we shall certainly be making them if it seems right, possible and necessary to do so; and we shall conclude by making suggestions and offering recommendations about what needs to be done if the teaching of history in our schools is to be improved. But there is one recommendation which can confidently be made at the outset, namely that no government should try to 'reform' history teaching in schools without some awareness of what has gone before, and of how things got to be the way they now are. Like any other classroom subject, from mathematics to music, French to biology, the teaching of history in English schools has its own history – indeed, it has many histories – which politicians and policy makers have all too often ignored or disregarded. But they will no longer have any excuses for doing so, for here that history is, and here many (though not all) of those histories are.

1 History Goes to School, 1900–18

It is surprising to find how little real knowledge of history is possessed by the average Englishman, or even by the average educated Englishman.

(Address by Miss M.A. Howard on 'The Teaching of History',
London, 5 January 1906.[1])

The teaching of history in English state schools first became widespread as the nineteenth century turned into the twentieth, and as elementary and secondary education were increasingly funded by the state in tandem with local authorities.[2] In 1870, W.E. Forster's Education Act permitted every child to have access to 'a school place in a building of reasonable quality and with a qualified head teacher'; and a new category of elementary schools, overseen by elected school boards, was created to complement the denominational or 'voluntary' schools, which might be Church of England, nonconformist or Roman Catholic, and which already received some state support. Across the next 30 years, this hybrid provision, via 'board' and 'voluntary' elementary schools, was further extended: in 1880, attendance was made compulsory up to the age of ten; in 1891, free education became available for all pupils attending elementary school; and eight years later the compulsory attendance age was raised to twelve (albeit with exemptions).[3] During the 1890s, the old system of school finance, known as 'payment by results', which had been tied to the teaching of reading, writing and arithmetic, was replaced by the 'block grant' scheme, which made it easier to include additional subjects, and thus made possible the enhanced provision of history teaching. In 1900, the Board of Education was created, superseding the lowly Education Department that had been established under the Privy Council in 1856, and the President of the new Board was given a seat in cabinet.

As late as 1890, history had scarcely counted as a classroom subject, even at the higher levels of England's 22,500 elementary schools. In that year, English was taught in 20,300 schools, geography in 12,300 – and history in a mere 414, so that most boys and girls received no formal teaching in the subject. But the abolition of the system of 'payments by result' meant that the numbers of schools teaching history started to rise: by 1899, it was on the curriculum in nearly 6,000 of them, and for the first time, one third of those of school age were receiving some form of historical instruction.[4] When the 'block grant' funding scheme was introduced in the following year, it was 'recommended' that for 'older scholars' (of seven years and upwards) there ought to be 'lessons, including object lessons, on geography, history and common things'.[5] There was nothing compulsory about this: history might be taught for two lessons a week, but if there was 'good reason', it could be omitted altogether. Yet this rarely seems to have happened, and by 1903 most elementary schools were offering it: 23,295 of them taught the compulsory subjects of reading, writing and arithmetic, and 23,053 taught history – but only 719 taught French. Here was the 'great turning point' in the standing of history in the elementary school classroom, and with it our inquiry properly begins.[6]

There was nothing uniquely English about this development, for the general expansion of school facilities, and the increased attention given to history, were part of a broader pattern across the western world, as the mass society of the last quarter of the nineteenth century both required and compelled the provision of an appropriate form of mass education.[7] As more people lived in towns and cities, and were employed in industry and factories, there was a growing need to train and discipline a labour force that would be qualified, co-operative and productive. In the era of the second industrial revolution, with new businesses based on chemicals, electricity and petroleum, there was an increased demand for trained experts, who needed a general education before specializing in scientific and technical subjects. As the franchise was regularly extended and more people exercised the right to vote, it seemed important to create an informed, engaged, responsible and educated citizenry. And in a tense phase of imperial expansion and international rivalry, it was considered essential to instil into the populace, while at their most impressionable age, a shared sense of national identity, national loyalty and national pride. In order to raise national consciousness, knowledge of national history was deemed of the first importance, and the classroom was regarded as the place to instil it. So when, in France, in 1897, candidates for the *baccalauréat moderne* were asked to discuss the purposes of history in education, 80 per cent replied that it was primarily to exalt patriotism.[8]

In England, the educational reforms of the late nineteenth century culminated in what is often known as the Balfour Education Act of 1902, named after the politician who became Tory leader and Prime Minister during the course of its passing.[9] It abolished the elected school boards that had been set up in 1870, and placed education under the jurisdiction of the already-existing local authorities, namely counties and county boroughs (the London school board, the largest of them all, was abolished by separate legislation in 1903). For the first time, all elementary schools with approved educational standards were deemed eligible for support from the rates, including those under direct religious control. And the local authorities would not only be responsible for educating children in elementary schools up to the age of twelve, but also for new secondary schools that would be built for pupils continuing their education beyond the elementary level. The bill's passage through parliament was protracted and disputed: by some Conservative Anglicans who resented the public subsidy of Roman Catholic and Nonconformist schools, and by secular Liberals who objected to the subsidizing of any kind of religious activity. But the act was finally passed, and although it was one of the reasons the Conservative Party went down to heavy defeat in the election of 1906, it set the framework within which the state oversaw education, including the teaching of history, until 1918 and in many ways beyond.

The Government Suggests and Recommends

The Education Act of 1902 was much influenced by the first President of the Board of Education, the eighth Duke of Devonshire, who had insisted it must encompass elementary and secondary education.[10] After scarcely two years the Duke was succeeded by the sixth Marquis of Londonderry, but he was a lightweight, excessively deferential to his civil servants, and spoke in the Lords with 'voluble vagueness'.[11] On the fall of the Conservative government, the first Liberal President of the Board to be appointed was Augustine Birrell, but he held the post for scarcely a year, and failed to pass a measure to modify Balfour's Act, which many Liberals thought too favourable to the Church of England. Birrell's successor was Reginald McKenna, another short-term appointment, although he did set up a separate Welsh Department. When Asquith became prime minister in 1908, he put Walter Runciman in charge of education, but he, too, was unable to modify the 1902 Act; and his successor, Joseph Albert Pease, also failed to get through any major reform. In May 1915, Asquith reconstructed his flagging Liberal government as an all-party coalition, and the Presidency of the Board was allotted to Arthur Henderson of the Labour Party. He held the job for 15 months, but his prime concern was the mobilization of labour for the war economy. Henderson's successor was the Marquis of Crewe, but he was a stop-gap, for Asquith's government collapsed in December 1916, and the new Prime Minister, Lloyd George, summoned H.A.L. Fisher to take charge of Education; his uniquely long presidency belongs to the next chapter.

Eight presidents in 16 years was a high turnover, which made it difficult for any of them after Devonshire to make their mark, and this pattern would continue throughout the twentieth century. Between them, they well reflect the culture and personnel of Edwardian high politics. Three were authentic grandees: Devonshire, Londonderry and Crewe. Four were middle class: Birrell was a barrister, McKenna a banker, Runciman a shipping magnate, and Pease was the scion of a north-country industrial dynasty. Only Arthur Henderson was working class: the son of a cotton spinner, who was apprenticed at the age of twelve in a locomotive factory. The three grandees had been to public schools; the four middle-class figures had attended a minor public school, an independent school, a local high school, and a Quaker boarding school; and Henderson's education was confined to elementary school. As such, he was the only President of the Board during this first phase of its existence who had any significant first-hand experience of the schools for which he was briefly responsible. Apart from Henderson, all of them had been to university (overwhelmingly Oxbridge) and one of them had studied history as an undergraduate. Perhaps because of the long years of Liberal hegemony from 1905 to 1916, they were a slightly more diverse group than their inter-war successors, when Etonians and aristocrats were more in evidence.

Between 1900 and 1918, the Presidents of the Board were supported by three permanent secretaries. The first was Sir George Kekewich, the son of a Devon landowner, who had joined the Education Department in 1867, when appointments were still made by patronage. He had helped carry the principle of free elementary education in 1891, but he was hostile to the Conservative Government's determination to abolish the school boards, and he was prematurely retired in 1902.[12] Kekewich may have been forced out by his successor, Sir Robert Morant, who had spent eight years as a tutor to the Crown Prince of Siam before he joined the Education Department in 1895. As permanent secretary, his prime aims were twofold: to reorganize the Board of Education into an effective instrument for the implementation of the 1902 Act; and politically to thwart the attempts made by successive Liberal Presidents to carry legislation modifying that Act. Eventually, Morant's excessive zeal brought him into conflict with teachers and local authorities, and in 1911, he was compelled to resign. But Beatrice Webb considered him to be the 'one man of genius in the civil service'; and H.A.L. Fisher regarded him as the most valuable public servant of his time.[13] Morant's successor was Sir Lewis Selby-Bigge, another scion of a landed family, who was an Oxford don and Assistant Charity Commissioner before transferring to the Board in 1900. Lord Haldane thought him 'very jealous and full of red tape and sealing wax'; but his style was more emollient and consensual than his two predecessors, and he remained permanent secretary until 1925.[14]

These were the ministers and mandarins in charge of the Board during its first phase of existence: but as a recently created department, Education ranked low in the Whitehall hierarchy, and the only President who was a front-rank politician was the Duke of Devonshire. The three permanent secretaries were of undoubted ability, but the first two were disputatious and controversial, and Morant not only quarrelled with Kekewich, but also with another senior civil servant, Sir Michael Sadler; and his relations with his ministers were often strained (he treated Lord Londonderry like a 'backward pupil').[15] Before 1914, the most high profile and time consuming business of the Board was the passing of the 1902 Act, and the three failed attempts to modify it. Beyond that, little was accomplished: in 1906, the provision of school meals for elementary school pupils was given statutory sanction; in the following year, a free-place scholarship scheme was introduced to give promising children from elementary schools the chance to go to secondary school; and the regular medical inspection of schoolchildren was begun. But as this low level of activity suggests, the Board's political weight and its budget were both limited, and since school funding was primarily in the hands of local authorities, its power was distinctly circumscribed. As Selby-Bigge recalled, it did not administer education in 'categorical imperatives' but merely 'superintended', and after 1914 it was increasingly peripheral to the task of fighting and winning the war.[16]

But once the 'block grant' scheme was in place, the Department, and subsequently the Board, did issue guidance as to what and how teachers should teach. The first such *Code of Regulations for Day Schools* appeared in 1900, and suggested that the history taught to pupils aged between nine and fourteen should be wholly concerned with England, centring on great figures from King Alfred to the Duke of Wellington, and on great events from Magna Carta and the Wars of the Roses to the Crimean War and the Indian Mutiny. There should be a chronological progression from ancient to modern times, and a corresponding intellectual progression, as the 'simple stories relating to English history' should be superseded by a more analytical approach, exploring the evolution of parliament and the acquisition of the colonies.[17] To this *Code* was added *Instructions* for Inspectors, who were exhorted to allow teachers 'the greatest freedom possible' in 'planning and carrying out courses of instruction'. The *Instructions* also declared that 'time spent during school hours in visiting museums, art galleries, and other places of educational value, or of national or historical interest, may count towards the time required for attendance at school'; and HMIs were urged to encourage such visits, with the proviso that there should be only 15 pupils per teacher, and a maximum of 20 such visits a year. It was also suggested that 'some person competent to give information of a kind interesting to young children' should be present, and that children 'of a proper age to do so should write out an account of what they have observed'.[18]

In 1905, the Board published the first of its *Suggestions for the Consideration of Teachers and Others Concerned with the Work of Public Elementary Schools*. Once again, the Board urged that 'each teacher shall think for himself, and work out for himself such methods of teaching as may use his powers to the best advantage, and be best suited to the particular needs and conditions of the school'. The aim of elementary education, the *Suggestions* continued, was 'the establishment of character', in which history should play an important part; and it should also teach 'how the British nation grew up, and how the mother country in her turn has founded daughter countries beyond the seas'.[19] Younger pupils should be taught the subject orally, 'through a series of biographies of typical heroes or heroines', with a view to 'illustrating in the action of real persons the principles of conduct and qualities of character which promote the welfare of the individual and of society'. But they must be 'from all stations in life', and while their 'higher qualities' should be proclaimed and extolled by their teachers, they should take care 'not to raise them too far above the level of common humanity by the omission of their faults or shortcomings'. There was also a warning that 'the teaching of history in the past has been too much confined to accounts of wars and battles, and narratives of the doings of great kings and nobles', and that insufficient attention had been given in the classroom 'to the life of the people as a whole'.[20]

Accordingly, lessons should deal 'with the triumphs of peace as well as those of war', including 'the discovery of America, the invention of printing, the abolition of slavery and the change of life in recent times'; and while the 'chief interest' would 'centre in the stirring events and in the striking qualities of the central figures of our own history' it was important, 'in dealing with times of conflict with other peoples', to 'do full justice to those who are national heroes in other countries'.[21] For those in their final years, from eleven to fourteen, the Board offered three new proposals: one conveying 'a basic idea of the development of British history', utilizing 'patriotic poems, historical tales and national songs', while also engaging with the history of the school's locality; another stressing chronological periods (up to 1485, 1485–1688, and 1688 to the present), stressing 'the sequence of cause and effect, so that reason as well as the memory may be trained'; and a third devoting one year each to European history, to local history and the British Empire, and to citizenship and a special period such as the reign of Elizabeth. In each case, 'various aids' would enhance 'the effectiveness of the teaching', including pictures, photographs, lantern-slides, old coins and maps. There should be readings of 'striking passages' from 'original authorities' and from 'the brilliant pages of writers like Macaulay', and visits to 'historic spots' such as castles, abbeys, battlefields or hill camps.[22]

Such was the Board of Education's initial notion of the history to be taught in elementary schools, and they remained essentially unchanged for the next 15 years.[23] The *Codes*, *Instructions* and *Suggestions* stressed national history, chronological ordering and long-term narrative, with the aim of forming pupils' characters, of giving them a sense of the nation to which they belonged, and of training them for citizenship. But there were significant qualifications: history ought to be about peace as well as war, about women as well as men, and about ordinary people as well as kings and queens; and it should recognize that England's greatest heroes had their weaknesses, while other nations, which might sometimes have been England's enemies, had their own heroes, too. It was repeatedly suggested that there should be chronological progression and intellectual development across the years, and that every attempt should be made to arouse their curiosity by using up-to-date teaching aids and taking them on outside visits. History was not just about character or patriotism or citizenship, it was also about curiosity and imagination and life-long learning, for the aim was 'not only to impart information but also to stimulate in the pupil an appetite for increased knowledge of the subject which will outlast their school life'.[24]

The same views inform the Board's recommendations about how history should be taught at a higher level, as set out in two documents produced in 1908: Circular 599, on *Teaching History in Secondary Schools*, and an accompanying *Memorandum in Explanation and Expansion of the Board's Circular*.[25] Both were the work of James Wycliffe Headlam, who became one of the most influential figures in the teaching of history during the early twentieth century. He was born in 1863, his father was a clergyman in County Durham, and his elder brother would become Bishop of Gloucester. Headlam was educated at Eton and at Kings College, Cambridge, where he took a double first in Classics; from 1894 to 1900, he was Professor of Greek and ancient history at Queen's College, London; he was also a regular visitor to Germany, and published a book on Bismarck in 1899. Soon after, he was appointed a Permanent Staff Inspector of Secondary Schools at the Board of Education, and there he remained until 1914, when he took up war work in intelligence and propaganda, moving to the Foreign Office in 1918, when he changed his name to Headlam-Morley, on inheriting property in the West Riding.[26] He attended the post-war Paris peace conference, was one of the founders of the Royal Institute of International Affairs, and was knighted in 1929, the year of his death.

Although never Permanent Secretary, Headlam was a substantial figure at the Board of Education. He began Circular 599 by repeating the mantra that in history there was 'room for the greatest variety of treatment', and he had no wish 'to lay down strict rules either as to the arrangements of the course or as to the methods of teaching.'[27] By the age of twelve, Headlam believed, boys and girls 'should have some idea of the nature of the great nations and stages of civilization, centering in each case around certain individuals or events in their chronological succession'. This they should have learned through stories, not just concerned with England, but 'from the history of the most important nations', which might include Alexander the Great, episodes from Roman history, the early Church, Attila, Charlemagne, Columbus and other explorers, Galileo, George Washington and Garibaldi. Such stories, Headlam continued, 'afford excellent material for training the imagination', and they should be illustrated by 'plans and pictures of armour, dress, castles, etc.' Much of the teaching would be given orally, but books should also be used. As for dates: they were significant, but they should be taught with care, content and context: 'It does not seem desirable,' Headlam noted, 'to give up the traditional system by which boys [sic] are expected to know the kings [sic] of England.' But, he went on, 'the dates and names of the kings should be learnt in connection with some important events of the reigns, and not by rote'.[28]

However, his prime concern was with pupils aged between twelve and sixteen, who should take 'a formal course covering the whole of English history from the invasion of the Romans to the present day', to give them 'a clear apprehension of the general chronological sequence of the cardinal events'. They should not attempt 'to learn all the names and facts which are mentioned in the ordinary school text books', nor should they be crammed with detail about 'the political history of Charles II's reign' or 'the internal history of the eighteenth century'. Instead, they should concentrate on major episodes such as the Crusades, the reign of Elizabeth or the Civil War, along with 'reference to the great inventions, such as gunpowder, printing [and] the steam engine', which had had a great 'effect upon the history of the nation', and which were also 'especially characteristic of European civilization'. Headlam also wished 'to remove the complete ignorance of history outside England', by urging that European history 'must' be taught whenever it was 'necessary for the understanding of English history', as with the Viking invasions, the French wars, and the voyages of discovery; and this should be balanced by giving attention to 'the history of the locality', especially in terms of old buildings such as castles, monasteries and city walls. 'It is far more important', he insisted, 'that pupils should leave school with their eyes trained to observe the historical remains which are to be found in almost every part of England, than that they should attempt to remember the whole of the political history which they cannot understand.'[29]

Headlam admitted this was an ambitious programme, but there was considerable overlap in the information and concepts found in history with those in 'allied subjects, especially literature and geography.' It would, for example, be possible to co-ordinate with what was read in English classes: Froissart's *Chronicles* or Chaucer's *Canterbury Tales* would align perfectly with history classes on the Middle Ages; while the study of the geography of Asia would be incomprehensible without 'some elementary facts as to the rise and spread of Mohammedanism'. He was generally in favour of history textbooks, but distinguished between those with 'a well arranged narrative' and those that were 'merely a chronological summary or compendium of facts to be used for reference'. Headlam also believed that written work should be set even in the lowest forms: to afford 'practice in original composition, writing essays and answering questions, sometimes in exam conditions'; and to give 'systematic practice in the taking of notes, graduated according to the age of the pupils', so they would be able to make 'a well-arranged digest for themselves of all the information which they acquire both from reading and from teaching'. The whole purpose of teaching history at secondary level, he concluded, was to 'train the power of giving a connected narrative or explanation'.[30]

To this Circular, Headlam attached a *Memorandum*, which further elaborated his views. 'One of the chief reasons', he began, 'why much history teaching is so unsuccessful is that an attempt is made to teach too much', and the sheer amount of ground that had to be covered prevented teachers from 'dwelling with any detail on those events and ideas which are interesting and instructive'.[31] Headlam's main proposal was that for pupils aged from twelve to sixteen, schools should plan 'a course of three or four years in which there should be a consecutive study of English history ... with large digressions into foreign history'. But to cover the whole of the national past in three years, with attention to the history of other countries, would require careful selection, and pupils 'should be told what is being left out and why'. In the case of the Tudors, for example, it would be good to begin with the voyages of discovery, to leave out the greater part of the reign of Henry VII and most of the reign of Henry VIII, and to go straight to the empire of Charles V, and then take up the history of England with the Reformation. But Headlam admitted this selective, in-depth approach would only work if the pupils were already well grounded in the subject. As for external assessment: he believed that 'history is always a most difficult and unsatisfactory subject to examine in well'.[32]

These proposals were well received at the Board, and W.N. Bruce, the Principal Assistant Secretary responsible for secondary schools, welcomed the suggestion that 'some instruction on the history of other countries should be included in the history course in all secondary schools, and also that the interest of the pupils should be aroused in the history of the district or town in which they live'.[33] Sir Robert Morant agreed, wishing he had had such documents 'years ago when one had to try and direct that kind of study for varying ages'; he felt sure that they would 'carry great weight and be of immense help everywhere'; and he urged publication as soon as possible.[34] But neither Headlam's 'Circular' and his *Memorandum* concerning secondary schools, nor the *Codes* and *Suggestions* regarding elementary schools, were mandatory or 'categorical imperatives'.[35] This may have been how the civil servants in Whitehall thought history in English schools ought to be taught, but they had no first-hand experience of the state educational sector, and until the 1980s, neither they nor their successors could compel schools to do their bidding.

Nor, during these years, was the influence of public examinations on history teaching in state schools of much significance, since only a tiny minority of pupils stayed on long enough to sit them. Such tests had existed since 1858, when Oxford and Cambridge Universities organized 'local' examinations in different parts of the country: 'senior' for those under 18, and 'junior' for those under 16. (There was also a joint Oxford and Cambridge Examination Board, but this was concerned with public rather than state schools.[36]) The Oxford and Cambridge 'locals' were in response to the demand in middle class secondary schools, whose pupils did not usually go on to university, but who wanted some external validation of their studies. By the early twentieth century, several new examining bodies had come into being: the two biggest were the University of London Board and the Northern Universities Joint Matriculation Board, while the Universities of Bristol and Durham ran their own examinations, and there was a separate Board for Wales. There was confusion about the relative merits of these many and varied examinations, and a growing demand for standardization. In 1904, a consultative committee of the Board of Education vainly recommended a unified scheme of School Leaving Certificates and a Central Examinations Board. Five years later, the Committee returned to the matter, and in 1911 a national system of examinations at two levels was proposed: a School Leaving Certificate for 16 year olds, and a Higher School Certificate designed to allow entry to university.[37]

The recommendation was that these school certificates would recognize attainment across an agreed range of subjects, with Pass and Credit grades, which would provide consistency. The subjects would be arranged in groups, and to achieve a certificate, students would have to demonstrate their attainment across subjects in different groups. The university-based boards would be 'approved', and invited to set, mark and certify the exams under the jurisdiction of the Board of Education. The aim of the examinations would be to test 'the form and not the pupil', and this was agreed by the Board's Circular 849, issued in July 1914. It also decreed that 'the standard for a pass will be such as may be expected of pupils of reasonable industry and ordinary intelligence in an efficient secondary school'.[38] But the committee was not wholly in favour of exams, which it believed 'as ends in themselves have occupied too much of the thoughts of parents and teachers', and to 'their occupying too large a place in the system of national education'. The time had come for 'the curtailment of their numbers', and for an increased regard 'to those sides of school life which no written examination can ever test, and for which purely intellectual discipline is not itself a substitute'.[39] But the onset of the First World War meant these recommendations were put on hold, and the unregulated system of university-related examining boards continued.

In 1911, 14-year-olds in the lower forms of secondary schools might have taken the Cambridge Preliminary Local Examination, being asked to answer six questions on English history in one hour and a quarter. The periods covered were 1066 to 1485, 1485 to 1603, and 1603 to 1714, and the questions were factual and precise: 'Give a short account of Robert Dudley, Earl of Leicester'; and 'Write brief accounts of any *three* of the following: Laud, the Earl of Essex, Monk, Lord Danby, Admiral Rooke.' In a similar way, the Cambridge Junior Examination, for 16-year-olds, divided its English history paper into

1066 to 1509, 1509 to 1688, and 1688 to 1832. There were six questions in each section, candidates had to answer six questions in an hour and a half, and they could select them from across the whole span from the Norman Conquest to the Great Reform Act. Again, the aim was to test factual knowledge: 'Write a short life of Marlborough' or 'What were the subjects of dispute between England and France in 1756? How were they settled in 1763?' The 1911 Cambridge Senior Examination, for those aged 18, was much the same. The periods of English history were: up to 1509, 1509 to 1714, and 1714 to 1867. In an hour and three quarters, candidates were again expected to answer six questions, such as: 'Give some account of the career of Thomas Cromwell', and 'What were the Corn Laws? Give some account of the circumstances that led to their repeal.' For the time being, these exams were attempted by a tiny minority of pupils, most in public schools. But in years to come, they would be attempted by a broader spectrum of the population.

First Thoughts on Teaching History

The growing (but still limited) interest of central government in the teaching of history in schools was a sign of the state's suddenly enhanced involvement in educational provision, but it was also in recognition of what seemed to be the increased importance of history in national life. There was a powerful legacy of great Victorian writers, among them Lord Macaulay, J.A. Froude, Thomas Carlyle, J.R. Green and S.R. Gardiner, who wrote narrative histories that reached a wide audience. Degree courses in history had recently been established at Oxford and Cambridge and London Universities, and on the civic campuses of Leeds, Liverpool, Manchester, Birmingham and Sheffield. They employed a new breed of professional historians, who were often concerned with the development of the nation's constitution, among them Stubbs, Freeman and Firth at Oxford; Seeley, Acton, Bury and Maitland at Cambridge; A.F. Pollard in London, and T.F. Tout in Manchester; and they established both the Royal Historical Society and the *English Historical Review* as their professional organization and publishing outlet.[40] Popular engagement with the past also seemed more pronounced, as evidenced by the proliferation of historical pageants, the expansion of historical tourism, and the popularity of historical novels, and by the creation of the National Trust, the *Dictionary of National Biography*, the *Victoria County Histories*, the *Survey of London*, and the Royal Commission on Historical Monuments.[41]

Yet these fledgling institutions, organizations and activities were not so much a sign that history was flourishing, but rather an indication that history needed all the help it could get. In 1900, only 200 graduates from Oxford and Cambridge had taken degrees in history, and the total number of graduating historians across the whole of England can scarcely have been in four figures. Throughout the university system, there were at most one hundred people teaching history, and the majority of them were tutors and instructors, with no first-hand experience of research or writing, since there was little systematic training available in historical research methods. There was Tout in Manchester, and Pollard in London, and there were pockets of such activity in Oxford and Cambridge; but there was no national research culture in academic history in England as there already was in France and Germany and on the eastern seaboard of the United States. As for the organizations that had come into being to practice public history and to proclaim the importance of the national heritage: their memberships were limited, their finances were precarious, and they wielded little influence in Westminster or Whitehall. From this perspective, England in 1900 was a nation with little seriously developed or widely shared sense of the past, and what else could have been expected, given that scarcely any history was taught in state schools up to that time.

It was in this uncertain context that the Historical Association was established in 1906, following similar organizations set up for mathematics (1870), geography (1893), modern languages (1893), the classics (1903) and English (also 1906). The idea originated with two members of the London Day Training College, one of whom was Dr Rachel Reid, who had joined the College after teaching history in secondary schools. 'I had', she recalled, 'literally no one to consult about syllabus, choice of text-books, methods, etc.'; and since the Geographical Association had been founded to help teachers, she 'did long for an Historical Association to do the same for me and for others placed like me'.[42] Dr Reid discussed her idea with Miss M.A. Howard, head of the History Department at the College, and she mentioned it to Professor A.F. Pollard who taught constitutional history at University

College, London. On 5 January 1906, at a conference of elementary schoolteachers, and at a session that Pollard chaired, Howard proposed the 'formation of an Historical Association to do for the teaching of history what has been done for the teachings of other subjects by ... similar Associations', namely to 'co-ordinate the efforts of all who are working in England towards the improvement of history teaching in our schools'. Pollard supported Howard's proposal, calling for 'an association which should be comprised mainly of teachers of history in the schools and in the universities, and an association the objects of which should be that history should be properly recognized by universities and that history should be properly taught in schools'.[43]

Four months later, Pollard convened a meeting where he deplored the 'present inadequate and haphazard provision for the teaching of history in England', and proposed the establishment of an organization that would not encroach upon the provinces of the Royal Historical Society or the *English Historical Review*. At the meeting, which was attended by Professor C.H. Firth and G.M. Trevelyan, the Historical Association was formally established to facilitate 'the interchange of ideas and information with regard to the methods of historical teaching'. There was a heavy weight of academics among the original officers (Firth was the first president), but there were nine secondary school teachers on the Council, and Reid and Howard were the first honorary secretaries. The new Association's aims were as follows:

(a) The collection of information as to existing systems of historical teaching at home and abroad, by getting together printed books, pamphlets and other materials, and by correspondence;

(b) The distribution of information amongst the members of the Association as to methods of teaching and aids to teaching (viz maps, illustrations, text-books, etc.);

(c) The encouragement of local centres for the discussion of questions relative to the study and teaching of History;

(d) The representation of the needs and interests of the study of History and of the opinion of its teachers to governing bodies, government departments, and other authorities having control over education;

(e) Co-operation for common objects with the English Association, the Geographical Association, the Modern Languages Association, and the Classical Association.[44]

Accordingly, the Historical Association was conceived as a national organization to give history teachers a shared sense of identity and practical support, and to lobby central and local government on their behalf and on behalf of their subject. Non-teachers were encouraged to join, and in 1917, membership was widened to include all those 'interested in the study and teaching of history'. Originally, there were only 100 members, paying an annual subscription of five shillings, but by the end of the First World War, there were more than 1,300, and they were distributed among 15 branches that, in addition to London, ranged from Sheffield to Southampton, and from Bristol to Bradford.[45] They held meetings, addressed by eminent historians, they went on outings to places of historic interest, and they organized joint ventures with other learned societies. Every year, the Historical Association held a general meeting, and the Council established committees to deal with publications, the use of illustrations in teaching, examinations and syllabuses. Almost immediately, the Association began publishing leaflets devoted to practical teaching issues, including bibliographies for British history, Irish history, general history, ancient history and European history. In 1912 it began to publish the *Annual Bulletin of Historical Literature*, and four years later, the Association took over the periodical *History* as its house journal: edited by A.F. Pollard, it published articles about teaching practice and teaching issues, as well as papers based on original research.[46]

Like the Board of Education, the HA was making up guidelines about how history should be taught, for as Miss Howard had explained in January 1906, it was 'a comparatively new subject in schools', and teachers were 'feeling our way towards a satisfactory treatment of it'. But the essential starting point was the recognition that 'the average Englishman knows no history', either because he had never been taught any, or because 'most of the matter taught is totally forgotten in adult life'. History teaching might recently have improved, but there was still a long way to go: 'we try to teach too much, and so we teach nothing properly'; the 'unintelligent memorizing' of too many facts and dates was a 'barren exercise'; there was insufficient chronological progression, which meant the Norman Conquest and the Stuart period were too often repeated; the balance between local, national and general history was rarely well struck; and most classes were too big, which meant pupils were passive spectators rather than active participants. As a result, they learned little history at school, forgot it as soon as they left, and evinced no interest in the subject thereafter: 'the average Englishman or Englishwoman has never read any standard book on history, and never touched a historical book of any sort after leaving school'. Most people might know the date of the Battle of Trafalgar, but it was, she lamented, 'startling to find how few people have any real grip of the salient points of the history of our own country and Empire', and 'how few have even ... a "bowing acquaintance" with the great men of general history, or the haziest notions about the landmarks in the story of the world'.[47]

There was, Howard insisted, 'room for great improvement' in the teaching of history: 'We want our pupils to leave school with a firm grip on what they have learned, with a thorough realization of how little they know, with a strong desire to learn more, and with minds so trained that they will know how to learn more.' It was important 'to make the past real' to schoolchildren, and she urged the extensive use of pictures, illustrations, lantern slides, time charts, maps and visits to places of historical interest. Pupils should be encouraged to read, there ought to be 'a good school library', and 'regular tests and examination papers' were of the highest importance. Stories, people and a strong narrative were the ways to 'make history intelligible', and the curriculum should be planned over several years as a 'carefully organized whole' to avoid repetition and ensure chronological development. 'Every child of ordinary capacity' should leave school with 'a clear knowledge in outline of the main course of English history'; and strengthened and broadened by the study of some local, foreign and general history. All this would enable children to 'develop intelligence, patriotism, and citizenship', and to retain an interest in history for the rest of their lives; but it would also enable them to learn how to think, to understand the importance of historical truth, to cultivate a sense of proportion, and to acquire the quality of 'sympathy' by 'exercising his imagination, projecting himself backwards into the past, looking at things from other people's point of view, and picturing circumstances widely different from his own'.

A year later, in February 1907, James Bryce addressed the first annual meeting of the Historical Association, 'on the teaching of history in schools'. In the course of his long and distinguished career, Bryce was by turns a lawyer, a journalist, an explorer, a mountaineer, an academic, an historian, a Liberal MP, a cabinet minister, British Ambassador to the United States, chairman of several Royal Commissions, President of the British Academy, and a member of the Order of Merit. He was a fully paid-up member of the establishment, and like many of those who belonged to the 'liberal and literary' intelligentsia of the time, he regarded history as a demanding academic discipline and as an essential component of the national culture. Among his own books was a classic history of the Holy Roman Empire, and in one of his presidential addresses to the British Academy, he celebrated and encouraged the wide-ranging and accessible approach to the study of the past which he believed was becoming ever more widespread.[48] Bryce was a big catch as the keynote speaker for the fledgling Historical Association, and though he claimed to offer nothing more than 'a few scattered thoughts', because he would soon be departing to the British Embassy in Washington, his speech engaged with many of the issues that had arisen since history had become a serious subject in English schools.[49]

Fifty years ago, Bryce recalled, 'there was practically no teaching of history at all', but 'the present state of things' was 'incomparably better and more promising', since in recent years, an 'immense deal has been done to introduce the study of history into all secondary schools and into the higher elementary schools'.[50] Ideally, teachers of history should have well stocked minds, and know a great deal more about their subject than their pupils. Bryce admitted this might be 'a counsel of perfection', since many teachers had no serious training in the subject, and he wondered whether 'it is worthwhile to try to teach much history to young children'. For those under 13, it was probably better 'to give them the main facts and dates which it is essential they should know, and for the rest to give them stories and anecdotes'. But when it came to older pupils, Bryce believed there were important challenges and exciting prospects in the way history could be taught: he welcomed the increasing use of 'books which contain extracts from original sources'; he agreed there should be more 'unity and co-ordination' in school examinations, but cautioned against making them too rigid or uniform; he thought it better for history to be presented in terms of 'broad outlines' rather than special periods; he noted that 'the importance of studying history in relation to geography and geography in relation to history has been more and more appreciated in late years'; and he urged the value of relating 'historical teaching to the teaching of literature'.[51]

In the manner of many single-issue lobbyists, Miss Howard and James Bryce may have exaggerated the problems and challenges that history teachers faced. But their comments, criticisms and proposals seem to have been inspired by, and lent support to, the early *Suggestions* and *Recommendations* about the teaching of history emanating from the Board of Education; and at its annual general meeting in January 1910, the Council of the Association set up a committee to draw up a list of questions suggested by the recently issued Circular no. 599. Miss Howard's initial ideas were further reinforced at the HA's meeting in January 1911, when the Council declared that 'the time has come when it behoves the Historical Association to formulate a policy with regard to the place that should be taken by historical teaching in various types of schools'. It went on to assert 'that in every school of sufficient size there should be ... one teacher specially qualified to supervise the history teaching of the school, and that the history lessons should only be entrusted to those who are competent and interested in such work'. A second resolution demanded that British history be made compulsory in 'all school-leaving, matriculation and professional entrance examinations', and that it should embrace the growth of the British Empire, and aspects of European history and geography. It was also decided that at the next annual meeting, there should be a discussion on 'The Teaching of History in Elementary Schools'.[52]

By the early 1910s the Historical Association was established as a forum where a wide range of opinions were expressed at the annual general meeting and at branch meetings. According to Professor F.J.C. Hearnshaw, the most important task for any teacher 'in the modern democratic state should be the training of citizens', and history should occupy a prominent place, as a school of political method, as a storehouse of political precedent, and as a basis of political progress. But C.H.K. Marten (who was a history teacher at Eton, a founder member of the HA, and the author of best-selling history text books) disagreed: he believed 'we do not yet attach sufficient importance to the history of other countries', because of the 'tendency to exaggerate our own achievements and belittle those of other nations', when what was needed was 'a due sense of proportion of our own importance compared to that of other nations', which could be encouraged by reading 'the history of other countries from their point of view'.[53] By contrast, the main concern of the medievalist C.G. Coulton was that there ought to be 'a definite and official syllabus, drawn up by some body of sufficient authority to secure its general recognition throughout the country'. Only in terms of what constituted the current teaching method did there seem to be a measure of agreement: boys and girls learned history from what they heard, what they read, what they saw, and what they wrote. It was as simple as that: as yet, pedagogy was a largely undeveloped field.[54]

There were some more adventurous views put forward during the years before the First World War, which reflected the growing opinion that children were not miniature adults, but had their own personalities and distinct needs. These views were set out by psychologists such as James Sully who, in his *Studies of Childhood* (1895), argued that it was a stage of life characterized by heightened emotional sensitivity, which meant that imagination and play were important elements in the upbringing and education of boys and girls. One indication of this changed perspective was the proliferation of Edwardian fiction directed at children to evoke and stimulate their magical thought-world, including Beatrix Potter's *Tales of Peter Rabbit* (1902), Edith Nesbit's *Five Children and It* (1902), James Barrie's *Peter Pan* (1904), Kenneth Grahame's *The Wind in the Willows* (1908), and Walter de la Mare's *Peacock Pie* (1912). Another sign was the expanding market in such toys as teddy bears (named after President Theodore Roosevelt) and Meccano (first produced in 1908), and the publication of magazines such as the *Boy's Own Paper* and the *Girl's Own Paper*.[55] Yet a third was an increased awareness that children should be properly cared for and protected, as evidenced by the founding of the National Society for the Prevention of Cruelty to Children in 1884. And in 1907, the establishment of the Child Study Society provided a forum for a new and increasingly influential profession of child psychologists, who would argue that childhood should be understood in 'psycho-medical terms'.[56]

One figure influenced by these developments was Harriet Finlay-Johnson, an elementary schoolteacher in Sussex, where she pioneered the 'dramatic' method of pedagogy. In 1910, she retired, and published a book opposing the widespread practice whereby a teacher recited names, facts and dates to a bored and inattentive class. Her aim in her teaching had been to get children to learn for themselves, by actively engaging with the subject, on the grounds that 'a child learns, and retains what he is learning, better by actually *seeing* and *doing* things'.[57] In the case of history this meant creating and enacting plays about great events and personalities from the past, which were constructed from historical novels such as those by Sir Walter Scott and a wide variety of history books. The children would organize most of the drama themselves, in such a way that 'we would be quite astonished at the originality and individuality shown'. As a result, the young pupils 'would bring out, apparently quite casually and without effort, the salient points of the history they were engaged in *learning* without being taught formally'. Creating and acting in a play about the past thus became the way to learn history, and Finlay-Johnson's pupils had done so with an enthusiasm and excitement lacking in dull, conventional lessons.[58]

Another innovator in teaching methods was M.W. Keatinge, a former schoolmaster and Reader in Education at Oxford, who shared Finlay-Johnson's concern that history was taught in the wrong way. In 1910 he published *Studies in the Teaching of History*, advocating the use of original sources. This was not a novel idea, since Bryce had mentioned it in his address of 1907, and in the same year, the Historical Association had published its inaugural leaflet on just this subject.[59] But Keatinge was the first to set down a systematic justification for using sources as a way of getting beyond the taking of notes from the teacher or the textbook, and as an opportunity to encounter history as something concrete and specific rather than vague and generalized. 'A few documents carefully studied', he insisted, 'will be impressed on the boys' minds and will serve as centres around which historical facts may be grouped.'[60] Why were such documents written? What were the motives of the author? By asking such questions, Keatinge believed history could be brought alive, and he urged that source-based exams could be introduced. As with Finlay-Johnson's advocacy of drama, Keatinge's aim was that 'the pupil may and must always be contributing to the development of the subject, instead of the teacher always doing the maximum and the pupil the minimum of work'.[61]

In retrospect, the growing concern about the need to understand childhood on its own terms, and the attention given by Finlay-Johnson to the use of drama and by Keatinge to the use of sources in teaching history mark the beginning of the 'progressive' approach to educational theory and practice. This fledgling movement received a further boost in 1911, when E.G.A. Holmes, the recently-retired Chief Inspector of Elementary Schools, published *What Is and What Might Be*, a radical critique of the elementary education he had spent his professional life observing. Across the country, he complained, the atmosphere in most classrooms was cold and stultifying, there was no attempt to engage with children in ways they could understand, and many left elementary school without ever having had their curiosity aroused. Holmes was an unusual figure among HMIs, in that he was a bohemian, a spiritualist, and a nature-worshipping poet. But he knew what he was talking about, he expressed enthusiasm for the ideas of Harriet Finlay-Johnson, and would-be reformers 'gained unexpected support, and defenders of the status quo were shaken, when so eminent an educationalist joined the ranks of their attackers'.[62] Holmes would spend the next 20 years involved in progressive education movements, and in 1914 he helped organize a conference out of which eventually grew the New Education Fellowship and its house magazine *The New Era*. During the inter-war years, the Fellowship and its journal would achieve worldwide importance as the champions of progressive education.

Such were the conventional (and unconventional) wisdoms about teaching history in English schools as they were developed and debated by members of the historical and the teaching professions. But the Historical Association was a small and unrepresentative organization, and most of its members were university academics, or on the staff of teacher training colleges, or secondary school teachers – of whom the majority came from the public school sector. So when history teaching in elementary schools was duly discussed in Manchester in January 1912, the majority of the speakers had no first-hand experience of teaching younger pupils.[63] To the extent that elementary schoolteachers were involved with the HA during these early years, it was at the local branch level, as at Leeds, where an HMI and a university professor ran a local study group specifically for them. Yet the over-riding impression remains that most members of the Association were little more in touch with history teaching for the vast majority of English children in state schools than were the politicians at Westminster or the civil servants in Whitehall. As for the innovative methods proposed by Finlay-Johnson and Keatinge: they had some admirers and supporters, and hers made some impact before 1918, but his required a fundamental rethinking of curricula, text-books and examinations which few teachers were prepared to contemplate.[64]

Teachers and Resources for History

The years from 1870 to 1914 have been described as the age of the elementary school, and England was no exception.[65] By the first two decades of the twentieth century, there were over 20,000 of them, which makes it exceptionally difficult to generalize about what it was like to teach or to be taught history. It has been argued that terrible buildings, which were slum-like in cities, and squalid in the countryside, combined with sadistic and authoritarian teaching, made schooldays at best a drudge and at worst a torment, to be escaped from as soon as possible. Orderliness and conformity were paramount, and they were imposed by drill and corporal punishment, along with much rote learning. The result, according to H.C. Dent, was that 'with relatively rare exceptions ... teachers and taught were sworn enemies. The latter resisted by every means known to them ... the dessicated diet of irrelevant facts that the former persisted in pressing upon them; teachers retaliated with incessant applications of corporal punishment.'[66] Truancy, disorder, disobedience and even 'dumb insolence' were signs of continued resistance by boys and girls to the authority and the message of teachers. There were even strikes, as in 1911 when protests spread to 62 towns, with children picketing schools and marching through the streets, demanding an end to homework and caning, better meals, and a warmer environment. [67]

This Dickensian world was scarcely a nurturing or stimulating environment in which to be taught history – or any other subject. But it was not the only picture of life and learning in Edwardian elementary schools. Jonathan Rose analyzed the interviews conducted in the late 1960s by Paul Thompson and Thea Vigne of 444 people born between 1870 and 1908, and concluded that 90 per cent of them had derived some benefit from their education, that two thirds remembered their time at elementary school as a positive experience, that only one in seven had unhappy memories, and that few regarded their teachers as enemies.[68] Corporal punishment was less widespread than was claimed, and Board schools offered a structured learning environment, recognition for academic achievement, and (often) sympathetic and (sometimes) inspiring teachers, as well as proper heating, lighting and plumbing. Girls enjoyed school more than boys, but many members of both sexes remembered their time with pleasure and appreciation.

Even the rote learning of mathematical tables or the reigns of kings and queens had its attractions and defenders. 'The continuous chanting', recalled the son of a Suffolk factory foreman, 'of so many facts was a hopeless mumbo jumbo to me at first, but gradually light dawned, and I began to see what it was all about and enjoyed finding out more.' 'Did we', another interviewee asked rhetorically, 'find it drudgery?' Her answer was 'Not so. There was pride in achievement, and we all worked to get a word of praise that would follow our "best work".'[69]

But however good or bad or varied their experience of elementary school, most boys and girls were taught history for a mere two hours a week, such teaching only began at the age of seven, and while attendance was made compulsory to the age of twelve in 1899, many children had departed in spirit or in body sometime before then.[70] Exploiting various loopholes in the law, many parents continued to take their children away from school earlier, or only let them attend part time. In the countryside, the leaving age remained generally lower, because of the demands of agricultural labouring, and in the industrial north, the 'half-time' system meant many children combined schooling with factory employment, and boys also worked as street vendors and messengers. In 1903 the government passed the Employment of Children Act, which allowed local authorities to make by-laws prohibiting many of these practices; but one third of them did not adopt the legislation, while others did not enforce their own by-laws, and in 1914 it was estimated that there were over 600,000 children working in shops, agriculture and domestic service, or employed as half-timers in factories and workshops, or doing casual errands as street traders or helping their mothers in home industries. Nor do these figures include poor working-class children occupied in tasks set by their parents: young girls sharing domestic chores with their mothers, boys running errands, and both sexes involved in 'outwork' such as matchbox making.[71]

In practice, then, the amount of history learned by many pupils in Edwardian elementary schools was significantly less than is suggested by the limited amount officially recommended for teaching it; and few of them went on to advanced schooling beyond the age of twelve. There were some higher grade schools, higher elementary schools, technical schools and continuation and evening schools, but they only catered for a tiny percentage of the school going population (there were a mere 36 higher elementary schools in 1913[72]). More important were the secondary schools, which were also placed under the control of local authorities by the 1902 Act, and which Sir Robert Morant was particularly eager to promote.[73] But again, the numbers were tiny: by 1912, there were 5.5 million boys and girls in elementary schools, yet fewer than 50,000 former elementary school pupils in secondary schools. So while the Board of Education lavished considerable time and thought on promulgating suggestions and teaching codes for secondary schools, most English children never attended them, and those few who did only spent a total of four and a half hours a week on English, geography and history combined, which meant that two lessons devoted to history was the most that was realistically possible.[74]

But it was not just that there was little time in the classroom for learning history: it was also that the schoolteachers rarely knew much about it. Most of the instruction in elementary schools was undertaken by former 'pupil teachers', who had been apprenticed to a head teacher at the age of 13, and who may (or may not) have gone on to obtain qualifications at a pupil-teacher centre or a training college. There was a noticeable expansion in the demand for and the supply of such teachers in the aftermath of Forster's Education Act; but since they had been in elementary school at a time when history had rarely been taught, they often knew little more about the subject than those whom they were abruptly called upon to instruct in the subject after 1900. Most elementary school teachers came from working-class backgrounds, their morale was low and their circumstances often precarious, and teaching was generally regarded as a low status profession, which helps explain why 75 per cent of them were women.[75] By the 1900s, when there were more than a quarter of a million of them, most elementary teachers were earning below 150 pounds a year, significantly less than most professionals or skilled industrial workers. Their collective organization (the National Union of Teachers) was weak, many of them lived in circumstances that were little better than genteel poverty, pension schemes scarcely existed, and the inflation of the war years eroded both teachers' incomes and their savings (if they had any).[76]

At the elementary level, Sir Robert Morant was determined to tighten up the regulations governing pupil teachers by requiring that they must be educated at secondary school, by raising the age level at which they could begin, and by insisting on 'appropriate courses of instruction' at pupil-teacher centres or day training colleges. In 1907, he introduced a 'Preliminary Examination for the Elementary School Teachers' Certificate', the second part of which included compulsory papers in history. This was the first attempt to give future elementary teachers any training in the subject, but the Chief Examiner's report was damning.[77] 'There were', he began, 'a considerable number of papers which may be passed over as worthless.' As for 'the great mass of papers which in marks reached a fair standard': there was 'a fair acquaintance with the subject in its concrete phases' and 'some of the broader and more important points were understood by many'. But the overall verdict was devastating: 'they do not know history, but only know the answers to certain questions'; there was 'no evidence that any, or hardly any, have read any serious book on the period of the kind to which an adult would naturally go for information'; and most had mugged the subject up 'out of the ordinary school text book, and not always the best at that'. 'I hope', the Chief Examiner concluded, 'that we may remedy this by degrees.' But Morant had been determined to end the pupil-teacher system, and by the outbreak of war, he had effectively done so.[78]

During the same period, there was also a notable advance in the provision of teachers for the (slowly) expanding secondary school sector, and the result was a growth in teacher training colleges, under the auspices of local authorities, and often affiliated with the new redbrick universities. The most famous was the London Day Training College, founded in 1902, controlled by the London County Council, which eventually became the Institute of Education.[79] Until 1905, there were no specialist historians in any teacher training colleges, and the subject was left to 'general tutors'; which meant that the proper instruction of would-be teachers in history was essentially one of 'hope deferred'.[80] Thereafter, matters did improve, but the formal instruction in history left much to be desired. One Chief Examiner regretted that the students failed to demonstrate 'the sense of humanity in history, of continuity, of picturesqueness', let alone the qualities of 'reverence and imagination', they ought to have learned. Part of the problem lay with the lecturers, who often went on too long, bored their audience with too much detail, and failed to excite their curiosity or capture their imagination. But it was also that college libraries were often deficient, reducing the students to 'a painful dependence on the text book, often of the most elementary character'. In any case, teachers trained in history were a small proportion of a very small cohort:

until 1914, the number of trained secondary school teachers averaged fewer than 200 a year.[81]

The result was that most history teachers were excessively reliant on textbooks for facts, details and information. In the lower years of elementary schools, these publications were generally called 'readers', whose main purpose was not to impart information or excite curiosity, but to improve the reading skills of boys and girls. Some readers were quite general, containing snippets of information about a range of topics – geography, literature, myths and legends, and history. Or they might be specifically historical readers, containing such stories as Alfred and the cakes or Robert Bruce and the spider. Among the most popular were *Nelson's Highways of History*, and the *Piers Plowman Histories*, which provided accessible stories, along with vivid illustrations, for use by pupils from six onwards.[82] According to an LCC report on history teaching, overseen by A.F. Pollard and published in 1911, history readers should 'consist of graphically told and picturesquely illustrated biographies and stories drawn from the history of England and the world'. They should also contain 'summaries and marginal notes, and accurate, plenteous and appropriate illustrations', along with 'some copies of old documents'. Moreover, they should not 'consist merely of the lives of kings (an arrangement unfortunately too common), but should be a living story dealing with men and movements in continuous progression'. Compiled and constructed in this way, readers would enable pupils to acquire 'an intelligent view of the main lines of historical development'.[83]

For senior pupils in elementary school, and for those few at secondary school, readers were superseded by textbooks and general surveys, which in their modern form date from J.R. Green's *Short History of the English People*, published in 1874; but the first phase in the major growth in the provision of history textbooks dates from the early years of the twentieth century. Most of these new textbooks were concerned with England, Britain and the British Empire, and paid little heed to the rest of the world.[84] Some were written by people who have vanished into obscurity, such as O.M.E. Edwards's *A School History of England*, and Mrs Ransome's *First History of England* (1903), and *Primary History of England* (1905). Some were by reputable academics, such as S.R. Gardiner's *A Student's History of England* (1891), and T.F. Tout's *An Advanced History of Great*

Britain (1909). And some were by famous authors, such as C.R.L. Fletcher and Rudyard Kipling's *School History of England* (1911). They were primarily concerned with the story of the English nation as constitutional progress and ordered liberty; but some were also concerned with the growth of the Empire. The most popular textbook in London secondary schools was Miss C. Linklater Thompson's *A First History of England*, which appeared in 1902, and was described by one reviewer as 'an admirable piece of work', based on original authorities, written in a clear and simple style, and with an enthusiasm that should 'carry the pupils along with her'.[85]

But these history readers and textbooks needed to be chosen and used carefully, and some of them were severely criticized. The LCC committee of 1911 concluded that only one reader seemed vaguely acceptable, but it was 'lacking in many respects'. No doubt A.F. Pollard had a hand in this damning verdict, and he was no more friendly to text books: they may, as a genre, 'be necessary, but are certainly evil', for they preferred 'knowledge to understanding, and seem expressly designed to nip the bud of historical interest and to clip the wings of historical imagination'.[86] He was not alone in this opinion: according to G.F. Bridge, who had surveyed several of them, history text books were 'dreary deserts of bald facts', characterized by 'their inhumanity, their deadness, their coldness, their incapacity to touch the springs of feeling and imagination'. Tout's *Advanced History* was criticized for 'signs of haste' and needed 'careful revision', while Fletcher and Kipling were condemned for their 'inconsistency and crudeness of political thought', and for their 'imperialist judgments' that were 'uncontrollable and irresponsible'. Even Miss Linklater Thompson's *First History* was taken to task for concentrating on the reigns of kings and queens and the doings of politicians to the virtual exclusion of all else. Not surprisingly, the LCC concluded that 'reliance should be placed less and less upon the text book, ... and more and more upon ... other aids'.[87]

The Board of Education also urged the use of maps and pictures, coins and models, lantern slides and visits to museums, galleries and historic sites, and many of these 'novel equipments' were on display at an exhibition of history teaching held at King's College, London late in 1914.[88] Lantern-slides were the first example of technology transforming the history classroom. In 1901, six elementary schools in East London began to use them 'to give particular force and vivacity' to the teaching of history, and a similar consortium was set up among ten schools in Stoke Newington. The LCC inherited a large collection of historic slides from the London School Board, and in 1908 an Historical Association leaflet was devoted to illustrations and lantern slides, and provided lists of suppliers. Visits to historic sites also proliferated: in 1907–08 the top class at Sherington Road School in south-east London went to the Tower of London and Westminster Abbey; in 1914, Windsor Holy Trinity School took pupils to Runnymede and five years later to the State Apartments in Windsor Castle.[89] There was also drama: some schools followed Harriet Finlay-Johnson by creating renditions of such iconic episodes as King Alfred burning the cakes, while others drew on historical playlets provided by *The Woman Teachers' World*. And there was re-enacted history outside the classroom: civic pageants became popular after one held in Sherborne in 1905 celebrating the town's 1,200th anniversary; and there were dramas furnished by the Village Children's Historical Play Society established in 1911.[90]

But beyond the confines of some atypically well-supplied and well-supported schools in large cities or comfortable county towns, it is not clear that these resources were readily available. Readers and textbooks were not only criticized for being boring and inaccurate: pressure on funding meant they were often used when they had long since become out of date, in many schools there were not enough of them to go round, and some schools were completely bereft.[91] For whatever reason, many schoolchildren would later recall that they had used no such books in class, or if they had, they could not remember anything about them. Maps, wall charts, pictures and lantern-slides also cost more than many schools could afford, and so did outings to museums, galleries, castles, churches and other places of historic interest. In 1906, a headmaster in Bethnal Green noted how difficult it was for many of his pupils to manage even the few pence needed for a trip to the City of London. As so often, there was a large gap between the best of governmental suggestions and pedagogic intentions, and the chronically underfunded and under resourced classroom reality.[92] Indeed, it was precisely this gulf, between what was prescribed and what was actually being taught and experienced, that HMIs repeatedly encountered on their visits to evaluate history teaching in state schools.

History in the Classroom

As in all subjects taught at elementary and secondary level, the Inspectors provided the crucial link between the Board and the schools, and in 1903 they consisted of one Senior Chief Inspector, nine Chief Inspectors, and 88 Inspectors. Like the civil servants at the Board, most HMIs were Oxbridge graduates from an upper middle-class background, they were recruited by patronage, they had not been educated at the state schools they were employed to inspect, they were often independently opinionated, and they tended to remain in post until well into their sixties.[93] In 1903, Sir Robert Morant prepared a memorandum on the subject of Inspectors for the new President, Lord Londonderry. It was highly critical: he doubted whether many HMIs were of the calibre or standing to deal with the responsible local authorities, and he thought too many were old men, 'who have been … upwards of thirty years doing the same thing in the same way'. Local authorities needed to be shown the Board was determined to increase the efficiency of the Inspectorate, and to this end, he proposed to weed out weak and incompetent HMIs. But in practice, Morant's so-called 'purge' amounted to very little: a few elderly inspectors retired, and some women were appointed – but only to specialist posts. The preponderance of male Oxbridge graduates remained, as did anxieties about their ability to engage with elementary schools or with the new local authorities.[94]

Just as the Board had its problems with the aged and reactionary HMIs, so the Inspectors had their problems with what they saw as the limited and blinkered outlook of the Board.[95] Unsurprisingly, one of them was E.G.A. Holmes, who was not only hostile to the stultifying atmosphere of many elementary school classrooms, but also to the 'handful of officials in Whitehall', whom he denounced for their 'bureaucratic ignorance and imbecility'. Holmes may have been atypical among HMIs, but his hostility to the London-based mandarins was not unusual. Yet he also admitted that he found it difficult to engage with the schools, and especially with the pupils, he was employed to inspect – in part because of the social distance between them and him, but also because it was exceptionally difficult for HMIs to get close to the experience of what it was like for boys and girls being educated in the classroom. As Holmes went on to explain, 'neither the teacher nor the inspector could get into living touch with the child, or make any serious attempt to understand his character or take measure of his capacity'. This meant 'the mind, the heart, the whole personality of the child, was an unknown land which we were forbidden to explore', as a result of which he 'took little or no interest in my examinees either as individuals or as human beings, and never tried to explore their hidden depths'.[96] The reports of HMIs are often the only evidence available of how history was taught in the classroom; but they rarely enable us to see things from the pupils' point of view.

How, then, did children experience the novel phenomenon of being taught history for two hours a week during the early years of the twentieth century? And what impact, if any, did it have on them, at the time and in later life? According to Jonathan Rose, most boys and girls found the subject less appealing than English literature or geography, because it rarely dealt with modern times, and focused so heavily on kings and queens. This had certainly been true in the closing decades of the nineteenth century, when history had only been taught in a tiny minority of elementary schools, as one inspector explained:

> Children invariably answer better in geography than they do in history, and at first sight this seems inexplicable. Our school histories record many stirring scenes which are certainly more attractive to the scholars than lists of capes and bays with which geographical primers abound, yet children know the capes, but they do not know history.[97]

The constant stress on dates and reigns and kings and queens was arid, narrow and stultifying. As another HMI observed at this time:

> The chief events of the period selected are generally satisfactorily known, and the most important dates are committed to memory, but the causes and results of these events, and the social and political life of the time, are not well taught. The biographies of famous men are not sufficiently studied, and good notes by the teacher are rarely forthcoming.

Even worse, 'this subject, more than any other, suffers from the indiscriminate use of readers', and they were 'almost devoid of interest, and such dry bones as these simply kill the love of reading'.[98]

It was hoped that the new block grant scheme, combined with the *Code* promulgated in 1900, with its stress on teachers' independence, would result in history being taught in all elementary schools, and on better and broader lines, and there was soon evidence that this was happening. The freedom given to teachers to design their lessons 'according to the staff and appliances of the school, the circumstances of the neighbourhood, and the capacity of the scholars', was widely welcomed.[99] One HMI reported that in some schools 'greater attention' was now being paid to 'English history', with 'the basis of instruction being a brief outline of the main events for the lower classes, and a more detailed knowledge of the period – usually the reign of Victoria – for the upper classes'. A second inspector found it 'gratifying to note how children now begin to learn to use dictionaries, atlases etc instead of uselessly trying to convert themselves into ... lists of names, places etc.' Yet a third believed history was now 'one of the most interesting subjects', and 'some of the history readers' were 'delightful for children'.[100] There was, another inspector concluded, 'no doubt' of history's popularity 'with children where it is well taught"[101]

But how often and widely was it 'well taught'? Some HMIs complained that many teachers were still using 'crabbed and tedious old books', which were in 'too good a condition to be changed for newer ones', but which were 'responsible for a good deal of the lack of interest in the subject, which is often evident'. They were concerned that 'a proper sequence of study from year to year is not provided for', and that boys and girls were often overwhelmed by 'too much detail'. There was criticism of the lack of time and effort devoted to school excursions: either because there was 'nothing interesting in the neighbourhood', or (as in Cambridge) because teachers feared taking their pupils to museums or galleries where their limited knowledge of the objects on display might be shown up by expert curators.[102] And the HMIs worried that 'the teacher is sometimes very little ahead of the class, and very often the oral exposition is weak and the questioning puerile, not calculated to appeal to the child or stimulate further reading'. But even when the teaching was better, the outcome was not necessarily better. 'The children are attentive and interested while their teachers are talking to them', one Inspector noted, but 'except in the best schools, very little information is returned to the teacher', while 'the children appear to remember scarcely anything'. Another HMI agreed: 'the results of the teaching cannot yet be considered satisfactory'.[103]

There are many recollections by former pupils that bear out these official criticisms. According to C.H. Rolph, the teaching of history in elementary school lacked coherence and conviction, even when it took the recommended form of tales and stories. 'The history lessons', he remembered, 'were, it seemed, judged to be sufficiently human if they were larded with fancy legends like Alfred and the Cakes, Bruce and the Spider, Canute and the Tide, and Turnagain Whittington'. But none of this captured Rolph's imagination. 'What history I ever learned', he went on, 'I was to get, in due course ... from Gibbon, Froude, Macaulay, Wells, Toynbee and the marvelous reams of scholars who compiled the Oxford and Cambridge modern histories.'[104] A further frequent criticism was that (despite repeated official exhortations to the contrary) there was no sequence of chronological progression or sense of intellectual development. When the young Jack Common was bought a second hand biography of Dr Johnson, the history he had learned was of no help as he tried to make sense of the great lexicographer's life:

> Our history lessons, you see, had nowhere near reached the eighteenth century. We were still bogged among the Plantagenets, and by the same method of slow torture employed in the issue of books for class-reading, it was all too likely that next term would find us starting the Plantagenets all over again. In fact it might easily take us as long to get down the centuries as it did the folks who originally made the trip, except that in one class or another we were bound to encounter a teacher who dropped us quickly down a ladder of dates into an era he had been reading up on.[105]

Not surprisingly, for many in elementary school, English literature remained more appealing than English history. 'Scratch us even now, and we'll break into a rash of Browning, Wordsworth, Shelley, Milton; and, of course, the Bard', recalled Amy Gomm, born in 1899, the daughter of an Oxfordshire electrician. But while lessons in English literature left a lasting and positive legacy, English history was merely a matter of battles and kings, and trying to remember their dates. We'd hear, in passing, of certain villains who 'rose up in revolt.' It was years before we realized that they might have had a point of view. We didn't learn real history.[106]

Gomm's unhappy experience seems to have been widely shared, especially the revulsion at the rote learning of the reigns and names and dates of kings and queens, an activity devoid of any broader context, or of any feeling for the passing of time. Along with large classes, the absence of homework, an inadequate supply of suitable textbooks, and the widespread ignorance and indifference on the part of teachers, the tedium of rote learning was one more obstacle to generating enthusiasm for history. And according to Frances Collie, one of the earliest lecturers in education, the result was that 'instead of acquiring those estimable moral, aesthetic and intellectual virtues which codes and educational text books assure us are the inevitable consequences of introducing history into the curriculum', the reality was that bored and indifferent pupils were 'apt to derive a permanent dislike for the subject'.[107]

Against these negative recollections and comments should be set a report on 'a certain Liverpool Girls' School' compiled in 1911, where the inspector was struck 'with the unusual freedom and spontaneity which characterizes the children in all departments of their work, and especially in English and History'.[108] It was a Roman Catholic school near the docks, it enjoyed 'no striking advantages by way of premises', and there was 'nothing striking or unusual in the equipment'. But the rooms were clean, bright and tidy, and it possessed 'a large library'. The 250 girls were 'for the most part daughters of labourers', ranging from eight to 14, and the history teachers took 'a real interest in their work', while 'the girls show a surprising keenness in their historical study and an exceptional grasp of the material that has been presented to them'. Lessons were never 'uninteresting lectures', the acquisition of information was never regarded as an end in itself, and the note-taking and essay-writing were of a very high standard. This made possible debate and discussion between the girls and their teachers on such questions as 'No representation, no taxation – were the Americans justified?' and 'Who was greater, the younger or elder Pitt?' The inspector was especially impressed that 'the absence of dogmatism and the encouragement of free expression of opinion have produced independence of thought and judgement in a marked degree', which meant the children were 'able and eager to attack intellectual problems of some difficulty', and thereby obtained 'some insight into the controversial and problematic nature of historical study'.

At secondary level, the initial standard of history teaching was again low. In 1902, a Board report looking into the 'literary subjects' in selected boys' schools was damning: many had no libraries, no atlases and taught solely from one textbook. Teaching was geared to the syllabus of whatever examination was being taken, and too many boys were 'studying the Wars of the Roses who are quite ignorant of all previous history, so ignorant that they did not know who William the Conqueror was'.[109] Thereafter, there seems to have been gradual but uneven improvement, as evidenced in the report on the Roan Boys School at Greenwich, inspected in May 1907. None of the masters were specialists in history, but they were 'sufficiently well qualified for the work they are called upon to do', their lessons 'gave evidence of careful preparation', and the syllabus was 'planned so as to ensure that a boy shall during his passage through the school acquire a good general knowledge of the subject'. But there were also serious shortcomings. 'The general level of knowledge in the various forms' was not 'at all high', and when questions were put by the Inspector, 'the answers came almost entirely from two or three of the best boys, the vast majority making no attempt at all'. 'The equipment for history teaching' was also 'very meagre': 'insufficient use' was made of maps and diagrams; there ought to be 'a supply of illustrations of historical events and portraits of famous characters'; and the 'Teachers' Reference Library should contain a good collection of standard histories'. Such resources, the report concluded, would help 'give life and zest to the teaching'.[110]

Thereafter, the guidance offered in Circular 599 seems to have had a definite impact. Two years later, the new County Secondary School in Kentish Town was inspected; it was 'still in a transition state', but the work 'appears to have been very well planned': history was well 'correlated' with other subjects, there were 'plenty of good reference books', translations from original sources were used, and 'both teachers and taught seem interested in their subject'. The balance between English, European and general history might be better struck but, 'having regard to all the circumstances of the case, it does not seem necessary to advise an alteration which might not ... be for the better'.[111] At the same time, the County Secondary School in Fulham had received an even more glowing report. The headmistress and her staff were 'specially qualified' in history, and they had worked out a detailed and coherent syllabus, balancing English and European history, and covering both over a long chronological span from the lower to the higher forms. Special stress was given to ancient Greek and Roman history, to setting the Tudor period in the broader context of the European Renaissance, and to institutions of government and the evolution of the British constitution. The 'oral methods' of teaching were 'generally effective', and essay writing was 'well directed and supervised'. Maps and diagrams were given sufficient attention, and the reference library was being added to. 'Altogether,' the Inspector concluded, 'the teaching of history seems to be particularly well schemed and carried out.'[112]

The only generalization that can be ventured is that across the twenty thousand state schools, history teaching ranged from the excellent to the deplorable. By the same token, opinions differed as to how far history teaching instilled patriotic sentiments and imperial awareness into Edwardian youth. According to Robert Roberts, growing up in the Salford slums, it did so with considerable success:

> Teachers, fed on Seeley's imperialistic work, *The Expansion of England*, and often great readers of Kipling, spelled out patriotism among us with a fervour that with some verged on the religious. Empire Day, of course, had special significance. We drew union jacks, hung classrooms with flags of the dominions, and gazed with pride as they pointed out those massed areas of red on the world map. 'This, and this, and this', they said, 'belong to us.'[113]

Robert's view is corroborated in some working class memoirs, but this was not the whole of the picture. This was partly, as Frederick Willis explained, because the teaching of English history rarely got beyond the Tudors, which meant there was no opportunity to celebrate imperial greatness or to raise imperial consciousnesses. 'History', he recalled,

> as taught by the board school, left us with a vague impression that up to the time of Elizabeth this country had been occupied exclusively by kings and queens, good, bad and indifferent, and from Queen Elizabeth onwards were the Dark Ages, since we never heard of anything happening in that period.[114]

The lack of attention given to the nineteenth century was one reason why history teaching was less imperialist in its message than some supposed, and others would have wished, and why later recollections of such propagandistic pedagogy are relatively rare. Many readers and textbooks in use during the 1900s and 1910s had been produced in earlier decades, and their imperial content was meagre; and although it increased in works published thereafter, some textbooks were critical of Britain's conduct vis-à-vis the rest of the world, while most teachers had received no training in imperial history, and were ignorant of the British Empire's recent past.[115] Moreover, many were thought to be left wing and hostile to empire: 'they are the children of working people', complained one critic in 1908, 'and bring to their work all the prejudices and limitations of their class'.[116] This may explain why, in 1902, Lord Meath, the inventor of Empire Day, was dismayed to discover that school leavers knew nothing of the Indian Mutiny; he was concerned at the lack of teaching about the history of empire, and regarded its inadequate coverage in textbooks as 'positively dangerous'. In 1911, at the Imperial Education Conference, Halford Mackinder urged that geography rather than history was the way to teach Empire, while Richard Lodge conceded it was 'absurd' to try to 'frame an ambitious scheme of historical study embracing the whole of imperial history' for children leaving school at fourteen. The result, as C.P. Lucas lamented, was that 'nine out of ten workingmen' were ignorant about the history and geography of the British Empire, because 'they have never been systematically taught to know or care'.[117]

The evidence concerning the substance and impact of history teaching in Edwardian England is thus spotty and inconclusive. But even allowing for the outstanding examples afforded by the elementary school in Liverpool and the County Secondary School in Fulham, there was often a wide gap between the thoughtful suggestions made about how the subject might be taught by the Board of Education and the Historical Association, and the gloomy and unexciting reality of history as experienced in the classroom. As the Board conceded in its *Suggestions* of 1914, 'schools vary widely in their circumstances', and 'the teaching of history in elementary schools presents great difficulties', among them 'large classes, restricted time and the want of good text books'.[118] The professoriate agreed. According to C.H. Firth, history was taught in elementary schools by staff with virtually no training in the subject, while for the few who stayed on to secondary level, instruction was 'neither thorough nor systematic'. And Ramsay Muir, from Liverpool University, was even more scornful: 'he would rather', he told the Imperial Education Conference, 'see history dropped from the curriculum of elementary and secondary schools altogether than have pupils coming to him with the kind of knowledge that that have in their heads and the kind of detestation they have in their hearts for the subject'.[119] Matters may have improved since 1906, but the anxieties entertained in that year by Miss Howard still retained their force.

Against this must be set a survey, undertaken in 1913 by E.O. Lewis, into the relative popularity of different school subjects.[120] He obtained his data from 5,000 boys and 3,000 girls, the majority of whom attended elementary schools in London. He asked the pupils to rank the subjects they were taught in order of preference, and history emerged as the third most popular subject, with a high interest-level and 'general appeal to all pupils', which vindicated his view that history should be 'universally taught'. 'History', Lewis concluded, 'is a subject that appeals greatly to pupils; and our data frequently suggest that the appeal is strongest to young pupils.' But he also expressed concern that the popularity of history was of 'dubious value' if the reasons given for liking it were viewed from 'the moral standpoint'. Some boys, he noted, 'state without reservation that the massacres, battles, strategies, and pillaging are the chief charms history has for them', and their 'chief heroes' were 'Drake, Raleigh, Hawkins, Nelson [and] Frobisher'. Lewis was also less than happy with the 'deductions' some pupils draw, of which he offered two examples: 'history teaches us to be civil, because people were always fighting with one another [in the past]'; 'we all cannot go like Drake and rob Spain, but we can all do our duty to our country'. Within a year, hundreds of thousands of former schoolboys would be doing just that. To what extent had their school history predisposed them to do 'our duty to our country'?

History Goes to War

If the Hackney shoemaker Arthur Newton is to be believed, history teaching had accomplished this objective. 'The population of the country', he recalled, 'had been schooled in the glories of the British

Empire and the deeds of her victorious armies.' This, he believed, was why so many young men volunteered in 1914 in such large numbers, to fight for 'King and Country'. Thus regarded, the enterprise of 'exalting patriotism' by teaching history, which had been begun in English schools as the Boer War ended, had been an outstanding success; and this was not only true in England, but also throughout the United Kingdom, and across other belligerent nations, where millions flocked to their country's colours.[121] Yet it is not clear that the teaching of history is the prime explanation for the jingoistic euphoria that greeted the outbreak of war, because as a means of inculcating patriotism, history had not been effectively taught. In France, a survey carried out in 1901 reported that six out of every ten recruits to a cavalry squadron had never heard of the Franco-Prussian War, and five years later, a similar inquiry revealed that barely half the recruits knew of the loss to Germany of Alsace-Lorraine. Historians of German education have also concluded that there was only a weak link between government intentions and pedagogic reality; that nationalist messages varied according to different regions; that they were less important than the promotion of proper social roles; and that their influence on adult attitudes and behaviour was very limited.[122]

The same was true in England, where teaching the reigns and dates of kings and queens did not necessarily inculcate feelings of patriotic loyalty or promote shared national identity in the classroom, and where, as J.W. Headlam noted, history was 'for most pupils a by-study; it gets a scanty two hours a week, and it is difficult to see how this can be increased'. Insofar as young Englishmen were fired up with patriotic zeal in 1914, this owed more to the influence of youth organizations, to the cult of Empire Day, to the songs of the music hall, and to the royal ceremonials that proliferated at this time than to the eighty hours of history teaching that they may (or may not) have received until the age of fourteen.[123] And just as the time given to history was a small part of the time spent at school, so the time spent at school was a small component of the time spent growing up. The ruling elites may have thought that elementary education was 'an instrument for conditioning and controlling the lower orders'; but in England as elsewhere in Europe, it is not clear that schools were successful agents of propaganda or vehicles of social control. As F.M.L. Thompson has written, 'school was a significant part of growing up, and an important influence on a child's ideas about the world and how to behave in it'. But 'it was only one strand among many, and for the working-class child with only a short time in school, that was likely to end by the age of twelve, it was not the dominant or decisive element'. On the contrary, it was 'the home and the neighbourhood, and later on the workplace and the pub' that 'had superior influence in shaping the outlook of working class youths and young adults'.[124]

In any case, the Board of Education had always set its face against the teaching of history as crude, patriotic propaganda, and on the outbreak of the First World War, it reaffirmed its position in Circular 869, a *Memoranda on Teaching and Organization on Secondary Schools*, as related to 'Modern European History'. 'The events now proceeding in Europe', it began, 'and the crisis the nation has to face, call for knowledge as well as courage and devotion.' Those responsible for teaching history, it went on, 'will be considering how this, like other subjects of instruction, may best be made to serve national purposes'.[125] But what the Board offered was an embellished version of Circular 599 on the teaching of recent European history. The years from 1815 to 1871 were relatively straightforward, witnessing the beginnings of 'the modern history of nearly every European nation'; but the subsequent period 'presents little that is suitable for school work, and it is doubtful how far it would be desirable to carry on the narrative in a systematic way'. Attention should be given to the establishment of the Kingdom of Italy and the German Empire, to the expansion of the British Empire and to the decay of the Ottoman Empire, and the part played by the royal navy and the British army deserved more notice. But in dealing with the recent past, 'everything should be avoided which would encourage national animosities', and although 'there is no surer source of courage than the study of past achievements', there was also 'no better school of wisdom than the recognition of past mistakes'.[126]

This remained the Board's position throughout the conflict, and it was reaffirmed by J.W. Headlam in a minute of September 1917. To begin with, 'the amount of time' that was 'available for the teaching of history' in schools 'is and must remain very small', which meant it was 'quite impossible to make room for all which it is suggested we should do.' Moreover, there were 'the most strenuous objections to the Board using its influence to give any definite political bias' to history teaching, 'for if we once admit the principle, we shall get into the intolerable position that we shall be asked to change the advice which we give to schools as one party or another succeeds to power.' Such 'definite propaganda', Headlam concluded, was wholly inappropriate, and it should be left to 'each individual school' to decide what aspects of history should be taught.[127] In the following year, Headlam-Morley (as he had become) again made the same point, expressing his hostility, in another minute, to 'the possible dangers arising from the use of teaching history in schools for immediate political purposes'. Moreover, in the case of the history of the British Empire, there had never been any enthusiasm for it: indeed, 'the history of the colonies' had been regarded by most schools and schoolchildren as 'extraordinarily uninteresting. We cannot get boys and girls to be interested in subjects such as the establishment of the Commonwealth of Australia.' 'Hitherto', another official noted, 'the British Empire has not been seriously treated in school history.'[128]

As the war drew to a close, the Board's *Suggestions* for elementary schools continued to hope that pupils would acquire 'a tolerably connected view of the main outlines of British history, some knowledge of the government of the country, the growth of free institutions, the expansion of the Empire, and the establishment of our position among nations'.[129] But recent history was problematic: treating it 'reign by reign' would never be 'really interesting and attractive', while constitutional and economic changes would be difficult to teach and might prove controversial. Topics such as 'the industrial revolution' or 'the growth of empire' or 'social reform' might be possible, especially if looked at through 'the lives and careers of men and women who played a principal part in them'.[130] But the reality was that history was often not being well taught. In 1917, Charles Jarvis, a lecturer in education and history at the Leeds Training College, claimed that 'many teachers' were 'not convinced' of the 'value' of history, and had 'no definite objective in the work, no enthusiasm, and little historical knowledge', which meant it had 'been more neglected than any other subject of the curriculum'. There was also a growing concern that chronology was being neglected: one HMI complained that 'the reaction against the 'dates of the kings and the queens' had 'gone too far', and many pupils left school not knowing 'any dates', and with 'little appreciation of historical time'.[131]

This was partly because the circumstances of wartime teaching were decidedly adverse, as education was subordinated to the greater endeavour of fighting the enemy. Any further attempts to reform the Balfour Act of 1902 were put on hold, the recruitment of new inspectors was suspended and school inspections were halted, and the Board of Education became an increasingly marginal department. Before the first year of war was over, it came under heavy pressure from local authorities anxious to suspend school attendance by-laws, and there were pleas for the release of children into the labour force on the grounds of economic necessity when their fathers were wounded or killed on active service. The result was that during the first three years of war, 600,000 children were put 'prematurely' to work.[132] Nor was this the only disruption. Many male teachers volunteered, many more were conscripted, and by 1918 the number of men training to be teachers was less than one tenth what it had been when war broke out. This sudden decline was only gradually compensated for by an increase in the number of women being trained to enter the classroom, and it became increasingly clear that when the war was over, a large number of additional teachers would be urgently required. There was also growing disquiet at the 'slight esteem' in which teachers were still held, and at their inadequate salaries and limited benefits.[133]

Yet these general concerns about education, and specific anxieties about history, co-existed with increased excitement about the prospects once the fighting was over. As the Board of Education made plain in its report for 1917–18, the war 'has certainly brought a clearer and wider recognition of the value of education', and had also strengthened the nation's 'resolution to improve it'.[134] Members of the Historical Association seized the opportunity to urge the rethinking and scaling-up of history in the classroom. The war had ended as a triumph for Britain and its Empire, but this made it essential to teach the neglected nineteenth century, and give more attention to imperial, military and naval history. It also seemed important to teach in a less insular way, giving time to Britain's relations with European powers, and the United States. The passing of the Fourth Reform Act in 1918 brought the county closer to mass democracy, which made it essential to educate voters in the responsibilities of citizenship, which could only be done by teaching more history, including economic and social history. And with the establishment of the League of Nations, there were calls to present the subject in a more internationalist perspective.[135] In the brave new post-war world, the possibilities for history in the classroom seemed almost limitless, and with an historian in office as President of the Board of Education, there seemed good grounds to hope they might soon be realized.[136]

2 History in Peace and War, 1918–44

Of all subjects in the curriculum, history in the larger sense of the term, is the most difficult for young people to comprehend: yet it contains materials which should make it most interesting.

> (Board of Education, *Report of the Consultative Committee on the Education of the Adolescent* (London, 1927), p. 195.)

When the First World War ended, the President of the Board of Education was H.A.L. Fisher, who had been in post for almost two years.[1] He had been invited to join the coalition which Lloyd George formed in December 1916, and held office until it fell in October 1922. Fisher was President for longer than any of his predecessors; none after him would equal his length of tenure; and nor would any subsequent Ministers of Education or Secretaries of State. He was also the only holder of the office who had been a full-time educationalist, for he began his career as a Fellow of New College, Oxford, then moved to be Vice-Chancellor of the University of Sheffield. Although a classicist, Fisher's preferred subject was history, and by the time he joined the government, he had published on a wide variety of topics.[2] He also belonged to the nation's 'intellectual aristocracy': Leslie Stephen was an uncle, F.W. Maitland and Ralph Vaughan Williams were brothers-in-law, and Virginia Woolf and Vanessa Bell were cousins; and after leaving government, Fisher would be Warden of New College, Oxford, President of the British Academy, a member of the Order of Merit, and the author of a three-volume, best-selling *History of Europe*. Like James Bryce (whose biography he wrote), he was a quintessential ornament of the British liberal establishment.[3]

Fisher adapted easily to the House of Commons, to the cabinet, and to the social life of London; he got on well with his civil servants at the Board, especially Sir Lewis Selby-Bigge and William N. Bruce, who admired him for his emollient manner, administrative efficiency,

61

and commitment to reform; he was also the first President to establish a close rapport with schoolteachers, whose pay and conditions he was determined to improve.[4] History remained important to Fisher throughout his years in government: he helped establish the Institute of Historical Research at the University of London, and he pondered how the subject might be appropriately presented in the classroom. 'My general view', he told Francis S. Maude, an HMI for history and classics, 'is that the best result is obtained by strengthening and enlightening the teacher in that side of historical teaching in which he already feels most interest and with respect to which he already possesses most instruction.' Subject to this 'general principle', Fisher hoped to see 'infused into our school teaching a broader appreciation of the general development of human civilization than at present prevails', and he wanted history teaching improved along these lines.[5]

Fisher also enjoyed the advantage of the engaged support of the Prime Minister. Lloyd George's preoccupations from 1916 to 1922 were with foreign affairs, and he and Fisher came from very different social backgrounds and educational worlds; but the Prime Minister believed that reconstruction must be carried forward on the home front, and he regarded the increased provision of educational facilities as of the highest importance. He was the son of an elementary schoolteacher, and although he left school at 14, Lloyd George had been taught by an inspiring mentor, David Evans, who had vainly urged him to become a pupil-teacher. Moreover, history was one of the subjects to which Lloyd George had been attracted, and his interests ranged from the Peloponnesian War to the American Civil War.[6] When urging Fisher to take on the Presidency of the Board, Lloyd George declared that educational reform was a top priority, and that it would come better 'from an educationalist than from a politician', and during the early years of his coalition, he never wavered from this undertaking. Indeed, when he came to write his war memoirs, Lloyd George devoted a whole chapter to the 'constructive statesmanship' Fisher had displayed in his 'wise and far-seeing' work – a compliment he paid to no other former colleague in the coalition.[7]

There were other good reasons why the time was propitious for a renewed initiative in educational reform.[8] There were growing concerns about national efficiency and national welfare, which cast doubt on the adequacy of the current educational provision, especially for working-class children, while many local authorities found they were paying proportionately more towards the cost of schooling, whereas central government was paying less. At the Board of Education, the need for reform was the conventional wisdom, and this remained the view when Lewis Selby-Bigge succeeded Robert Morant as Permanent Secretary. In parliament, there was continuing Liberal resentment that their attempts to modify the Balfour Act had been unsuccessful, and when Haldane became Lord Chancellor, he took the lead in pressing for additional legislation. Finally, the First World War exposed the limitations in scientific and technical education, and strengthened the arguments that the nation's youth should be better trained and taught. So the tide was with Fisher, and between 1918 and 1922, he steered a mass of reforming legislation through parliament. 'The nation is awakening', he proclaimed, 'as never before, to the possibilities of education.'[9]

The State and the Schools

The school scene for which Fisher had taken responsibility was deeply unsatisfactory and highly challenging. There was no single national system, and although the nominal school leaving age was 14, many pupils left before then: nearly half of England's children did so at 13 and often 12, and for many pupils, the last two years in school were wasted, since nothing of significance was taught to those who were anxious to leave.[10] Moreover, the supply, quality, conditions and pay of teachers were all unsatisfactory, and they had been further aggravated by the war. Although the pupil-teacher system was running down, many elementary school teachers had been trained in this way, which meant they had not been well trained, and few were proficient in the subjects they were called upon to teach, history included. In rural areas, and in inner cities, school buildings were cold, insanitary and unwelcoming places in which to work, pay was inadequate and further eroded by wartime inflation, while pensions did not exist for secondary school teachers, and the situation was little better among their elementary school colleagues. And the war had placed 'a steadily escalating strain on the archaic system' of educational provision, both at the Board itself in Whitehall and also among local authorities and in schools across the country.[11]

Fisher was determined to rectify these matters, and between 1918 and the fall of the coalition, he carried a succession of interconnected pieces of legislation, beginning with the Education Act of that year, and ending with a measure which consolidated all the legislation passed since Forster's Act of 1870, with the aim of improving every aspect of English state-supported education. In future, central government would contribute 60 per cent of teachers' salaries – the major part of any education budget – and local authorities only 40 per cent. He also sought to improve the material circumstances of teachers, and to raise their social standing and self-esteem: in part by introducing what became known (after its first chairman) as the (Lord) Burnham scale, which would provide a national pay structure for teachers, and in part by instituting a state-funded pension scheme. As far as the pupils were concerned, Fisher wanted to establish 'the great principle that all young people in this country, boys and girls, should receive some form of education through the whole period of adolescence': the school leaving age was compulsorily raised to 14, all previous 'exemptions' were abolished, and local authorities were also required to make available 'a sufficient supply of continuation schools' which were to teach 'suitable courses of study, instruction and physical training' to all children between 14 and 16, and to the age of 18 by 1925.[12]

Fisher's Education Act rightly bears his name, but apart from the abolition of exemptions, the raising of the school leaving age, and the creation of the Burnham scale of salaries, scarcely any of his major reforms survived. Despite Lloyd George's support, the cost of Fisher's reforms far exceeded what the government was willing to pay – or in the end, could afford to pay. When he became President, the Board's annual budget was still below 20 million pounds; by 1921 it had exploded to 51 million.[13] But the economic downturn after the war ended brought about a crisis in public finance; the Board's much-expanded budget was under constant attack, from the Treasury, in the Commons and by the press; and the 'Geddes Axe' of 1922 reduced education funding by almost 7 million pounds. Having earlier been acclaimed as a great reforming president, Fisher now found himself reviled by the teaching profession, his efforts to minimize the damage brought him no thanks, and his last years in office were 'a discouraging period of disappointed hopes'. His attempt to establish a national system of public education went unrealized, and the pre-1914 system remained intact, with the majority of England's children still spending the whole of their education in elementary school.[14]

Fisher's successors rarely held office long enough to make an impact, they often had no wish to do so, and they did not have the chance to do so in the straitened circumstances that governments found themselves in throughout the 1920s and 1930s. During the brief premierships of Bonar Law and Stanley Baldwin, Fisher was followed for 15 months by the high church, fox-hunting Tory, Edward Wood: he was a Yorkshire grandee, who had read history at Oxford, and was a prize Fellow of All Souls. But Wood's imagination was never stirred by the cause of elementary and secondary schools; he had no interest in educational policy; he was aloof and inaccessible to his civil servants; and he made no reference in his autobiography to his time at the Board. Moreover, he had little to do but implement the spending cuts already insisted on by Geddes, recognizing the need to 'pursue economy having regard to the general exigencies of the public service'; and the estimates he carried for 1923–24 were 3.3 million pounds less than the previous year, and 9 million less than those for 1921–22. Wood consoled himself by getting out of London as often as he could, weekending with his fellow grandees in the country, and hunting in Yorkshire twice a week.[15]

Edward Wood was succeeded by Charles Trevelyan, another northern landowner. He had studied history at Cambridge, and he held office during the first, brief, minority Labour government. He vainly attempted to reverse the earlier spending cuts, sought to renovate or rebuild 'blacklisted' elementary schools, tried to increase the number of free places at secondary schools, wanted to reduce the large class sizes, and encouraged local authorities to raise the school leaving age to 15.[16] But after less than twelve months, the Labour government fell, and Trevelyan was succeeded by yet a third north country patrician, Lord Eustace Percy, a younger son of the Duke of Northumberland. He had read history at Oxford, was seriously interested in education, and was President throughout Stanley Baldwin's Conservative government of 1924–29.[17] But despite Percy's unusually long tenure, which ranks second after Fisher's, the times were unpropitious for creative (and thus expensive) reform. He sought to honour the Labour government's commitment to renovating elementary schools, to reducing class sizes, and to expanding secondary education; but he became a target for Conservatives who disliked his progressive views. Moreover, Percy was aloof, superior, portentous and pedantic in the Commons; he was easily dismissed as 'Lord Useless Percy'; and after the Conservative defeat at the general election of 1929, his political career fizzled out.[18]

Percy was followed by the man who had been his predecessor, Sir Charles Trevelyan (as he had become on inheriting the family title and estates); and during the second minority Labour government, he sought to carry an Education Bill to raise the statutory school leaving age to 15. Trevelyan introduced the measure three times, but each time it failed, on the last occasion, in February 1931, because the financial climate was again rapidly deteriorating.[19] He resigned, and was followed by another history graduate, Hastings Lee-Smith, who held office for barely eight months in 1931, when he was forced to accept another round of cuts as a result of the financial crisis in August that year. On the creation of the National Government, Lee-Smith was replaced by Sir Donald Maclean, a Welsh solicitor and Asquithian Liberal, whose chief task was the unenviable one of soothing the angry teachers and administrators who were suffering reductions in spending on salaries and schools. His sudden death opened the way for the return of Lord Irwin, as Edward Wood had become when he went to India as Viceroy. But he was no more interested in education this second time around, and his view of the purposes and limitations of state-supported schooling was well revealed when, on a visit to his estate at Hickleton in Yorkshire, he announced, 'we want a school to train them up for servants and butlers'.[20]

When Stanley Baldwin replaced Ramsay MacDonald as Prime Minister in June 1935, Irwin was moved to the War Office; and he was succeeded as President by another grandee, Oliver Stanley, younger son of the seventeenth Earl of Derby. But he had been shifted sideways from an unhappy tenure as Minister of Labour, and he performed no better at the Board, where he stayed for less than two years. In 1936 he steered through an Education Act, which aimed to raise the school leaving age to 15 on 1 September 1939. But it was a limited piece of legislation, for children could be 'exempted' from attending school for an extra year, and in very large numbers: indeed, *The Times* calculated that 86 per cent of them would be 'eligible for exemption'.[21] When Baldwin retired in May 1937, he was succeeded by Neville Chamberlain, and in the ensuing reshuffle, Stanley was replaced at the Board by the seventh Earl Stanhope, another minor Conservative politician of aristocratic pedigree, who had previously been First Commissioner of Works. His main interests were in naval matters, the Presidency was 'a post for which he had had no previous experience or possibly even aptitude'; and he was put there to promote the cause of physical education.[22]

Stanhope was at the Board for only 17 months, before moving on to the more congenial post of First Lord of the Admiralty; and in October 1938, he was succeeded by the ninth Earl de la Warr, who had been demoted from the grander post of Lord Privy Seal by Neville Chamberlain, because of his heretical views on appeasement. De la Warr was at the Board for only a few months longer than his predecessor, and with the worsening international situation in Europe, there was less scope than ever for action. Indeed, the very day when the school leaving age should have been formally raised to 15 also turned out to be the day when Germany invaded Poland, as a result of which the Education Act of 1936 was suspended for the duration of the Second World War. When Winston Churchill became Prime Minister in May 1940, he dispensed with the services of Lord de la Warr, and appointed the even more obscure Herwald Ramsbotham as President. Unknown to Churchill, Ramsbotham was determined to restore coherence to education in the aftermath of wartime evacuation, and to develop plans for long-term reorganization. But the Prime Minister wanted the home front kept quiet until Germany and Japan were defeated, and he replaced Ramsbotham in July 1941 with R.A. Butler, believing he would be as inactive as most inter-war Presidents.[23]

With the exception of Lees-Smith and Maclean, all these men had attended public school, and most had gone to Oxford and Cambridge: like the majority of their predecessors, they had no first-hand experience of the schools of which they had been put in charge. Only three were seriously interested in education, but none of them achieved much: Fisher because his efforts were nullified by the Geddes Axe; Trevelyan because his terms of office were so short; and Percy because he lacked the financial resources and political clout. Edward Wood, later Lord Irwin, and subsequently Lord Halifax, was a major figure, at least by the time he returned from India, but his first tenure was brief, and he was more interested in India and international affairs during his second. As for Lees-Smith, Maclean, Stanley, Stanhope, de la Warr and Ramsbotham: none were politicians of the front rank, and none held the presidency for even two years, which scarcely gave them time to master their brief, or to get to know their civil servants, or the educational world beyond Whitehall. Of the eleven Presidents from Fisher to Butler, five had been to Eton, five had read history at university and two more were lifelong devotees of the subject: Fisher as a writer and an academic, and Stanhope as the initiator of the National Maritime Museum and as a Trustee of the National Portrait Gallery. But with the exception of Fisher, this did not lead them to take a special interest in how the subject was taught in schools.

As in the 1900s and 1910s, education was not a high priority for inter-war government, and its organization in England remained highly decentralized by international standards. Lord Eustace Percy would later describe it as an example of 'indirect rule' transplanted from the empire to the metropolis, and the Board did not manage schools, employ teachers, prescribe textbooks or provide school buildings.[24] In the early 1920s, the organization of the Board was assimilated to the civil service as a whole, but there was no fundamental change in the background, numbers or outlook of the staff. All four permanent secretaries who held office during this period, Sir Lewis Selby-Bigge, Sir Aubrey Symonds, Sir Edward Pelham and Sir Maurice Holmes, were educated at public school and Oxford University, and had excelled in such traditional subjects as classics, mathematics, philosophy and the law. None was as assertive as Sir Robert Morant, and Symonds gave insufficient support to Lord Eustace Percy against Conservative demands for more economies. As for the rest of the senior staff: until 1919, recruitment had been by patronage; thereafter it was assimilated to the standard procedure of open competition which operated across most of Whitehall; but most of those appointed had been educated at public school and Oxbridge.[25]

Between the presidencies of Fisher and Butler, there was no effective reforming initiative in the Board at ministerial level, and insofar as educational policy and practice were moved forward, it was thanks to reports issued by the chairmen of the Board's Consultative Committee. The first of them was Sir William Hadow who, from the early 1920s to the early 1930s, produced six reports: *The Differentiation of the Curriculum* (1923), *Psychological Tests of Educable Capacity* (1924), *The Education of the Adolescent* (1926), *Books in Public Elementary Schools* (1928), *The Primary School* (1931), and *Infant and Nursery Schools* (1933). In 1924 Hadlow endorsed the current trend in educational thinking which was increasingly against attendance at one school up to 14, and in favour of dividing schooling at eleven, and he urged an increase in secondary school accommodation and in the supply of free places.[26] Two years later, he developed these proposals: all-age elementary schools should be abolished, to be replaced by two distinct forms of education, 'primary' and 'post-primary', the one to end, and the other to begin, at the age of eleven plus; the school leaving age should be raised to 15 by 1932; and there ought to be five different types of post-primary education: ranging from secondary (or grammar) schools, following a literary and scientific curriculum, to vocational technical and trade schools.[27]

Hadow's recommendation that the school leaving age be increased was not realized before the Second World War broke out; but from the mid 1920s to the mid 1930s, there was a growing separation between elementary and secondary schools at the age of eleven, and an expansion and reorganization in secondary education along the lines that Hadow had recommended. It was, to be sure, a matter for local authorities to decide what to do and how to do it, and the Board had no powers of compulsion, but it did make encouraging noises and publish a favourable pamphlet about reorganization.[28] By 1933, the Board was claiming that 50 per cent of pupils over the age of eleven were in reorganized schools. This was an overly optimistic figure; but by 1937 40 per cent of local authorities had reorganized their schools for pupils aged eleven and upwards, and since these authorities were more likely to be in towns and cities than rural areas, this probably included a majority of the classroom population. But these arrangements were by no means universally adopted, there were marked regional and local variations, there was never sufficient funding, and in any case, the majority of pupils who stayed on after the age of eleven only had three years of secondary education until they left school at 14.[29]

In the mid 1930s, Will Spens, who had succeeded Hadow as chairman of the Board of Education's Consultative Committee, was asked to undertake a further inquiry, published as *Secondary Education with Special Reference to Grammar Schools and Technical High Schools* (1938). Spens recommended rationalizing secondary education from a five-strand into a tripartite structure, according to the varying capacities and prospects of pupils, namely grammar schools, technical high schools, and (secondary) modern schools, each of them providing a complete curriculum of education for pupils above the age of eleven, and all of them to enjoy what was termed 'parity' of staffing and esteem. (The alternative model, providing secondary education for all boys and girls under the same single roof, in all-encompassing 'multilateral' – or comprehensive – schools, was considered at some length, but rejected.) Such 'parity' between the three types of school meant that it was 'inevitable' that the leaving age would have to be raised to 16, although Spens admitted this was not 'immediately practicable'.[30] In the straitened financial climate, and on the very eve of war, his report was shelved, although it would later be of great influence when the pressure for reform built up during the early 1940s.

Meanwhile, the partial and piecemeal implementation of the Hadow recommendations meant that the 20,000-odd elementary and secondary schools were more varied than ever.[31] Where local authorities did not draw a firm line between 'primary' and 'secondary' education, there were advanced classes in some elementary schools, for those aged eleven and above; or an elementary school might bring in children from other schools to what was termed its advanced 'senior class'. Alternatively, there might be a complete break at eleven, with some pupils going on to selective secondary ('grammar') schools, some to 'central' schools which might be selective or semi-selective, and the least academic to 'senior' school, with different priorities, curricula and leaving ages. There were also technical and trade schools, part time day continuation schools, and art schools. The physical and intellectual quality of these many different types of school varied enormously. Secondary schools tended to be better funded than elementary schools, urban schools than rural schools, schools in prosperous areas than schools in poor areas; but there were many exceptions.[32] Overall, there was little money available, and there was still a 'blacklist' of schools whose conditions were officially admitted to be unacceptable, which numbered 1,500 in 1932. Some schools were also warm, welcoming and well funded; but this was not the general experience.[33]

Prescribing History for Peacetime

Beginning in 1918, the Board of Education continued to offer its *Suggestions* as to the kind of history that should ideally be taught in English schools. As far as elementary schools were concerned, it remained a matter of policy that the Board insisted 'each teacher should think out and frame his own scheme, having regard to the circumstances of the school'. The Board admitted that 'the teaching of history in the elementary schools presents great difficulties', and this reinforced the view that 'in history, perhaps more than in most studies, the personality of the teacher and his own reading are of the first importance'.[34] But the Board did concede that the study of history should enable the pupil to acquire, 'by the time he leaves school', a 'tolerably connected view of the main outlines of British history', which meant 'some knowledge of the government of the country, the growth of free institutions, the expansion of Empire, and the establishment of our position among nations'. History was also 'pre-eminently an instrument of moral training', which would enable children to 'learn naturally in how many different ways the patriot has helped his country', and 'by what sort of actions nations and individuals have learned the gratitude of posterity' – lessons which 'will be at work long after the information imparted to them has been forgotten'.[35]

For both juniors and seniors, the Board again recommended that 'the picturesque element which quickens imagination and gives life and reality to persons and events' should be conveyed in the classroom by the use of stories and biographies. It was a good idea to teach recent history, but it not easy: to do so 'reign by reign' would never be 'really interesting and attractive', while looking at constitutional and economic changes would be either too difficult or too controversial. Topics such as 'the industrial revolution' or 'the growth of empire' or 'social reform' might be possible, as would the investigation of changes through 'the lives and careers of men and women who played a principal part in them', or through the study of local and social history and visits to historic sites.[36] Maps and drama should be essential parts of lessons, and as for dates: 'they should not be regarded as separate facts but as a means of tracing the course of events', and there was 'much to be said in favour of committing to memory the dates of the accessions of English monarchs as a useful framework of chronology in addition to the dates of outstanding events'. There might, the *Suggestions* admitted, be criticisms of the emphasis on dates in lessons and in some textbooks, but such an approach was well justified, because the stories and personalities which a knowledge of their dates helped to establish appealed to children, and because the character of the sovereign and the duration of his reign 'has often been the determining factor in the story of our country'.[37]

These recommendations remained essentially unaltered in the second instalment of post-war *Suggestions* produced in 1927; but there were significant modifications. In recent years, the *Suggestions* lamented, some teachers had tried to do without dates, 'with the result that many children lost all sense of historical sequence'. But it was now recognized by 'all good teachers' that 'some dates are necessary and can easily be memorized by children'.[38] There was also a proposal that by the time pupils left elementary school, they 'should have gained a connected and definite knowledge of the story of Britain and of the British Commonwealth of Nations', along with an awareness of 'the growth of free institutions at home and overseas', which would also give them 'some idea of the place of the British story in the story of the world', and also 'the bearing of this story on everyday life'.[39] Now that the League of Nations seemed successfully established, there was a strong case for setting British history in more of an international perspective. It was important to teach the history of ancient Palestine, Greece and Rome, 'from which modern civilization can trace a direct descent'. Later episodes such as the Crusades, the Reformation and the scientific discoveries of the seventeenth century should be taught in a European-wide perspective. And when it came to modern times, the League of Nations should be introduced to children as an organization where 'the peoples of the world' combined 'their natural sense of local patriotism' with a new 'conception of their common interest and duties'.[40]

Four years later, the Hadow Report on *The Primary School* took a different view, urging that the curriculum should be thought of 'in terms of activity and experience, rather than of knowledge to be acquired and facts to be stored'. By the time they finished their primary education, children should be 'beginning to have a lively sense' of the bearing of history on their 'everyday life and environment'; but it was more important to instil an interest in the past, by telling romantic stories, than to burden them with 'a knowledge of historical facts which properly belongs to a later stage'.[41] Hadow thought less history could be taught in primary and elementary schools than the Board's circulars had optimistically supposed, and its next *Suggestions*, published in 1937, were much more cautious about what might realistically be achieved. They still hoped boys and girls might acquire some knowledge of the last 1,000 years of British history, and of the growth of the Empire and Commonwealth. But while they admitted this was 'the ideal', the *Suggestions* conceded that 'to attain it fully may be beyond the reach of many schools', especially those 'where conditions are difficult'. In such places, the best that might be hoped for was 'the maintenance of interest in the subject', by omitting many topics 'in themselves of great importance, in which the children can feel little interest', and by focusing on stories and biographies, 'so that the pupil shall leave school with at least some knowledge of those outstanding characters in our national story whose names are commonplaces of our daily life and thought'.[42]

At secondary level, there were strong feelings by the end of the First World War that pupils should know much more history than had previously been the case. That was the conclusion reached by the Historical Association at its annual general meeting in January 1918, and it was also the message conveyed in three 'memorials' sent to Lloyd George early in 1919, which urged the Prime Minister to set up an inquiry into the teaching of history, as had already been done with natural sciences, modern languages, classics and English.[43] Fisher was eager to reform history teaching in the schools, and the Board of Education called a conference, attended by academics and by teachers from public and state schools; it was chaired by C.H. Firth, the President of the Historical Association, and he conveyed its conclusions to Fisher. The war had made it imperative that more European, imperial, economic and contemporary history should be taught in the classroom; there should be a closer connection between the teaching of history in elementary and secondary schools; the amount of time given to the subject in secondary schools should be increased from two periods a week to three; there should be a 'definite syllabus'; and 'the training of history teachers should be improved'.[44]

Fisher responded in January 1920 by setting up three small committees.[45] The first looked at the relations between history as taught in elementary and secondary schools, and concluded that secondary school history teachers would be content if children came to them, 'with an interest in the subject, with some respect for the past and a desire to know more about it', though it would also help if they had some grasp of major events and individuals. The second explored the idea of establishing complete syllabuses in history for all schools, but concluded that it would be a mistake, on the grounds that they 'would become stereotyped, would exclude exploration and initiative, and would be provided for by specially written text-books of a uniform and narrow type'. But they conceded that 'specimen' syllabuses might be useful, and offered some suggestions.[46] The third committee investigated the training of history teachers in colleges and in universities (of which more later). The reports should have been the preliminary to a full-scale inquiry, but the deteriorating economic situation meant it never happened.[47] Instead, Fisher set up a small committee of HMIs, reinforced by J.W. Headlam-Morley. Their *Report on The Teaching of History* appeared in 1923, and although no longer President, Fisher wrote the introduction.[48]

It was published as a pamphlet not an official document, on the grounds that it reflected the views of the writers but did not carry the authority of the Board, but its recommendations were little more than a selective summary of what had been said on the subject during the preceding five years. It continued to advocate the teaching of 'a complete survey of English history' in secondary schools, 'with European history as ancillary to it'. But it suggested additional lessons on the ancient world, and 'world history', which should be made 'as interesting as possible by good preparation, abundant illustrations and so forth'. This was the conventional wisdom of the time, namely that had there been more awareness of global history, disasters like the First World War might have been averted.[49] The *Report* also urged that more attention be given to naval history 'especially in its connection with the building-up of the Empire', and to social history, because it 'allows a fairer treatment of the part played by women in the historical process than is possible with the ordinary political outline'. But the *Report* worried that by extending the subject in this way, the 'great landmarks in history' might be lost, namely politics and war and kings and queens, and it reaffirmed the view that history should be taught so as to ensure that pupils had a full knowledge of appropriate dates and facts in chronological order.[50]

This view was largely endorsed in 1927 by the Hadow Report on *The Education of the Adolescent*, which offered some observations on teaching history to those who were educated in central, senior or modern schools, or in the senior classes in elementary schools. The 'whole period' of English history should be taught, 'at least from the time of the Romans to the present', and the aim must be to give pupils 'a definite framework of knowledge in chronological sequence'.

To be sure, much of this framework would be 'lost in later life', but this made it all the more essential that 'a few vital dates and facts should be driven home at every opportunity – preferably by the use of a time chart'. Hadow also urged the use of appropriate textbooks, historical novels, maps and atlases, and educational visits to historic sites. As for the very recent past: it should certainly be taught, and 'such material as is selected should be linked up with current events, and the growing sense of the interdependence of communities, as shown, for example, in the work of the League of Nations, should receive due prominence'.[51] Hadow also supported the idea of teaching some world history, along with social history and economic history, especially for those pupils who would soon be going on to earn their living. Economic history was particularly relevant to their 'immediate interests' and 'future occupation', but it was important to ensure 'this work should be simple, and that the economic factor in history should not assume a disproportionate importance in the minds of the learners'.[52]

The calls for a broader conception of history in secondary schools continued to co-exist with the traditional view that the chronological history of England was the most essential subject – a view unforgettably parodied by W.C. Sellar and R.J. Yeatman in *1066 and All That*, published in 1930, gently sending up the prevailing stress on dates, monarchs, the national narrative, and examination questions.[53] This tension between two different approaches to teaching was exemplified in two reports on junior technical schools which appeared just before the outbreak of the Second World War, urging that the history taught should 'have regard to the origins, causes and results of important economic and commercial movements', while also insisting that it would be 'a great mistake for other aspects of history to be ignored'.[54] As for modern times: the Spens Report asserted that 'recent political and economic history is the best introduction to the study of politics', because it supplied 'the necessary information', and because it could be taught to 'induce a balanced attitude which recognizes differing points of view and sees the good on both sides'. It was 'by precept or still more by the breadth of their own sympathies, that teachers can best educate pupils to become citizens of a modern democratic country'.[55]

By this time, history teachers were not only being called upon to educate their pupils to be responsible citizens in a mass democracy, and to take the more internationalist view: they were also expected to educate the growing (though still limited) numbers staying on to sit public examinations, and these syllabuses influenced and constrained the sort of history that was being taught to those aged 15 and over. In order to give belated effect to its Circular 849, the Board had set up the Secondary School Examinations Council in July 1917, to co-ordinate and oversee the different examining bodies. Their reports revealed that at School Certificate level, sat by candidates aged 16, most papers were in English history, usually beginning at 55 BC, and ending not later than 1914. They were divided into familiar periods, and at familiar dates, such as 1485, 1688, 1714 and 1815, and most candidates took only one period. Some boards also offered separate papers in Greek and Roman history, European history, the history of the British Empire, and world history.[56] In order to receive their School Certificate, candidates had to pass in a range of subjects, chosen from different groups, of which history could be one, but did not have to be. At the level of Higher School Certificate, which was for 18-year-olds, most examining boards expected candidates to take one paper in English history and a second in European history, and some boards also required a third paper on a special subject.[57]

It was not easy for teachers to prepare their pupils, for the exam questions were often very ingeniously set, to be as unlike the previous year's as possible. As a result candidates had to prepare a very wide range of topics, and the papers were often difficult to the point of being 'exasperatingly unsuitable', as exemplified by these questions: 'Estimate the relative importance of the economic and social conditions producing the French Revolution'; 'Indicate the chief economic and political reactions on Great Britain of the development of her overseas empire'; 'Indicate how England's policy in the Near Eastern Question is illustrated by three of the following: a) the war of Greek Independence; b) the career of Mehemet Ali; c) the Crimean War; d) the Russo-Turkish War'. (The second and third of these questions had to be answered in no more than 20 minutes.)[58] Moreover, teachers had no idea what level of historical knowledge and technique was expected from their pupils by the examiners, many of them believed the marking was unduly severe, and they were obliged to try to reconcile two very different aims: to provide a general education about the past, in accordance with the suggestions and circulars emanating from the Board of Education; and to prepare their pupils for taking their exams by concentrating in detail on one particular period. Indeed, the Spens

Report claimed that whereas in theory the curriculum determined the content of examinations, in practice the content of the examinations determined the curriculum.[59]

History Teaching in Theory and in Practice

As Fisher had noted in a memorandum to Lloyd George on assuming the presidency, 'the teachers were shockingly paid. Their salaries were so slender as to make it impossible for them to enjoy the benefit of travel or to purchase books.' During the war he had raised salaries, before it ended he had launched the superannuation scheme that further stabilized the profession, and he established a post-war system of national salary scales for teachers in elementary, secondary and technical schools. As a result, the average teacher's salary rose from 104 pounds in 1917 to 251 pounds in 1922, an increase of over 150 per cent, which helps explain the unprecedented enthusiasm immediately after the war, as many men, often returning home from the front, applied for teacher training. 'The whole teaching service', Fisher informed Lloyd George in his final letter as President, 'has been lifted out of the pit and placed upon a secure bed of comfort.'[60] But the ensuing economic crisis brought the earlier enthusiasm to an end, many recently-qualified teachers could not find jobs, salaries were cut, and so were grants to teacher training colleges. In the aftermath of the second economic downturn in 1931, teachers' salaries were again reduced by 10 per cent. They were cushioned from the worst effects by the general fall in prices, and their real incomes may have risen; but teachers remained under-esteemed during the inter-war years, as 'lower-grade professionals'.[61]

In the mid 1920s, there were almost 165,000 teachers in English state schools: nearly 147,000 of them in elementary schools, and 17,000 in secondary schools. Of the secondary school teachers, almost 12,000 were graduates, and of the elementary school teachers, slightly more than 80,000 had received some college training.[62] But few had degrees in history, and most had at best a passing acquaintance with the subject. The third of the inquiries into school history appointed by Fisher in June 1920 had investigated training colleges, and training departments attached to universities, and their role in preparing teachers of history. The committee made little comment on history graduates from university, but it was very critical of the limited grounding that those who went from school to two-year courses at training college received in the subject. Many arrived with limited qualifications, they learned little history from staff who knew scarcely anything about it, the libraries were often inadequately supplied with essential books, and the courses were so short that serious study of any subject was impossible.[63] Teachers from training college had received hardly any education in history, while history graduates went into the classroom with little if any training in teaching.[64] Here was an emerging debate. Should teachers be experts in their chosen field, or should they be professionally trained for the classroom? Should their teaching be subject-centred, or child-centred?

As the organization representing history teachers in schools and historians in universities, the Historical Association took a subject-centred view: the best way to improve history in schools was to make the case for it to government, and to encourage teachers to be intellectually more ambitious. At the end of the war, the Association's membership stood at 1,500; by 1939 it was 4,494. The HA's officers were fully involved in the consultations and committees that H.A.L. Fisher inaugurated, and in 1923 the Board of Education's *Report on the Teaching of History* paid tribute to the Association's part in 'increasing the opportunities of historical research, in assisting and stimulating the teachers, and spreading in a wider circle among the general public a sense of the profound and increasing importance of history in national life'. Nor were the HA's horizons confined to 'national life': after 1918, branches were established in Montreal, Colombo, Rangoon and Pietermaritzburg and other imperial cities; *History* gained enhanced credibility as the Association's notice board and as an academic journal; and a series of pamphlets were published, by distinguished academics, making the latest scholarship available to teachers, including R.G. Collingwood on *The Philosophy of History* (1930), F.M. Stenton on *Norman London* (1934), N.H. Baynes on *The Political Ideas of St Augustine's De Civitate Dei* (1936), and J.N.L. Myers on *Roman Britain* (1939).[65]

During the inter-war years, the Association became concerned at what seemed to be the distorting effect of School Certificate on the curriculum, and in 1925 it set up an Examinations Committee. These matters were debated at the annual general meetings of 1927 and 1928, and C.H.K. Marten summed up these discussions in an article in *History*, where he drew attention to the variability in marking, the low marks awarded in history compared to other subjects, and the deadening effects of examinations on teachers and pupils. He also urged that questions should be set on a broader range of topics, that more teachers should be used in examining, and that 'before sending their questions to be printed, the examiners should try to do them themselves – and submit their answers to their fellow examiners for criticism. It might', Marten impishly concluded, 'be, some say, a salutary, if humbling experience for them!'[66] In 1928 and in 1938, the HA sent out a questionnaire to establish what history teachers thought about history exams. The completed forms have not survived, but their findings were summarized in *History*. In the case of the School Certificate, teachers were divided as to what sort of exam they would prefer, while at the Higher level, there was criticism of the papers set by one board where the detailed knowledge required encouraged cramming rather than understanding, but most papers were considered to be 'not unsatisfactory'.[67]

The inter-war years also witnessed the growing impact of the 'progressive' approach to education, which was child-centred rather than teacher- or subject-centred. By then, progressive education had become a worldwide movement: indebted to the work of educational-ists and psychologists such as Maria Montessori and John Dewey, it was championed internationally by the New Education Fellowship, and its advocates in England included the retired HMI E.G.A. Holmes, who lived on until 1936.[68] The central tenet of 'progressive' education was that it was wrong to teach children by regimenting them in the classroom, passively absorbing large amounts of factual information imparted by the teacher. Instead, they should be encouraged to learn for themselves in an active, creative and engaged way, drawing on their own experiences. By the 1930s, such views had been embraced in England by many who were concerned with elementary education. The McMillan sisters, Margaret and Rachel, urged the importance of child-centred learning, nursery schools, and primary teacher training; and such views soon made their way into official circles, where the Hadow Report and the *Suggestions* emanating from the Board of Education began to commend the encouragement of curiosity and enthusiasm in primary teaching, rather than the strict instilling of information. This was a very different view from that advocated by the LCC school psychologist, Cyril Burt, who favoured selection by examination at the age of eleven, on the basis of what he believed to be a reliable method of intelligence testing.

Among educationalists and officials, progressive ideas made some impact on primary education, and they began to percolate upwards towards the secondary schools. One of the earliest advocates was Helen Madeley, who produced a guide to teaching in 1920, setting aside 'the battles and genealogies of the Wars of the Roses, the ministries of George III [and] the terms of some defunct treaty or some long-repealed bill' in favour of 'craft history which might give new life to our technical training, studies in social life which might bring a new sensitivity into human relations, and political discussion which would give both a new zest and efficiency to citizenship'. At around the same time, Helen Parkhurst's 'Dalton Plan' was taken up by some schools in England. It urged teaching on the basis of individual assignment and personal initiative on the part of the pupil; boys and girls should be given a syllabus to complete in their own time, as they embarked on the novel experience of self-directed study.[69] Later in the decade, another history teacher, F. Crossfield Happold, argued that teaching should not be concerned with filling pupils' heads with a mass of unrelated facts: instead, history should train their minds in the art of thinking, and encourage them to imagine themselves as eye witnesses to past events. And in the mid 1930s, M.V.C. Jeffries urged that history should be taught in terms of themes and topics rather than names and dates, along what he termed 'lines of development.'[70]

Although Happold and Jeffries published under the auspices of the Historical Association, theirs were not mainstream views among secondary school teachers. But at the elementary level, their impact was greater, as a new generation of textbook authors began to treat history more imaginatively and appealingly, among them Eileen and Rhoda Power's *Boys and Girls of History* (1929), the *Mayflower Histories*, and C.B. Firth's *History Series*, which began with a volume on *Children of Athens, London and Rome* (1931). Three years earlier, the Board of Education's Consultative Committee had looked into the textbooks used in elementary schools, and concluded that those on history had recently improved. Before 1914, 'they were too much confined to political history'; the generalizations 'presumed a background of knowledge and experience the children did not possess'; the illustrations were 'crude and inaccurate'; and 'the vocabulary and diction were often too difficult for children'. But since then, books had been produced that were 'suitable for quite young people': greater prominence was given to economic, social, cultural and local history; there was a more 'adequate recognition of English history as part of European and world history'; and the illustrations were of 'first-rate historical value'. But the Committee was not wholly satisfied: insufficient attention was given to the dates that were essential for any understanding of the sequence of historic time.[71]

In secondary school classrooms, the most popular series was the three-volume *Groundwork of British History*, by G.T. Warner and C.H.K. Marten. They would later revise it as *The New Groundwork of British History*, published in 1943, which would be reprinted 21 times until 1961. The other textbook widely used during the inter-war decades was R.B. Mowat's *A New History of Great Britain*, which first appeared in 1926. According to an international survey, both Warner and Martin, and Mowat, were traditional textbooks 'dominated by the conception that history is mainly concerned with the actions of politicians and with the details of wars'.[72] A different perspective, but a similar conclusion, was offered by F.H. Johnson, the senior history master at Barrow-in-Furness Secondary School for Boys, in a survey of textbooks he published in *History*. He happily used Miss C.L. Thomson and the *Piers Plowman* series for junior forms, but regretted there was no 'really good text book for Matriculation forms'. Warner and Marten worked 'quite successfully' for those forms taking the Cambridge syllabus, with its shorter periods, but not for the longer periods required by the Northern Matriculation Board. He had also tried Mowat, but the chapters were long, and were 'apt to over-emphasize unimportant biographical detail at the expense of historical causation'.[73]

The use of illustrations in the classroom remained popular: in 1930 the Historical Association produced a leaflet listing thousands of pictures for schools to borrow or buy, and recommended post cards and small photographs, 'which can be put into the child's own hands' rather than 'the wall picture, which is expensive and cumbersome and does not command individual attention'. Lantern-slides were also appealing: by 1938 the London County Council's library contained half a million of them, which were lent out to schools at the rate of 60,000 a month.[74] Enterprising local authorities and schools invested in more sophisticated projectors, such as episcopes and epidiascopes which were more versatile and could project postcards and photographs as well as slides. And after a decline in the 1920s, school visits to museums, galleries and historic sites seem to have picked up during the next decade. According to a report commissioned in 1938 by the Carnegie Trust, such places were 'actively encouraging school visits', and were providing 'special facilities with extensive school loan collections'. Of approximately 800 museums in the United Kingdom, nearly half received visits from school parties, and more than a third made arrangements for them to be accompanied by a curator or staff member.[75]

There were also two major innovations, of which the first was film. As early as 1919, some Birmingham schools had begun to hire cinemas to show films to their pupils, and four years later, the Historical Association set up a Cinema Subcommittee to investigate its teaching potential. Soon after, *History* published the scenario for an educational film dealing with woollen manufacturing in Yorkshire, and in 1931 the Association published a report on films in the classroom. But not everyone in the HA was impressed by this new medium, least of all A.F. Pollard, who remained convinced that 'you cannot make visible to the eye the really vital things. You can portray the king, but not the monarchy.'[76] But the main reason film made little headway was the lack of equipment, and the lack of films to show. In 1930, scarcely 250 schools had their own cinema projectors, and seven years later, fewer than one in ten schools were suitably equipped. And although in 1937 the British Film Institute listed 2,250 educational films, only 28 were concerned with historical subjects. But in that year, the Board of Education decided to encourage film in schools, and offered to pay half the cost of the equipment, and by 1940, the number of projectors in schools had doubled.[77]

The second major innovation was the wireless, and the growth in BBC schools broadcasts was more marked than the development of educational films. In 1924, scarcely 200 schools were listening to the BBC; by 1927 the number was close to 3,000; and by 1939 it was approaching 10,000, nearly half of all schools in the country. In the early years, the programmes tended to talk down to children, with the result that in 1927, the Carnegie Trust funded a major study of educational broadcasting.[78] Thus began an extended period of consultation between the BBC, HMIs and the schools, with the Corporation carrying out its own surveys to discover what teachers and pupils thought of their broadcasts. As a result, the BBC began to publish pamphlets to accompany its programmes, and improved the quality of its broadcasts by telling stories rather than giving lectures; and Rhoda Power, who had recently co-authored a history book with her sister Eileen, began a series of programmes entitled *Boys and Girls of Other Days*. In 1929, the BBC established the Central Council for School Broadcasting; the first chairman was H.A.L. Fisher, and the second was Lord Eustace Percy. Subject sub-committees were established, and that for history was chaired by G.T. Hankin, an HMI who was committed to the use of film and the wireless in history teaching in schools.[79]

In 1931, a new series was begun entitled *Tracing History Backwards*, as 'an attempt to deepen knowledge of current problems by examining them in historical perspective'. The earliest programmes were devoted to such topics as 'The Budget', 'The British Empire' and 'Disarmament', and they were aimed at the senior classes in elementary schools. In the same year, another new series was inaugurated, devoted to *World History*, and the first broadcasts were concerned with 'Empires, Movements and Nations'. Meanwhile, Rhoda Power was developing a new sort of programme that would be an illustrated history lesson, using dialogue, music and sound effects to bring the subject alive. Here was a potential revolution in the teaching of history in the English classroom, but it was constrained by the cost of wireless sets. Lord Eustace Percy tried to persuade the Board of Education to provide the money, but they were unwilling to do so, and it was left to local authorities and individual schools. Many found the funding somehow: in 1935, nearly 1,000 schools were listening to British history on the wireless (and half that number to world history); whereas by 1938 pupils at more than 3,500 schools were listening in, to world history for pupils aged 9–11, and to British history for those aged 11–14.[80]

Yet these developments only affected a minority of history classes. Among our correspondents, some recall the *Piers Plowman* series from primary school, and some from secondary school remember Mowat. But others have no memory of using a history textbook. One interviewee attended a non-selective senior school, leaving at 14. She loved history, but could not 'remember us having any books. Any history books at all. I can't remember many books at all in our school … I don't remember any textbooks.'[81] Many teachers continued to teach with little help from aids of any sort, beyond the blackboard and chalk (and cane). Such was the recollection of another former pupil, who attended a central technical school in south London. It was 'all very formal. As far as I remember you had blackboards which slid out one behind the other', on which the teacher entered 'all sorts of notes and things'. A third contemporary, has similar recollections: 'there were no visual or audio aids at all ... You listened to the master ... you took it in from what he was saying.'[82] And while museum visiting may have been more common by the 1930s, there were children whose parents could not afford it, as one woman we interviewed explains: 'There were no outside activities except visits to museums and these all cost our parents money. This meant that these trips were impossible for pupils who, like me, had parents who could not possibly afford the cost.'[83]

Once again, generalization is hazardous. By the second half of the 1930s, there was an increase in the schools building programme, and new methods of teaching and new aids to teaching were making an impact in some classrooms. But these were the exceptions to what was on the whole a much grimmer reality. For many boys and girls,

1. Infants class, Lavender Hill School, SW London c1925 or 1926 (courtesy of John Geddes who is standing on far left)

their education was sketchy and uncoordinated, as a morning's lessons might include scripture, arithmetic, history, and current affairs, further broken up by break time and the 'endless distractions' of visits from the nurse and the collection of dinner money.[84] Moreover, classes were large, which made teaching hard and concentration difficult. In 1932, the official standard size for elementary school classes was 50 pupils; but in 1934 there were still over 6,000 of them with more than that number. In the case of secondary schools, the maximum class size was officially 30; but there were 52,000 with more than 30, and another 60,000 that were above 40. Two thirds of all children attended schools built before 1900, and many were gaunt Victorian fortresses, which were cold, ill-lit, badly ventilated, and with primitive sanitary arrangements. For many pupils attending such unwelcoming establishments in inter-war England, their closest encounter with history would have been dispiriting and depressing: not due to the subject they were taught in class, but to the antiquated buildings in which they received their education.[85]

History Inspected, Remembered and Examined

In 1918, the inspection of elementary and secondary schools was resumed, and soon after, the recruitment of HMIs was assimilated to the general civil service pattern. The structure of the Inspectorate was subsequently rationalized, and more women were recruited, but throughout the inter-war years, the Inspectors remained overwhelmingly male, and public school and Oxbridge educated, with little first-hand experience of the classrooms they were called upon to assess.[86] They were the only way in which the Board connected directly with the working of the schools, and as such, HMIs remained controversial: as Sir Lewis Selby-Bigge conceded, there was the 'difficulty of maintaining a constant standard of inspection', and it was 'inevitable' that their reports were 'not always consistent or command approval'. But he dismissed the charge that Inspectors preferred uniformity to originality, and were against initiative and experiment, and he was adamant that 'any extensive study of Inspectors' reports would convince an impartial reader that they do not err on the side of excessive fault-finding'.[87] In reality, it is impossible to know whether that is true: in any assessment of history in the classroom during the inter-war years, Inspectors' reports are undeniably important, but they are necessarily imperfect evidence.

The flavour of these appraisals is well conveyed in the report on the teaching of history in 41 elementary schools in London in 1927. As taught to younger pupils, the subject often lacked interest, and it was not always presented in the right sequence: in one school a lesson devoted to Florence Nightingale was followed by one on Captain Scott, which made chronological sense; but then it doubled back to 'Stephenson and the railway', and skipped more than half a millennium to get to Joan of Arc. The report also regretted that syllabuses for older children were 'almost without exception, overloaded with material': indeed, in one school, 50 different topics were studied over the year, but only one hour a week was allowed for history. Most syllabuses were too narrow, and there was a lack of 'historical aids' in most of the classrooms: only two schools possessed adequate history libraries, 13 had no history books whatsoever, and not one possessed an historical atlas. Few schools made much use of historical illustrations or visual materials: 15 used none at all, and only 12 used lantern-slides. Their conclusion was gloomy: the majority of the older children 'spend at least seventy five per cent of their time during the history periods as passive listeners, and in some schools it is difficult to ascertain what else they do'.[88]

How far was the teaching of history modified to take account of the popular support of the League of Nations? The report of 1927 regretted that most London schools still taught syllabuses 'concerned too exclusively with the story of Britain and the British Empire'. Recommendations by the LCC, that pupils should receive some notion of world history, 'appear to have had little effect', although it did admit that in about a quarter of the syllabuses there was at least some reference to the League.[89] A few years later, the Board carried out an inquiry, and concluded that, with 'a few exceptions, every local authority in England and Wales encourages League instructions in its schools'. The form this encouragement took varied widely: from a circular approving such teaching to granting leave to teachers to take courses on the League at its headquarters in Geneva. But teaching about the League in schools also varied: exhibitions, essay competitions, intensive two-week courses on the League, direct teaching of its aims and developments in the last year in history lessons. Some teachers who supported the League sometimes felt unease about what might be seen as propaganda; but they declared that the League's influence was so pervasive anyway that it was taught 'indirectly' through references particularly in history lessons, but also in geography, scripture, English and science.[90]

As before, history was taught in England's inter-war elementary schools in a variety of ways; but it was sometimes not taught at all, and there was often a large gap between what the Board suggested, and what happened – or did not happen. Some of our survey pupils had no recollection of learning any history before eleven. According to one, 'as far as I can remember, there were no history lessons or projects. I left primary school knowing nothing at all about history. All our lessons concerned the three Rs.' Another had a similar experience: 'there was not much history taught at primary school. The headmaster would try, but with large mixed classes in small surroundings, they tended to concentrate on the three Rs.' It was the same for a third: 'there was no teaching of history at either the infants or junior school. The syllabus was limited to the three Rs ... My only recollection is an incident in my last year at infant school when I drew a Viking longboat in chalk on my slate.'[91] Others just recall the drudgery of rote learning: one glosses 'over my junior school in the twenties because it was the old traditional kings, queens and battles theme'; and for another, 'the teaching was straightforward – kings, dates and the main events'.[92] Although the Board hoped those who were taught history would heed its lessons all their lives, many pupils remembered nothing about the past from their classroom days.

But others were taught history, and they did remember some of it. A few studied the ancient Greeks and Romans, although Vikings and Normans figure more prominently. One correspondent learned 'about the Anglo-Saxons, the Celts, the Gauls, the Norsemen, etc., and then the Romans. We would draw their helmets, their weapons, and their boats.' Another recalled being 'introduced to the history of Greece and Rome, [the] Roman invasion of Britain and their influence. Bath and Hadrian's Wall featured mainly, but in those days it would be rare for a Liverpool child to have visited either, or even dream one day of doing so.'[93] A close contemporary remembers being taught 'quite a lot about pre-history and probably the Romans onward', as well as 'the way the Anglo Saxons and Normans lived', and also 'the medieval three field system'. And a fourth remembered 'the Stone Age and the Romans ... I believe we were taught about the Tudor period and also about the Civil War. Guy Fawkes, of course, and also Robert the Bruce and the spider. Stonehenge in the ancient history. Henry VIII and his wives. You get the picture – anything to appeal to children.'[94]

Many teachers made an effort to make history 'appeal to children'. Some told 'stories, vaguely biographical, about historical characters', or provided pictures of Anglo-Saxon houses for their pupils to copy. Others showed lantern-slides of prehistoric sites and fossils, and encouraged boys and girls to collect historic artefacts to display on 'show tables'.[95] Several former pupils remember the occasional use of drama:

> Every summer day there was an open day when the Juniors performed a play and/or tableaux with singing and/or dancing. It always seemed to be a hot sunny day. The Burghers of Calais, Queen Elizabeth's speech at Tilbury, and a medieval market with folk dancers, I recall. Garments were borrowed or old curtains draped, sometimes crepe paper cloaks – all very cheaply made.[96]

There were also historic events and reconstructions taking place outside. One pupil, who grew up in Manchester, recalls a civic anniversary, perhaps the centenary of incorporation in 1938: 'I remember my elder sister being dressed in Tudor costume for a pageant in a nearby large park.'[97] All this was a very different world from the history-starved education endured by some young pupils, or the lifeless rote learning inflicted on others in the mistaken and ineffectual belief that this was an appropriate way to educate and excite them about the past.

In the case of secondary schools, where only a tiny minority of English boys and girls were educated, the picture was equally varied. In 1923, an inspection was made of Wandsworth Technical Institute Secondary School, where history was part of the curriculum in all forms except the science sixth, where an 'adequate' amount of time was allowed to it throughout, and where two of the seven teachers concerned with history were graduates in the subject. But the Inspectors were unhappy: 'stories of history' were being taught to junior boys who had already passed beyond that stage; and greater attention should be given to 'taking into account the main European movements as and when they influence events in England'. The recent appointment of a specialist history teacher had improved matters, but 'much remains to be done before a satisfactory standard is reached', and the exam results in 1921 and 1922 had been 'very unsatisfactory'. There was an urgent need to 'raise the standard of accurate knowledge'; there should be 'constant revision of past work, not only from term to term but from year to year'; and steps should be taken to provide 'a larger supply of books in the school library'. 'In the absence of a sufficient supply', the Inspectors concluded, 'the boys have to depend too much upon the teacher's lectures, and consequently they miss the opportunity of becoming independent workers'.[98]

But even teaching that was 'good and indeed excellent' did not necessarily produce corresponding results, as the Inspectors discovered who visited Parliament Hill County School for Girls in St Pancras in 1926. The syllabus, which extended to Higher School Certificate, included Greek and Roman history, and English and European history were both taught from early times until 1914. The lessons were 'entirely pleasing', 'the interest of the children' was 'aroused throughout', and the provision of 'maps, plans, illustrations and models' was 'quite unusually good'. But the teaching was less 'successful in getting "home"'. Questions put to many of the forms 'revealed that very much had been forgotten that ought to have been remembered', and this was confirmed by 'the unsatisfactory examination results of the last three years'. Accordingly, the teachers were urged to 'satisfy themselves that the children have really assimilated what they have been told', by getting the class to give back 'as far as possible in connected form, the subject of every lesson at the end of the teaching period'. Methods of revision should be improved, and the inspectors urged 'the desirability of laying down an irreducible minimum of knowledge to be exacted from even the weakest member of the form'. The teaching had 'so many good points' that the HMIs were disappointed 'to find that the results are not better'.[99]

There was less cause for concern at Roan Secondary School for Boys in Greenwich. The buildings were excellent, and the library contained four thousand books, where history was well represented. The history masters were 'keen, conscientious, knowledgeable and quietly effective teachers, whose object is to create a living interest in the subject, while obtaining the maximum of effort and response from their pupils'. They had devoted 'much thought' to the syllabus, which was 'interesting, enlightened and more realistic than is often the case'. The youngest boys were given 'stories from British and world history', which led on 'to some study of early civilizations'. Two years were given to British history up to the present day, which was treated topically and with emphasis on social and economic history as 'preparation for life'. The pre-Certificate year combined a short course in Citizenship with an introduction to European history from the Renaissance to the end of the nineteenth century. This paved the way for a more detailed study of a period in European history during the following year. The textbooks and atlases were satisfactory and well used, there was an abundance of illustrative material, and there were successful visits to historical sites and museums.[100]

The recollections of former pupils reflect the differences in the syllabuses of the different kinds of schools, and they were especially varied in the case of the central schools. One of them attended one such establishment in south-west London, and regretted that the course ended too early and was narrowly conceived. 'We didn't touch on anything after the Crimean War', he recalled. 'That was the end of history. It was political after that, and you couldn't teach anything about politics in schools.' If he had been taught social history, he 'would have been much more interested'.[101] But another respondent, who went to another central school in south London, was taught quite differently, using the 'lines of development' method. 'I loved the way in which history was taught', he told us. 'We started with a subject such as money and traced its development from pebbles to coins, letters of credit and on to the banking system and the stock exchange.'[102] The recollections of a third former pupil were different again: 'history was extensive, each term covered a set period. Homework was set weekly.' Nor in his case were history and politics kept separate: 'we had to read a newspaper each week and give a "write up" of prominent news items complete with photographs and maps cut from the newspaper and submit it for marking'.[103]

In the case of grammar schools, the syllabuses were less varied, and concentrated on a narrative history of England. An Oxford schoolgirl remembers being taught '1066 and Harold's arrow in the eye. The Crusades. Stephen and Maud (there were connections with Oxford). Caxton's printing press. The Agricultural Revolution.' And they were followed by 'The Industrial Revolution. The Black Country. The Luddites. Pitt the Elder. Pitt the Younger. Lord Salisbury. Victoria Regina. Disraeli. The Crimean War. Florence Nightingale.'[104] And these are the similar recollections of one interviewee, who attended a school in Stepney, where history was 'an important subject':

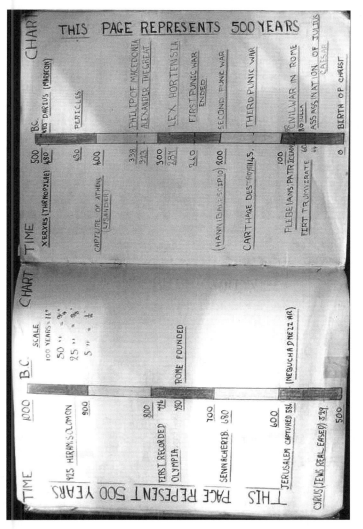

2. Time chart in exercise book from Bermondsey Central Technical School, c1935 (courtesy of Norman Roper)

91

3. Exercise book showing use of illustrative material including cigarette cards, Westborough Senior Girls' School, Southend, c1935 (courtesy of Irene Eaton)

4. Revision list from exercise book, Raine's Foundation School for Boys, East London c1939 (courtesy of Kenneth Kelsey)

Our history syllabus for the General School Certificate covered the period 1485 to 1815, and we were taught the history of that period progressively through five years. We retained the same history master throughout, and his method was to concentrate mainly on political history. As we studied each monarch's reign in sequence, we had to learn by heart the dates and two or three 'anchor points' in the reign. For example (and from memory): Henry the Seventh, 1485 to 1509, Star Chamber, foreign marriages; Henry the Eighth, 1509 to 1547, Wolsey in power, breach with Rome; and so on. It was very effective, and left us with the confidence that we would never be completely nonplussed in the exam room.[105]

As this suggests, the history that was taught to enable pupils to pass exams was often very narrowly focused: European history before 1700 was virtually disregarded, English history began with the Tudors, and few schools entered their pupils for ancient history or the history of the British Empire. There was concentration on political, constitutional and diplomatic history, but insufficient attention was given to 'the study of social and economic affairs and the everyday life of the people'. When the Secondary Schools Examination Council investigated the School Certificate examinations in 1931, it concluded, in the case of history, that 'the mass of scripts which have been placed before the investigators affords convincing evidence that by encouraging the reproduction of lifeless text book formulae, the existing type of examination deadens the pupil's interest in what should be one of the most stimulating subjects in the school curriculum'.[106] And when they looked into the Higher School Certificate six years later, they were no more impressed: 'candidates often achieve their results by a more intensive and detailed knowledge of a common textbook, rather than by wide reading and originality of mind. The approach of even the best candidate to the examination is hardly distinguishable from that to the School Certificate.'[107] Indeed, it was widely believed that cramming boys and girls to pass these examinations had a deadening effect on teachers and pupils alike.[108]

Between 1918 and 1930, the number of pupils taking School Certificate in history nearly trebled, from 23,000 to over 63,000, and by 1938 it had risen to 77,000, which meant it was the fourth most popular subject after English, mathematics and French.[109] The examination was conducted on the principle of easy papers and a high standard of marking, and because candidates were obliged to take a certain range of subjects, a minimum aggregate of marks had to be reached in the exam as a whole, and if a higher overall standard was reached, candidates were deemed to have passed 'with credit'. The only officially published pass rates were for those who did so 'with credit', which in history was generally somewhere between 45 per cent and 50 per cent. But the numbers taking School Certificate in history were always less than 10 per cent of their age cohort, and those taking Higher School Certificate during this period amounted to less than 1 per cent: there were a mere 2,673 of them in 1926, and only 3,880 in 1938, but with the pass rate generally between 75 per cent and 80 per cent. For much of the period, one third of all Higher School Certificate candidates were offering history, which meant it was also the fourth most popular subject, and if the numbers taking ancient history are added on, then in some years it was the most popular examination subject of them all.

But the experience of history teaching and of exam-taking beyond the age of 14 was exceptionally rare for boys and girls in inter-war England. Here was a potential pedagogic paradox: for in theory, it was easier to teach history in a broad-ranging, innovative and imaginative way to those pupils who were *not* taking examinations than it was to teach it to those who were. Then, as since, being educated in history, and being examined in history, were not necessarily the same things. In practice, however, there was rarely such a discrepancy, since most of the history that was taught at all ages and stages was English history, and it was built around dates and names, kings and queens, politics and war. In 1924, Hilaire Belloc had called for a 'return to an old fashioned method which had governed the teaching of history for generations' – methods which he defined as giving the highest priority to 'dates, conventional divisions and an insistence upon mechanical accuracy'.[110] It was neither the first nor the last time that such a call would be made. But during the inter-war years, there was no need to call for a *return* to such pedagogic practice, for it had never yet been significantly abandoned. *Pace* Belloc, the result was that history as taught in inter-war state schools was widely regarded as being dull and unexciting; and it did not make pupils proud to be English or British.

From the very beginning, the Board of Education had been against history teaching that was xenophobic or excessively 'Empire-minded', and the British Empire loomed less large in the nation's consciousness and classrooms during the 1920s and 1930s than it had before 1914: it was not a popular subject for School Certificate, and in 1937 some educational authorities banned the celebration of Empire Day, although it continued to be observed in many schools.[111] There was also the countervailing pacific internationalism encouraged by supporters of the League of Nations. It may not have been as significant or subversive a force as its critics alleged, but it was bad news for those who believed schools existed to promote patriotic values. In March 1918, H.A.L. Fisher noted that George V talked 'of French revolution in schools and also of a boy not knowing the union jack'. Two years later, the king was 'much disturbed about Labour Colleges, socialist Sunday schools, also illiteracy in Grenadier Guards; also lack of patriotic teaching in the schools'. This was a widely held Conservative view, and even a liberal Tory such as Lord Eustace Percy regretted that the reaction against 'drum and trumpet' history had gone too far, and he feared that the stress by many teachers on the 'serenities of the League of Nations', which downplayed the horrors of war and the importance of patriotism, amounted to 'a flight from reality'.[112]

5. Empire Day at Mauldeth Road Primary School, Manchester, c1938 or 1939 (courtesy of Enid Deeble who is 'England' second from the left)

History Goes to War – Again

In 1938, the last year of pre-war official statistics, there were just under twenty thousand elementary schools in England, and 1,244 secondary schools.[113] All boys and girls attended elementary schools, but the majority still left at 14 with no qualifications, and never having even attempted any official examination. Little had changed since the early twentieth century, and this was a measure of the inability or indifference of successive inter-war governments to engage seriously or significantly with these issues.[114] By 1939, there was considerable disquiet about the educational system in England, and by the early 1940s, there was a general consensus that if the nation survived the war, there must be put in place a reformed system of free secondary education for all children, although there was already serious debate as to what its structure should be: the tripartite system which had been advocated by Spens in 1938, or the multilateral (or 'comprehensive') school which he had dismissed, but which was gaining support among some teachers' associations, educationalists, trades unionists and Labour supporters. There was also a widespread belief that the raising of the school leaving age could not be further delayed, and that it must certainly be advanced to 15 and preferably to 16.

Meanwhile, the state schools were subjected to the disruptive stresses and unprecedented strains of total war, as the military requisitioning, the widespread bomb-damage, the enforced evacuation, and the increasing shortages of staff and supplies, combined with severe financial restrictions, meant that by the end of 1939, state education seemed on the verge of complete collapse. Half a million children were getting no schooling at all, and by early 1940, the Board of Education was not only being criticized for ignorance and incompetence, but both the civil servants and the politicians also faced the well-grounded charge that they did not understand the problems of state education in peacetime, let alone in war, because they themselves had all been taught in very different sorts of schools.[115] Although matters later improved, and although it is impossible to quantify the problem, it is clear that a substantial number of children lost out heavily in terms of their limited and disturbed education. By 1943, early concerns about the effects of wartime educational disruption had begun to receive a measure of official recognition, when tests in arithmetic, English, geography and history, given to 3,000 children, revealed an overall rate of educational retardation of about one year.[116]

Ironically, while Winston Churchill invoked the nation's past in his rousing speeches, many boys and girls in wartime Britain were receiving less historical education than their inter-war predecessors. This was certainly the case in elementary schools, as one teacher explained in a letter to *History* in the summer of 1940: 'Insofar as it functions at all, either in the neutral, evacuated or reception areas, I think it is true to say that history as a distinguishable, formal and integral part of the curriculum has been wiped out.' If taught at all, it was 'spasmodically at irregular intervals, whenever an odd quarter- or half-hour can be snatched by the zealous teacher'.[117] Several of our interviewees confirm this. One was evacuated twice to different primary schools, but has no recollection of being taught history at either of them. Likewise, another could not 'recall any specific history lessons': most of the staff had been called up, the classes were huge (48 children), and the retired teachers who were brought back 'concentrated almost entirely on the "three Rs"'.[118] But one correspondent does remember getting 'a good grounding in English history at primary school, mainly from age eight to eleven ... Heroes and heroines were greatly stressed, e.g. Florence Nightingale, Nelson, Wilberforce ... Hitler was of course a hate figure.'[119]

For boys and girls in secondary education, the disruption seems to have been less, and serious efforts were made to ensure that the teaching of history was carried on. But there were repeated interruptions from air raids, and 'having a lesson sitting on benches in the school basement, writing notes in pencil', was scarcely a good way to learn about the past, or about anything else.[120] Wartime shortages were also very constraining: 'few or no new books were available', and there was 'very little writing paper', which meant that history had to be learned 'very largely from out-of-date text books and lectures from teachers'. Moreover, fuel rationing meant that school trips were no longer possible, and in any case most of the nearby museums were closed or semi closed. The war also seems to have 'very much restricted' the teaching of recent history, which had been so strongly urged in secondary schools during the 1920s and 1930s. 'Anything post-1910', one correspondent recalls, was never mentioned' – least of all international harmony or the League of Nations. Like many others, her teachers may have been 'heroic in their efforts', but even in such stirring times, when history was unfolding before their very eyes, the wartime teaching of the subject was more stale than scintillating.[121]

This view was captured in an article published by M.V.C. Jeffreys in the summer of 1940. 'History', he observed, 'is one of the worst taught school subjects, if it is not still one of the best hated. Teachers whose annual task is to prepare pupils for public examinations might well conclude from their painful experience that history is not a suitable subject of study for boys and girls.' Part of the problem, he insisted, was the sheer complexity of the past: for children lacked the experience to understand much of what had happened except in impossibly simplified versions. Moreover, the curriculum had been so extended during the inter-war years that there was too much history to teach: 'Today', Jeffreys observed, 'we all subscribe to the doctrine that the syllabus should somehow span the entire evolution of human society in its length, from the dim subhuman past to the very brink of the future, as well as in its breadth of cultural variety.' At least, 'when history syllabuses complacently followed the lines of *1066 and All That*', we 'knew where we were'. There was also insufficient direct access to the past, because all too often, 'the materials for its reconstruction' were 'fragmentary and confused'. Yet children showed great delight and enthusiasm when they were presented with panoramas in the Science Museum illustrating the history of transport, or the fun they had doing research to make a model of a Roman galley.[122]

Jeffreys was scarcely a disinterested observer, since he had devised the 'lines of development' method of teaching history. But there were also criticisms that the history being taught was not so much stale as unpatriotic. In September 1940, *History* published an article by J.D. Mackie, lamenting the fact that insufficient attention was devoted in schools to imperial and naval history. Mackie was both a soldier and a scholar: had served in the Argyll and Sutherland Highlanders during the First World War, and he also held history professorships at the Universities of London and Glasgow. 'Our Empire', he observed, 'seems to have become suspect in certain quarters', and there seemed to be 'a school of thought which attributes our every action to low motives – usually economic – and takes no account of the valour by which an empire has been won, or the benefits it has conferred upon great peoples'. He also regretted that during the inter-war years, too much contemporary history had been taught, with the result that 'the student inevitably reads into the past his own opinions, or the opinions of his teacher, upon the questions of the day'. And nowhere, he insisted, had 'the triumph of theory over fact been more evident than in the treatment accorded by historians to the League of Nations'. From Mackie's perspective, the pacific internationalism of the 1920s and 1930s had distorted rather than enhanced the teaching of history in schools.[123]

But Jeffreys and Mackie may both have been in error in overestimating the lasting impact of history teaching in the classroom. Such was the conclusion of Alfred Hanson, who had been a history teacher, and would later be professor of politics at Leeds University. During four years in the army, he talked to many 'ordinary men' in the ranks about their experiences of being taught history, and he reported his findings in a letter to *History* in the early autumn of 1945. 'The general impression', he concluded, 'has not been very gratifying', since 'nearly all those who have talked to me about history' remembered 'nothing more' than a few 'outstanding events', to which they refer with 'jocular condescension'. But 'of history as a process of social evolution, and as a treasure-house of human experience', they had 'no conception'. In particular, Hanson criticized the 'excess of period study' that those from eleven to fourteen had endured; and as for the minority who took School Certificate:

> They are immersed in an effort to memorize sufficient factual information about a very small part of history to enable them to pass the examination. The tragedy of this situation is that they receive the false idea that history is nothing more than a confusing and indigestible mass of facts, dates, causes and results just when they have reached the stage of development at which they can begin to perceive its real importance.[124]

Meanwhile, there were few official pronouncements on history teaching from the Government, and the reiterated view was that it would be 'ill-advised to mix up education with what may be regarded as propaganda'. Between 1939 and 1943, the Board published a series of memoranda on 'The schools in wartime', suggesting ways of studying the history, literature and geography of Britain's allies, the USA, the USSR and China.[125] And the inquiry into secondary education chaired by Sir Cyril Norwood (of which more later) devoted only a brief chapter to history, and once again left it to the teachers to decide how to approach the subject: 'Many will not wish to omit a survey of civilization from ancient times; others no doubt will shape part of their course on the basis of biography or social history, or regard a chronological framework of history as indispensable, omitting long stretches of events and concentrating on outstanding features.' But 'an overcrowded syllabus must be avoided', the 'history of Britain must remain at the core of the history syllabus, and to that core the history of other peoples must be organically related'. Only in the sixth form, Norwood went on, was it possible for 'real historical study' to begin, and this should be devoted to 'the history of Britain at home and overseas in the latter part of the nineteenth and the twentieth century', to which should be added the history of the British Commonwealth, the United States and the USSR.[126]

The Historical Association dismissed Norwood's proposals as 'sedate and uninspiring', expressing disappointment 'with the history sections in which they had the right to expect inspiration, if not some advanced views on method and matter'.[127] The author of these comments was S.M. Toyne, who had taught history at Bedford School and Haileybury College, and he had recently drafted the Association's own proposal for a history syllabus with Dr Rachel Reid, a former LCC Schools Inspector and a history lecturer at Girton College, Cambridge and University College, London. But although Toyne and Reid's report was more detailed, their proposals were scarcely more exciting than Norwood's. Younger children should take a 'preparatory course', in which 'stories of great men and women of the past' loomed large. Thereafter, there would be ancient and local history, followed by the nation state to 1485, British and European history from 1485 to 1715, and finally the modern world since 1760.[128] But as the Second World War neared its end, the general view remained that it was difficult to teach history to children under 14 or even 15, and there was scarcely any discussion of how it should be taught to those older boys and girls who would soon be staying on at school in unprecedented numbers.[129]

3 History and the Welfare State, 1944–64

It is right that all boys and girls should be introduced to historical studies, although the time available for their pursuit is limited.
(Ministry of Education, *Teaching History* (pamphlet no. 23, London, 1952, 4th impression, 1960), p. 12.)

For much of the Second World War, R.A. Butler was responsible for education, as the last President of the Board, from July 1941 to August 1944, and as the first Minister of Education until the end of Churchill's coalition government. Butler's stint of almost four years puts him behind H.A.L. Fisher and Lord Eustace Percy among his predecessors, and below George Tomlinson, Sir Keith Joseph and David Blunkett among his successors (and also David Eccles if his two separate terms are added up), but it places him ahead of everyone else. As his promotion from President of a board to Minister of a department suggests, Butler was one of the most influential figures in charge of education, carrying reforms which were more lasting than those of H.A.L. Fisher.[1] Like Fisher, Butler was a member of the nation's 'intellectual aristocracy': for generations his forebears had been academics, his father had risen high in the Indian civil service, and when Rab graduated in history at Cambridge, he was immediately elected to a Fellowship at Corpus Christi College, where the Master was Sir Will Spens, whose report on secondary education would significantly influence him. Having been found a safe parliamentary seat at Saffron Walden in Essex, Butler spent much of the 1930s as a junior minister at the India Office and then at the Foreign Office, until Churchill moved him to Education.

Unlike Lloyd George and Fisher, relations between Churchill and Butler were far from being close and constructive. Both were Conservatives, but during the 1930s they had disagreed on Indian constitutional reform and on foreign policy towards Germany. Butler

102

was an ardent appeaser and supporter of the Tory establishment, as embodied in the figures of Stanley Baldwin, Lord Halifax and Neville Chamberlain, and he regarded Churchill's advent to power in the spring of 1940 with unconcealed horror, dismissing him as the greatest adventurer in modern political history.[2] But the new Prime Minister kept Butler on at the Foreign Office – whereupon he promptly indulged in some exceptionally indiscreet conversations with the Swedish minister in London, expressing his hope that no opportunity for a compromise peace with Germany would be neglected. He was lucky to survive, and a year later Churchill sent him off to the Board of Education, removing him from any further involvement in the war. It was marginally better than a sideways shift, but the Prime Minister wanted Butler to behave like most of his predecessors in the office, and do as little as possible, avoiding both party politics and religious controversy for the duration of the war.

According to Butler, Churchill's interest in education was 'slight, intermittent and decidedly idiosyncratic'. The Prime Minister was enthralled by the English past, but to him history was more a matter of religion and sentiment than of education and pedagogy, and he knew nothing first-hand of the elementary and secondary schools in the state sector. Although Churchill had held a variety of domestic portfolios, he never had much interest in local government, and his imagination was not caught by trying to improve what he once called 'village schools with a few half-naked children rolling in the dust'. Early in his career, he had been dismayed by the religious controversy surrounding the passing of the Balfour Act, and as Chancellor of the Exchequer from 1924 to 1929 he did all he could to cut government spending on schools. According to Lord Eustace Percy, Churchill seemed to dislike education 'so cordially that he might seem to revenge some personal injury'.[3] So when he offered Butler the post of President, he did not think it 'a central job', though he felt the schools could do more to raise morale. 'I should not object', he told Rab, 'if you could introduce a note of patriotism in our schools.' 'Tell the children', he went on, 'that Wolfe won Quebec', to which Butler properly replied that he 'would like to influence what was taught in schools but that this was always frowned upon'.[4]

'Come and see me to discuss things', Churchill said to Butler, 'not details, but the broad lines.'[5] Yet Rab was soon thinking on very 'broad lines' indeed, as he determined to carry a major piece of reform, and his civil servants were fully behind him.[6] For by the time he became President, there was widespread concern within the Board about the state of education, as evidenced in this damning report:

> The full time schooling of the children of our country is in many respects seriously defective. It ends for some ninety per cent of them far too soon. It is conducted in many cases in premises which are scandalously bad. It is imparted in the case of some schools by persons who need have no qualifications to teach anybody anything.[7]

There was a developing consensus that secondary education must be made freely available to all children, and broad agreement that the school leaving age must be raised, preferably to 16, but certainly to 15. Among those in favour of reform was the permanent secretary, Sir Maurice Holmes, son of the former HMI turned radical educationalist, E.G.A. Holmes, and it was he who had produced the so-called *Green Book*, which put forward many of these proposals, just before Butler arrived.[8]

The Butler Act and Beyond

Butler now seized the opportunity to push educational reform forward, convinced that he would be able to carry the Prime Minister, the Conservative back benchers, and the churches with him.[9] But he took his time, and it was not until the middle of 1943 that two major documents appeared on the subject. The first was a White Paper entitled *On Educational Reconstruction* which recommended that free secondary education should be made available to all; that the school leaving age should be raised to 15 and eventually to 16; and that the day continuation schools vainly proposed in the 1918 Education Act should be revived, but 'adapted to meet the requirements of the post-war world', as 'young people's colleges'.[10] Butler had succeeded in bringing along with him not only the Conservatives, but also the Labour members of the wartime coalition, including his own junior minister, James Chuter Ede, and Ernest Bevin at the Ministry of Labour, and he was also able to reach agreement with the churches over the fate of the denominational schools. The White Paper was well received, although some Tory backbenchers feared it was proposing too much change too quickly, while some on the left worried that the proposed time frame was too long.

Ten days after the appearance of the White Paper, the Board published another report by Sir Cyril Norwood, whom Butler had asked 'To consider suggested changes in the Secondary School curriculum and the question of School Examinations in relation thereto.' He did not have much to say about the curriculum (especially history), but in other ways took a broad view of his remit, urging that 'pupils of a particular type of mind' should 'receive the training best suited for them and that training would lead them to an occupation where their capacities would be suitably used'.[11] This meant that a schoolchild could be placed in one of three categories. The first were those who were 'interested in learning for its own sake, who can grasp an argument or follow a piece of connected reasoning'. The second were those 'whose interests and abilities lie markedly in the field of applied science or applied art ... He often has an uncanny insight into the intricacies of mechanism whereas the subtleties of language construction are too delicate for him.' Finally there was the third group, which formed the majority, where pupils dealt 'more easily with concrete things than with ideas. He may have much ability, but it will be in the realm of facts.'[12]

Following the proposals sketched out by Spens in 1938, Norwood recommended three different kinds of secondary school: grammar schools, technical schools and (secondary) modern schools, providing appropriate education for the three different kinds of mind exhibited by children. They would be allocated to the most appropriate school at the age of eleven on the basis of examinations which would test intelligence, and there might also be a second such allocation at 13.[13] In reaching these conclusions, which started from the presumption that it was impossible to re-structure the school curriculum without restructuring the schools, Norwood, like Spens before him, had come out against the 'multilateral' or comprehensive alternative. Along with the White Paper, the Norwood Report provided the essential underpinnings to the Education Bill which Butler introduced at the end of 1943, and which received royal assent in August 1944. It was the one major piece of reforming domestic legislation passed by the Churchill coalition, and it came into force on 1 April 1945.[14] Within two months, the government broke up, and in Churchill's caretaker

Conservative administration, Butler was moved to be Minister of Labour, and Richard Law was briefly Minister of Education.

The legislation of 1944 was always known as the Butler Act, and most of its provisions were implemented, even though there was another severe economic downturn once victory was won. Local authorities had to provide separate primary and secondary schools, where the major divide would be at eleven-plus, they would be 'sufficient in number, character, and equipment to afford for all pupils opportunities for education offering such variety of instruction and training as may be desirable in view of their different ages, abilities, and aptitudes', and this would include grammar, technical and secondary modern schools (although the wording of the Act did not preclude alternative schemes), as well as 'young people's colleges'.[15] The Act also proposed raising the school leaving age to 15, and for it to be increased to 16 as soon as this was 'practicable'. Here was a new beginning for education, and although some Labour-controlled local authorities soon began to push for multilateral (i.e. comprehensive) schooling, the incoming Labour government followed the plans laid down in the Butler Act, including the tripartite system of secondary schools, and the raising of the school leaving age to 15, which was implemented in 1947. As Ellen Wilkinson, the Labour Minister of Education, explained: 'To put this Act as a whole into effect is really a job for a generation.'[16]

Wilkinson had worked briefly as a pupil teacher, then studied history at Manchester University, and she was Attlee's Minister of Education from August 1945 until April 1947. Even in a period of economic austerity, she won the resources to ensure free school milk and school meals, smaller classes, and extensive school building, as well as raising the school leaving age; but she was handicapped by persistent ill health, and died in office.[17] Her successor, George Tomlinson, was a former Lancashire mill worker, and he would stay in post for more than four years, until the fall of the Attlee government in October 1951. The job fulfilled his ambitions, he was determined to help provide for young people the sort of educational opportunities he had been denied, and he established the provision of new schools and extra places as a government priority.[18] Throughout this time, the permanent secretary at the Ministry of Education was Sir John Maud, previously an Oxford politics don and Master of Birkbeck College, London, who was a skilled, persuasive and enthusiastic administrator, and it was his view that 70–75 per cent of all secondary school places 'should be of the modern type', and that the remaining 20–25 per cent should be allocated to grammar and technical places.[19] There would also be 'parity of esteem' between the three types of school, so that all of them would be equally attractive to parents and to pupils.

Thus began a revolution in English education. During the next five years, 1,000 new primary schools were constructed. The old senior elementary schools were renamed 'secondary moderns', and local authorities began to establish new schools of the same type. Technical schools would accommodate about half the selective intake, between 10 per cent and 15 per cent of all pupils; and by the late 1940s a system of grammar schools was generally established, although provision varied enormously across the country.[20] But there the revolution stalled. Scarcely any resources were made available for the creation of technical schools, and the grammar schools received more funding than the secondary moderns. In practice, there was no parity of provision, and there was never any 'parity of esteem'. By 1951, secondary modern schools catered for 65 per cent of the secondary school pupils, and grammar schools for 29 per cent. By contrast, technical schools educated only 4 per cent. This was not what the Butler Act had intended, and the 'young people's' or 'community colleges' also fell by the wayside. Nor had the Butler Act, or the Labour Government, brought the public schools within the state system. These criticisms were muted during the immediate aftermath of the war, but by the early 1950s they were being vehemently voiced on the left.[21]

In October 1951 the Conservative Party won the general election and Florence Horsbrugh became the Minister of Education in Winston Churchill's last administration. She had not been to university, had only held minor office beforehand, and she was regarded as weak and indecisive. She was not even a member of the cabinet until well into her three-year tenure, a clear indication that the Prime Minister, who did not much like her, was no more enthusiastic about education in peacetime than in wartime: indeed, his private view was that the recently-raised school leaving age should go back to 14.[22] In terms of government spending, defence and housing were the top priorities, and this necessitated cuts elsewhere, so while Harold Macmillan could boast about building hundreds of thousands of new homes, Horsbrugh was obliged, under pressure from the Treasury, to oversee economies which reduced the school-building programme the Labour government had begun, and which left her vulnerable to attacks about the overcrowded schools, the sub-standard classrooms and the antiquated buildings still in existence.[23] This did not endear Horsbrugh to local authorities, teachers or parents, and the sudden increase in the birth rate in the post-war years added to the pressure, for these baby-boomers were now swelling pupil numbers to unprecedented levels.

Horsbrugh resigned in October 1954, and she was succeeded by David Eccles, who was rich, grand, self-confident, a product of Winchester and Oxford, and strongly committed to the cause of education.[24] His arrival coincided with an improvement in the economy so there was more money to spend on the schools; and in a way that even Butler had never managed, Eccles succeeded in persuading the Conservatives that education was a sound economic investment, because a well-schooled workforce would be more efficient, productive and innovative. In addition, Eccles set out to conciliate the local authorities and the teachers who had resented the low priority and the limited funding accorded to education during Churchill's last government. Even in 1956 when the Suez crisis led to renewed pressure on the education budget, Eccles held firm, and although he left office in January 1957, expansion continued under his successors, Viscount Hailsham and Geoffrey Lloyd. Eccles returned to Education for a second stint in October 1959, and he continued to oversee expansion until Macmillan sacked him in July 1962. But it was an indication of Eccles's success that between 1947 and 1958, spending on education doubled in real terms and increased as a proportion of the national income by 75 per cent.[25]

By the early 1950s, there was growing criticism of the eleven plus: the selection process varied from authority to authority, and ultimately depended on the number of grammar school places rather than any fixed performance in the exam; while the view that intelligence could be tested, propounded by Cyril Burt, was increasingly criticised. By 1953 the Labour Party was committed to a policy of non-selective, comprehensive schooling, and the Tory Education Ministers were also guardedly equivocal. Florence Horsbrugh was firmly in favour of grammar schools, but she did allow some comprehensives to be established; David Eccles grudgingly accepted the principle of comprehensive schools, but his preferred policy was to improve the secondary moderns. He was determined to achieve that 'parity of esteem' between grammar, technical and secondary modern schools that had been envisaged in the 1940s, so that parents would not feel disappointment and anger if their child 'failed' to win a place in a grammar school. 'To allow 4 out of 5 of our children and their parents to feel that the children who go to the secondary [modern] school start life impoverished in education', he observed, 'would be to sow the seed of discontent throughout their lives.' If secondary education was not improved, especially at the 'lower' end, the tripartite system might be in jeopardy, and even 'the grammar school, highly regarded for its success in coping with academic pupils, might face extinction'.[26]

Between Eccles's two terms as Minister, Lord Hailsham and Geoffrey Lloyd followed a similar policy. In 1958, Lloyd issued a White Paper on secondary schools that sought to reassure parents about their children's chances even if they did not pass the eleven plus. It admitted there were 'too many children of approximately equal ability who are receiving their secondary education in schools that differ widely both in quality, and in the range of courses they are able to provide'. But the solution was not to abolish grammar schools and impose comprehensives: rather, the government was encouraging a range of schools which would provide 'a full secondary education for each of its pupils in accordance with his ability and aptitude'.[27] A year later, the Central Advisory Council for Education (which had been established under the Butler Act to succeed the Consultative Committee that had advised the Board of Education) published a report on education for pupils aged between 15 and 18. It called for the school leaving age to be raised to 16, and for a widening of the scope of sixth forms beyond those intending to go to university. In 1963, a further report was published, named after its chairman, John Newsom, which Eccles had commissioned during his second period as Minister, on 'the education of pupils aged thirteen to sixteen of average and less than average ability'.[28]

By this time, a number of local education authorities had introduced comprehensive schools, but in 1961, more than 70 per cent of 13-year-olds were being educated in secondary moderns, almost 20 per cent in grammars, and the remainder in technical schools – or, increasingly in comprehensives. The attempt to create technical schools had clearly failed, and the move to comprehensives was gaining momentum. From 1962 to 1964, the Ministry of Education was in the hands of the liberal Conservative, Sir Edward Boyle, an

Old Etonian who had studied history at Oxford. He would later recall that in 1963, two thirds of the local education authorities in England had either finished or were working on partial or complete schemes of comprehensive reorganization – and they were not all Labour-controlled.[29] Boyle's foreword to the Newsom Report famously rejected the notion of fixed intelligence levels, and this made him the most sympathetic Conservative Minister of Education yet towards the idea of comprehensive schools. Meanwhile, the Labour Party had fully embraced the policy of moving to universal comprehensive secondary education during its years in opposition, and it successfully campaigned on this platform in the general election of 1964.[30]

By then, it was almost exactly 20 years since the passing of the Butler Act which, despite its limitations and failures, was the most important legislation passed since the Balfour Act of 1902, and it puts Butler in the limited pantheon of politicians who significantly changed the course of state education in twentieth-century England. None of his successors was in the same league, though most Ministers of Education were more influential than their inter-war predecessors, because schools were now taking a larger slice of government spending. Richard Law was in office for only a few months at the very end of the war, and made no serious impact; Ellen Wilkinson (the first former teacher to hold the office) and George Tomlinson sought to implement as much of the 1944 Act as the limited resources of post-war austerity allowed; and Florence Horsbrugh tried, but largely failed, to accomplish the same objective under Churchill. David Eccles reconciled the Conservative Party to the cause of educational investment and expansion; Lord Hailsham and Geoffrey Lloyd followed in his footsteps; and Sir Edward Boyle went further than any of his Tory predecessors in expressing his sympathy to comprehensive schools. Indeed, by the early 1960s, the conventional wisdom in the Ministry of Education had begun to embrace comprehensives – of which, from 1958, that at Holland Park in London was widely regarded as the flagship.[31]

Holland Park was one of more than 2,000 schools constructed between 1954 and 1963: light and airy, built in glass and concrete, and often located on green-field sites, they were very different from the unwelcoming Victorian buildings of old, and education was intended to be exhilarating and enjoyable, rather than oppressive and overbearing. Yet though the number of pupils grew from 5.3

million in 1951 to 7.6 million in 1970, and per capita expenditure also rose during the same period, there were limits to progress. In 1952, more than 5,000 all-age elementary schools still existed in all but name; and at the end of the decade, many schools had to accommodate their pupils in classrooms that were prefabricated huts with concrete floors and corrugated roofs.[32] As such, the ambiguous state of the schools mirrored the uncertain state of the nation: there was euphoria at the coronation of Elizabeth II, and unprecedented prosperity by the late 1950s and early 1960s; there was a gradual relaxation in Victorian moral and religious codes, and a growing influx of immigrants from the former colonies; and as Britain's Empire dissolved and its armed forces downsized, it became a lesser force in a bipolar world dominated by the United States and Communist Russia. What kind of history was appropriate in the classrooms of the welfare state? How might it be presented to the unprecedented numbers of pupils who were staying on at school for longer than ever before?

History Justified, Encouraged and Examined

The only mention of history teaching in the White Paper of 1943, *On Educational Reconstruction*, was neither precise nor subject-specific: 'A new direction', it urged, 'in the teaching of history and geography and modern languages will be needed to arouse and quicken in the pupils a livelier interest in the meaning and responsibilities of citizenship of this country, the Empire and of the world beyond.'[33] But this was just a vague aspiration, for no government between 1944 and 1964 had any intention of imposing its own syllabus on the schools – in history or in any other subject.[34] Instead, the Ministry of Education continued the practice of the former Board, by sending out recommendations and suggestions, beginning with a substantial pamphlet published in 1952, entitled *Teaching History*. It was reprinted several times up to the early 1960s, and it began with a broad survey of history teaching in England since the nineteenth century, which opened with the resounding claim that 'teaching about the past is one of the constant elements found in the education of all societies'. In England, it went on, 'it has been the general feeling over the centuries that to ignore the experience of the past is not merely folly but a sort of impiety'; and although nowadays such reverence no longer characterised the 'contemporary cast of mind', history rightly remained important.[35]

At primary level, young children were 'introduced at the junior school stage to some history', when they 'made the acquaintance of some of the great characters and stories of all ages'. But there was 'less stress than there used to be upon any fixed content', and the teacher's aim now was 'first to feed his pupils' imaginations with good stories, and secondly to arouse their intellectual curiosity about the past'.[36] During the early years, 'when fantasy and reality may not always be distinguishable, and when interest in fairy tales is at its height', it was appropriate to focus on stories combining 'myth and legend'. By the age of eight or nine, children were more interested in fact and truth: they were ready for 'heroic stories' in which 'they can see in action the virtues they esteem – skill, audacity, courage and loyalty'. Finally, in their senior years, there might be 'a concentration of stories mainly about our own country, arranged in some sort of chronological order for the sake of those boys and girls who are developing an idea of time'. Such stories should awaken 'historical curiosity', they should enlarge 'imaginative experience', they should give children a sense of 'the mental and spiritual background of their country', and they should establish a 'foundation for the history that is to follow'.[37] These arguments would be reiterated in 1959, when the Ministry produced an updated version of its *Suggestions for the Consideration of Teachers and Others Engaged in the Work of Public Elementary Schools*, which had last been published in 1937, and reprinted in 1944.[38]

As far as secondary level was concerned, *Teaching History* went into considerable detail appropriate for the new tripartite system. At grammar school, the growing importance of public examinations 'tended to create a pattern of well-defined historical periods', which was being 'followed by some three-quarters of these schools today'. Those aged 11 to 12 studied pre-history, ancient civilizations, and medieval history. For boys and girls between the ages of 12 and 13, the Tudors and the Stuarts predominated. From 13 to 14, eighteenth-century England was very popular, with some American and Empire history, and occasionally Europe; and from 14 to 16, the syllabus consisted of nineteenth-century English and European history (and sometimes American history), which would be taken for the School Certificate examination.[39] For those studying the nineteenth century, the topics covered were familiar: the Napoleonic Wars, the Great Reform Act, Palmerston and the Crimean War, the Irish problem, and the Boer war; and the French Revolution, Greek independence, the revolutions of 1848, the Franco Prussian War and the scramble for Africa. The one suggestion the authors ventured was that, since the aim was to give 'those who are leaving school their practical bearings in our contemporary world', teaching should encompass as much of the twentieth century as was practicable, including 'the Soviet Union, India, Pakistan [and] China', though 'we shall have to wait for a long time for a balanced appraisal of Fascism or Nazism'.[40]

In secondary modern schools, efforts were also made 'to cover in outline the political history of Britain, with at least some reference to that of Europe, the Commonwealth and the United States'. Indeed, in some secondary modern classrooms, 'attempts to cover the entire history of the world are to be found'. But unlike the grammar school, the pedagogic tendencies were 'away from any formal political outline' and towards subjects deemed more appropriate, namely those 'concrete things' that were 'relevant to the present'. There was more social and economic history, and there was 'a strong disposition to treat of separate topics, such as the histories of clothing, trade, food or government', and also 'to study distinct phases of historical development: feudalism, the industrial revolution and so forth'.[41] Moreover, the study of many of these topics did not end in 1914, but was often brought close to the present time: 'George Stephenson's Rocket turns not merely into the Flying Scotsman hauled by an "Atlantic" in 1911, but into the Flying Scotsman hauled by a blue "streamliner" in 1939'; 'the sailing ship turns not merely into the Mauretania of 1905, but into the Queen Mary of 1936 or the Queen Elizabeth of 1942'; and 'the League of Nations and the United Nations emerge, not infrequently, at the end of the World Survey'.[42]

Having dealt with both grammar and secondary modern schools, the authors of *Teaching History* concluded that 'all boys and girls should be introduced to historical studies, although the time available for their pursuit is limited'. Yet across the twentieth century, there had been 'little change in the status of the subject in the school curriculum or in the amount of time devoted to its study'. Since the 1900s, two periods a week had generally been allocated to history for those aged over eleven, from which two deductions might be made, one encouraging, the other less so. The first was that 'educational opinion

6. Exercise book showing topics studied in the early 1950s; some grammar schools did topic work in the first and second year, Minchinden Grammar School, North London, c1950 (courtesy of Monica Wafford)

evidently believes some school course in history to be important'. But the second was that 'despite the faith of some historians that their subject provides the natural core of any sound curriculum', history had not yet succeeded 'in assuming a role comparable to that occupied in the olden days by the classics'. Nor, in the secondary modern schools, did it 'show signs of assuming any preponderant position such as that traditionally occupied in the old elementary school by any one of the "three R's"'.[43] History was important, but not a core subject.

Nevertheless, the authors offered three compelling reasons why history was worth studying, the first of which they termed the 'moral motive', namely that it was 'good for boys' and girls' character that they should hear or read about great men and women in the past and so learn gradually to discriminate between disinterested and selfish purposes, or between heroism and cowardice'. The second justification was that children should be 'introduced to their heritage', by which they meant 'their own environment, in which they will have to live and to act'. To be sure, it was no longer convincing to depict the history of England in the terms of *1066 and All That* as a 'march towards national greatness and political liberty'. But it was still important to introduce pupils to 'the sweep of history, even if it is almost all forgotten, even if it has been grasped in the most confused way, [it] has this value, that it puts our life in some sort of perspective'. Finally, the pamphlet urged that history enabled schoolchildren to enter 'into an entirely different atmosphere and point of view from one's own', by studying periods and places which had 'no obvious or continuous connection with any present-day institutions or preconceptions'. By cultivating this quality of 'sympathetic imagination', history enjoined 'a certain humility about one's own age and the things to which one is accustomed'. Such were the justifications offered for teaching history in English schools in the early 1950s.[44]

There was another reason, to which the authors alluded only indirectly, namely that many boys and girls studied history so as to pass the public examinations in the subject; but this was a controversial issue they preferred to leave alone. The Norwood Report of 1943 urged that the School Certificate should be replaced by an internal form of testing, 'conducted by the teachers of the school on syllabuses and papers framed by themselves'; it proposed a seven-year transition period between external public exams and internal school exams, but it was vague about how and when the final transition would occur. Norwood also urged that the Higher School Certificate should be abolished, and be replaced by a school leaving examination that would be conducted twice a year for pupils aged 18 who required external validation so they could enter university or the professions.[45] Initially, these proposals received a warm official welcome, and in May 1946, the Ministry of Education issued Circular 103, advocating the abolition of external examinations for 15- and 16-year-olds, and announcing that regulations would be put in place ensuring that only grammar schools could enter their pupils for any external examination under the age of 17, thereby excluding those at technical schools or secondary moderns.[46]

But opinion soon turned against Norwood's proposals and Circular 103: the examining bodies argued for the advantages of external testing, and grammar school teachers were critical of the additional burdens that would be imposed on them, and on the impossibility of establishing a national standard.[47] Moreover, with the prospect of the leaving age being raised to 15 in 1947, some secondary modern schools hoped their pupils might stay on longer, so they, too, might sit the School Certificate exams, and they were critical of proposals that would prevent them doing so. So when the Secondary Schools Examinations Council reported in September 1947, it hedged its bets. It continued to advocate the eventual phasing out of the School Certificate, and urged its replacement by internal assessment; but in the meantime, it proposed the abolition of the School Certificate and the Higher School Certificate examinations, and their replacement by a new General Certificate of Education, which would be set at Ordinary Level (the equivalent of the School Certificate) and at Advanced Level (approximating to the Higher School Certificate). But it was this interim measure which became government policy when, in 1948, the Ministry issued Circular 168, declaring that the new system of examinations would consist of the GCE at O and A Level, beginning in 1951.[48] They would be organized by the university-based boards that had previously set and marked the School Certificate papers, and in 1953 they were joined by a new body, the Associated Examining Board which was established at the behest of the Corporation of London.

By the time the GCE replaced the old School Certificate exams, the Ministry had accepted that pupils at secondary modern schools should be allowed to take O Levels, 'provided that the curriculum for the remaining pupils of the school did not become distorted'. Yet the early

1950s also witnessed the substantial growth of other school-leaving examinations.[49] By the end of the decade, more than a quarter of secondary modern schools were entering candidates for the GCE O Level, and more than half of them were putting some of their pupils in for examinations conducted by the Royal Society of Arts, the College of Preceptors, the Pitman Examinations' Institute, and the General Nursing Council. The result was a chaotic situation, and in 1958 the Secondary Schools Examination Council appointed a sub-committee to advise on the possibility of establishing an alternative exam, both to the recently-established O Level, and also to the many other tests which secondary school pupils were taking. The Beloe Report appeared two years later, and proposed a new examination, to be sat in the fifth year of secondary schooling by the 40 per cent of pupils below the top 20 per cent (who were taking O Level), although it proposed no examinations for the bottom 40 per cent. Sir Edward Boyle accepted these recommendations, and the new examination, which was called the Certificate of Secondary Education, would be taught from 1963 and sat for the first time in 1965.[50]

More Teachers and More Technology

In 1956 the Historical Association, which now numbered more than eight thousand members, celebrated its fiftieth anniversary, and did so by mounting an exhibition, staging a conference and publishing a book of articles about its own history. In one of the essays, Professor A.C.F. Beales described how teaching practices had improved during the intervening half century. Back in the 'bad old days' of 1906, history was taught by a '"conscript army" in the elementary schools, sprinkled with pupil-teachers who taught all subjects, frequently to classes of over 100', and by a '"professional army" in a quite separate and privileged world of secondary schools'. All had taught by the traditional method combining oral instruction with copying notes from the blackboard: 'chalk-and-talk'. This was scarcely an environment in which history thrived, but Beales admitted that even then, some teachers already had 'the reality (though thank God not yet the label) of visual aids', and their use had become more widespread since.[51] Yet he also conceded that even in 1956, it was difficult to know what was happening across the country in the majority of classrooms. The exhibition mounted by the HA was a vivid celebration of developments since the Second World War: 'syllabuses, charting, local and social studies, films, models, all the rest of it'. But it was unclear how widely these had 'taken' in grammar and secondary modern schools, and it was no easier to know how widespread were the modern methods of teaching, pioneered during the inter-war years, and taken up in some quarters since then.[52]

As during 1914–18, the Second World War was traumatic and transformative for teacher training.[53] Many colleges were evacuated, and many of the men who wished to be teachers were called up. There was continuing concern about the quality of the staff and level of instruction, and in 1942, R.A. Butler had appointed Sir Arnold McNair, Vice Chancellor of Liverpool University, to inquire into the recruitment, supply and training of teachers. His report, published two years later, criticized many colleges for being too small, poorly housed and ill-equipped, and condemned the existing system as 'chaotic and ill-adjusted even to present needs', let alone to the likely increase in future demand consequent upon Butler's intended reforms. McNair recommended there should be only one grade of teacher, who had 'satisfactorily completed an approved course of education and training', and who would be recognized as a 'Qualified Teacher'. He also proposed that approved training colleges should be federated on a regional basis, and be overseen by a local university through a department of education.[54] Meanwhile, an emergency training scheme for new teachers was instituted, aimed particularly at ex-service people, and by December 1945 applications were pouring in at the rate of 5,000 a month. Within two years, the scheme would produce an extra 35,000 qualified teachers, ranging from their twenties to their fifties, and it was these emergency-trained teachers who made practicable the raising of the school leaving age in 1947.[55]

Meanwhile, the training colleges had been reorganized along the lines suggested by McNair, and institutes of education were established in universities to oversee the training courses in member colleges; and in 1946, Ellen Wilkinson announced that it would be government policy to require the appointment of Qualified Teachers in state supported schools. By 1951 nearly 25,000 men and women were training to be teachers, the number rose again towards the end of the decade, and an extra 24,000 places were authorized between 1958 and 1960. By then, the two-year course had been lengthened to three years, which made teacher training more attractive, because there was time for more focused and less hurried study. The number of formal classes and lectures was reduced, while opportunity for seminars, tutorials and private study increased. The two main elements of teacher training would be maintained – the professional study of the theory and practice of education, and the academic study of one or two subjects normally included in the school curriculum. But there was no agreement as to whether emphasis should be on professional training or academic study, or whether the professional training should stress theory or practice, or how much time should be allocated to teaching practice, or what it should include and involve. The result was that, for all their regulation by universities, teacher-training courses varied widely across the country, in both their content and their standard.[56]

Nevertheless, most teachers were now being trained in the child-centred method that carried forward the inter-war 'progressive approach', where the emphasis was for boys and girls to discover things for themselves, in an informal setting, lending priority to inquiry over memory, imagination over instruction.[57] In the history classroom, this gave rise to the so-called 'patch method' of studying a short period in depth, enabling children to enter 'into another time' with its 'different habits and different scales of value', with the aim of discovering 'the character of life in some other age for its own sake', thereby 'greatly extend[ing] the imaginative experience of those who pursue it'. The Ministry of Education briefly became enthusiastic about this approach, and warmly commended it in *Teaching History*.[58] So, too, did the medieval historian and former teacher, Marjorie Reeves, who wanted all pupils to sit down 'in a good rich patch of history and stay there for a satisfying amount of time'.[59] Conscious that this method could lead to children knowing only random disconnected areas of history, Reeves urged that the 'patches' or 'beads' of history must be connected by 'a thin string' of narrative which would enable children to see how the pieces fitted together, and thus to understand how societies developed, evolved and changed over time. Yet the lack of connection and continuity were seen as a major drawback: children might know only certain pieces of the past, and would have no idea of how they cohered in an overall pattern. So while the 'patch method' had its supporters and practitioners, it did not catch on widely.

It was in this context that the Ministry of Education set out, in *Teaching History*, to explain how history might be brought alive in the classroom. For primary schools, it recommended the provision of 'lively biography, good imaginative stories in a historical setting, and simple books of information'; it urged the importance of mime and movement, speech and drama, drawing and painting; it encouraged teachers to help their pupils get to know their own neighbourhood; and it noted that children's hobbies often furnished 'the bridgehead from present to past'.[60] As for secondary schools: 'the oral lesson' had an 'essential place', encompassing a broad range of activities from story-telling and exposition by the teacher to class debate and discussion. Nowadays, many textbooks were 'well written, well illustrated and interesting, covering a chronological period or a historical theme'. Time charts were important, because 'memorization must have its place, whether it is achieved by rote learning or otherwise, and the framework of a few dates, even of kings and queens, need be no serious burden to young children'. Visual aids, from wall maps to atlases, illustrations to films, were essential, since they enlisted 'another sense in the effort of understanding'. School broadcasting was warmly recommended: 'the radio set is the aid, and the lesson is what is made of the broadcast by pupil and teacher', who were thus in the 'unusual situation' of 'learning together, reacting differently to the same material'.[61]

The claims that there were 'well-written, well-illustrated and interesting' textbooks would certainly be borne out by the end of the 1950s. To be sure, many schools immediately after 1945 were still reliant on ageing pre-war publications, but there was a major change in primary schools with the publication of the first Ladybird biography of Alfred the Great in 1956, which was soon followed by books on William the Conqueror, Sir Walter Raleigh, Nelson, Queen Elizabeth I and Captain Cook, and on topics such as Stone Age Man, Roman Britain and Kings and Queens. Copiously illustrated, and produced in a standard 56-page format, the books sold at the relatively low price of two shillings and sixpence, and proved to be extremely popular with pupils and teachers (and with parents) in the senior classes of primary school. Many of the Ladybird histories and biographies were written by Lawrence du Garde Peach, who was by turns an academic, an actor-manager and an author. He was one of the pioneers of radio drama, and he also utilized similar material when putting together ambitious pageants for Sheffield, Manchester and other cities. His experience in drama and his feel for a young audience served him well with the Ladybird books, and between 1956 and 1975, he produced 38 of them. Although he occasionally ventured into overseas subjects, the majority of his work was confined to British historical figures. The Ladybird books were accurate and written in a lively style calculated to awaken interest in the national past.

Another popular author, who was a generation younger, a trained teacher and a primary headmaster, was Robert John Unstead. Disenchanted by the turgid tone and dull appearance of many history textbooks, Unstead's were arrestingly written and lavishly illustrated, with artists' impressions of historical events. His first series, the four-volume *Looking at History*, published from 1953, sold over 8 million copies, and in more than 50 subsequent books he ranged from ancient Egypt, Greece and Rome to the British Empire and the English-speaking world. Although later derided by progressive history teachers, Unstead's books were a welcome novelty in the primary school classrooms of the 1950s, and they remained indispensable for the next two decades.[62] This new emphasis on the appeal to the imagination in teaching history was also embraced by historians such as Marjorie Reeves, who wrote several books in a series entitled *Then and There* that were intended for older primary children.[63] They combined contemporary accounts, photographs and well-researched but simple texts to give a vivid account of life in a monastery, castle or country house. In contrast to the artists' impressions in Unstead, Reeves believed that verisimilitude was a vital part of the 'activity revolution' in the classroom: 'to understand', she insisted, 'is to respond, for gaining understanding is never a passive process ... No learning is complete without some activity of body, mind or imagination.'[64]

Some of the more advanced books by Unstead and Reeves were used in the junior forms of secondary schools; but with increasing numbers in these classrooms, as the baby-boomers reached their teens, and with the compulsory school leaving age having been raised, this was another burgeoning market opportunity for publishers and authors alike. Pre-war textbooks such as those by R.B. Mowat remained in widespread use, but many new titles were published, usually focusing on the conventional periods of English or European history. One such author was another schoolmaster, Sidney Reed Brett, who produced a string of books for those taking School Certificate and subsequently O Level, such as *The Tudor Century, 1485–1603* (1962), *The Stuart*

Century, 1603–1714 (1961), and *A History of the British Empire and Commonwealth* (1959). For those staying on to A Level, the works of the Rev. Leonard W. Cowie were widely read, such as *Seventeenth-Century Europe* (1961), and *Eighteenth Century Europe* (1963), as were two books by the Oxford historian V.H.H. Green, *Renaissance and Reformation: A Survey of European History between 1450 and 1660* (1952), and *The Hanoverians, 1714–1815* (1954). But they were far outsold by G.R. *Elton's England Under the Tudors* (1955), and by his *Reformation Europe, 1517–1559* (1963).

As history textbooks gradually became more user friendly, so technological developments further enhanced the potential appeal of the subject, one indication of which was the unprecedented use of the 'magic lantern' in many classrooms. The LCC continued to lend hundreds of thousands of slides from its library, and the Historical Association enlarged its own collection for schools to borrow. Enterprising (and well-financed) schools and local authorities were investing in more sophisticated projectors, such as episcopes and epidiascopes, which could project postcards and photographs on to the screen as well as slides. 'Filmstrips' were also being widely used; despite their name they were a novel way of projecting still pictures. By 1960 there were 30,000 filmstrip projectors in schools, and 4,500 filmstrips available covering most of the subjects in the curriculum. The strips were cheap enough to be purchased by schools, the projection equipment was comparatively simple, and many history teachers who completed our survey forms remember using them during the 1950s and 1960s. At the same time, these decades witnessed the introduction of duplicating machines known as 'gestetners' and 'bandas', which represented a considerable advance on the earlier mimeograph or cyclostyle processes. Magazines and books of guidance for history teachers advocated copying original source materials and maps for the classroom; but they do not seem to have been widely used before the 1970s.[65]

This was also a period when the use of moving pictures in schools, and educational visits to the cinema, were more widespread. During the war, film was enormously valuable, for instruction as well as entertainment, and film shows proved useful as a way of conveying information and providing distraction to schools that were short of teachers and overcrowded with evacuees. As one wartime grammar school pupil recalls, 'spare cash' was 'almost non-existent, but if there was a film at the cinema depicting an event relevant to the curriculum, we were taken'.[66] Not surprisingly, the Olivier production of Shakespeare's *Henry V* was a great favourite, though this was as much on account of its high-flown language and patriotic appeal as its historical resonance. Such was the importance of film that at the end of the war, the Ministry of Education hoped there would soon be one projector in every school.[67] This was over-ambitious, but by 1960 half the schools in England were so equipped. By then the Educational Foundation for Visual Aids, established in 1948 by the Ministry of Education in conjunction with local authorities, had collected 6,000 films and filmstrips made specifically for teaching purposes, and it was making 60,000 loans to schools every year.[68]

During the Second World War, schools broadcasting had kept going, and at a time of unprecedented educational disruption, the programmes were seen as crucial when children were evacuated or kept at home with limited schooling: and they also kept boys and girls engaged and distracted when they were 'compelled to spend many uncertain hours in air-raid shelters'.[69] The long-running series *How Things Began* which dealt with life on earth up to the first settled civilizations was started during the war, and after 1945, schools radio became increasingly available and increasingly popular. In 1938–39, there had been about 9,000 schools where pupils could listen to broadcasts, which was less than half of the total number. By 1952–53 there were more than 21,000, and by 1960–61 there were more than 23,000, which was virtually all schools, and over 9 million pamphlets accompanying the programmes were sold.[70] Throughout the 1950s there were four weekly history programmes running every term, which were aimed at different age groups between eight and fifteen, and they were keyed in to the subjects and periods most commonly taught: in addition to *How Things Began*, there were broadcast *Stories from World History*, *Stories from British History*, and *Modern History* for older children.[71] But at the very time that radio seemed to have become indispensable, it was challenged by the new medium of the small screen.

The BBC's general television service had begun in 1936, but it was suspended during the war, and it was not until 1952 that schools television tentatively started. But the results were not encouraging, television sets were expensive, the Ministry of Education remained unenthused about the whole idea, and for the next few years nothing happened.[72] Eventually it was Associated-Rediffusion, one of the newly established Independent Television companies, which started serious school broadcasting in the summer of 1957. Later that year, both ITV and the BBC began transmitting an extended service, although they were still called 'experimental', and for all its novel appeal, the new medium was slow to catch on: in 1960 only 2,000 schools possessed televisions, even though there were nine weekly programmes running each term. A year earlier, the BBC ran its first schools history broadcasts, a series called *The Twentieth Century*, aimed at 13–15-year-olds. In 1960, it began broadcasting *Men of the Past – From the Remotest Past to Roman Times*, which was intended for those aged between eleven and fifteen. And in 1961, it premiered *A Century of Change – 1860–1960*, for 13–15-year-olds, which was 'designed to illustrate the major changes in the social history of Britain and her relationships with other countries during the last hundred years'.[73] The connection between these made-for-television series and the school syllabuses was immediately clear.

While there was change inside the history classroom, there was also the continuing appeal of doing things outside school. Most pupils attending after the Second World War remembered going on at least one class trip to an archaeological site or historic town or castle. One of them attended a small girls' grammar school, and went on several such expeditions, including a long weekend away when she was 16. There was, she recalled, 'just a small select group of us', eight pupils with 'two teachers, our history teacher and our art teacher'. They spent the February half-term weekend in York, and that 'further increased' her 'fascination with the Middle Ages'.[74] In the same way, a teacher whose career spanned the years from 1946 to 1984 remembered that every year each form would go on a day visit to historic places such as Verulamium and St Albans, and there were also residential trips to cities such as Norwich, 'when everyone stayed in a local youth hostel'.[75] But from the late 1950s, the increase in car sales, the improvements in the road system, the opening of stately homes to the public, and the expansion of the National Trust meant many children could visit an unprecedented number of historic sites with their parents, at just the time they could now watch historical dramas and historical documentaries at home on television. With such novel and powerful competition, it is not surprising that local civic pageants, which had previously brought history alive, became less popular, as the small screen and the stately home made history outside the classroom more real, vivid and immediate than ever before.

In many grammar schools, and in some secondary moderns, the impact on the teaching of history of these extra-curricular activities, combined with the new technologies in the classroom, was both reinforcing and liberating. As Asa Briggs explained, they helped contribute to 'a revolution of educational provision and technology', which encompassed 'books, pianos, projectors, and materials for art and crafts as well as wireless sets', and they also helped bring about 'a revolution of educational aspiration and ambition, associated with the widening of curricula, the use of experimental teaching methods, and the relaxation of purely external discipline'.[76] From these developments, the teaching of history must have benefitted, yet as before, this was only part of the overall picture, and it was probably not the preponderant part. In many secondary modern schools, the grim realities were similar to those described in Michael Croft's novel, *Spare the Rod*, published in 1954, whose fictional Worrell Street school reflected the author's own teaching experiences: an ill-equipped struggle in seedy premises to foster civilized values among sullen and disorderly pupils, and where his colleagues urged that 'You don't need a degree for this job', but rather 'common sense and discipline'. A year later, Edward Blishen produced *Roaring Boys*, which was revealingly subtitled *A Schoolmaster's Agony*, and eloquently portrayed the plight of the conscientious secondary-modern school teacher, beset by his pupils' alien and anti-intellectual out-of-school culture, yet well aware of their academic potential if only he could find the time and energy to elicit it.[77]

History Assessed and Recollected

As during the First World War, no new Inspectors were appointed between 1939 and 1945, and no schools were inspected: HMIs were seconded to other government departments, or they were busy surveying the provision of education among evacuees, and assisting in the preparation of the official reports that the Board of Education commissioned during these years. HMIs were closely involved in the production of the *Green Book*, and one of them, R.H. Barrow, was secretary to the Norwood Committee, which may explain why the Report declared the Inspectors to be 'the eyes and ears' of the Board of Education. After 1945, recruitment and inspection were resumed, and HMIs were charged with such additional tasks as reporting and encouraging new educational developments, and with supervising the emergency teacher-training scheme. Between 1945 and 1949, the number of HMIs increased from 364 to 527, they were recruited from broader social and educational backgrounds, and in 1961 equal pay for men and women was established.[78] But there were problems of adjustment to the expanded world of schooling in the aftermath of the Butler Act. There were some who claimed the HMIs were too independent, while others alleged they 'conscientiously measure the size of classrooms, count the number of lavatories and washbasins, and pace out the size of the playground', but that 'the art of assessing standards of work seems to be lost'. Indeed, one commentator concluded that 'the modern Inspectorate no longer inspects and in giving advice is no more expert than many others in the educational system'.[79]

There is little official material on junior and infant schools for this period, but one non-ministerial inquiry was a survey of history teaching carried out in May 1955 by the BBC, to which more than 500 primary schools replied.[80] This was scarcely a random or statistically significant sample, but the findings are suggestive. A few schools had no history syllabus at all but introduced the subject through topics, projects or social or environmental studies. In most schools where history was taught, it began in the third year, usually for two 30-minute periods a week, when it mainly consisted of story-telling, often concentrating on earliest times and ancient civilizations. Thereafter, it was taught within a chronological framework, although some small schools continued with story-telling. In the later years, all the schools concentrated on British history, the majority dealing with 'Modern Times' by the end of the sixth year and a few introducing some world history, while one tenth of the schools included some local history.

Yet the majority of respondents to our survey who were at primary school during the late 1940s and 1950s remember very little about the history they were taught, although those who do most frequently recall Greek and Roman myths and stories of great British men and women. 'My memories,' notes one of them who was at primary school in the late 1950s and early 1960s, 'are of learning about famous people such as Elizabeth Fry, Florence Nightingale and Capability Brown. We had no textbooks but listened to the teacher talking. I really enjoyed history because these people came alive to me as the teacher spoke about them.' Another former pupil recalls how his teacher 'really brought the stories to life, and stories of torture, murder, divorce and battles really seemed so exciting to us all'.[81] Here was a vindication of the official view that telling stories was the best way to engage boys and girls with history, but it bears repeating that few of our respondents can remember any of the history they were taught in primary school, and that amnesia certainly mirrors the experience of one of us in the late 1950s.

At secondary level, the HMIs' reports are a vivid reminder of just how hard it is to generalize about history teaching in post-war grammar schools. 'This subject does not seem to provide much intellectual stimulus', they noted of Reigate Grammar School in Surrey. 'Some of the notebooks suggest that the owners have not taken a great deal of pride in them and that the written work has been rather casual.' The whole treatment was 'too abstract', the Inspectors complained of the Joseph Rowntree Secondary School in New Earswick, Yorkshire, and in the library there was 'a serious shortage of reference books and monographs'.[82] The Inspectors regularly reported that the teaching was too detailed and too dense, and was dominated and distorted by the public examinations. So, while at Hastings High School for Girls, there was 'a lively interest in the subject throughout the school', in the middle forms, 'the external examination overshadows the course, and there is too much lecturing by the teachers, accompanied by a good deal of unnecessary note taking by the pupils'. But at Lady Lumley's Grammar School in Pickering, Yorkshire, 'the staff were devoted', and history was 'in a healthy state and shows much promise'. The subject was taught even better at Northallerton Grammar School, where the history master was a 'vigorous and attractive teacher with an infectious enthusiasm', with the result that 'a number of pupils have been inspired to a successful continuation of their studies after leaving school'.[83]

Most HMI reports make plain that grammar school history in this period was English history, taught chronologically from ancient times in the first year to the nineteenth century for School Certificate and then O Level, sometimes (but not often) with added episodes of imperial and European history. The recollections of our respondents bear this out. Here is one such reminiscence:

First year in High School we started with the Romans and spent the next five years working through to the end of Queen Victoria. No social history, just political, and nothing European or global, except where it impinged on Great Britain.[84]

For those who sat O Level, the fourth and fifth years typically completed the national narrative by covering English (and sometimes European) history from 1815 to 1939, or English social and economic history from the eighteenth century onwards.[85] In most grammar schools, the history curriculum was relentlessly focused on preparation for O and A Level, and many teachers regarded their prime function as being to prepare their pupils for the narrow yet specific requirements of an examination based on memory, fast writing and cogent prose. For O Level history, pupils were generally required to write five essays in two and a half hours. Teachers tried to anticipate the questions that would be set, and to train their pupils to answer them by committing to paper as much historical information as they could remember on the day.

Yet in some grammars, the history teaching was very good. One female respondent went to such a school in Nottinghamshire, where she

had one history teacher only from 1950–1955. She introduced each topic by talking to us. We had history textbooks, but did not follow them slavishly. We were encouraged to find things out for ourselves. The homework our teacher set often involved us in imagining ourselves in a particular historical event/period/scenario … I especially enjoyed medieval architecture and the Tudor and Stuart periods. Along with a fair proportion of my class mates I really enjoyed the 'Imagine yourself living in the Civil War' type of homework. Fourteen-year-old girls in the 1950s were not sophisticated young ladies![86]

Another attended grammar school in the Cotswolds during the late 1950s, and had 'an absolutely inspirational teacher':

This was when the real love of History as a subject began … He made all of it come alive, so much so that I took my O Level a year early and then once in the sixth form, [I] went on to do A Level history. It was a small Grammar School, and [he] taught us all the way through from the First Year. Although we were made to learn dates, it was mainly to hang the facts on and we had discussions rather than lessons from him ... His success rate was excellent mainly because he just loved the subject. He made us think in the discussions we had, not just take down facts and learn them ... We learned to ask why things went the way they did rather than just learn facts.[87]

Those who recall their time at grammar school with pleasure and fondness almost invariably do so, not for any particular period they studied, nor because they did well in their examinations, but because their attention had been caught and their curiosity stimulated by imaginative and inspirational teaching. One respondent remembers being given homework 'where we had to pretend that we were reporters, writing for a newspaper about early battles', and the written-up stories had to be 'complete of course with drawings of maps with plans of attack, people fighting, etc.'. Another recalls their teacher being 'highly innovative and getting us to work in groups to produce newspapers of Tudor times'. Such activities often won children over to the subject who might otherwise have been sceptical, but even the traditional methods of 'chalk-and-talk' could be captivating with a good teacher who had a passion for the past. One former pupil remembered that 'we started with the Babylonians and worked through chronologically, learning important dates'. In the classroom, 'we sat in rows, facing the teacher', and 'kept quiet, listened, asked questions. We had text books and homework and, I think, weekly informal tests on what we had been studying.' But despite this rigorous regime, the teacher was 'fantastic': she 'had a good degree and loved her subjects [and] made lessons fun and interesting'.[88] In the same way, another respondent remembers being taught political history, and initially feared the 'dryness of various Acts of Parliament etc. that we had to learn'; but the schoolmistress responsible was 'energetic and refreshing' in her delivery, and 'it's a great testament to the teacher that I enjoyed the subject'.[89]

But as practiced by an uninspiring and unimaginative teacher, 'chalk-and-talk' was utterly dispiriting, as this disenchanted recollection makes plain:

On arrival at the history classroom, which had a 'wall' of four blackboards at the front of the room, we would find the master busy with his chalk, writing reams of words on the fourth board. The first three were already filled. We had to desperately copy down all of the notes in 'rough' making sure that we had completed the first board before he finished the fourth because he would then erase the first and start to write the fifth and so on ... His style was to underline names in red, significant places in green and dates in blue. We were expected to write up the notes in our 'best' books as homework and he expected his style to be copied meticulously. Once a week there was a test before we started writing. The test was to remember all of the dates copied from the previous week ... Punishment was severe for failure in the tests running from detention, through the punishment of writing out 100 dates, to being beaten with a cane![90]

Not surprisingly this pupil 'hated the whole process of learning history and dropped the subject as soon as school procedures allowed me to'. He was not alone. One woman recalled the tedium of 'always sitting in rows and taking copious notes from the board'. The teacher gave little explanation of the notes, there was no class discussion of the work, and the pupils understood 'very little'.[91] Another woman vividly remembered how each history lesson 'commenced with the whole class standing by their desks reciting, with dates, the kings and queens of England from 1066'.[92]

For many grammar school pupils, history meant tedious hours of dictation, copying from the blackboard, uninspiring teacher-talk and note-taking, and essay-writing and practice examinations. One of our respondents remembers that the teacher rarely faced her class, because she was too busy 'writing notes on acts of parliament, battles, treaties etc. on the blackboard for us to copy'. To make matters worse, 'there were no teaching aids and no enthusiasm for her subject. It became very boring, I lost interest and then made no effort'. Another regrets there was no opportunity for their class 'to think for ourselves, no independent learning as there is now, and revision for the exams consisted of trying to memorise as much of [the teacher's] notes as possible'.[93] Yet a third recalls becoming 'disenchanted with history' because 'the teacher read from her notes, we copied them down, she wrote dates and names on the board so that we could copy them correctly, there was no discussion and at the end of the lesson she left the room'. As a result, 'there was no interest sparked or encouraged and no suggestion that we should do anything but learn the facts she put in front of us and pass our exam'. Such experiences were by no means unusual: for many grammar school boys and girls, bad history teaching 'completely destroyed' any interest in the subject that they might have possessed.[94]

Technical schools were few and far between after 1945, and given their practical concerns, history was rarely a high priority. The HMIs were unimpressed with how the subject was taught at Stanley Technical Trade School in Croydon where, in his eagerness to cover the syllabus, the teacher 'uses methods of teaching that demand very little effort on the part of the class', and it was no better at the Walton County Secondary Technical School in Liverpool, where history was 'a rather unpopular and dull subject'.[95] But in other schools, attempts were made to teach history in a way that was relevant: as at Worksop Secondary Technical School, which had building, technical and commercial streams, and where teaching included the history of construction, technical and engineering advances, and domestic life, costume and banking.[96] In a similar vein, one correspondent recalls the history she was taught at a junior commercial school in Bristol:

> We covered the whole period from Romans to about 1918, seen mostly from the point of view of how people lived, and, from the late eighteenth century, major legislation passed. We spent some time learning about Factory Acts, Trade Unions and the Agrarian and Industrial Revolutions ...

She could also remember learning 'about the Elizabethans and the contrasts in Elizabethan times between poverty and riches'. The picture of the Tudor nation divided between 'the haves and the have nots' remained vividly with her; and when studying the late eighteenth and early nineteenth centuries, 'we did a lot about factories and trade unions and that sort of thing, [and] a lot of social history'.[97]

Comprehensive schools were also in a minority during this period, and little was yet written about how history was taught in them. One person who did record his impressions was the historian George Rudé, who spent his early career teaching in English public schools and grammar schools, and then at Holloway comprehensive in Islington, about which he wrote in 1957. Rudé argued that history should be part of the common core of subjects to the end of the third or fourth year, for a minimum of two teaching periods a week; but he thought history should be an optional subject for O Level in the fifth year. Throughout the school, he believed there should be a common syllabus 'for every form in a given age-group, irrespective of the level of attainment or presumed intelligence of the classes into which pupils are divided', and it should attempt to integrate all aspects of human activity (such as economic, social, political and religious) into a single pattern rather than confining itself to one particular area.[98] 'It does not seem to me,' Rudé wrote, 'that any one of them can in itself be an effective substitute for the systematic study of man's history as a more or less chronological sequence in its many-sided aspects, proceeding by stages of development (including both failure and achievement) from the distant past to the present day.' Accordingly, he argued for the kind of syllabus that he had devised and taught at Holloway, which was chronological from 'Early Man' to 'Modern Britain', but with themes for study specified for each year, which gave scope for looking at social, military or economic history in addition to the conventional political narrative.[99]

The majority of boys and girls in post-1945 England were educated in secondary modern schools, and there was considerable discussion about what sort of history should be taught there, or whether it should be taught at all. The Labour Minister of Education, Ellen Wilkinson, was a history graduate, and was eager to see more children educated to a greater age, but she feared that pupils in secondary moderns would be steered 'away from the humanities, pure science, *even history*'.[100] A few years later, the authors of *Teaching History* were concerned that 'history itself [is] on the defensive; it is not uncommon to find it abandoned in the fourth year of the course in favour of some kind of civics or social studies of a more or less contemporary kind'.[101] Indeed, in some secondary moderns, courses in social studies were sometimes substituted for history and geography entirely, dealing in successive years with homes, communications, agriculture and industry, and citizenship. The case for such a syllabus was that 'some real integration of history and geography' might be effected, that many of the topics were treated from an historical perspective, and that social studies evoked 'useful effort from children in a variety of different directions'. But the authors of *Teaching History* believed much was lost in the process: first, 'the unfolding story of men and women and nations, of particular men and particular women and particular nations, the strange unfolding of individual destinies and of worldwide movements'; second, the evocation of individual character and achievement, and even the overall general story itself; and third, the sense of a complex era or age as a whole. 'These dangers and limitations', the authors concluded, 'have to be squarely faced by those of us who abandon history as traditionally understood and embark instead upon social studies of this kind'.[102]

The idea of merging history and geography and introducing elements of civics and economics in a new subject called social studies was briefly fashionable after 1945, but by the mid 1950s, 'many

7. A first-year grammar school pupil's notes on 'Alfred the Great', Morecambe Grammar School, 1961 (courtesy of Ian Colwill)

schools' had 'returned to a traditional curriculum'.[103] This was borne out in 1956, when the BBC carried out a survey of history teaching in secondary schools, and 300 replies were received from secondary moderns. Nearly 80 per cent of them spent at least 70 minutes a week on history, and over 10 per cent spent over 100 minutes a week; and the curriculum bore striking similarities to those of the grammar schools, with its focus on English history. In the first year, history began with prehistoric man or the Romans, and went as far as 1485; in the second year, the chronological approach remained, but the periods studied were more diverse. By the third year 30 per cent of schools were adopting a less chronological method – usually 'patches', 'topics' and special subjects, but with starting dates ranging from 1485 to 1900, and with closing dates varying from 1485 to 1956. As for the teaching: the HMIs who visited secondary moderns often reported that facilities were woefully inadequate. Many schools had no library books, or lacked film projectors, or were unable to receive programmes from the BBC. Sometimes the teaching was good despite these drawbacks, as at Norbury Manor County Secondary Girls' School, Croydon, where there was 'hard work and enthusiasm on the part of both staff and girls'. Sometimes the teaching was effective with the more able pupils but, as at Nechells County Modern School in Birmingham, a greater effort was needed to stimulate the interest of those who were less academically inclined. Sometimes, as at Harborne Hill County Modern School in the same city, the teaching was just not very good.[104]

One of our survey participants taught in secondary moderns from 1951 to 1967. He believed that most of those teaching history in such schools had some degree of interest in the subject, but few had any extensive knowledge of it, and even fewer had a degree in it. The aim, he recalled, was to give pupils an outline: the ancient world and Roman Britain in Year 1, the Saxons and Middle Ages in Year 2, the Tudors and Stuarts in Year 3, and 'the Industrial Revolution to today' in Year 4. World history and politics 'were largely omitted and war was too close for comfort'. Such textbooks as there were mirrored the school syllabus, and towards the end of term, a class might be broken up into groups to research separate topics which would be displayed in 'a voluminous timeline for the school open day/parents' evening'. These activities 'demanded library access, class movement and discussion and a teacher able to cope with multifarious questions off the cuff', but 'not all teachers had the knowledge and many schools were reluctant to let pupils out of desks'. Those teachers whose knowledge of the subject was wider than the history textbook went beyond giving an outline, and tried 'to arouse interest and feed it when aroused'. Our respondent did so by getting the pupils 'to use their imagination and to connect their own lives with those of people in the past'. For his first lesson on the Tudors, he asked them to draw their own family trees, and then asked questions such as 'who was Queen Elizabeth's granddad?' He also took his classes to historic sites: those studying the Middle Ages went to a monastery, where they ate 'sandwiches in the refectory in silence except for monkish sign language they have been told about'.[105]

Just as the teachers in secondary moderns varied greatly in their knowledge and commitment, so did the range of pupil experience. Children who were not expected to take leaving exams were spared the rigours of intensive note-taking, but many teachers fell back on a watered down version of the grammar school curriculum, as one of them recalls:

> I think I taught a bit of everything. Certainly I'm quite sure I did the Stone Age, the Greeks, the Romans, up to the Norman Conquest in the first year and then you did, not much on the medieval period to be fair, but probably then the Tudors and the Stuarts and so on. And in the last year you tried to do what you could to get them up to the present day.[106]

The result was that many secondary modern pupils found history as boring as their contemporaries in grammar school did: 'a grey, mechanical tangle of drudgery'. 'The teacher', one of them recollects, 'simply read long passages from books which we dutifully wrote down. No explanation was given. It felt like "these are the facts you must remember".'[107] But this was not everyone's experience. Another correspondent greatly enjoyed his two years in secondary modern school, where he 'liked all topics of history as I was fascinated by the different style/expectation of life during the different periods'. He then sat and passed the thirteen plus examination, but he was disappointed to discover that history at grammar school was much less interesting and engaging.[108]

As in earlier periods, the only generalization that can be safely made about the experience of boys and girls learning history during the 20 years after the end of the Second World War is that no generalizations can be safely made. There seems to have been a fairly even division between those with positive recollections and those with negative memories of their time in the classroom, and in most cases, it was the personality of the teachers and the quality of their teaching that were of especial significance in determining how they responded.[109] It is also clear that while teachers remained sovereign in their classrooms, the increased numbers of pupils sitting O and A Level exams meant that there was a growing uniformity in what was being taught, not only across grammar schools, but across secondary moderns, too. In 1965, Martin Booth completed a set of interviews with history teachers and their pupils at five different secondary schools. Most of them followed a traditional chronological pattern of study from Year 1 to Year 5 with an O Level examination at the end that tested how many facts the children could remember. Even though the teachers claimed to use local studies and sources in history to enliven their classes, the pupils regretted that they spent so much time taking notes, and also the lack of opportunity for discussion in class. History in school, Booth concluded, appeared to be 'a dreary desert where as far as the eye could see row upon row of school children sit, writing endless notes'. What, he wondered, 'can be done?'[110]

Many of these 'endless notes' were written down by boys and girls who were being entered for examinations in greater numbers than ever before. The years from 1947 to 1950 were the last of School Certificate, and more than 85,000 pupils were entered for history, which was much higher than during the inter-war years, and it remained the fourth most popular subject.[111] Yet the total number of children aged 15 was well in excess of half a million, so those taking School Certificate in history were less than one sixth of boys and girls in their age group. During 1951 and 1952, which were the first years of the new O Level GCE, the history numbers dipped to below 70,000; but they exceeded 80,000 again in 1953, and peaked at almost 160,000 ten years later. Unlike School Certificate, O Levels were examined separately not in groups, and the pass rate for history ranged from 60 per cent in 1955 to 55 per cent in 1964. As the total number of children aged 15 continued to increase, reaching nearly 700,000 by 1960, those taking O Level in history remained at approximately one sixth of all the boys and girls in their age group; but history declined from being the fourth to the sixth most popular subject, behind English Language, mathematics, English Literature, French and geography.

Yet this picture of apparent relative decline is also deceptive: for English was divided into two separate papers; while if the pupils taking ancient history and English economic history were added in, then history would again rank higher than geography. Meanwhile, at A Level, history was between the fourth and sixth most popular subject; but if other historical subjects were added, its position would have significantly risen, though the overall numbers remained very small. In 1951, 10,230 candidates took history A Level, and after a brief dip, the number of entries rose slowly through the decade, to 15,685 in 1960, and then doubled to 30,580 in 1965; and during the same period, the pass rate fell slightly from 77 per cent to 73 per cent.

School History at Empire's End

As in earlier times, the Ministry of Education did not direct schools to teach history with the aim of inculcating an enhanced sense of national identity and imperial pride. Whenever these issues were raised in parliament, and ministers were asked to prescribe the history that should be taught in schools, they invariably replied that this was not their job, and nor should it be. In the summer of 1944, Viscount Bledisloe, a former Governor General of New Zealand, moved an amendment to R.A. Butler's Education Bill, urging that a clause should be added making teaching about the 'geography, history [and] ideals' of the British Empire compulsory in all schools. But Lord Addison's reply, on behalf of the government, was crushing: 'we here are not constructing a school syllabus. We are constructing an Education Act.'[112] Four years after Bledisloe's unsuccessful effort in the Lords, Brigadier Rayner told George Tomlinson in the Commons how appalled he was that a recent survey had revealed that 50 per cent of those questioned could not name a single British colony, and 75 per cent could not tell the difference between a colony and a dominion. The Minister declined to be drawn.[113] In any case, by then, the British Empire was already in dissolution, and its liquidation would be virtually complete by the mid 1960s. Indeed, by then the prevailing mood, in the aftermath of such embarrassing episodes as the Suez fiasco and the Profumo scandal, was more one of national malaise than of national pride.

This was not a mood that R.J. Unstead shared. 'At a time when it is fashionable in some quarters', he wrote in 1962, 'to belittle England's achievements in the past and to doubt her place in the future, I have tried to show that whereas England has often acted foolishly or badly, her history shows the persistence of ideals which good men have lived by since Alfred's day.'[114] In the same way, Allen Lane's *Pelican History of England* was a product of the Attlee years, which were more patriotic than some Conservative critics allowed, and the most eloquent volume in the series, S.T. Bindoff on Tudor England, was drenched in the language of Shakespeare and the Bible; while Elton's book on the same period celebrated the nation he had come to venerate as a Jewish refugee fleeing from Nazi Germany.[115] But it is not clear whether any of this rubbed off on the schoolchildren who might have read them, and more than ever, they were learning history in many ways and in many places beyond the classroom: in visits to stately homes and National Trust properties; in reading magazines such as *Look and Learn* or *Knowledge*, which carried extensive amounts of historical material; in watching A.J.P. Taylor's lectures on television or in subscribing to *History Today*; and in reading the best-selling books of Arthur Bryant, J.H. Plumb, A.L. Rowse, Steven Runciman, C.V. Wedgwood, and Taylor himself. In any case, throughout the apparently radical Attlee years, and even more so under the Tories from 1951 to 1964, the prevailing tone of English public life and political culture remained overwhelmingly conservative, whether embodied in Harold Macmillan's faux-patrician Edwardian style, Malcolm Sargent's 'Last Night of the Proms' jamboree, or Richard Dimbleby's reverential commentaries on great state occasions.[116]

But as in the early 1940s of wartime, so again in the early 1960s of affluence, pressure for change was building up, with a new generation and new policies, epitomised by the Labour leader Harold Wilson, and his commitment to modernizing Britain. The implementation of this agenda would change school education, and would change school history, but in many ways that next phase of educational reform had already been anticipated in the last years of Conservative rule. In 1962, during his second stint as Minister of Education, David Eccles had set up the Curriculum Study Group, which was later superseded by the Schools Council for the Curriculum and Examinations, and which would prove extremely influential in modernising many subjects, including history. The following year, the Robbins Committee published its report urging the expansion of higher education, including teacher-training colleges. By then, the tide of educational opinion, and of local authority practice, was running strongly in favour of comprehensive schools, and the new Certificate of Secondary Education was just around the corner. In terms of educational reform, Labour was pushing at a door that was already open when it came to power in 1964. But as change gathered momentum during the second half of the decade, there would be significant implications both for the types of schools in which history would be taught, and for the sort of history that would be taught there.

4 History for a Nation 'In Decline', 1964–79

Students should be taught a European history, related to the history of the whole world, rather than the narrowly British history, which is still all too common. Too many French children are familiar only with battles that Napoleon won and British children only with the battles he lost. No one would want children exposed to any controversial propaganda while the question is still disputed, but schools will, when the settlement is final, have to educate for a European future.

(*The Times*, 29 October 1971.)

These words appeared in a leading article, published by *The Times* on the day after the House of Commons voted to join the Common Market. They recognized both the importance of teaching history in schools, and the need to change the history that was being taught, in the light of Britain's attempt to reposition itself, no longer as the metropolis of a global empire, but as a European nation whose future lay across the English Channel.[1] This reorientation was one response to the problem of 'decline', which was widely perceived as the defining national predicament and political challenge of the 1960s and 1970s. For Harold Wilson's Labour government, the solution was to modernize, by embracing the 'white heat' of the technological revolution, by supporting legislation to loosen the still-prevailing Victorian moral code, and by aligning his administration with the newly emerging culture of youth; while for Edward Heath's Conservatives, the answer was to turn the nation away from its disintegrated imperial past towards what seemed a brightly beckoning European future, and to spend as never before on industry, hospitals and education.[2]

But while these two leaders sought to grapple with the challenges and consequences of national decline, the fact they so often seemed unable to do so merely intensified the problem, and the perception, that once-great Britain had become the 'sick man of Europe'.

Wilson oversaw an unprecedented expansion in universities, and in scientific and technological education; but the white-hot modernizing revolution failed to eventuate, and his government never recovered its prestige or its purpose in the aftermath of devaluing the pound. Heath successfully took Britain into 'Europe', but his economic policies were ineffective and contradictory, he failed to stand up to the trades unions, and having called an early general election on the question 'who governs Britain?', he was dismissed from office by disillusioned voters. The ensuing years from 1974 to 1979 were widely regarded as the worst since the Second World War, as growing industrial unrest was compounded by a stagnating economy and soaring prices: Wilson had neither the energy nor the capacity to address these issues during his short second term; and James Callaghan, who briefly followed, fared no better, as his minority government was defeated after the 'winter of discontent' of 1978–79.

England was not at ease with itself during the 1960s and 1970s, and one indication of the general mood was that education became controversial in a way not seen since the disagreements surrounding the passing of the Balfour Act of 1902. This was less so in the case of higher education, where the unprecedented expansion of universities was widely welcomed; but in the case of secondary schools, the disagreements were both bitter and protracted. There were many, especially on the left, who were convinced that the tripartite scheme of grammar, technical and secondary modern schools had failed, and that it must be replaced by comprehensive schools which catered for all abilities and social backgrounds under the same roof. But there were others, usually on the right, who believed that since 1945, the grammar schools had provided unprecedented opportunities for bright children from lowly backgrounds. Yet although this was often a party political issue, some senior Conservatives were not opposed to comprehensive schools, while there had always been support in sections of the Labour Party for grammar schools.[3] But from the mid 1960s to the early 1980s, the tide of opinion was moving overwhelmingly in favour of comprehensive schools.

As *The Times* editorial had noted, the implications of these developments for the teaching of history in English schools were considerable – and controversial. How did the national narrative, which had previously culminated in the nineteenth century era of global greatness, now look when those supremacies seemed to have vanished? What version of English history, if any, might plausibly be put in its place? In two decades when stress was increasingly laid on the importance of science, technology and enterprise, and on looking to the future rather than to the past, how would history teachers face the mounting challenges to their subject on the timetable and in the classroom?[4] What was the appropriate form of history syllabus and history examination for pupils who were being educated, not separately in grammar or secondary modern schools, but together in comprehensive schools? And what sort of history did newly-minted teachers, arriving from new campuses with new ideas about their subject, want to teach in the classroom? Here was a veritable ferment in history education in schools, over which Westminster and Whitehall still exercised only a general supervisory role. As Britain faced the unprecedented challenges of decline, history faced unprecedented challenges in the classroom.

The Comprehensive Revolution

When Harold Wilson led Labour to victory in 1964, his tiny parliamentary majority precluded the introduction of any major legislation concerning education in the near future. Moreover, Wilson was a grammar school boy, who was alleged to have said that such institutions would be abolished over his 'dead body'; and there were those in his government, such as James Callaghan and George Brown, who regretted their lack of university education, and who were highly respectful of grammar schools.[5] But there were others, including former Oxford dons (as was Wilson himself) such as Tony Crosland, Patrick Gordon Walker, Richard Crossman, Douglas Jay and Lord Longford, who had been educated at fee-paying schools, and who felt no such loyalty to the grammar schools. In the first instance, Wilson appointed Michael Stewart to be Secretary of State for Education and Science. He had attended Oxford University, he was the first holder of the office since Ellen Wilkinson who was a former teacher, he was eager to further the cause of comprehensive schooling, and at the end of his brief period of office, in January 1965, the Commons passed a motion approving 'the efforts of local authorities to reorganise secondary education on comprehensive lines which will preserve all that is valuable in grammar school education for those children who now receive it and make it available to more children'.

The motion also recognized that 'the method and timing of such reorganization should vary to meet local needs' but urged 'the time is now ripe for a declaration of national policy'.[6] Stewart thereupon departed to the Foreign Office, but he had already prepared a draft circular, urging local authorities to reorganize secondary education on comprehensive lines, which would be issued that summer by his successor, Anthony Crosland, under the famous number 10/65. Crosland had attended Highgate School and Oxford University, after the war he established himself as a Labour thinker and politician, and in *The Future of Socialism* he declared that 'the school system in Britain remains the most divisive, unjust and wasteful of all aspects of social equality'. On being appointed Secretary of State, he famously told his wife that 'If it's the last thing I do, I'm going to destroy every fucking grammar school in England ... And Wales ... And Northern Ireland', and the circular 10/65 made plain the government's intention 'to end selection at eleven plus and to eliminate separatism in secondary education'.[7] But in conformity with the policy of leaving such decisions to local authorities, Crosland decided that he would only 'request' and not 'require' them to submit plans to reorganize their schools. In fact, many of them were already in the process of doing so, and the changes towards comprehensive schooling would probably have occurred whether Crosland had issued his circular or not.[8] In any case, after less then three years, he left Education to become President of the Board of Trade.

Crosland's successor was Patrick Gordon Walker, who had been educated at Wellington College and Christ Church, Oxford, where he subsequently became a history tutor.[9] He should have been Foreign Secretary in Wilson's Labour government, but his defeat in the 1964 general election meant he was out of the Commons for two years; following his return, he was put in charge of the Department of Education, but he only held office from August 1967 to April 1968. He was on the way out, and cuts in public spending in the aftermath of the devaluation of the pound in October 1967 meant he had to postpone the raising of the school leaving age to 16. This had been one of Labour's election pledges, and as the minister who had reneged on it, Gordon Walker felt compelled to resign. His successor was Edward Short, who came from the north country, working-class wing of the

Labour Party, having attended Durham University and subsequently qualified as a lawyer. He had been a secondary school headmaster, and he served as chief whip and Postmaster General in the early years of the Wilson administration. Short was passionately in favour of 'a more democratic education system', and in February 1970, he introduced a bill that, against all precedent, would have *compelled* local authorities to end selection at eleven; but it had not been enacted when the Labour government was defeated at the general election later that year.[10]

The proportion of secondary school pupils in English comprehensives had increased from below ten per cent in 1964 to just under one third by 1970, and there were some who hoped that the return of the Conservatives, under Edward Heath, would halt this trend; but this was not to be.[11] Throughout his administration, the Secretary of State for Education and Science was Margaret Thatcher: she had recently shadowed the Department in opposition, and she would become one of the longest-serving holders of that office, her continuous tenure having only been exceeded since 1945 by George Tomlinson. Heath sent Thatcher to Education because it was a suitably domestic job for the only woman in his cabinet, and with the precedents of Ellen Wilkinson and Florence Horsbrugh in mind, he thought that it was the upper limit of what she was capable of achieving. Like Heath and Wilson, Thatcher was a product of grammar school and Oxford, and she would later give a vivid and affectionate account of her time at Kesteven and Grantham Girls' school, where the 'teachers had a genuine sense of vocation and were highly respected in the whole community', and where she 'had a particularly inspiring history teacher, Miss Harding, who gave me a taste for the subject which, unfortunately, I never fully developed'.[12]

Yet despite these happy memories, in which history ranked second only to chemistry, it was on Thatcher's watch that the comprehensive revolution carried virtually all before it in England (and Wales), as she authorized more local authorities to go comprehensive than any Education Minister before her or after.[13] To be sure, Thatcher had been one of the prime Conservative opponents of Edward Short's abortive bill, and within a few days of taking office, she also withdrew Crosland's circular 10/65. This was fully consistent with the non-doctrinaire policy of leaving such matters to local authorities, but it was also the Tory policy at the elections of 1966 and 1970, and the speed with which Thatcher acted, without the customary consultations, suggested a determinedly doctrinaire coup against the prevailing orthodoxy.[14] But the withdrawal of circular 10/65 made little difference, for by 1970 comprehensivization had acquired a momentum that was impossible to stop, and no Secretary of State could realistically have impeded it. The result was that during her spell at Education, she approved all but 326 of the 3,612 schemes that were put up to her by local authorities. Nor did Heath interfere: he shared Thatcher's regard for grammar schools, but they both 'bowed before the spirit of the age'.[15]

Thatcher was also eager, like any determined departmental minister, to obtain a larger slice of government funding for schools, and to defend her patch vigorously against the threat of spending cuts which emerged in the aftermath of the energy crisis of 1973. In June 1971, she announced a new primary school construction programme, costing 132 million pounds over three years, which would replace the many antiquated and squalid Victorian buildings not yet swept away.[16] In December 1972, she introduced the Department's white paper, entitled *Framework for Expansion*, which projected a five per cent real increase in education spending during the next half decade. The document had long been in the making, but Thatcher made it her own: 'when it talked about expansion', she told the Schools Council, 'it meant expansion and not contraction', and she intended that an extra 1,000 million pounds would be earmarked for education by 1981.[17] In 1973, she raised the school leaving age to 16, which had been in the Tory election manifesto, and honoured a promise on which Labour had earlier reneged. Despite occasional confrontations, her officials soon warmed to her: she was hard-working, she read the papers and mastered her briefs, she left the local authorities to get on with things, she was forthright, determined and decisive, and she fought her department's corner.[18]

But Thatcher regretted that Education was not 'a mainline political job', and in retrospect, her time there would become an embarrassing episode she preferred to forget: for in what was her only cabinet post before becoming Premier, she had been as un-Thatcherite as Heath himself and the rest of his administration, and she and Sir Keith Joseph were the two biggest spenders.[19] Such was her record, but by the time she was Prime Minister, she had come to believe that the Department of Education and Science had been 'self-righteously socialist'; that its officials were determined to railroad through comprehensive schools at all costs; and that she had constantly been misled, thwarted, deceived, opposed and let down by her civil servants: all of which meant she had been prevented from doing what she had really wanted to do, namely reverse the trend towards comprehensives and safeguard the grammar schools. Yet the facts are incontrovertible: when Margaret Thatcher became Secretary of State, less than one third of all schools in England were comprehensives; by the end of her period of office, the figure had more than doubled.[20]

Thatcher's stint at Education ended when Heath's government fell in March 1974, and during the brief Labour administrations of Harold Wilson and James Callaghan, a succession of economic crises meant her expansionist plans were put into abeyance. For the rest of the decade, money for schools was tighter than since the mid 1950s, and once again, a succession of Secretaries of State held office for brief periods. The first was Reg Prentice, who had studied at the London School of Economics, and had already served as a junior minister under Michael Stewart and Tony Crosland. Prentice was disappointed to be given Education, he soon fell out with Wilson over the European referendum, and he was demoted to the Ministry of Overseas Development in 1975. He was replaced by Fred Mulley, whose background was authentically working class, but he had won an adult scholarship to Christ Church, Oxford, and on graduation he became a Fellow in economics at St Catharine's College, Cambridge. But he was only at Education for 15 months, because on Wilson's resignation, James Callaghan moved Mulley to Defence, and replaced him at Education with Shirley Williams – another woman given this 'domestic' portfolio.

Williams had attended a fee-paying school before going to Oxford; but she was an ardent champion of comprehensives, and during her time the Labour government passed the reform measure that had fallen in 1970 when the Wilson government had been defeated at the polls. Soon after taking office, Fred Mulley had introduced a new education bill, and it became law in November 1976, by which time Williams had succeeded him. It gave the Secretary of State the *compulsory* means to require all local authorities to plan non-selective school systems, which meant abolishing both the eleven plus and their grammar schools. Even Crosland, who was as much a comprehensive supporter as Williams, had only 'requested' not 'required' local authorities to act in this way; but the Labour governments of 1974–79 were more to the left than those of 1964–70, and the Education Act of 1976 was the most radical action yet taken to force comprehensive schools through, even in those areas where the local authorities remained reluctant. But Williams's tenure at Education was also brief, as Callaghan's government fell in May 1979, and one of the first acts of the incoming Conservatives was to repeal the 1976 legislation.[21]

Between 1964 and 1979, there were eight Secretaries of State for Education and Science, and all of them except Thatcher held office only briefly. As in earlier times, most of those in charge of England's state schools had little first-hand experience of such places, for five of them had attended fee-paying schools before going on to Oxford University. But there were some significant changes: no Secretary of State during this period was a patrician, or an Old Etonian, or a member of what had once been called the 'intellectual aristocracy'; only one of them had studied history at university; two of them had been teachers earlier in their careers (in Short's case as head of a secondary modern school); and for almost half of the time, the post was held by a woman. Yet there were limits to change: Mulley and Short were the only Secretaries of State from an authentically working-class background; Thatcher and Prentice were from the petit bourgeoisie; and the remainder came from the comfortable middle classes. But all accepted the conventional educational wisdom of the time, and allowed comprehensive schemes to proceed, with the result that by 1980, more than four fifths of those attending state secondary schools were being educated in comprehensives.[22] Here was a veritable revolution, as the grammar schools and secondary moderns virtually disappeared.

From one perspective, this was essentially a domestic matter, unconnected with the broader issues of national 'decline' that were so unsettling during the 1960s and 1970s. The widespread support for comprehensive schools, among politicians, civil servants, educationalists, teachers and the public, was the result of the growing dissatisfaction with selection based on the eleven plus examination, and also with the education that was provided by secondary moderns, which had been attended by 80 per cent of the population after leaving primary school. As a result, the ideological, political and bureaucratic momentum for educational reform gradually built up, until it became irreversible. But in other ways, this move towards comprehensive education *was* informed by the broader concerns about national 'decline'. In order to reinvigorate the economy, there needed to be a better-educated workforce than that which the secondary modern schools seemed able to produce; and there was also a need at a senior level for more scientists and technologists, who could provide the necessary innovation in business and industry, and for economists and sociologists who would increase understanding of the limitations and possibilities of contemporary society. But where did history fit into this brave new world, and how should it be taught in the comprehensive classroom?

History for the Comprehensive Classroom

From the 1960s, the Department of Education and Science ceased to issue the *Recommendations* and *Suggestions* to schools that had appeared in a continuous, if irregular, flow since the first decade of the twentieth century. One reason may be that in an era of national anxiety and introversion, it no longer seemed either possible or appropriate even to suggest the sort of national history that should be taught. To be sure, the men in Whitehall had repeatedly deprecated the teaching of history as national propaganda; but there had always been a quiet assumption that the national story was worth telling in an appropriately understated way; yet even this may have been harder to believe in or to sustain from the mid 1960s onwards. But in addition, the comprehensive revolution carried with it such significant implications for the teaching of history and for the content of the curriculum that it was no longer appropriate to continue refining and developing the earlier suggestions. Were there consequences for history in primary schools of the gradual phasing-out of the eleven plus? And what were the implications for history in secondary schools of the virtual disappearance of the grammars and secondary moderns, and their replacement by comprehensives? These questions took time to come into focus, and it is not surprising the Department gave up its traditional form of guidance and advice, leaving these matters to the Schools Council and local education authorities.

Some indication of official thinking came from two inquiries undertaken on behalf of the Department at the behest of the Central Advisory Council for Education. The Plowden Report, investigating primary schools, was published in 1967, and took a long perspective, going back to the original *Suggestions* that had been published in 1905, which had urged that teachers should be free to use their 'powers to best advantage and be best suited to the particular needs and conditions of the school'. Since then, the Report observed, 'the use made by teachers of their growing freedom' had 'varied considerably'. During the inter-war years, the force of tradition and 'the inherent conservatism of all teaching professions' had often 'made for a slow rate of change'. The requirements of selection examinations for grammar schools 'also exercised a strong influence towards uniformity'. For much of the time, HMIs had been 'restraining influences on innovation', although this may have changed in recent years. Only a 'minority of teachers ... particularly in the infant schools, responded eagerly to freedom', and only since the Second World War had 'child-centred education' become more (and sometimes excessively) fashionable; but 'the schools which continued on traditional lines to emphasise instruction exceeded the number of those which erred by excess of innovation'.[23]

As for history in primary school classrooms: the Plowden Report conceded this was 'a subject on which it is not easy to reach agreement', not least because since the 1900s, 'many new problems have arisen in the teaching of history to children'. This was partly because the subject had changed and developed: personalities had receded from the centre of the stage; their motives had become much more difficult to disentangle; and economic influences had come to the fore. This had made it harder to teach the past to infants and juniors: 'history, it is said again and again, is an adult subject. How then can it be studied by children without it being so simplified that it is falsified?' There was a 'further problem', namely that 'it is not until the later years of the primary school, if then, that some children develop a sense of time'. But this did not necessarily mean the subject could not be well taught below the age of eleven. Indeed, the committee had learned of one infant school 'where several of the older children became absorbed in historical matter of the most varied kind', while at another, 'one exceptional child had memorised the dates of the kings and queens of England – "all except the muddling Anglo-Saxons"'.[24]

Yet when it came to recommending the history that should be taught in primary schools, the Report said little that was new. In the case of infants, there should be no separate timetabling for the subject, because they should approach history through stories that were indistinguishable from literature: 'Odysseus, Beowulf, the Norse stories, Roland, some of Chaucer's tales, Arthur, Robin Hood'.[25] At junior level, history continued to appear 'as a separate subject in the timetable, certainly in the last two years and often before', though it suffered the disadvantage of 'being confined to two periods a week'. Much of this teaching, Plowden urged, should be built around topics or projects or discoveries, which might be introduced by the teacher 'because the subject matter is interesting', or in response to 'a child's questioning arising from a local antiquity or from an historical novel'. Once interest was aroused, materials would be collected from the school or the public library, collections of documents and illustrations might be obtained, photostats could be acquired from the local record office, and visits might be arranged to houses and churches of the period, or local museums. Class discussion should help clarify the topics that individuals or small groups of children might investigate, and an essential task for the teacher was to help 'individuals and groups to clear their minds as to what they want to find out'.[26]

Having described how history should be taught, the Plowden Report offered several justifications for doing so, though none were concerned with inculcating a sense of national identity or pride. By learning stories about the heroes and villains of the past, boys and girls might begin to understand that just as history made legend, so legend helped to make history. By acquiring 'some landmarks in chronology', they might begin to obtain an idea of sequence and change in the past, and to appreciate its implications for the present and the future. By exploring past times, people and places, especially with reference to their own locality, children should begin to understand the difference between the past and the present, and to escape temporarily 'from their own world', and to be 'confronted with a different world'. Some of them might even obtain 'an imaginative intuition' of past periods and earlier eras, and in so doing come to appreciate that 'men are the creatures as well as the creators of their time'. Having looked at different sources and read different books, 'even primary school children may begin to glimpse that history is in part created by the historian'.[27] More prosaically, Plowden noted that history 'frequently provides a successful starting point for spontaneous drama', and that its spilling over into 'other aspects' of the primary school curriculum was a recent development that it sought to encourage.[28]

The second of these inquiries was the Newsom Report, which had published its findings in 1963: it had been limited to the average and less able aged eleven and above, the overwhelming majority of whom left secondary school with no qualifications. The Report addressed two questions: what subjects could and should be taught to such pupils, and how might the teaching be done? Literacy, numeracy, religious instruction and physical education were deemed essential, and had the Report been concerned with all secondary modern pupils, including the more able, it would have urged that they should acquire 'some experience in mathematics and science, and some in the humanities.' But the 'wide range both of capacity and of taste' among those with whom Newsom was concerned made it impractical and inappropriate to propose any 'universal fixed curriculum'. The prime criterion of the least gifted was often the relevance of the subjects they studied to what they would be doing once they left school, and even for those who were more able, there was 'no compelling educational reason' why they should choose one subject rather than another. As a result, many boys and girls regarded history as 'expendable': 'they cannot buy anything with this kind of knowledge as they can with physics and shorthand'. Had any of them ever heard of Henry Ford, the Report opined, they would have agreed with him that history was 'bunk'.[29]

Nevertheless, Newsom urged that 'the customary division of the curriculum into certain traditional subjects should be retained', including history, but it did not venture far beyond the last *Suggestions* produced in Whitehall during the 1950s. One way of gaining the interest of younger secondary modern pupils was by using such mechanical aids as the 'projector, record player, tape recorder, radio and TV'. By focusing on particular episodes from the relatively recent past – for instance the life and impact of Mahatma Gandhi – it might be possible 'to set ordinary minds working on world problems'. Or by looking at family histories – 'uncles and aunts settled or working overseas, new neighbours from abroad' – there might be a chance to 'secure an intellectual and emotional breakthrough from the classroom with its textbook to the real world of human problems'.[30] It was equally important to teach pupils 'to enter imaginatively into other men's minds'. In some cases, this would mean keeping 'good company and great company' with such titanic figures as Abraham Lincoln. But it was also important to teach boys and girls 'to know bad company and to avoid it'. For 'evil men also have power ... Were those who followed Hitler necessarily worse men than those who rallied to Churchill? Why did they do so? Might we not have done the same?' 'These', Newsom observed, ambitiously, 'are sobering questions which ordinary young people ought to face.'[31]

As for more senior pupils: the Report suggested that teachers should 'choose contemporary themes' which would help them 'understand the world in which they live, not only the world in which their fathers were born'. History 'now often ... reaches 1939 and edges towards 1945'; but at the end of the Second World War, India was still part of the British Empire, China was not yet Communist, and Africa was 'still a network of colonies and mandated territories with only a distant prospect of becoming anything else'. History teaching, Newsom went on, which 'does not take account of these and similar revolutionary changes will not seem to the limited minds of our boys and girls to be the history of their world'. Yet the Report also stressed that 'some of our very modern history will take us back to ancient times', and the history of the nation needed to be set in a long term as well as a contemporary perspective: 'in British history, perhaps the most important thing to do with pupils before they finally leave school will be an assessment of Britain's true position in the world today, an assessment which must be based on knowledge of the past as well as the present'. Newsom conceded this was 'material for a life study, not for a year's work however generous the time allowance', which meant any teacher 'will have to choose between the barest outline of events and the selection of limited topics which can be studied in sufficient detail to bring them to life'.[32]

Four years later, the Department of Education published a pamphlet, *Towards World History*, which attempted to chart the directions in which history in secondary schools might be going. 'For nearly a century', it began, 'we were agreed in teaching mainly British constitutional history', and the authors did not advocate the abandonment of 'teaching ... our own history', since that would 'gravely weaken our very sense of national consciousness' which was constituted by 'our memory of our past'. But this was no longer enough, for in the changed circumstances of the 1960s, British history needed to be up-scaled into the broader panorama of world history, which was more relevant for the 'rising generation' which was 'less insular than we were in the past, more internationally minded, more tolerant, more appreciative of the special qualities and attributes of

8. The dismantling of the British Empire coincided with an increase in the teaching of the nineteenth century and emphasis on such episodes as the 'Scramble for Africa', Littlehampton Comprehensive School, 1977 (courtesy of Julie Johnson)

different peoples and different races'.[33] Moreover, since world forces had controlled events in every country from the late nineteenth century, this meant that 'twentieth century history *is* world history, with the result that new and considerable attention which our schools are beginning to give it appears to be providing the catalyst by which the insularity of our syllabuses may be dissolved'. Thus understood, 'world history' was 'an important new development and one worthy of consideration by teachers of history generally', which would 'encourage a better understanding of world affairs today'.[34]

The pamphlet then considered the world history courses recently devised by the examining boards. At O and A Level, there were syllabuses on 'world affairs' from 1919 to the present, while the new CSE examinations had resulted in a broadening of what was being taught. According to one board, the aim of world history was 'to help the school leaver to understand the society of which he forms a part'; another offered a paper dealing 'with some important aspects of British history, seen in a steadily widening context of European and world affairs'; while yet a third began with the assumption that 'the history which today's pupils need is the history of their own world in recent times'. Thus understood, 'world history' enabled teachers to bring school courses up to date, and to give 'relevance to their work by relating past to present affairs'; and it also enabled them to extend the vision of their pupils 'out into the world as a whole and away from too close a preoccupation with British politics'.[35] Of course, there were challenges and risks: 'the very large number and wide variety of the topics and events required for study' meant that there was an inherent danger that pupils would be asked to study 'too many topics, too superficially, in the context of too few decades'. The solution was to select a limited number of topics, and to ensure they gave the course an overall unity and coherence.[36]

Like Plowden and Newsom, *Towards World History* was very much a product of its time. All three were infused by an awareness that Britain's place in the world had diminished: 'we live in an entirely different world from that of our grandfathers'. But they also accepted that the current system of state schooling would continue, and none foresaw the scale or speed of the comprehensive revolution that was gathering pace by the late 1960s. Plowden lamented that even the 'meagre time' allowed to history in the top classes of junior schools was 'occasionally sacrificed to coaching for the eleven plus'; Newsom's concern was to improve the experience of the less able, rather than advocate the abolition of the secondary modern schools they attended; while *Towards World History* was concerned with school syllabuses not school structures.[37] But the comprehensive revolution, combined with the phasing out of the eleven plus and the raising of the school leaving age meant that by the late 1970s, the educational landscape had changed completely. Instead of suggesting the different sorts and levels of history that might be offered in grammar or in secondary modern schools, the challenge now became to devise a history curriculum that could be taught across the much wider range of ability found in the new comprehensives, where more pupils were staying on for longer than ever before.

The initial impetus towards curriculum change had been the introduction of the Certificate of Secondary Education in 1963, with the first exams being sat two years later. While O Levels catered for the top 20 per cent of boys and girls in ability, most of whom attended grammar schools, CSE was meant for the next 40 per cent, namely the brightest pupils at secondary moderns. The CSE was overseen by 14 regional boards, and was offered in three different 'Modes', providing a varied balance between examinations and coursework, and between external assessment and marking by the pupils' own teachers. Since each board could prescribe different syllabuses, there was a greater range than for O Level. There was more stress on local history, which was covered in Mode 2 (school-designed but externally marked) and in Mode 3 (school-designed and school-marked) syllabuses. Five boards offered medieval history, Commonwealth history and historical themes in Mode 1 (externally-designed and externally-marked), but they mostly focused on recent times, and all boards offered a syllabus on twentieth-century world history in Mode 1, which soon became the most popular. Although originally intended for pupils in secondary modern schools, by the end of the 1960s, the CSE had become the preferred examination for many teachers and pupils in the comprehensives.

'The general picture', J.W. Docking noted in 1970, when surveying the CSE courses, 'is certainly very different from one obtained by looking at various history O Level syllabuses, where bare chronological periods are often prescribed with little or no guidance in content or approach'.[38] He was undoubtedly correct. The O Level courses still focused overwhelmingly on English and European history, chopped up into such periods as 1485–1603, 1714–1815, or 1789–1914. But the initiative now lay with the CSE, and in response to its innovatory curricula, many O Level syllabuses were broadened during the 1970s to embrace world history. Soon after, for example, the Associated Examining Board came up with 'World Affairs from the Russian

Revolution to the Present', in which candidates would be expected to demonstrate 'an understanding of the interests and motives of the world's great powers in their relations with each other'. The range of topics was impressively (or intimidatingly) wide. 'Political developments' included Communism in Russia and China; the rise and fall of Nazi Germany; the League of Nations, the Second World War, the Cold War and Vietnam; and the end of the European empires and the growth of colonial nationalism. 'Economic and social developments' encompassed the international economy since the First World War; the growth of new industries and the rise of welfare legislation; race relations in the United States and South Africa; along with pollution, crime, housing, wildlife, and women.

The combined impact of the comprehensive revolution, the rise in the school leaving age, the advent of the CSE, and the changes in the O Level syllabuses had pushed the teaching of history to 15- and 16-year-olds away from the 'great tradition' of the national past and towards a global version of the twentieth century. For many teachers, the hardest challenges they now faced were how to select from a wide range of possible topics, how to cover them in sufficient depth, and how to bring them into relation with each other. But although they cascaded downwards to pupils aged between 11 and 14, these momentous changes made scarcely any impact in terms of the history that was taught to those staying on for A Level, where the traditional format of two papers, one in English history, and the other in European history, survived largely unaltered. In 1967, the English history paper set by the University of London Board divided the subject into three, from c450 to 1509, 1399 to 1714, and 1688 to 1955, and for each period, 30 questions were set, and candidates had to attempt four. It was the same for European history, where the divisions were from 800 to 1516, 1516 to 1789, and 1763 to 1954. By the mid 1980s, little had changed in the sixth form syllabus; but in most other classrooms, the history being taught had been transformed. At least, that was the aspiration and the intention.

New Teaching for New Schools

Despite the general anxiety about national (especially economic) decline, the late 1960s and early 1970s not only witnessed a massive expansion in primary and secondary education, but also in further and higher education: the post-war baby-boomers were moving from childhood to adolescence to adulthood, and Labour and Conservative governments believed that more graduates in the workforce would help economic recovery and national revival. The Robbins Report urged a substantial increase in the numbers going on to colleges and universities; it also recommended that more teacher-training colleges should be created, that they should be re-named colleges of education, that they should be closely linked to universities, and that they should offer new, four-year courses, leading to the award of the degree of Bachelor of Education.[39] More teachers were now being trained than ever (130,000 of them in 1972, the peak year), and there were more teacher-trainers and lecturers who were educating them. In colleges of education and in universities, educational theory was being energetically advanced, while the advent of comprehensive schools generated new demands and ideas about what to teach and how to teach it. The results of this 'pedagogic ferment' would profoundly affect how history was taught in schools.[40]

At primary level, telling stories had been the traditional way of introducing boys and girls to history, but the increasing popularity of child-centred learning, which put the interests of pupils first, offered new freedom for teachers. Moreover, the growing popularity of comprehensive schools meant the general phasing out of the eleven plus examination, resulting in a less rigid timetable which further increased the scope for pedagogic experimentation. At the recently established Bulmershe College of Education in Reading, John Fines encouraged his students to explore the use of drama and role-playing in the classroom, because he thought it more important for children to understand the ambiguities and complexities of history than to be introduced to the subject with unproblematized and often semi-fictional stories about heroes and heroines from the past.[41] A more accessible approach was the use of adapted original materials, and at Dudley College of Education, John West provided his students with a range of facsimile sources ready made for children to touch and feel as well as see, read and discuss.[42] As these examples suggest, the trend in innovative thinking about history in primary schools was away from traditional structure and chronology, towards more immediate and subjective methods.

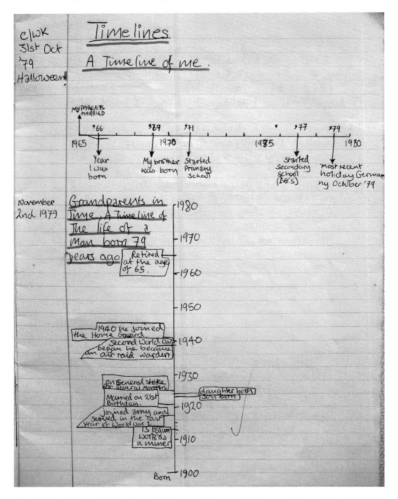

9. A 'Timeline of Me', from third-year history at Islington Green School, 1979, shows the influence of 'child-centred' history teaching – in contrast to the 1930s time chart in Fig. 2 (courtesy of Charlotte Crow)

Interest amongst educationalists in how children learned was not new, but the application of child psychology to the teaching of history was. The most influential theorist was Piaget, who defined stages of development according to the evolving capacity of children to think in logical fashion. Before the age of 11, he believed they struggled to understand abstract concepts, and that only thereafter did they gradually develop the skills of systematic thought and problem solving. But in the case of history, research appeared to show that most children were not capable of abstract thought and of problem solving until they reached the age of 15.[43] This did not matter if the aim was to spoon-feed factual information for O Level exams, leaving the treatment of complex topics and the embrace of abstract thinking until A Level. But it also meant that history was a particularly difficult and demanding subject, better suited to the able and senior school pupils rather than inflicted on those of lesser ability and at an earlier age. In which case there was a real danger that in the increasing numbers of comprehensive schools, where pupils were of a much wider ability range than in grammar schools, and where most of them left at 16, history might seem a subject suited only to a senior and elite few, and become marginalised as Latin had been.

In 1968, Mary Price published an article entitled 'History in Danger', warning that the growing number of comprehensive schools meant the subject was increasingly at risk.[44] Now that adolescents of all abilities were being educated under one roof, there was a growing need to provide less academic and more relevant subjects, either by integrating history, geography and religious instruction as 'humanities', or by focusing on contemporary issues by teaching 'social studies'. But the cross-curricular approach embodied in 'humanities' diluted history, while the current affairs content of 'social studies' threatened to disregard it altogether.[45] Accordingly, Price called for a massive exercise of 'self-help' on the part of history teachers, and for the establishment of a 'real forum for the exchange of experiment and thought in the teaching of history'; and the Historical Association duly established a new journal concerned exclusively with pedagogic practice, entitled *Teaching History*.[46] Within a year of her call to action, the Schools Council published *Humanities for the Young School Leaver*, exhorting teachers to 'find more successful methods of making history in its own right meaningful and attractive' to pupils; otherwise it risked disappearing from the curriculum altogether.[47]

Three years later, the Historical Association published a pamphlet entitled *Educational Objectives for the Study of History* by Jeanette Coltham and John Fines in which they described the attitudes, skills and abilities that they believed schoolchildren should display at all stages of learning history. Traditional history syllabuses specified *content*, namely periods to be taught and topics to be learned, but Coltham and Fines tried to identify the characteristic *practices* associated with doing history as an educational activity. 'Only as he masters the relevant skills', they wrote, 'will the learner come to know what historical method is (learning by doing).' From this perspective, the acquisition of detailed and substantive historical knowledge was less important than using the imagination as a means of understanding human actors in the past, along with different types of historical sources to produce 'truly their personal versions of history'.[48] In the early 1970s, such ideas sat awkwardly with the requirements of O Level examinations, focusing on factual recall and essay-writing skills, but the intention was that *Educational Objectives* would provide a 'working document' which teachers might use as a sort of 'check-list' for planning pupils' learning.[49]

In 1972, the Schools Council recognized the importance of applying these new ideas about children's capacity for historical thinking to the comprehensive classroom, and they initiated a project to create a new kind of history syllabus. It was led by David Sylvester, a member of the education department of Leeds University, who also taught in a local comprehensive school; he had never liked the traditional 'chalk-and-talk' classroom methods, and he had already co-authored a book about the challenges of teaching history to less able children.[50] Four years of work with volunteer pilot schools followed, resulting in a new course that was accessible to the ordinary teacher and met the needs of ordinary pupils, culminating in the setting of 'experimental' O Levels and CSEs in 1976.[51] The books produced to support the course were attractively presented, and included materials that could be used by pupils in their third year, before they decided on their O Level or CSE options. The topics prescribed were wide in their range, diverse in their methodology, and varied in their geographical scope, including a modern 'crisis' (such as the Arab-Israeli Conflict), a subject in social and cultural history (such as the American West), a theme traced over a long period (such as Medicine Through Time), and also local and regional history (with the fieldwork devised by the teacher).[52]

The driving force behind what became known as the Schools Council History Project (SCHP) was the recognition that in the new comprehensives, history had to justify its place in the curriculum by appealing to children across a wide range of ability: hence the stress on contemporary history rather than on earlier times; hence a subject like the American West, which was designed to subvert popular stereotypes not reinforce them; and hence the history of medicine, which emphasized the scientific and constructive aspects of human progress and development. The SCHP course was also innovative in its teaching methods, promoting a 'detective-style' approach, based on four underlying 'concepts': the significance and limitations of historical evidence, the balance between change and continuity, the problems of causation, and the importance of cultivating empathy. Boys and girls would be encouraged to 'investigate' historical questions, to interpret 'clues' from adapted original sources, and to understand that historical explanations were a matter of debate; and by learning about the perspectives and presumptions of people in the past, they would also begin to appreciate that their actions and views might be very different from those prevailing today. Accordingly, SCHP history would help adolescents 'to widen their experience in order to find themselves', by offering them 'the opportunity to experience vicariously an immense range of real human life and endeavour'.[53]

This required a more collaborative approach in class, involving games, simulation and drama, and with teachers 'supporting' pupils in their journeys of historical discovery: 'since the outcomes hoped for' were 'attitudes and abilities rather than the memorisation of facts', the aim in the classroom was to 'create an active learning situation for the pupil, rather than those which cast the teacher in the role of transmitter of information'.[54] As such, SCHP history was both 'more and less ambitious than traditional syllabuses at this age level': it did not set out 'to cover in detail the mass of content usually demanded', but it gave pupils 'the opportunity of sampling in some depth a range of historical content and adopting a wide variety of approaches to history'.[55] Accordingly, SCHP history was not so much justified on its academic merits, or as a form of moral instruction, but as a way of helping boys and girls to find their identity.[56] But to critics, SCHP history was a deliberate and misguided repudiation of the traditional O Level syllabus, sacrificing dates, names, content and coherence to chase after the chimera of historical skills and personal empathy. They also regretted that the stress on coursework, derived from CSE practice rather than O Level, meant that SCHP history was less academically rigorous.[57]

Even in terms of the original SCHP remit, Sylvester's project was open to criticism, in that it sought to introduce pupils of all abilities to ways of thinking about history at ages when most experts said that even the brightest would struggle to cope. Ironically, this might mean that less able children, for whom the course had ostensibly been designed, 'found a lot of the materials difficult'. But it also emerged that many children who took the course 'were better at explanations, better at evaluating sources, better at understanding historical thinking than people who hadn't'.[58] This was the attraction of SCHP for the newly-minted teachers emerging during the 1970s, some of whom became immediate converts: they saw it as a way of empowering their pupils by giving them 'the bricks' from which they could 'build their own history'. Teacher networks were established by the SCHP, and the scheme drew a strong following from local authority advisers.[59] The Southern Universities Board agreed to offer an O Level examination for the SCHP course, and by the mid 1980s, 20 per cent of schools were teaching it, while many more were using the SCHP text, *What is History?*, to provide an introduction to the use of sources for 13-year-olds. But the aim of the SCHP was more ambitious, namely to 'promote some re-thinking of the whole question of syllabus in history at the secondary level', and the approaches it had pioneered regarding the use of evidence and the cultivation of empathy influenced many lecturers and would-be teachers they were training.[60]

The SCHP was not the only force for change in the comprehensive classroom. As teaching methods developed, as new courses and syllabuses were devised, and as school budgets expanded, there were corresponding changes in the content and format of textbooks. At primary school level, the Ladybird books and the works of R.J. Unstead were gradually superseded: in the early 1980s, for example, Oxford University Press inaugurated its *Junior History* series, which focused on social history rather than on political events, and which presented the subject 'in a direct and exciting manner', which made history 'come alive for children by involving them closely with the people and periods they study'.[61] At secondary level, some publishers continued to cater for the traditional O Level courses, producing books by R.J. Cootes and L.E. Snellgrove, where the text was only relieved by a few black and white illustrations or maps; but there was also a growing market for the more vividly-illustrated books deemed appropriate for the CSE pupil, such as the *History Alive* series edited by Peter Moss, which used line diagrams and cartoons to depict historical events.[62] Publishers also hastened to provide anthologies of facsimile documents, most famously the *Jackdaw* series produced by Jonathan Cape.[63]

But teachers were also becoming less dependent on textbooks, thanks to the transformative effect of the photocopier, which meant they could mass-produce their own worksheets that were customised to courses of their own devising, and could be adapted to the varied needs of their all-ability classes. This 'worksheet revolution' seemed to portend the end of 'chalk-and-talk' classroom instruction, as it enabled each pupil to work independently at their own pace on the basis of individual contact with the teacher.[64] Nor did the revolution end there, as some teachers created their own 'home-made' workbooks, combining photocopied pages from text books and documentary packs, to which they added their own questions and tasks.[65] Even more adventurously, and seeing the opportunities made available by the new cheap printing technology, some teachers turned themselves into full-time publishers, among them John Simkin, who set up Tressell Publishing in collaboration with some colleagues. He produced books based on original sources appropriate to the new style of classroom teaching, and the volumes on the Industrial Revolution and the First and Second World Wars were particularly successful.[66]

There were also important developments in broadcasting. By 1960, the overwhelming majority of schools had radios, and two decades later, Oxford University Press published its *Junior Histories* to accompany the BBC series *History Long Ago* and *History Not So Long Ago*.[67] But by the late 1960s, the BBC claimed it was reaching a regular audience of 15,000 schools via television, with the aim of bringing colourful visual stimuli, evocative drama and authentic historical 'voices' directly into the classroom. Ideally, the teacher would prepare the topic beforehand and follow the broadcast with questions and discussion. As had been the case since schools programmes began, the supporting materials for the teachers and the workbooks for their pupils were as important as the broadcasts themselves, and in the 1970s, the BBC was selling 100,000 pamphlets a term.[68] All programmes had to be approved by the School Broadcasting Council, an advisory body of teachers and local authority representatives. Output and transmission were co-ordinated by the BBC and ITV and feedback was received from their schools' liaison personnel and also from teachers themselves.[69]

Most of the programmes were directed at the primaries, where scheduling was less of a problem, and many teachers looked to radio and television to provide the knowledge they themselves lacked. As a result, broadcasting provided the basis for history teaching in between one quarter and two fifths of all primary classes, and programmes such as *History Long Ago* and *History Not So Long Ago*, and the books that went with them, offered a sort of national curriculum for many boys and girls before the idea or the term had been invented: 'a railway track along which a teacher could take his class for two years', at the end of which 'the kids ... would have encountered ... a hell of a lot of history'.[70] There were also innovations in programming for those aged from eight to thirteen, particularly the widely watched historical drama, *How We Used to Live*, made by Yorkshire Television between 1968 and 2002. Almost 90 episodes were filmed, covering a family caught up in momentous historical events from the Elizabethan era to the 1970s. In these as in other programmes, the aim was to capture the attention of the young listeners or viewers with a dramatic story that would engage their emotions and excite their imagination rather than give them a sense of narrative development or chronological understanding.[71]

But teachers in the new comprehensive schools, faced with a broad range of abilities in the classroom, and with the increased competition from alternative subjects, could not rely on textbooks, technology and television to guarantee the continuing appeal of history. The use of drama undoubtedly increased, bringing alive episodes such as the murder of Thomas Beckett or the Peasants' Revolt, capturing the imagination of children at the age when they delighted in dressing up and showing off.[72] At a more senior level, many pupils taking the CSE in Mode 2 or 3 did coursework on local history topics, involving visits to museums, galleries and archives, or to historical or archaeological sites in the area. During the 1970s, the number of history trips increased significantly, and in response to this growing demand, more museums and county archive services employed education officers and produced special materials to support history in schools, while many local authorities established teachers' centres. One such was the History and Social Sciences Teachers' Centre in Clapham, established by the Inner London Education Authority in 1970, which for the next

20 years provided training for teachers and equipment and materials for history classes, and also acted as a forum for bringing together teachers, publishers and broadcasters.[73]

In all these endeavours, the aim was to enable children to discover the past for themselves, and it was one aspect of a much larger-scale transformation, described and celebrated as the arrival of the 'new history'.[74] The 'old history' had been the traditional national narrative, taught by means of 'chalk-and-talk'; the 'new history' was more varied and accessible. Out had gone the incessant note-taking, along with great chunks of the chronological syllabus, to be replaced by 'patch' and thematic studies, and the analysis of historical sources.[75] Many children were learning 'actively', by means of group discussions, through drama and on field trips, and they were also learning individually using worksheets or materials put together by the teacher from a multiplicity of original sources. At primary school level, the emphasis had shifted from learning history by listening to learning history by doing, while in the comprehensives, many teachers wrote their own courses for the lower years, often with a strong thread of local history.[76] For those taking CSE or O Level, the conventional English history syllabus, emphasizing politics, had for the most part been superseded by courses focusing on world history since 1900, or on recent British and social and economic history. Only at A Level did the traditional English and European history syllabuses remain largely unchanged.

But the 'new history' was not just about a change in historical *content* and in teaching, so as to help the subject compete in the new comprehensive schools: it was also concerned with historical *method*, in the belief that it was important to introduce children to the many ways in which history was constructed – and contested. From this perspective, the most important question was not 'what history should children be taught?', but rather, 'how should children be learning to think about history?' As such, the 'new history' drew on the long, but hitherto marginal tradition of progressive pedagogy, which had stressed the importance of promoting thinking skills and the use of sources in the teaching of history.[77] During the 1970s, the 'new history' became powerfully embedded in the comprehensive classrooms – thanks to the zeal of newly-qualified teachers, the growth in teacher networks, the new textbooks, television programmes and curricula, and the appeal of the SCHP; and also because of the commitment of many teacher-training lecturers, local authority advisers, school inspectors and examination boards. Such was the brave new world of advanced educational opinion, and of pedagogic practice, that had come into being. But what did this mean for teachers and pupils in the history classroom?[78]

History Remembered and Examined

In the case of primary schools, an HMI report of 1978 described history teaching as 'superficial' in 80 per cent of classes inspected, and noted that 'few schools had schemes of work in history, or teachers who were responsible for the planning and implementation of work in history'.[79] As always, the frequency with which the subject was taught and the style of learning adopted largely depended on individual teachers. Most had no specific training in history, and were under no compulsion to teach it. Moreover, the immediate interests of the children were deemed paramount, and in increasingly child-centred primary schools, such stories as boys and girls were told were more likely to be derived from their own everyday experiences than from the doings of past heroic figures.[80] And once the eleven plus disappeared, and the primary school curriculum was 'freed up' from exam preparation, history had to take its chance as increasingly popular projects were constructed by individual teachers. Such activities often lasted for days or even weeks, they cut across subject domains, and allowed children to do practical work, such as model-making or drama. At best, children might gain some disjointed historical knowledge, but the danger was they never encountered or recognized the subject itself.

Primary teachers amongst our interviewees confirm that project work often obscured the boundaries between history and other subjects, and few of our 54 respondents who attended primary school during this time remember being taught a structured history curriculum.[81] Thirty-five do remember being taught history in one of their primary school years, and for most of them it was an enjoyable experience, even though the knowledge they gained was patchy and eclectic, and they have little recollection of stories being told to them, or of the books they may have read. Some remember the historical aspects of their project work: drawing figures from the past in art classes, or painting the female pharaoh Hatshepsut modelling Tutankhamen's

10. The vivid experience of a history trip to Warwick Castle in 1977, as recorded in a seven-year-old pupil's exercise book (courtesy of Jillian Andrews)

mask for a project on ancient Egypt, or dressing up to re-enact the great plague of London.[82] Others recall the school trips, which gave them a rare opportunity to see and touch 'real' historical places and objects. In some cases there were short journeys to see 'traditional charcoal burning' in a nearby forest, or to celebrate the 500th anniversary of the town's charter. But there were also more extended visits: to the American Museum near Bath, or 'by train to the British Museum to see the Tutankhamen exhibition', where one respondent confesses the class were 'fascinated by the gory bits, of course!'[83]

In the aftermath of the disappointing conclusions that had been reached about the subject by the Inspectorate in 1978, it was only a matter of time before ideas for the 'revival' of history at primary level began to appear. Five years later, under the auspices of the Historical Association, two teacher-trainers with a strong interest in primary schools, Joan Blyth and Ann Low-Beer, published *Teaching History for Younger Children*, beginning from the premise that the subject's place in the primary curriculum had recently become 'uncertain'. To remedy this, they proposed a systematic school-wide approach covering all ages from five to eleven, and urged a return to regular, dedicated, lessons, initially focusing on local and recent history, then leading on to topics with a 'chronological coherence', which would be supported by the use of time charts. The aim would be to encourage 'the progressive development of skill and understanding together with knowledge', and the authors suggested a variety of appropriate topics: local and personal for infants, and ancient and world history for juniors, though they also recognized that teachers would want to be free to make their own choices.[84]

In the case of secondary schools, the HMI reports between 1964 and 1979 record the changes from the tripartite to the comprehensive system of schooling, and the revisions to the history curriculum and to the methods of teaching it. In March 1964, the Inspectors visited Eastfield County Secondary School for boys in Wolverhampton, which offered 'a full seven year grammar school course', but where 'the examination target emphasises the acquisition of knowledge rather than the use of it'. This meant insufficient attention was given to 'developing in the boys powers of independent thought and judgement'; although history was cited as one subject in which 'some progress' was being made.[85] The HMIs who visited Luton Secondary Technical School (which was developing 'as a mixed grammar school') in the following year found the same faults. 'External examinations', they observed, 'figure too prominently in the school's aims and thinking', with the result that 'a wider approach, giving more opportunities for discovery and personal development' was 'desirable'. History teaching was 'competent and conscientious', but relied 'mainly on oral exposition or note-taking', and was 'closely tied to the text book', which did not 'encourage independence of thought or provide enough opportunities for personal contact' with the subject 'through individual discovery, the use of local history, or original sources'.[86]

When it came to history in the secondary moderns, the picture was more varied. At St Chad's College, Wolverhampton, the Inspectors noted that 'the stimulating presentation of material by means of lively narrative, effective visual aids and other devices' attracted 'great interest on the part of the pupils'.[87] At Manor Secondary Modern School for Girls, in Cambridgeshire, there were 'a number of interesting features such as course work being produced by the fourth year and individual work elsewhere', but there was a need to concentrate teaching 'in fewer hands' which would 'enable some of the work to be taken to greater depth, especially by the more able pupils'. At St Edmund's Roman Catholic Secondary Modern School in Portsmouth, the 'scheme of work' was 'satisfactory', but it was 'not always carried into practice'. Too much class time was spent 'in writing dull summaries from a basic text book', there was a need for 'more training in the independent pursuit of knowledge', there were not enough historical atlases and 'collections of books for class reference libraries are lacking'.[88] Meanwhile, at Burwell County Secondary School in Cambridgeshire, and at Eastney County Secondary School for Boys at Portsmouth, history had virtually disappeared, having been subsumed into social studies.[89]

By the mid 1960s, many HMIs were less enthusiastic about the continued existence and purpose of grammar schools, they were increasingly eager for the full-scale advent of the comprehensives, they were more sceptical of 'traditional' teaching methods telling some version of the national story, and they preferred 'progressive' approaches to the subject. The Inspectors' reports from the late 1970s reveal how much had changed in the structure of schooling and in the kind of history that was being taught in the classroom; but they also concede there were corresponding problems, as they were reporting overwhelmingly on comprehensive schools or (just occasionally) on the few surviving grammars.[90] Instead of describing history syllabuses that were similar in many schools, they were recording much greater variety in what was taught and in how it was taught. Indeed, for many teachers, the biggest problem they faced was how to decide what to teach from the ever-growing range of available alternatives and how they should set about delivering content in the classroom, given the ever-widening range of materials and technological aids that were becoming available.[91]

In June 1976, the HMIs visited Featherstone High School in Ealing, which had become a comprehensive during the late 1960s. 'A majority of pupils' came 'from families who emigrated to the UK from India and Pakistan', which necessitated the provision of 'extra teachers for the special language needs of some of these children'. History was part of the faculty of humanities, where the aim was to promote 'skills, abilities and attitudes that will be required by the pupils within the context of their future working lives'. In the lower school, history and social studies were taught as a combined course, where the plan was that after 'teacher-centred work, emphasis should be increasingly on small group work, project work and especially resource-based and enquiry-based learning.' But in Years 4 and 5, pupils could take Mode 3 CSE courses, consisting of 'world history together with themes from British and local history'. History was also available in the sixth form, leading to A Level, but the HMIs declined to comment in detail, beyond remarking that 'students who are sometimes comparatively new arrivals in this country can be made more aware of their local area', which in turn would help them to appreciate that 'local events can be linked to world wide issues'.[92]

A similar picture emerged at Ravenscroft Comprehensive School in Barnet. For the first three years, the history syllabus provided 'a framework of mainly British history' from the earliest times to the twentieth century. Thereafter, history was an option: both the CSE Mode 1 and the O Level history courses covered modern world history, while the A Level course was concerned with 'British and European history, 1815–1939'. Pupils were 'encouraged to think logically for themselves, to see situations from contemporaries' points of view, and to argue constructively from evidence'. But there were problems about mixed-ability classes, the capacity of pupils to interpret evidence, and CSE and A Level results.[93] At Townfield School at Hayes in the London borough of Hillingdon, pupils in the first three years concentrated 'on

English history with occasional glimpses of European or world topics'. In the fourth and fifth years, those who stayed with history 'had GCE O Level or CSE Mode 1 British social and economic history as their target'. But at junior level, some classes began with the Romans, others with the Normans; the third-year courses were 'especially crowded' in a vain attempt to bring history into the twentieth century, tackling topics such as the French Revolution which were 'too complex and difficult for all but the most able'; the Industrial Revolution was studied in the third year and then repeated for O Level and CSE; and the A Level syllabus also 'repeated that of the fourth and fifth years'.[94]

Once more, the variety of circumstance makes it hard to generalize, but several themes stand out. One is the greater diversity of ethnic backgrounds and academic abilities that were often to be found in schools by this time, and the challenges this presented for teachers who had to devise syllabuses that would be appropriate and appealing to such a wide range of pupils. A second was the HMIs' stress on the 'progressive' educational agenda, built around the development and needs of the pupils themselves, with the aim of teaching boys and girls the skills to understand the complexities and evaluate the contradictions of historical evidence. A third was the corresponding disregard for the 'traditional' methods of pedagogy, where the teacher gave dictation to the class, and where the pupils took notes from textbooks – 'chalk-and-talk' practices which were still more widespread than might have been expected. The fourth was the recognition that the public examinations were not satisfactory: in part because teaching CSE history and O Level history required separate classes when the syllabuses did not coincide, and gave rise to uncertainty as to which exam pupils should be entered for; and in part because the 'traditional' A Level syllabuses of British and European history sometimes repeated topics that had already been taught at O Level or CSE or, alternatively, did not relate in any way to what had been studied before.

The changing reports of the HMIs are corroborated by the recollections of history in the classroom we have compiled. During the last years of the grammar school and the secondary modern, there were familiar complaints that the subject was dull, with too much note-taking and too many dates. One young teacher, arriving for the first day at his new school in the early 1970s, received from his head of department 'a set of seven exercise books of notes, and he said,

"There, that's what you've got to get into your children's exercise books"'.[95] Not surprisingly, pupils as well as some teachers found this boring. One of them, who went to a grammar school in Essex, spent the first two years just going over 'the Egyptians, the Romans, the Anglo-Saxons, the Vikings, etc.', which was merely 'repeating what we had done at primary school and the teacher was less than inspiring'.[96] A second, who attended a grammar school in Derby, 'didn't enjoy history, and didn't take it at O Level' because 'it wasn't presented to us in an interesting way', since 'some of our teachers tended to lecture rather than to teach ... We covered a lot of English history, but it lacked cohesion ... I never grasped the flow, as topics were presented in isolation.'[97]

Despite this bleak picture, a few grammar school teachers were attempting to vary the customary diet of chalk, talk and textbooks. One young teacher in the early 1960s sought to challenge the norms by introducing a one-term study of the American Civil War to his pupils. 'Most of the other staff thought, "How can you possibly spend a term on one topic?", but the kids loved it, and the parents loved it. When the parents came to the parents' evening, almost without exception they said: "For the first time my child is interested in history".' Another introduced project work, 'regarded with great suspicion by traditional teaching', using the old *Jackdaw* series and introducing pupils to documents twice a year: 'we studied Alfred the Great, the Black Death, Spanish Armada etc. and the Battle of Britain'.[98] In the secondary modern schools it was easier to break away from traditional methods, using local archaeological sites ('they'd suddenly realize that where they were actually had a history'), or getting pupils to act out historical drama (what did you think Beckett would say? What would Henry II say?').[99]

Some pupils fondly remember inspirational history teachers, even when they used 'traditional' methods. One of them went to grammar schools in Hove and Bletchley in the mid 1960s: 'I loved history and always did well in exams. The best era was 1815–present, and we had a very interesting teacher who taught us exactly how parliament worked ... I still read history for pleasure.' Another, attending a secondary modern school in Leicestershire at around the same time, has similar memories of 'an excellent teacher' who took the class through the Romans, the Anglo-Saxons, 'lives of the kings and queens plus major political figures', 'Guy Fawkes, Fire of London and Plague', the War of American Independence, the repeal of the Corn Laws and the trades union movement'.[100] Then, as always, much of the classroom experience depended on the quality of the teaching, which could change abruptly and with serious consequences. One woman, who attended grammar school at Taunton, remembers 'the most marvellous teacher, Mrs Motley, who took us on magical trips to Ancient Greece and Egypt through the power of visual aids and colourful stories', which meant 'our imaginations ran riot going back over several thousand years'. But after two years, Mrs Motley retired, and her successor was unimpressive by comparison: 'I cannot remember what she taught us, [and] I lost interest.' As a result, she gave the subject up, and 'I rue this act to this very day.'[101]

By the 1970s, under the impact of the comprehensive revolution, the 'new history', and the advent of the CSE, teaching had become more varied, in part because it involved 'history research – how we know what happened'. Several teachers we interviewed remembered bringing in 'new history' styles of learning to excite pupils about the past: 'I just got all the resources that I could find and experimented with doing source-based history'; 'We changed all our classrooms … so we could interact and work in groups, and it was all investigative.'[102] Not surprisingly, this was sometimes a conscious reaction against teachers' own experience of being taught history, as one interviewee recalled, 'you introduced the idea of history as an explanation – rather than as a definitive load of facts and that does require a more active involvement of students … as opposed to just sitting there listening to the teacher going on, which had been my experience'.[103]

Many pupils enjoyed the break from formality, and the variety. One recalls learning about 'Piltdown man and Roman artefacts' in the first year', the 'history of communication – postal service, smoke signals, telephone etc.' during the second year, and Christopher Columbus in the third. Another remembers studying 'the Tollund Man and the Boys in the Tower. We … had to decide if King Richard locked the boys in the Tower and killed them.'[104] Several who completed our survey forms recall school trips, which 'enhanced the classroom tuition', or being 'asked to imagine ourselves living in the period of time being studied and to relate our thoughts, reactions and experiences to our imagined surroundings'. And there was history as drama: one former pupil remembers 'an assembly of *This is Your Life* in which we chose Henry VIII. The Eamonn Andrews character would say "and here

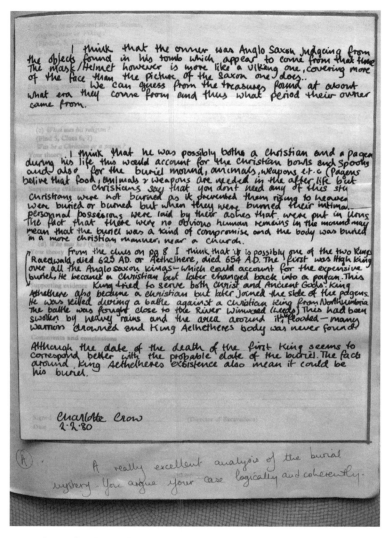

11. The results of a pupil's 'investigation' into the burial mounds at Sutton Hoo, showing how Anglo-Saxon kingship was taught via 'new history' methods, in contrast to the traditional treatment in Fig. 7, Islington Green School, 1980 (courtesy of Charlotte Crow)

she is, the love of your life, Ladies and Gentlemen, Anne Boleyn" and a headless student carrying a *papier mâche* head would walk onto stage, slap him in the face and sit down.'[105]

Our respondents who attended comprehensive schools during the 1970s generally remember their history lessons with more fondness than the earlier, Welfare State generation – though whether they were better taught, and/or learned and remembered more, is less clear (and probably impossible to know). There are also some dissenting memories. One correspondent recalls being taught Russian and German history, 'which I had very little interest in, and always felt I had missed out on an opportunity to learn about my own country: kings and queens etc. and the different periods which I probably was taught at primary school, but was too young to remember'.[106] Another 'detested [history] with a passion because I could not understand it', and 'remembers only a few things': the Egyptians in the first year, then some medieval history, and the Tudors in the third year. In the second year, there was a test 'about medieval kings or maybe Thomas Becket. I had one paragraph I had written about this in my exercise book. I was at a complete loss as to how to prepare for the exam. So I literally learned the paragraph parrot-fashion … I had no clue what else to do!' It was no better the next year: 'we had a dull dry textbook, and had to answer questions on the text, like a comprehension exercise. I loathed and detested it, and learned absolutely nothing at all.' He 'promptly and gladly ditched what I perceived to be an awful subject' at the earliest opportunity.[107]

When it came to making choices at the end of their third year, pupils were influenced by the nature of the teaching, and the content of the syllabus. Several of our correspondents took twentieth-century history for O Level: in one case, '1919 to the present day (which really did mean 1975) and I loved it – we did US, Russian, Chinese, European, Irish history'; in another 'First and Second World Wars, the rise of the trade unions and the labour movement, [and the] Russian Revolution'.[108] But those who chose history did not always enjoy preparing for examinations: in one case, having selectively studied the twentieth century, 'when it came to the exam we had missed out large chunks of the syllabus'; in another, where the syllabus covered the world since 1871, 'it was taught in a very dry way – all lists and dates'.[109] Reactions to A Level courses seem equally divided: ranging from a satisfied student who took Europe 1450–1650, which meant 'the Renaissance, Reformation and Counter-Reformation and the theory of history, with an oral history project and research project using archives (I covered "the persecution of the Catholic gentry in Suffolk under Elizabeth I")'; to a dismayed student who had been taught the Tudors but not the Stuarts, which meant 'when it came to the exam we were all shocked to see that there were hardly any questions on the Tudors and they were all on the Stuarts ... Out of a class of fifteen students, only three passed.'[110]

In 1966, the total number of boys and girls taking O Level history in England was slightly in excess of 140,000; in 1976, after the school leaving age had been raised to 16, it peaked at just below 150,000; but by 1979 it had declined to just above 135,000.[111] During this period, the pass rate remained fairly constant at between 56 per cent and 58 per cent, but the proportion of all O Level candidates who were taking history as one of their examination subjects fell from 55 per cent to 24 per cent. This relative decline (which was also experienced at the same time by geography) may in part have been because of the growth of new, competing subjects such as sociology and business studies that many large new comprehensives were able to offer. During the same period, the number of pupils entered for the new CSE examination in history grew from less than 17,000 in 1965, to almost 165,000 by 1979, again in part as a result of the raising of the school leaving age. Yet as a proportion of the whole CSE-taking cohort, history declined across the same period from around 40 per cent to 29 per cent, probably for the same reason as was the case with O Level.

There was a similar pattern at A Level. In the late 1960s, more than 35,000 sixth formers took A Level history, which was just above one fifth of all A Level candidates, and meant it was the fourth most popular subject after English, maths and physics. Thereafter, the numbers reached almost 40,000 in 1977, but they then fell away (the pass rate remained relatively constant and significantly higher than O level, at around 70 per cent). But in relative terms, the picture was more sombre: in a sixth form population which had doubled since the late 1960s, scarcely one in eight A Level candidates were now taking history. Many 17- and 18-year-olds preferred new subjects which had recently been added to the curriculum, such as economics and sociology, or psychology or computer science, which seemed more 'relevant' in their content and more 'modern' in their teaching methods, and which were often readily available in comprehensives and sixth form colleges. The result was that by the late 1970s, A Level history had declined among boys from being the fourth to the eighth most popular subject, and among girls from being the second to the fourth most popular.

These figures prompted some to insist that history in schools was still in danger, though whether this was because it had not become sufficiently 'progressive', or because it had ceased to hold to the 'traditional' content and methods, was not clear.[112] What *was* increasingly clear was the problems of maintaining the parallel examination systems of the GCE and the CSE. Moreover, the O Level boards were secretive about their procedures, and marking was often impressionistic. Indeed, Eric Evans, a senior examiner with two boards, considered 'the mark schemes were so risibly deficient as hardly to qualify as mark schemes at all'.[113] By contrast, CSE history exams were set and marked by regional consortia of local education authorities which involved teachers in the process at every stage, but this also meant that the setting of standards across a number of schools always presented challenges, and it was difficult to believe (or to prove) that standards across the whole country in particular subjects were uniform.[114] And while the top CSE grade (1) was considered equivalent to an O Level pass, this 'overlap' was difficult to measure or standardize. The result was that in 1970, the Schools Council proposed a common system of examinations at age 16, and having undertaken a series of studies to test the feasibility of a single examination structure covering the whole of the ability range, it recommended that a single system should be introduced.[115]

Between 1964 and 1979, history teaching was either liberated from the stultifying straitjacket of 'traditional 'chalk-and-talk' methods, or it was fragmented and endangered by the mistaken pursuit of the false gods of 'progressivism'. Either way, there were momentous changes, in schools and in schooling, and in teaching and in classrooms, which are partly to be explained by developments in the politics, theory and practice of education, but they must also be understood in terms of the changing domestic and international climate. Behind the rise of progressive, pupil-centred education lies the 1960s cult of youth, liberation and self-expression; and behind the weakening of the national history narrative lies the simultaneous eclipse of Britain as a great power. As early as 1964, C.F. Strong, who was a firm believer in the national history narrative, conceded that the growth of the nation had to be put in a broader world setting, and that this would help inculcate in boys and girls 'a sense of proportion and an attitude of tolerance'.[116] And none of the former pupils from this time who completed our survey thought they had been taught to be proud to be British, because insofar as they were taught about the national past, they were given a 'warts and all' picture instead.[117]

In any case, for many people during these years, including those attending school, the most significant developments in making history alive, engaged and accessible were not just in the classroom, but also on the adult television screen. On the 50th anniversary of the outbreak of the First World War, John Terriaine's 26-part series, narrated by Michael Redgrave, inaugurated a revolution in television history, which was consolidated ten years later by Jeremy Isaacs's *The World at War*, on the same ample scale, narrated by Laurence Olivier.[118] And in between there was not only Kenneth Clark's *Civilisation* and Alastair Cooke's *America*, each in 13 episodes, but also *The Forsyte Saga* and *The First Churchills*, which were the beginning of a new era in period television drama and adaptation.[119] These programmes brought history to an unprecedentedly large audience, and with unprecedented immediacy, and they were no less innovative in broadening the range of what history was about. This new form of history-as-television was also being joined by history-as-heritage, with a growing concern about the destruction of England's country houses, and a corresponding increase in National Trust membership.[120] Here, far beyond the classroom, but ultimately reaching back into it, was history in the public domain as it had never quite been before.

Towards a National Curriculum?

Meanwhile, the 'progressive' developments in comprehensive schooling and in classroom teaching soon provoked a critical reaction, and between 1969 and 1977 a frontal challenge was mounted by the *Black Papers*, produced by academics and educationalists who were disenchanted with prevailing educational trends. Among them were Brian Cox, A.E. Dyson and Rhodes Boyson, all originally on the left, two of whom (Cox and Dyson) taught English in universities, and one of whom (Boyson) was a former comprehensive school headmaster and a published historian, and elected a Conservative MP in 1974.[121]

Shocked by what they saw as the lax standards of comprehensive schools and the teaching that went on in them, and dismayed by the hostility their dissenting views provoked among the educational establishment, they inveighed against comprehensive schools and child-centred education. 'Children are not naturally good', the fourth *Black Paper* pronounced in 1975: 'they need firm, tactful discipline from parents and teachers with clear standards. Too much freedom for children breeds selfishness, vandalism and ... unhappiness.'[122] The authors urged an end to spontaneity and self-discovery in the classroom, and a return to discipline and instruction, and a revival of the grammar schools and their mission to promote equal opportunity.

The *Black Papers* captured a critical mood about education. Employers were objecting that workers hired from school were innumerate and illiterate, and some international comparisons suggested that English schools did insufficient to encourage science and technology.[123] Nor were such worries confined to the right of the political spectrum: as Labour Prime Minister, James Callaghan was concerned about standards of teaching in schools, the content of the curricula in the core subjects of English, mathematics and science, the need for ensuring basic standards of literacy and numeracy amongst schoolchildren, and the importance of promoting science and technology in the classroom. In October 1976, he launched what he called a 'great debate' about education in a speech delivered at Ruskin College, Oxford, in which he called for better ways of monitoring educational standards, for an inquiry into the theory and methods and aims of teaching, for an investigation into the role of HMIs in examining and assessing the competence of teachers, for better ways of managing schools and allocating educational expenditure in which parents should be involved as well as teachers, and for the establishment of a core curriculum of basic knowledge.[124]

Having left school at 15, Callaghan was 'a convinced believer in the importance of education'. He feared that the 'new informal methods of teaching' did not provide school leavers with the skills they needed if the nation was to become more competitive in global markets, and he also believed that 'public interest [in these issues] is strong and legitimate and will be satisfied. We spend six billion pounds a year on education, so there will be a discussion.' Some officials in the Department of Education and Science were resistant, and although Callaghan was determined to stay on good terms with them, the teachers' unions were hostile to proposals which they believed cast doubt on the competence and commitment of their profession. The Labour left regarded insistence on standards and quality control as a reactionary and traditionalist diversion from the progressive social engineering that a non-selective state system of schooling should embody, while the *Times Educational Supplement* complained that the Prime Minister was no expert in these matters, and should leave them to those who were. Undeterred by such 'appalling educational snobbery', Callaghan urged Shirley Williams to hold a series of regional conferences with teachers, employers, parents, trade unionists and other interested parties.[125]

These meetings broadened educational discussion beyond the professionals and the educationalists, and in the summer of 1977, Williams published a Green Paper that proposed a nationally-agreed and validated core curriculum that would occupy half the school timetable. (She also set up an inquiry into the O Level and CSE examinations which recommended they should be superseded by a new common system to be taken at 16.[126]) By this time, some HMIs were also beginning to develop ideas of curriculum reform, in the light of the comprehensive revolution, the raising of the school leaving age, and the 'bewildering diversity' of teaching practices, syllabuses and examinations which had come into being as a result, and which they believed necessitated the re-establishment of 'some common framework of assumptions ... which assists coherence without inhibiting enterprise'.[127] But Callaghan was unable to do any more to promote educational reform during the twilight time of his government. Nevertheless, his Ruskin speech had resonated widely, and it prepared the ground for the counter-revolution in education that Margaret Thatcher was determined to carry out after her victory at the polls in May 1979 – and in that endeavour the teaching of history would be high on her list.[128]

5 History in the National Curriculum, 1979–2010

I have always rather admired the French in a sense that they have never been bothered by these things, you know: 'this is French history, and get on with it, and that's it, folks.' I don't think that's good. I think we do these things rather better, if painfully, argumentatively, with difficulty.

(History in Education Project, Gillian Shephard interview, 14 October 2009, p. 6.)

At the end of her time as Minister of Education, Margaret Thatcher told a colleague she would 'always retain my interest in education, and I hope that one day I may be able to do something for it once again'. In the autumn of 1979, she returned, not just to power but to 10 Downing Street itself, convinced that destiny had called her to stop the rot of national decline, and make Britain great again. To this end, she sought to reassert the nation's position in the world, strengthening the Anglo-American alliance, winning back the Falklands, and going into battle against the bureaucracy of the European Union. And domestically, she sought to roll back the state, to tame the trades unions, and to curb the power of those professions she believed had sapped the nation's spirit of enterprise, among them clergymen, academics, intellectuals (apart from those who supported her), civil servants – and educationalists.[1] In seeking to restore Britain to the earlier greatness of 'Victorian values', Thatcher was espousing what she believed was a historically-validated policy, owing much to writers such as Martin Wiener and Correlli Barnett, who insisted that the nation's nineteenth-century greatness had been undermined in the twentieth century by those very groups she was determined to defeat.[2]

Among the civil servants Thatcher had come to dislike were those at the Department of Education and Science who, she believed, in alliance with educationalists, HMIs, local authorities, teachers and the trades unions, had railroaded through schemes for comprehensive

181

schools during her time as Secretary of State. As a grateful grammar school product, she also deplored child-centred teaching and firmly believed in traditional pedagogy: the teacher instructing the class in what they should know and what they should learn.[3] And although she was 'not an historian myself', she strongly believed that history was a simple, uplifting, important 'account of what happened in the past'. She believed British history was a narrative of advancing progress and imperial greatness, at least up to the end of the nineteenth century; and she had no doubts that it should be understood in terms of monarchs and politicians and great events. She deeply regretted the disappearance of this approach from classrooms, and when she turned her attention to the reform of education, its restoration was something she cared about very much.[4] But on taking office, she had more urgent concerns, including the economy, industrial unrest, and the high level of government spending, so the counter-revolution in education had to wait.

Accordingly, and as Heath had previously done with her, when Thatcher became Prime Minister, she moved her shadow education spokesman, Mark Carlisle, to be Secretary of State. He had been educated at Radley College and Manchester University, where he read law, and like so many of his predecessors, he would be in the job for less than three years. He immediately introduced legislation to repeal the Education Act of 1976, but while this saved some local authorities determined to keep their grammar schools, scarcely any that had gone comprehensive took advantage of its provisions to return to the earlier structure. Soon after, Carlisle established the 'assisted places' scheme, which allowed bright children from less well-off backgrounds to attend independent schools. But throughout his period of office, education was a high priority for cuts in government spending, and the White Paper published in March 1981 announced a reduction of 7 per cent over the next three years, while more than 30 per cent was knocked off capital expenditure.[5] As a result, Carlisle was caught in the crossfire between his own officials, who were not enthusiastic about his reforms, the Treasury mandarins who pressed for further reductions, the teaching unions who opposed him, and the Prime Minister who did not think him 'particularly effective'. She dismissed him in September 1981, and he never held office again.

It was a sign of Thatcher's growing wish to sort out education that she replaced Carlisle with Sir Keith Joseph, a born-again

Conservative, who had recanted his high-taxing, high-spending, interventionist heresies as a member of Heath's cabinet, and was now the ideological godfather of Thatcherism – in his commitment to reducing the spending and reach of government, to curbing the power of the trades unions, and to attacking the anti-business ethos of the churches, the universities, the schools and the civil service, so as to bring about a return to the bracing rigours of the free market and a liberation of the spirit of enterprise.[6] Appropriately, he was a successful businessman in his own right; but he was also a baronet, and an Old Harrovian, who, after Oxford and war service, had been elected a Fellow of All Souls College.[7] He had been a major figure in the founding of the Centre for Policy Studies, he had backed Thatcher to succeed Heath, and he was her closest soul-mate in her cabinet.[8] His first post, as Secretary of State for Industry, was scarcely congenial, for he wondered whether such a department should even exist. But having sacked Carlisle, Thatcher moved Joseph to Education, where he held office for four years and eight months, a span only equalled by Lord Eustace Percy and surpassed by H.A.L. Fisher.

At Education as at Industry, Joseph's starting point was his concern at the country's relative economic decline, and he believed one of its chief causes was the hostility to the enterprise culture inculcated in schools. Another was that the state education system had never worked effectively, and a third was that the recent rush towards comprehensivization (in which his own Prime Minister had played such an embarrassingly complicit part) had been a mistake, sacrificing the needs of children to the wrong-headed pursuit of equality, regardless of their abilities. To Joseph, the evidence of systemic educational failure was clear: in 1979, he was fond of saying, of 915,000 school leavers aged 16, almost half had departed without a single O level.[9] No wonder the nation was failing to compete with continental countries whose education systems were better! In reaching these conclusions, Joseph had been influenced by the arguments advanced in *Lessons from Europe: A Comparison of British and West European Schooling*, which he had commissioned for the Centre for Policy Studies from the educational journalist Max Wilkinson. Indeed, on his first meeting with his civil servants, he was dismayed – but unsurprised – to discover they had not read it, and he urged them to do so, for it now became his foundation text.[10]

A Counter-Revolution in Education?

In practice, Joseph's agenda at Education bore some similarity to that which Callaghan had sketched out at Ruskin College, Oxford: the greater provision of information about how schools were doing, more stress on vocational training and practical skills, an insistence on high academic standards, the inauguration of a core curriculum, and a shift in the balance of power away from the local authorities, the teachers' unions and the educationalists towards parents. But while Callaghan had appreciated the need to carry the educational establishment with him, Joseph's style was more confrontational. When further cuts in government spending were announced, he welcomed them, and made no effort to try to fend them off. He appointed extra HMIs to check on teaching ability, and pressed for the publication of indicators of school performance. He abolished the progressively-inclined and teacher-dominated Schools Council, urged local authorities to sack incompetent teachers, and made it plain he regarded many teachers as below standard. Not surprisingly, Joseph soon became involved in bitter disputes with the teachers, and having lost their confidence, he never regained it. His one piece of advice to his successor was 'Don't make the same mistake I did of attacking the teachers.'[11]

As early as 1973, the Department had warned of dramatic cuts in the number of trainee teachers that would be needed in the coming years, as the birth rate fell in the aftermath of the immediate post-war baby-boomer generation, and by the early 1980s, the number of trainee teachers had fallen by as much as one half.[12] This period of shrinking numbers and declining opportunities had a lowering effect on teacher morale, as did what many regarded as the unrelenting attacks on their competence and professionalism that they believed were being waged by Joseph. In 1983, his Department produced a White Paper, *Teaching Quality*, which set out major changes in the pattern of teacher training, reflecting the government's view that schools should play a larger part, and not only by ensuring that apprentice teachers spent more time learning their job in the classroom rather than in the lecture room. In future, all those who trained teachers would be required to have 'recent and relevant' hands-on experience of successful school teaching, amounting to one term in every five years. The aim was that by sending teacher trainers out of their academic environments, and back into the demanding realities of the classroom, they might be disabused of the more outlandish and misguided 'progressive' educational theories, and might begin to appreciate – and thus pass on to their own students – the benefits of more traditional pedagogic approaches.[13]

By the early 1980s, opinion in the Department of Education and Science, as well as outside, was beginning to move in favour of establishing a national curriculum.[14] That was even true in 10 Downing Street. Margaret Thatcher had previously been opposed to it, on the grounds that she believed in rolling back the reach of the state rather than extending it, and that such regrettable centralizing and authoritarian practices were more appropriate to the French than to the English. But she now came to believe that the condition of the schools was such that the state had to intervene. Thus supported, Joseph published a White Paper, *Better Schools*, in 1985, outlining the government's plans to reform the curriculum, to give more emphasis to vocational learning, to improve the quality of the teaching workforce by training and appraisal, and to reform school governing bodies as overseers of educational effectiveness by giving power to parents. Joseph would later describe *Better Schools* as a 'far-reaching programme for improving the performance of our schools' focused on 'ways of identifying the expectations against which we can measure educational achievements, and ways in which educational achievements can be assessed'.[15] It was his major achievement as Secretary of State: the manifesto for a counter-revolution in schooling, and a blueprint for education for the twenty-first century.[16]

By then, Joseph had reluctantly presided over another major change, namely the belated implementation of the recommendation that had been made to Shirley Williams in 1978, that O Level and CSE should be abolished, and that they should be replaced by a new single public examination at the age of 16, to be known as the General Certificate of Secondary Education. Williams had been in no hurry to accept these recommendations, in part because she worried about the proposed abolition of O Levels, which many parents and pupils regarded (perhaps with more sentiment than good reason) as the gold standard of public examinations, by comparison with which the CSE was merely an upstart and undemanding exercise. In 1980, Mark Carlisle had accepted the need for such a reform, but Joseph was less sure, and he spent several years agonizing over what to do. Like

Williams, he worried that the introduction of continuous assessment would result in a dilution of academic standards; but in the spring of 1984, he decided the change should go ahead, on the grounds that whatever the dangers, the GCSE would allow a better comparison of pupil performance across the whole country, across all schools, and across all pupils, and the first GCSEs would be sat in the summer of 1988, ten years after it had initially been recommended.[17]

Two years before then, in May 1986, Joseph retired from front-line politics, and was replaced at Education by Kenneth Baker, who had been to St Paul's School and Oxford University, where he had studied law. But literature and history (and political cartoons) were his abiding interests, and he would later devote considerable effort to the (thus far unrealized) endeavour of promoting a museum of national history in London.[18] Like Joseph, but unlike any other previous holder of the office, Baker came to Education having already held a major cabinet post as Secretary of State for the Environment. Like Joseph, Baker was determined to ensure the Department maintained a high political profile, and he was determined to implement the proposals outlined in *Better Schools*. Like Joseph again, Baker believed that the DES was 'in league with the teacher unions, university departments of education, teacher-training theories, and local authorities'; that it was a place where 'the interests of the producer prevailed over the interests of the consumer'; that it was 'devoutly anti-excellence, anti-selection, and anti-market'; and that it was in thrall to '"progressive" orthodoxies'. But unlike Joseph, Baker was a skilful politician and an engaging, self-confident personality, and this enabled him to carry the Education Reform Act of 1988, the most significant piece of legislation concerning schools since Butler's measure of 1944.[19]

From one perspective, Baker's legislation was a measure of unprecedented centralization, which abandoned both the principle and the practice that Westminster and Whitehall did not interfere with local authorities and individual schools. But it was also a populist display of educational devolution, taking the financial management of schools away from local authorities, and putting it in the hands of the school governors. (Subsequently, Baker also abolished the Inner London Education Authority.) By such means, education's consumers, namely the parents and the pupils, would gain over education's producers, namely the HMIs, the local authorities and the teachers and their trades unions.[20] As Thatcher, Joseph and Baker saw it, the educational freedoms locally enjoyed since the beginning of the twentieth century had been irresponsibly abused during the 1960s and 1970s: by local authorities, who had mistakenly ditched the grammar schools and embraced comprehensives, and by heads and teachers who had abandoned 'traditional' pedagogy, and fallen for 'progressive' methods. The aim of the Education Reform Act of 1988 was to halt and reverse these developments, and one of its key provisions was the creation of a national curriculum, which would outline what schools should teach, and ensure they did so to a required standard which was testable and comparable.[21]

Within a year, Kenneth Baker was moved from Education to become Chancellor of the Duchy of Lancaster and Chairman of the Conservative Party, with a remit to win the Tories the next general election. He was replaced in July 1989 by John MacGregor, a graduate in history and economics from the University of St Andrews, who had been Minister of State for Agriculture, Fisheries and Food. He lacked the stature and status of his immediate predecessors, and he did not stay long. In November 1990 Thatcher herself departed from Downing Street, but just before she did, in her last and rather frantic cabinet reshuffle, she moved MacGregor on, after less than a year and a half at Education, to be Leader of the House and Lord President of the Council. His replacement was Kenneth Clarke, a heavyweight figure, who had previously been Secretary of State for Health, who would serve under John Major until April 1992. Clarke had been educated at Nottingham High School and at the University of Cambridge, before qualifying as a lawyer. Like Carlisle, Baker and MacGregor, and like so many of his predecessors and successors, Clarke was not long in post, indeed for less than a year and a half; but unlike so many of his predecessors, he would go on to higher things, for following John Major's election victory in the spring of 1992, he was moved on to be Home Secretary.

But by then Clarke had carried through one significant reform, and that was the sidelining of the HMIs, and the opening up of school inspection to the free market. Neither Thatcher nor Joseph had much liked the HMIs, regarding them as in league with the rest of the 'progressive' educational establishment. But there was an additional line of criticism, to which Clarke was sympathetic, which was that there were insufficient Inspectors, there were insufficient inspections of schools, and there ought to be more of both. If the government wished to increase the amount of inspection, there were only two ways it could be done: the first, for which there was no enthusiasm, was to employ more HMIs; the second, and preferred solution, was to open up inspection to the market, and to have it overseen by a regulator.[22] The result was the ending of the structure of school inspection dating back to the first half of the nineteenth century: HMIs largely ceased to fulfil their traditional function, and their numbers were much reduced; school inspectors were now privately contracted, and were often part-time; they were (if possible) trained by former HMIs; their findings were brought together in subject reports; and the whole enterprise was monitored and overseen by a regulator called the Office for Standards in Education, (or Ofsted), where some former HMIs were employed. Both primary and secondary schools were more frequently inspected, and the intention was to produce regular subject-specific reports.[23]

Kenneth Clarke was replaced by John Patten, who had been educated at Wimbledon College and Cambridge University, studying history, before moving to Oxford as an historical geographer, where he was elected for one of the city's constituencies in 1983.[24] He had held junior office during the Thatcher years, but he did not bring the standing or experience to Education that Joseph, Baker and Clarke had done, he would soon be out of his depth, and he did not last long. In the summer of 1994, he stepped down, after little more than two unhappy years: he never held office again, and he retired from the Commons in 1997. His successor, Gillian Shephard, was the first woman to hold the post since Shirley Williams; she had been educated at North Walsham Girls' High School, and Oxford University, and had spent her pre-political career as a modern languages schoolteacher and as a local authority education inspector. Like Joseph, Baker and Clarke, she came to Education having held a major cabinet post as Secretary of State for Employment; and after a year, the Department of Education was merged with Employment, and she was put in charge of this new Whitehall conglomerate. But the Conservatives' defeat in 1997 meant she was in post for less than three years, she had insufficient time to stamp her mark on education, and the revealing subtitle of her memoirs was *Illusions of Power in British Politics*.[25]

In addition to the creation of Ofsted, the other educational initiative of these later Conservative years was the further reform and improvement of teacher training, a decade after Joseph's paper on *Teaching Quality*. In 1992, the basic requirements for all teachers were formalized with the introduction of common training 'standards' related to the National Curriculum, and the need for demonstrable subject expertise. The role of schools in training was also increased, as they now took 'joint responsibility' for those who came to practise in their classrooms, along with university departments of education and colleges of education, and higher standards were laid down for the training of primary school teachers. In 1994, the Teacher Training Agency was set up which, like Ofsted, was directly answerable to the Secretary of State. Its mission was to 'secure diversity of high-quality and cost-effective initial training, which ensures that new teachers have the knowledge, understanding and skills to teach pupils effectively', and it soon developed its own National Curriculum for teacher training.[26] Thereafter, colleges of education and university departments were regularly inspected by Ofsted.

Gillian Shephard was the fifth person in charge of Education since Sir Keith Joseph, the seventh to hold office in Conservative administrations between 1979 and 1997, and the only woman. Apart from Joseph, whose background was rich and titled, and who attended Harrow, the remainder of these Conservative Secretaries of State were remarkably similar in circumstances: middle class, mostly schooled in the independent sector, and for the most part attending Oxbridge. Two of them had studied history at university. Having held office for more than four and a half years, Joseph stands out as one of the most significant Education ministers of the twentieth century, in terms of his creative input and political importance. Baker was also a major figure in carrying the Education Reform Act which implemented many of Joseph's ideas, and Clarke's establishment of Ofsted also made a lasting impact, despite his brief tenure of office. The remainder, as so often, had little time to accomplish much. But the Thatcher years did witness significant changes in educational policy and a no-less significant assertion of central government in bringing them about: and as the figure driving these changes, Thatcher herself had a more decisive (and divisive) impact on education as prime minister than she had earlier as Secretary of State.

Before Tony Blair became Prime Minister, he claimed that 'education, education, education' would be his top priority in government.[27] Unlike Thatcher, he was not much interested in history, and after his landslide victory in 1997, he was more concerned with moving the country forward than with showing much interest in its past: from 'New Labour' to 'new Britain' would be but a step. Having emancipated his own party from the anachronistic shackles of class consciousness and Clause Four, he hoped to liberate the nation as a whole from being an 'old country': hence the absence of any history in the millennium dome, and hence the cult of 'Cool Britannia'. 'There never has been a time', Blair grandly informed the US Congress on the eve of the invasion of Iraq, 'when … a study of history provides so little instruction for our present day.'[28] Indeed, much of New Labour's domestic agenda, built around concern for ethnic minorities and the disadvantaged, and around access, citizenship and social inclusion, was predicated on the belief that the past was primarily a rubbish-heap of ills and wrongs that urgently needed to be cured and righted. This view was not shared by Blair's Chancellor, Gordon Brown, who had obtained a PhD in history, and who was particularly interested in Britishness – past, present and future – and its relation to devolution. But for the most part, history was not a big item on the New Labour agenda of 1997, educational or otherwise.

In appointing David Blunkett to be Secretary of State for Education and Employment, Blair was giving office to someone whose social background and personal experience of education was very different from that of most of his predecessors. Blind since birth, and from a poor family in one of Sheffield's most deprived districts, Blunkett had educated himself at night school and on day release, he had studied politics at Sheffield University under Bernard Crick, and he had trained to be a teacher. He soon became a major figure in local government in Sheffield, and was elected to parliament in 1987; he made his reputation as an expert on such domestic issues as local government, the environment and health policy, and he had been Shadow Education Secretary since 1994. Not surprisingly, Blunkett saw education in large part in terms of its potential for social engineering and social mobility: of the constraints it imposed on those from disadvantaged backgrounds like his own, but also the possibilities and opportunities it might offer for such people to advance and escape. He was in charge of Education and Employment for four years, which made him the longest-serving Secretary of State since Sir Keith Joseph, and he obtained large sums of government money to spend: on free nursery places, cutting class sizes, increasing teacher numbers, further enhancing teacher training, improving school buildings, and giving priority to the teaching of literacy and numeracy.

After Blair's second electoral triumph of June 2001, Blunkett moved on to become Home Secretary, and his successor was Estelle Morris, appointed Secretary of State of the renamed post and reconfigured Department of Education and Skills. She is the only Secretary of State to have taught in a comprehensive school, however, she resigned in October 2002 after a mere 16 months. For the next two years, the post was held by Charles Clarke, educated at Highgate School and Cambridge, who oversaw the introduction of legislation enabling universities to charge top-up fees; then by Ruth Kelly, who was the youngest woman to sit in the cabinet, but who lasted barely a year; then by Alan Johnson, who was an orphan, left school at 15, and worked as a postman and as a full-time union official. In June 2007, when Gordon Brown succeeded Blair, Johnson was moved from Education to Health, and was succeeded by Ed Balls as Secretary of State for Children, Schools and Families; higher education having been hived off to the newly-created Department of Innovation, Universities and Skills. Under Brown as under Blair, spending on education increased significantly, and failing inner-city schools were rebranded, refinanced and transformed into academies. The Conservatives would later want to make all schools into academies, and by 2011, it was reported that one third of England's secondary schools had become academies or were converting to academy status.[29]

During the years of New Labour government, from 1997 to 2010, there were six ministers in charge of education and between Blunkett and Balls there were four of them in less than five years, an even more rapid turnover than among the Conservatives after Sir Keith Joseph. Two of them were women, two had trained as teachers, none of them who attended university studied history. In terms of their backgrounds, they were more varied than their Conservative predecessors: indeed, they were the most varied ministerial cohort to date: three were comfortably middle class, attended independent schools, and went on to Oxbridge; three were from much less secure backgrounds. By virtue of his long span in office and his own political weight, Blunkett was the most significant; thereafter, there were too many ministers and (as some saw it), too many new and ill thought-out initiatives. But spending on education continued at a high level until the election of 2010, and even a disaffected Labour MP like Chris Mullin conceded this had made a real difference, as the GCSE pass rate in many schools significantly improved.[30]

The GCSE and the National Curriculum

The establishment of the GCSE and the National Curriculum had important implications for history in the classroom. In February 1984, Sir Keith Joseph addressed the annual conference of the Historical Association, in which he urged that history should be 'an essential component in the curriculum of *all* pupils', and should form part of primary and secondary education for boys and girls up to the age of 16. Joseph even sought to reassure proponents of 'progressive' teaching by stressing the importance of imparting 'knowledge, understanding and skills', by recognizing the value of offering children different interpretations of the past, and by accepting the significance of empathy or 'sympathetic understanding'. But he also sought to reassure the traditionalists, expressing concern about recent trends towards the fragmentation of the nation's 'island story', which was no longer continuously told or celebrated in schools; and he urged the importance of teaching children to take a 'proper pride' in the country's past and in the 'development of the shared values which are a distinctive feature of British society and culture' – though he recognised the sensitivities involved in teaching pupils from 'a variety of social, cultural and ethnic backgrounds'.[31]

Soon after, Joseph announced the establishment of the GCSE, which radically changed the teaching of history to 15- and 16-year-olds from 1986. Unlike the O Level and CSE, it was intended for the whole ability range of comprehensive school pupils, with exam papers that would stretch the most able yet also be answerable by the less gifted. In outline, the GCSE history syllabuses were familiar: in 1988 the Associated Examining Board offered a choice of five: British Social and Economic History since 1750; World Powers since 1917; British History, 1485–1714; British History, 1815–1983; and Britain, Europe and the World, 1848–1980. But a minimum 20 per cent of the assessment was to be based on coursework, which had never been the case with O Level, although from the beginning it had been part of the CSE. In the examination, segmented questions were set using edited historical sources – often cartoons or quotations –

to test candidates' skills in evaluating them for bias and meaning, and short-answer questions superseded the long essays that had characterized O Level. In some cases multiple choice questions were used and, in line with recent HMI thinking, and with Joseph's address to the HA, the GCSE exams included the assessment of 'empathy' as a significant and demonstrable skill.[32]

The GCSE was considered a 'triumph' for the principle of teacher control over the curriculum, giving all staff who prepared their pupils for examinations a chance to be involved in the assessment process. Yet it also signalled greater government involvement, imposing curriculum revision, and the GCSE's content and assessment were governed by national and subject criteria and regulations.[33] Moreover, examination boards had to collaborate to approve syllabuses, and use national guidelines for setting and marking their papers. As a result, GCSE exams were more standardized than O Levels or CSEs had been 'in terms of approach, expectations and the sorts of questions' that were set. But while these developments were welcome to the Thatcher government, the GCSE was in other ways less congenial. For it had been more influenced by the CSE than by O Level in its general design, and the GCSE in history bore the imprint of the Schools Council History Project, whose 'progressive' ideas were applied to the history syllabuses and examinations.[34] Just as the grammar-school loving Thatcher had presided over the greatest growth in comprehensive schools, so the 'traditionalist' Joseph approved an examination giving unprecedented scope to 'progressive' teaching and the approach pioneered by the Schools Council – which he had earlier abolished.

The year 1988 was doubly portentous for history in schools, witnessing the implementation of the GSCE and the establishment of the National Curriculum, including the three 'core' subjects of English, mathematics and science, and seven 'foundation' subjects. Benchmark tests would be sat at ages seven, eleven and fourteen, at the end of the first three 'Key Stages', and there would be a final test at the end of Key Stage 4, namely age 16.[35] Kenneth Baker was determined that history should be one of the 'foundation' subjects, and hoped it would provide 'a timeline from whenever you started whether it was pre-Roman Britain or Roman Britain up to today', to give schoolchildren 'an idea of the continuum of history' in a way that he believed the 'progressive' teaching, focusing on sources, brief periods, and self-discovery, did not.[36] In January 1989, he called in a group of 'experts' to form a History Working Group, with the remit to produce a curriculum. But despite consultation with HMIs, and although determined to avoid representatives of the Schools History Project, Baker found it difficult to make these appointments, as Thatcher vetoed some initial choices because they had too close a connection with 'progressive' teaching and the 'new' history.[37]

As eventually established, the Group comprised an eclectic mix of 'lay' members with an interest in history, two teachers (one primary and one secondary), two teacher-trainers from colleges of education, and two academics. The result was 'a very varied group and in some respects a quite innovative group', who were essentially 'starting from scratch'.[38] They were willing to comply with Baker's demand that half the curriculum should be devoted to British history, but they did not necessarily agree with him as to what that history should be. They were not generally in favour of a traditional national narrative, built around kings and queens. Some members thought it important that the subject in schools should be broadened to include women's and black history, along with a substantial amount of social and cultural history, to reflect the recent changes in British society. There was also, in an era where demands for devolution were growing in Wales and Scotland, a view that British history should be taught from the perspective of Ireland, Wales and Scotland as well as England.[39] This may explain why, when the interim report of the History Working Group was published in August 1989, Thatcher was 'appalled', and insisted more time be devoted to British history and more emphasis be placed on chronology.[40]

She pressed her new minister, John MacGregor, to modify the proposals of the History Working Group, and he asked them to give more attention to chronology, and to include more British history in the projected compulsory units of study.[41] The Group acceded to both requests, but refused to specify the historical knowledge on which pupils would be tested at each of the four key stages, where they were expected to meet 'attainment targets'. Their rationale was that, unlike mathematics or the sciences, historical knowledge was not cumulative, so there was no hierarchy of factual information that could be related to the key stages and tested as such.[42] So while historical knowledge would be the *medium* for the tests, the marks would be awarded for the demonstration of skills, such as 'acquiring and evaluating historical information'. Thus did the Group try to bridge the gap in the long-running 'knowledge versus skills' debate, by arguing that one was dependent on the other, and that in any case, the knowledge to be taught was already set out on a yearly basis in the proposed programmes of study.[43]

Determined to get her way, Thatcher insisted on additional public consultations, which she hoped would reflect her own preference for 'traditional' history, and give her and MacGregor the opportunity and the justification to impose the changes they wanted.[44] More than 1,000 responses were received to the interim report, mainly from groups of teachers and from local authority advisers. Their concerns were overwhelmingly practical, including the unfamiliar subject knowledge expected for some of the proposed study units (such as Mughal India and Classical China), and the quantity of time assumed to be available to teach them. Yet many respondents also commended the proposals for the attainment targets, and for the decision not to specify particular factual knowledge which would be tested. Meanwhile, the Historical Association organized a series of regional conferences, where objections ranged from particular issues such as the need to include a study unit on the Second World War to the restrictions that would be imposed on the hitherto-sacrosanct autonomy of teachers to develop the curriculum they thought appropriate. Concern was also expressed at the amount of content prescribed in each study unit, the costs of providing new materials, and that some proposed units were just too boring.[45]

There was also a public debate in which professional historians revisited the issues of 'skills versus content' in the syllabus, and 'traditional versus progressive' modes of teaching.[46] A leading traditionalist among them was Professor Robert Skidelsky, who had recently formed the History Curriculum Association to defend the subject as 'an account of what happened in the past', and to support the essay-style approach to history examinations which focused on the learning and recall of dates and details and facts. He conceded there had always been a tension between '"learning history" and "learning how to think"', but argued that recent trends had shifted too far towards the teaching of thinking skills with insufficient regard to the significance of the content that was being taught in the classroom. 'Factual knowledge', he insisted, in words that must have been music to Margaret Thatcher's ears, was 'still essential to most kinds of thinking'. He was happier with the Working Group's Final than with its Interim Report, and he applauded its emphasis on British history, even as he regretted the omission of specific knowledge from the attainment targets.[47]

The argument from the left was led by Raphael Samuel, who wanted an alternative form of national history, recognizing the impact of European, Imperial and world developments, the changes in national culture brought about by New Commonwealth immigration, British membership of the European Community, and the effect of Welsh and Scottish devolution and the 'Ulster' 'troubles', all of which had challenged traditional and secure conceptions of national identity since the 1950s.[48] From the opposite perspective, Skidelsky contended that the more ethnically and religiously diverse Britain became, the more important it was to socialize children into a common national heritage, which only history could teach. Despite their disagreements, the protagonists shared a concern about 'the status of the United Kingdom in the world and the nature of the relationships between the four countries of the United Kingdom', and about the importance of teaching history in schools, and when it appeared their squabble might lead to history being dropped altogether as a foundation subject, they promptly buried their differences.[49]

The Final Report of the History Working Group appeared in April 1990, and was passed to the history task group of the National Curriculum Council, to convert its proposals into a workable scheme. The Report's attainment targets were intended to guide children's progress in learning how to 'do history', while they were also supposed to be covering a very broad range of content. There was also the 'PESC formula', by which the Working Group sought to ensure that the specified content covered a full range of political, economic, social and cultural history at each key stage. But these requirements had resulted in an overloaded curriculum, which would be virtually impossible to deliver in the classroom, where only two or three periods of history at most were timetabled each week. By December 1990 the history task group had reduced the prescribed content in the study units, but it had not removed the Working Group's requirement that 'understanding' rather than just 'knowledge' should be the basis of assessment.[50] Within each of the four attainment targets were ten statements outlining the progress children should make during their years of compulsory education in history, which were due to extend from five to 16, and thus to GCSE.[51]

The National Curriculum for History eventually emerged in the form of Statutory Orders in March 1991, during Kenneth Clarke's brief period as Secretary of State. He did not share Margaret Thatcher's belief that one of the purposes of history should be 'to teach patriotic enthusiasm'. On the contrary, as a 'libertarian on all those things', he was 'very much against the curriculum being used to impart political views'.[52] Much more damagingly, he abandoned Kenneth Baker's earlier commitment that history should be a compulsory subject until the age of 16. Instead, he decreed that when they reached the age of 14, all pupils would be given the option of choosing between history and geography – a decision he would later come to regret – and with good cause.[53] For the result was that the carefully constructed curriculum which the History Working Group had designed to run chronologically from age five to age 16, culminating in two years devoted to twentieth-century modern British and world history at Key Stage 4 and GCSE, was upset and disarranged – indeed, decapitated. In consequence, the history of the twentieth century had to be moved from Key Stage 4 (those aged 15 and 16) to Key Stage 3 (those aged 13 and 14), so as to ensure that they knew something about the recent past and the modern world before they gave history up, as many of them would do, preferring to study geography instead.[54]

One regrettable result was that, by teaching the history of modern times to 13- and 14-year-olds, the many centuries that had to be covered prior to that were squeezed and truncated, and could only be superficially and selectively covered. Another was that pupils who stayed with history for the whole of their school lives into the sixth form, might now study the twentieth century once at 14, again to 16 for GCSE, and yet a third time to 18 for A Level – a degree of repetitiveness which was not only intrinsically indefensible, but also prevented them from learning about many other periods and people in the past. Finally, by truncating the national curriculum in history at 14, the subject was uncoupled and disconnected from the GCSE examinations, which completely undermined the original idea of an integrated curriculum, leading step by step from the infant school to the comprehensive school and then to the public exams. Many of the most problematic aspects of history teaching in secondary schools today thus stem from Clarke's deeply unfortunate decision.

The truncated history curriculum that eventually appeared was divided into 'Core Study Units' and 'Supplementary or Extension

Units'.[55] At Key Stage 1 (ages five to seven) the 'Core Study Unit' was '"everyday life" in the past with a focus on changes in their own lives and their families', changes in British life since World War II and the way of life in a period beyond living memory; the lives of famous men and women; past and commemorated events, such as the Gunpowder Plot and the Olympic Games'. No 'Supplementary or Extension Units' were specified.

At Key Stage 2 (ages seven to eleven) the 'Core Study Units' were 'Invaders and Settlers (Romans, Anglo-Saxons and Vikings); Tudor and Stuart times; either Victorian Britain or Britain since 1930; Ancient Greece; Exploration and Encounters, 1450–1550'. The 'Supplementary or Extension Units' were 'A study of a topic over a long period (eg transport, houses and places of worship); A local history topic; A past non-European society (eg Ancient Egypt, the Indus Valley, the Aztecs, Benin)'. At Key Stage 3 (ages 11 to 14), the 'Core Study Units' were 'The Roman Empire; Medieval Realms: Britain, 1066–1500; The Making of the United Kingdom: Crowns, Parliaments and Peoples, 1500–1750; Expansion, Trade and Industry: Britain 1750–1900; The Era of the Second World War'. The 'Supplementary or Extension Units' were 'A depth or thematic study in British history (eg Castles and Cathedrals, the British Empire and its impact in the late nineteenth century, Britain and the Great War, 1914–1918); A turning point in European history (eg the Crusades, the French Revolution); and A past non-European society (eg Imperial China, India under the Mughal Empire; indigenous peoples of North America; Black peoples of the Americas, sixteenth to early twentieth century'.

There had never been anything like this in English education, yet and apparently unknown to those involved with it, the new National Curriculum for history bore a more than passing resemblance to those *Suggestions* and *Recommendations* that had earlier emanated from Whitehall, both in terms of the time span and the balance between national and world history. At Key Stage 1 pupils would learn about famous men and women, and be told stories of specific historical episodes and events. At Key Stage 2, they would learn about two millennia of the national past; some ancient European history, and the early modern voyages of discovery; there would be 'lines of development' (though no longer called that) over a long period focusing on particular topics; and opportunities to learn about local history, and ancient societies beyond Europe. And at Key Stage 3, the aim was to cover much of Key Stage 2 again, but in greater depth, looking at the nation's history from the Romans to the Second World War, to which were added topics in European, third world and American history. As in earlier times, national history predominated, some attention was given to Europe, and there was significant provision for studying far-off peoples and places.

Despite the lengthy period of gestation and consultation, and the later work of the National Curriculum Council history task group, there were problems with the National Curriculum in history from the outset, and during the first 18 months of its implementation, two key issues emerged: the overwhelmingly overloaded content and the difficulties of the assessment stages and targets.[56] Many teachers were confused about how to evaluate their pupils against the newly-imposed attainment targets, and the training they needed so as to do this was necessarily rushed. Moreover, there were 51 so-called 'statements of attainment', which seemed an impossibly large number – although there were many more for other subjects: 159 in the case of English and 295 for mathematics.[57] At all levels, there seemed too much content to cover, given the limited number of hours a week that could be devoted to history, and Key Stage 3 was particularly loaded with content, since additional topics had been transferred there from Key Stage 4 to accommodate the Clarke truncations. And since it was expected that all pupils would be tested in history at the end of Year 9, when they were aged 14 and the subject ceased thereafter to be compulsory, this added to the pressure on teachers to try to cover everything that had been specified in the mandatory study units.

In fact, history was not the only subject where the National Curriculum soon looked distinctly 'shaky', and many teachers were also becoming increasingly critical of the Standard Assessment Tests (SATs), which were an additional requirement beyond the attainment targets. The result was that John Patten's two-year period of office saw 'the relationship between the teaching profession and the government plummet new depths of antagonism and distrust', culminating in the 'infamous boycott of National Curriculum testing arrangements in 1993'.[58] Patten responded by appointing Sir Ron Dearing, the new Chairman of the recently-established Schools Curriculum Assessment Authority, to conduct an immediate review of the National Curriculum, and his Interim Report, published in July 1993, recommended that SATs should be limited to the core subjects of English, maths and science. But his Final Report, in January 1994, proposing a 'slimmed down' National Curriculum, was even worse news for history than Kenneth Clarke's earlier decision: for it countenanced the scrapping of the requirement that pupils must study either history or geography after the age of 14, and increased the pressure on the time allocated them in class by urging that more space be freed up in the curriculum to allow greater choice of subjects, including vocational courses.[59]

In addition, Dearing recommended the appointment of Key Stage oversight groups to ensure the requirements for the whole curriculum were manageable across all subjects, and new subject working groups were appointed, and given nine weeks to come up with further revisions.[60] The history committee argued over issues of content and testing, and one member entered a minority report, regretting that the requirement to include social, cultural, religious and ethnic diversities within the topics studied amounted to 'a great deal of sociological baggage' that should be removed, and objecting to the attention given to the testing of thinking skills, when it was children's factual knowledge of history which more important.[61] But the majority report did slim down the compulsory content and the attainment targets. The 'Core Study Units' were simplified, the 'Supplementary or Extension Units' were removed or in a few cases added to the 'Core Study Units', and there would be only one overall attainment target, expressed in a succession of ten 'level descriptions' against which pupils' progress would be judged.[62] The decision to remove all history and geography from the National Curriculum after the age of 14 was understandably deplored by educationalists, not least because it severed any remaining link between the National Curriculum in history and the GCSE in history. But it did seem as though history could now be realistically taught in the time available, and the syllabus did retain many 'essential features' of the Working Group Report of 1990.[63]

Three years later, Labour came to power, with its own agenda, an early indication of which was the introduction of 'citizenship' as a compulsory element in the National Curriculum to the age of 16.[64] It contained little in the way of historical subject-matter, but many history teachers were reluctant to teach citizenship, fearing it might squeeze out their own subject. And this was only the first such adjustment. In primary schools, literacy and numeracy 'hours' were introduced, occupying most mornings, relegating subjects such as history to the sidelines. At secondary level, the initiative *Every*

Child Matters, enjoining pupils to 'be healthy, stay safe, enjoy and achieve, make a positive contribution, achieve economic well-being', was a further super-imposition on the National Curriculum, taking time away from the subject-specific curriculum, history included.[65] In the case of primary schools, Blunkett defended 'putting emphasis on literacy and numeracy' on the grounds that they should have been a way 'of getting into subjects like history and bringing them alive, making them something that would inspire youngsters to have an enquiring mind'. But he conceded this had not often happened, and that the additional subjects imposed on secondary schools meant time was further squeezed for subjects such as history. 'I've got this niggle inside me,' Blunkett recently observed, 'that we really ought to have said that everybody should study history through to sixteen.'[66]

Meanwhile, the National Curriculum for history was reviewed twice: in 1999, which included all Key Stages, and again in 2007, which was confined to Key Stage 3.[67] In 1999, Key Stages 1 and 2 were slightly adjusted, to give more scope to local history and to Britain and the wider world; and in Key Stage 3, more attention was given to global history. The 2007 revision to Key Stage 3 was more fundamental: influenced by the Ajegbo report on citizenship, it introduced a new requirement called 'cultural, ethnic and religious diversity', and the curriculum was amended to give more attention to such topics as 'the impact through time of the movement and settlement of diverse peoples to, from and within the British Isles' and 'the role of European and international institutions in resolving conflicts' (shades of the League of Nations).[68] Especial attention was given to two highly controversial episodes, the Slave Trade and the Holocaust. These had both been specified in the original National Curriculum of 1991, but the emphasis given in 2007 highlighted the fact that teachers were being asked to address momentous historical events with an eye to current concerns about genocide and racial discrimination. These subjects were undeniably important, but they were complex and controversial, and the Historical Association issued a report noting that some teachers avoided them in the classroom, for fear of causing offence in local communities – or because in an 'all white' school there was thought to be no need to discuss them.[69]

In terms of the development of the National Curriculum for history, the signals under New Labour were contradictory: in some ways an enhancement of teacher autonomy, by lessening listed content and targets to be achieved; in other ways greater intervention from the centre, as schools were urged to deal with historical topics of current concern and contemporary relevance. At the same time, the Labour governments responded to wider social 'issues', such as youth crime or the decline in voting participation, by imposing further burdens on the already-overcrowded National Curriculum – as when schools were asked to respond to the obesity 'epidemic' by providing opportunities for their pupils to learn cookery and understand the importance of healthy eating; or when, in recognition of the importance of immigration, they were called upon to promote 'community cohesion' through the curriculum.[70] As more subjects and tasks were imposed on the National Curriculum, and as it was increasingly expected to fulfil immediate social agendas, the time left for teaching history came under increasing pressure. Yet this made it even harder to teach such topics as slavery and the Holocaust, to which the government attached great significance, because they could not be rushed, and required teaching at length and in detail if pupils were to understand their magnitude and significance.[71]

Classroom History across Two Millennia

There can be no doubting the determination of Thatcher, Joseph, Baker and Clarke to initiate a counter-revolution in education. They disliked teacher-training colleges, educational theorists, HMIs, comprehensive schools, progressive teaching methods and the cult of 'empathy', and they were determined to rein them all in both by exerting the power of the state in education as never before, and also by invoking and involving what they believed was the sympathetic force of parental preference. But the limitations to what they accomplished are a vivid reminder of the constraints on any government's power, by which is meant the capacity to bring about an intended state of affairs. To be sure, teacher training was made more practical, the HMIs were replaced by Ofsted, both the Schools Council and the Inner London Education Authority were abolished, and a National Curriculum was established. But the comprehensive revolution was not reversed, the GCSE and later revisions to A Level history courses were in some ways a victory for 'progressive' education, and the creation and implementation of the National Curriculum were not well or deftly handled in general, and were particularly botched in the case of history. Nevertheless, the Thatcher governments did change the educational landscape, and New Labour very largely accepted it. What, then was the impact of these reforms on the teaching of history in the classroom?

At the level of primary schools, it was considerable and for a time distinctly positive. In 1988, an HMI survey of 285 such schools reported that standards of work in history were 'disappointing' and that it was 'under-emphasised' or not taught at all in half of the sample inspected. Less than a third of the schools had a member of staff responsible for history across the whole school, and most teachers 'chose topics autonomously', making it difficult to achieve any co-ordination or progression in the children's learning even within the same school.[72] History in primary schools had been relegated to the status of a marginal or non-existent subject, the province of the rare enthusiastic and confident teacher, and was experienced in the classroom as an occasional 'extra' by most boys and girls. By contrast, the National Curriculum required primary school teachers to move from a relatively unstructured approach in the classroom to dealing with ten distinct subjects all specified in detail, of which history was one. This meant teaching it explicitly and directly in a way that had not been the case for many years, and also assessing pupils' progress in this subject as in the other nine, via attainment targets. These were serious challenges, and in response to them, the Primary History Association was set up, with its own journal and conferences, to offer professional support to teachers of infants and juniors.

The response to the National Curriculum was a mixture of anxiety and excitement, as primary school teachers needed more resources and more guidance. Training courses, lasting several weeks, were put on at colleges of education, to get them 'up to speed with the National Curriculum'; and more resources and new textbooks were produced, sometimes by primary school teachers themselves, in the hope of getting both the classroom content and the required assessment right.[73] The result was a significant restoration of history in primary schools: the Romans, Anglo-Saxons and Vikings returned to the classroom; and there were even teachers whose approach harked back to the days of R.J. Unstead – reading a page, talking about it, and drawing a picture. But there was a more nuanced debate about how to teach young children about major figures from the national past: should King Alfred be described as the monarch who burnt the cakes, 'whether it was true or not' because the story was 'part of English heritage', or should there be an effort to tell the 'truth and make sure that people knew what a great king he was and about the navy and the English laws'. There were also some new topics for which initially there were very few resources, such as a unit on the history of the African kingdom of Benin, added as an optional unit by the National Curriculum Council history task group.[74]

At primary level, the 1990s were a burgeoning and buoyant time for history, and publishers, museums and heritage sites all started to focus on supporting the core units which the majority of schools were now teaching. The economies of scale were obvious, and the survey responses of pupils who had been at school in that decade reflect the common topics remembered from Key Stage 2, between the ages of seven and eleven: the Ancient Egyptians (chosen as a non-European civilisation by many schools), the Romans and the Vikings and, most vividly of all, the Victorians. One correspondent remembers being 'encouraged to imagine what it would be like to travel on a train for the first time. It was hands on, with a dramatic element – some role play.' Another recalls 'a class assembly where we all dressed in Victorian clothes'. Yet a third still talks with his school friends about 'sitting in a Victorian classroom and writing on a slate, going down the mine in pitch darkness, and buying barley sweets with old money'.[75] All of which lends support to John Fines's claim that as a consequence of the upgrading of the subject through the National Curriculum, 'young children [were] doing an enormous amount more history than ever before'.[76]

The Nuffield Primary History Project was one manifestation of the new confidence that history for infants and juniors now had a better footing and a brighter future. Lasting from 1991 to 1996, it explored ways of delivering the history required by the National Curriculum using small-scale schemes with individual schools. But the ethos was far from compliant with any return to 'traditional' teaching methods – in the words of Jon Nichol, who worked in primary teacher training, 'We were so fed up with the wretched National Curriculum that we [said] "let's try and get something else going on primary … history".' Accordingly, they were insistent that children should try to explore topics in depth, using authentic historical resources and sites, with the work focused on 'doing' history by investigating and questioning.[77] But according to *Primary History*, there was 'growing confidence in teaching the subject' at infant and junior level thanks to the increased status the National Curriculum had given it. More schools were allocating specific time to history and to teaching it separately rather than within integrated topics, and the establishment of the National Curriculum 'was a catalyst for that'.[78]

According to a local authority adviser in Staffordshire, the National Curriculum provided a basis for raising standards and 'eliminating … mediocrity', and certainly did so in his county.[79] His impressions were corroborated more broadly by the Ofsted report of 1998, completed after its first four-year 'cycle' of inspection of primary schools, where it summarized the progress in the teaching of history, noting that it was 'prospering' with a 'modest but steady improvement in standards' and 'steady improvement in the quality of teaching', compared to the dark days of the 1960s and 1970s, when history had seemed fated to disappear from primary schools altogether. Matters had significantly improved since the HMIs' concerned report of ten years before, but Ofsted also believed that too many schools were concentrating more on knowledge than on enquiry skills, and that primary school teachers often missed opportunities to stretch their pupils by 'playing safe' and by asking questions which required only factual answers; and it urged that more of them should go on the short training courses that were still available in many colleges of education.[80]

At secondary level, the impact of the National Curriculum was rather different: for unlike the primaries, it applied to schools where history was already being compulsorily taught up to age 14, and it seemed to threaten history teachers with a potential loss of autonomy, as they also faced a new regime of accountability under Ofsted inspection. Schools received a large binder for each subject, detailing both the curriculum and the attainment targets, and 'when receiving the document, people probably blanched at the sheer detail and size of it'.[81] Some teachers feared they would have to teach 'a very conventional curriculum', but this underestimated the extent to which the National Curriculum merely codified what many teachers were already doing, while also urging the importance and appeal of new subjects, such as the Aztecs or Mughal India.[82] More generally, the positive impact of the National Curriculum was that it gave to the first three years of secondary schooling in history, which had previously been seen merely as the preliminary to O Level, the CSE and the GCSE, a separate status and an autonomous importance they had previously lacked, as teachers were increasingly required to measure progress and 'level' their pupils' work.

Like their primary school colleagues, some secondary school teachers initially found this difficult and discouraging: 'levels' were 'so vague', and there seemed to be 'a lot of targets to be met and boxes to tick'.[83] But they soon came to appreciate that the National Curriculum justified and guaranteed the place of history in schools at Key Stage 3, and that there was more scope for selection and initiative than some initially thought, enabling them to 'pursue special interests'. In the words of one of our correspondents: 'the National Curriculum' was 'a hypothesis. It tells you what to teach, but not what the children have to learn, or how long you have to spend teaching it.'[84] It also placed greater stress on organization, forcing teachers to construct detailed schemes of work – an aspect of history teaching which had certainly been weak up to the 1980s. Even though its remit only extended, thanks to Kenneth Clarke's decision, to pupils aged 14, the National Curriculum in history at least helped ensure that they would leave school with a sense of some of the major developments in Britain's past, as well as some knowledge of the twentieth century, and thus of how the current world had come to be the way it was; while it also made history teachers 'think harder about what topics we taught and how we justified their inclusion'.[85]

The National Curriculum undoubtedly broadened history teaching, by encouraging more teachers to tackle subjects they might not have felt comfortable with before – such as the Aztecs in primary schools and Native Peoples of the Americas in secondary schools. Although 50 per cent of the National Curriculum had to be British history, and even more than that after the Dearing reductions of content, all primary schools were required to teach a non-European history unit, and in secondary schools, optional units at Key Stage 3 covered both European and world history topics. Despite the burst of enthusiasm for creating resources to accompany topics like the history of Benin, the most popular non-European subject in primary history has been Ancient Egypt, which is so well supported by resources and museum collections. At secondary level, world history, multicultural themes and the study of Empire and slavery have become more prominent than they were in the earlier versions of the National Curriculum.

12. A pupil's work on the French Revolution, taught in Year 8 of the National Curriculum, from a comprehensive school in the north-east of England, 1996 (courtesy of anonymous donor)

This is partly because of the reshaping of the curriculum in 2007 to emphasize the study of slavery in the context of the British Empire as a major topic, and also because of the inclusion of 'diversity' as a key concept in the curriculum.

These were not the only changes in the history classroom. The National Curriculum generated an unprecedented demand for new textbooks, especially for those covering the mandatory Key Stage 3 at secondary school. In the case of 'Medieval Realms: Britain 1066–1500', for example, there was a wide range of approaches on offer. For the more 'traditionally' inclined teacher, R.J. Cootes produced a dense narrative text, broken up by photographs and headings, along with sources and questions to develop the pupil's understanding of interpretations in history. For those preferring a more 'progressive' approach, Ian Dawson's book was focused on such questions as 'Was religion important in the Middle Ages?', supported by a larger selection of sources and a section entitled 'Historical Skills and Ideas'.[86] Such diversity was building upon a strong tradition in the 1970s and 1980s of teachers becoming textbook authors, and a new generation of writers with direct experience of the classroom included John D. Clare, Penelope Harnett and Michael Riley.[87] And although the academic links between schools and universities were less than they had been in the 1960s and 1970s, there was some continuing interest: Professor Eric Evans of the University of Lancaster was an O and A Level examiner, and in 1983 he inaugurated the *Lancaster Pamphlet* series, intended as a guide to the recent historical literature on major topics for those teaching and taking A Level.[88]

Many teachers also compiled their own materials to accompany television programmes, which could be watched live or (increasingly) as video recordings. The spread of video machines into most schools from the early 1980s was a major turning point in classroom technology, as the medium was sufficiently flexible for pre-recorded programmes to be shown in timetabled lessons, either as a whole or as short illustrative clips. Video made the screen the servant of the teacher rather than dictating the format and the timing of the lesson, as had been the case in the rigid days when schools relied on the inflexible scheduling of live television programmes. It became especially important for secondary history teachers offering courses in twentieth-century world history, for which there was a huge reservoir of documentary film in a way that was not true for earlier periods.

By the end of the decade, teachers were creating customized video selections to match and accompany their own reading packs, and some of them were also beginning to devise ways of using the emerging computer technology in the classroom.

But not many: for even when rooms of computers were installed in schools in the 1990s, and despite the early interest of the Historical Association, history departments were less likely than almost any other in school to make use of them.[89] Many teachers were initially reluctant and insufficiently expert to use them, and although some developed social history topics which required the processing of large amounts of census data, there was in general little need for the computer in the history classroom, beyond basic word-processing.[90] Even more fundamentally, the individual nature of the computer interfered with the interaction between the teacher and the class, rather than facilitated it. Whereas video had been taken up quickly as a way of supplementing history teaching 'from the front' in ways the teacher controlled, the computer distracted pupils from class learning. In most cases, history classrooms would be provided with one computer only, which only tended to emphasize its redundancy apart from the production of individual coursework. The real breakthrough came with the union between video and computer technology, via the ceiling-mounted data projector, which meant a whole class could be engaged and involved, and which quickly became an essential resource in the history classroom.

By 2002, Ofsted concluded that progress in the use of technology in history was limited, although teachers were beginning to realise the potential (and the perils) of the internet as an almost limitless source of historical information for pupils to use in their work.[91] Since then, use of the internet has had a transformational effect, increasing teachers' access to both historical materials and new ideas, whether from government, examination boards, publishers, professional networks, teachers' own websites or blogs with each other.[92] Many schools have virtual learning environments which allow teaching materials to be available outside lesson time and also at home for individual study. This has proved especially useful for A Level history, where pupils are expected to do more in their own time, and where a virtual learning environment can help sixth formers with their essay writing, and with collaborative learning: they can read and evaluate each other's work online, contact their teacher to ask questions, and participate in class discussion via a virtual forum.[93] With such tools at their fingertips, should pupils still be asked to learn the dates and reigns of English monarchy, when they can all be accessed via Google or Wikipedia?

The most recent piece of classroom technology is the interactive whiteboard, and almost all of the history teachers under 40 who responded to our survey used it.[94] As such, it is the latest instalment in a multi-media, interactive revolution in history teaching that was scarcely imaginable when the National Curriculum was introduced 20 years ago. Nowadays, teachers are less dependent than ever on textbooks (which, in any case, increasingly come with additional electronic or web-based visual resources), major collections of source materials have been made available online (some of them suitable for topics in the history National Curriculum), and the once-indispensable video now vies with YouTube as the most effective teaching aid in the classroom. The combined effect of projectors, videos, the internet and interactive white boards has been to change fundamentally the whole process of classroom learning about the past, away from the written word and towards visual images, which are now available in almost limitless supply.[95] Nowadays, history in the classroom often means engaging with and responding to interactive sites which invite participation, discussion and allow pupils to make their own collaborative podcasts or websites – a very different way of acquiring and communicating historical knowledge than from working on the individual handwritten essay.[96]

As with so many subjects, the effect of the (unfinished) revolution in ICT on history in the classroom has been to dissolve boundaries: between teachers and taught, readers and texts, viewers and screens, learning and leisure, schoolwork and homework. Nowadays as never before, history is instantly, everywhere available, all day, all night, 24/7, and learning about it in school is only part of the process of encountering and, increasingly, 'experiencing' the past. Is it just coincidence that the 1990s and the 2000s were not only the decades of the ICT revolution, but also when the membership of the National Trust surpassed that of the three major political parties combined? And that they also coincided with an unprecedented period in the production of television history, in the hands of a new generation of presenters, including Bettany Hughes, Michael Wood, David Starkey, Simon Schama and Niall Ferguson? For many people today, wanting to learn about the history of their country, either in the classroom or at home, Schama's millennial series remains their first port of call: on DVD as well as in book form. And in terms of their chronological span and geographical range, from the ancient world to modern times, and across all continents, the history offerings on television have never been so rich or so varied.[97]

Although many older history teachers consider their ICT skills under-developed, especially by comparison with their pupils, younger history teachers have overwhelmingly embraced the new technology at both primary and secondary level, and have been trained to incorporate it into their lessons, which often combine textbooks, worksheets, pictures, photographs, television clips, film footage, videos, CD recordings, digital projectors, PowerPoint presentations, and the interactive white board.[98] Yet some traditional elements of history teaching remain significant. Despite the rising costs of transport and the ever-tightening health and safety regulations, school trips are still important as 'highlights' in many history courses, and many teachers we interviewed still valued their role as story-tellers, especially in primary school and in the lower secondary years. Here is one teacher's account, from someone who is also an enthusiast for ICT and interactive learning, which must stand proxy for the others:

> Children love stories … I can sit down a set of the naughtiest and least able Year 9 pupils … and I can talk to them for an hour about the murder of Franz Ferdinand at Sarajevo, and I won't pause for breath and … not one of them will glance sideways; I can keep them absolutely thrilled. The story side of history is, I think, still the big power over children.[99]

As this suggests, in some comprehensive schools, the old 'chalk-and-talk' methods were still in evidence, and as was always the case, with an inspirational teacher, they could be enthralling. One of our correspondents remembers 'just sitting and listening. Mr Wade, our history teacher, was possibly my favourite.' He also recalls 'a good deal of copying from the board … I remember enjoying all of it, but I do think that the teacher had a lot to do with it.' He was 'enthusiastic and our lessons were always interesting and often good fun'.[100] Many of those who filled in our surveys found the subject came alive when they could relate to history in terms of local sites and artefacts, especially in the case of the Industrial Revolution: one recalls a 'field trip to local water wheels and a local working mill where we watched a loom in action'; another remembers studying 'education/travel/industry', which meant visiting 'viaducts/aqueducts and canals in the area'.[101] And for those who were particularly fortunate, there might be trips further afield: in one case to France, where one respondent recalls visiting the Bayeux tapestry ('I remember being mesmerised by the pictures and stories that unfolded on this fabric') and the Normandy beaches and graves ('thus began my fascination for all things to do with World War Two').[102]

Others recall with particular gratitude the range of their 'aids to learning': in one case 'maps, primary source materials, worksheets, posters/images, television (we regularly watched *The Way We Used to Live* at primary school), plays, poetry'; in another, 'videos, newspaper articles, textbooks mainly. I loved looking at old maps, particularly of my local area'; in yet a third, 'work books/TV series/maps/film strips/ videos/worksheets'.[103] (Although one correspondent does recall 'a concentration camp video and a girl in my class fainting, even though it was in black and white'.) And there were some who relished both the challenge of A Level and being treated as undergraduates in the sixth form: one correspondent remembers that 'we were taught like adults at university, it was great'; another recalls that 'we used books you might use at degree level'.[104]

Yet as before, there are those who look back on their time learning history with regret and disappointment. For some, 'chalk-and-talk' was deadly dull: history lessons meant 'textbooks [and] teacher standing in front talking', only relieved by 'occasional videos'; or a 'hated … year of World Wars One and Two. We were just taught from textbooks and had no field trips. I didn't understand most of what happened.' For others, history meant going over the same ground: material already covered at primary school taught again during the first years at a comprehensive school; or later of 'the same key topics' being taught, such as the Industrial Revolution or the Second World War, which created a feeling of 'a lack of progress due to repetition'.[105] There were regrets that their historical studies never brought them close to the modern world: 'It all seemed very boring and irrelevant and … we did not cover any modern history … There was no link with modern day living, and how learning of history is relevant.'[106] And there were those who chose history, and carried on to A Level, only to discover that the inspiring teacher they had expected had been replaced by someone new, who was 'bloody hopeless', with the result that both their examination performance and their enthusiasm for the subject suffered.[107]

This last example is a reminder that, while the effects of ICT in the history classroom have been pervasive at all ages, from primary schools to A Level, the National Curriculum in history has had no direct effect on GCSE or on A Levels – except insofar as future candidates for these examinations would themselves have first encountered history through the National Curriculum. The introduction of the GCSE prompted a rationalisation of syllabuses, as the former CSE and O Level boards were merged (and the connections which most of the latter had maintained with universities soon became attenuated), and as most of the less popular O Levels and themed CSE syllabuses were immediately dropped. At first, question papers covering long periods of English history remained, but they rapidly lost ground to those concerned with modern British economic and social history, the modern world, or the Schools History Project (as the Schools Council History Project had by now become). The skills-based methodology also remained embedded in the GCSE, though there was the suspicion that in some classrooms, 'skills' meant a formulaic approach whereby pupils learnt a few 'rules' for judging evidence ('Is it biased?; Is it a primary or secondary source?') just to pass the exam. This impression that source analysis had been stripped of its 'discovery' and 'enquiry' elements was reinforced by the use of brief extracts or heavily edited sources in some GCSE examinations. Alternatively, some schools immersed their pupils in in-depth studies using sources with insufficient historical background.[108]

In general, teachers were positive about the GCSE, although some were initially 'confused and unsure' about assessment.[109] But there was one part of the history syllabuses that proved seriously controversial, and that was the idea that 'empathy' could be taught. For a time, it became a 'big deal', but not all teachers were convinced it could (or should) be taught, let alone examined.[110] In 1987, at Priory School, Lewes, in East Sussex, two history teachers, Anthony Freeman and Chris McGovern, decided to enter some of their pupils for the Scottish Ordinary Certificate in history the following year, because they were particularly exercised about the idea of

differentiated historical empathy, which meant that in a good answer on your GCSE paper you had to show differing points of view, so as a Palestinian terrorist you had to give the point of view of the Palestinian terrorist and also the point of view, a recognition, of the point of view of the people you were blowing up ... Do you give them a grade A or send them to a psychiatrist?

The case became a *cause célèbre*, and was taken up by Robert Skidelsky, whose children attended the same school. Even though Sir Keith Joseph had spoken in favour of the cultivation of 'sympathetic understanding', it seems unlikely that this was what he had intended when he had agreed to the establishment of the GCSE.[111]

The first GCSE examination in history was taken in the summer of 1988, but it was against the background of a gradually declining trend in the numbers of exam candidates in the subject earlier in the decade: O Level numbers had peaked in 1982, at slightly above 130,200; CSE in 1983, at more than 176,000.[112] The first cohort of schoolchildren to sit history GCSE amounted to 217,300 pupils, and they achieved a pass rate of 45 per cent at A to C grades. This total was less than the number taking geography, and it was 36 per cent of all those sitting GCSE examinations. Between 1988 and 1997, the number of candidates sitting the GCSE in history dipped to 188,000 in 1992, it rose to 223,000 in 1995 (the largest number ever entered), but it fell back to 207,000 in 1997. During the 2000s, the number varied between 195,000 and 205,000, and for the first time history GCSE became more popular than geography, whose numbers fell sharply, while history's rose until 2006. Between 1988 and 1996, the proportion of GCSE candidates taking history increased slightly from 36 per cent to 38 per cent, but from 2000 to 2009, it fell from 36 per cent in 2000 to 33 per cent in 2009. At the same time, the proportion of history candidates passing GCSE with A to C grades has risen virtually year on year, from 45 per cent to 69 per cent.

Throughout the 1980s, most A Level history exams had continued to consist of two three-hour papers, concerned with a period of British and of European history, during which candidates wrote four 45-minute essays. One major change from the beginning of the decade was the setting of questions using original sources, but as before, A Level history was generally insulated from changes in the curriculum between the ages of 11 and 16. In 1990, the Associated Examining Board offered four syllabuses: English and/or European history from 1450 to 1760, sub-divided into roughly 100-year periods, of which candidates took only one; British and/or European history from 1760 to 1980, sub-divided into shorter periods, of which again candidates could take only one; the history of the United States from 1783 to 1974; and Aspects of World History since 1945. In practice, the Tudors and the Nazis have tended to dominate A Level syllabuses, and this has remained true since 2000, when all A Level examinations became 'modular', with the syllabus broken down into separate 'units' (initially six, more recently four), with a short examination for each one, which can be re-sat. As a result, assessment has become very complicated.

The number of candidates taking A Level history peaked for the first time in 1983 at just over 38,000, thereafter diminishing to 27,000 by 1988, after which the numbers began gradually to rise again. The reasons for this mid-decade dip are not wholly clear, but since the percentage passing increased from just below 70 per cent to just above 80 per cent, it may well be that weaker candidates were dissuaded from taking the subject. From a low point in 1988, when 27,190 candidates sat the examination, numbers steadily increased, until by 1997 the figure was 33,035. Since 1997, they have continued to climb steadily, reaching 39,000 by 2005, and passing 45,000 in 2010. So while the numbers taking GCSE have fallen slightly during its 20-odd years of existence, the trend at A Level has been significantly in the opposite direction. But just as the pass rate has gone up for GCSE in history, the same has been true at A Level: from 81 per cent in 1988 to 88 per cent in 1998, and to 99 per cent in recent years. Nowadays, and in part as a result of the modular syllabus and the opportunity to re-sit the examination in each 'unit', and in part because no self-respecting school lets weak AS Level candidates continue on, A Level history is a subject which it is almost impossible to fail.

History is Now and is England

When Kenneth Baker wrote his memoirs, he noted that, as Secretary of State for Education, he had been responsible for the oversight of '30,000 schools, 400,000 teachers, and 7.5 million children'.[113] These are very big numbers, and they are not only a reminder of the importance of education in the lives of millions of individuals and in the collective history of this country, but also of the extraordinary difficulty of venturing any generalisations about schools and teachers and history and the experiences of pupils. Nevertheless, it seems appropriate to try to tease out some general reflections, even if they must be, perforce, of a very general and interim nature. The first is that, despite what was originally their vociferous opposition, many history teachers recognize the position of their subject in schools has been strengthened by the imposition of the National Curriculum. This has certainly been true at Key Stages 1 and 2 at primary level, where history had seemed mortally marginalised, but where since the early 1990s it has been taught as a discrete subject and for a specified number of hours.[114] In secondary schools, the advent of the National Curriculum has also meant that history's place in the timetable has been secured, at least up until the age of 14, and that the subjects cover a good spread, both temporally and geographically.[115]

The most recent accounts of history teaching in primary and secondary schools come from two surveys by Ofsted, for 2003–07, and for 2007–10, and their verdicts, although based on a limited sample, are encouraging and yet equivocal in a way that will come as no surprise to anyone who has persevered thus far with this book. On the one hand, they report 'much to celebrate', and 'much that was good and outstanding in the history seen for this survey'. The overwhelming majority of schools were teaching history well or excellently, and at GCSE and at A Level, the pass rates were higher than the average for all subjects.[116] Apart from design and technology, there were more examination entries for history at GCSE level than for any other optional subject, and the proportion of pupils taking the exam has remained about one third since it was first introduced. The numbers taking the subject at A Level have risen in recent years, making it one of the top five subject choices. At secondary level, the teaching workforce was deemed to be of especially high quality, which helped explain why history was 'generally a popular and successful subject, and many pupils enjoyed it: according to one, it helped broaden horizons and thus served to 'liberate the mind'; according to another, it made it easier to 'understand the world in which we live'.[117]

But the news is not all good. At primary level, there has recently been a retreat from history and a return to 'topics' which cut across subject-specific boundaries, while younger primary school teachers receive little specialist training in history either before they qualify or as serving teachers.[118] And in secondary schools, at Key Stage 3, citizenship, vocational courses and other new specialist subjects and topics imposed by government have cut into the time previously allocated for history.[119] As a result, local history has been a noteworthy casualty, partly because there is little room for it in Key Stage 3 and also because GCSE syllabuses in social and economic history have recently declined in popularity.[120] Nor is there much enthusiasm to teach British history as the 'history of four nations', by giving more prominence to Scottish, Welsh and Irish history. Moreover, history is often seen as a 'hard' subject, suitable for the above-average pupil, whereas schools can improve their league table position by putting their pupils in for 'easier' courses which deliver more 'points'.[121] This means there has been a contraction of the time available for history in the classroom, and more pressure has been put on teachers to get good results in the subject at GCSE and at A Level. This in turn has led to increasing conservatism in the choice of topics, which helps explain why the Tudors, the two World Wars and the Nazis are so often taught from the ages of 15 to 18.[122]

As a result, the suggestion has crept back that history is again 'in danger', from being fragmented and disaggregated.[123] For as the time allocated to the subject in secondary schools has been reduced, this has often resulted in an increasingly 'episodic' treatment of the subject, with teachers hopping rapidly from one topic to another, without providing chronological coverage and coherence. At ages 11–12, pupils might begin with the Roman invasion or the Norman Conquest, move on to Henry II and Thomas Becket or the Crusades, followed by King John and Magna Carta and then skip to the Black Death and Peasants' Revolt. At 12–13, they can rush through the 'voyages of discovery', Tudor monarchs and English Civil War, and the British Empire and Slave Trade. As one head of department noted 'Lots of the work I saw had Roman centurions travelling to Australia and the Roman army using guns to impose its rule in Britain.'[124] The result is that too much history is taught 'in terms of disparate fragments ... Everybody can see ... that knowing a bit about the Tudors and a bit about Jack the Ripper and a bit about the Victorians is really not a history education.'[125] At both primary and secondary levels, 'too great a focus on a relatively small number of issues means that pupils are not good at establishing a chronology, do not make connections between areas they have studied, and so do not gain an overview, and are not able to answer the "big questions"'.[126]

Many of these shortcomings are to be explained by what both reports deplored as the 'limited place' history occupies in the school curriculum: in primary schools because of 'the necessary focus on literacy and numeracy'; in secondary schools because of the increasing pressure at Key Stage 3, where some schools are opting to teach history in two years rather than three; where only 30 per cent of pupils study the subject in Key Stage 4, and fewer still thereafter, 'which means that a substantial number never consider important historical issues when they are mature enough to do so'.[127] (And in new academies, as a recent Historical Association report makes plain, the time given to history has dwindled still further.[128]) 'Unlike the practice in most of Europe', the Ofsted report went on, 'history is not compulsory after the age of fourteen in English schools', and the pressure of other subjects on a crowded secondary school curriculum means that 'most of the history that pupils are taught is at primary school'. How odd this seems, 'particularly in an era when many people, including politicians, say that it is important for everyone to understand the past in order to understand the present'. The overall conclusion Ofsted offered in 2007 still seems valid: 'there is much to celebrate about current history provision in our schools, but there is no room for complacency'.[129] What, then, needs to be done?

Conclusion:
Perspectives and Suggestions

The biggest issue for school history is its limited place in the curriculum.
(Ofsted, *History in the Balance: History in English Schools,
2003–07* (London, 2007), p. 28.)

Education, it has been observed, functions in two ways: first, as a matter of formal pedagogy, namely what is taught, where it is taught, why it is taught, how it is taught, by whom it is taught, and to whom it is taught; and second, as part of the shared accumulation and passing on of a society's collectively accumulated knowledge, 'as the entire process by which a culture transmits itself across the generations'.[1] But education also needs to be understood as the interconnection between pedagogy and culture, and this book is a pioneering effort to do so, looking at history in twentieth-century England as a *taught subject*: at the arrangements and means by which schoolchildren come to learn about the past, but also at the sense of that past, if any, which they acquire, retain and remember in their later lives. All taught subjects, from mathematics to music, economics to English literature, have such double identities and overlapping histories, within the classroom, and in the wider world beyond. Yet they have rarely been written about in this way, in part because to do so requires the bringing together of two sub-disciplines which only infrequently conjoin: the history of education, and the history of culture.

But the histories of taught subjects have also been largely unwritten because, despite their undoubted importance, they are by their nature vague, protean, hard to grasp and difficult to pin down. As we have tried to show in the foregoing pages, the history of history, like any taught subject, needs to be approached, appreciated, understood, analysed and described at many different, overlapping, and interlocking levels: from prime ministers and cabinet ministers making educational policy (or not), via civil servants and HMIs (overseeing the nation's schools), educational theorists and psychologists (offering thoughts on how to teach), teacher trainers and teachers (doing the work in colleges and classrooms) to the pupils on the receiving end (who are the point and purpose of the whole enterprise). Thus approached, the history of any taught subject is more than the history of education (because it is concerned with power and knowledge broadly conceived), and also more than the history of culture (because it is concerned with institutions and policies). Because the history of a taught subject comprises so many things, there are many voices that need to be heard, and we have tried to give them appropriate attention in this book. Only by so doing is it possible to convey the complex nature of how history has been taught in the state schools of twentieth-century England – and that complexity would equally apply to the teaching of other subjects in this country, or to the teaching of history in other countries.

But there are also ways in which history is not like most taught subjects. Some of them are virtually the same the world over: economics and physics, Spanish and engineering, Latin and astronomy. Even allowing for linguistic variation and cultural differences, teaching them in a school in Beijing or Moscow or Cairo or Caracas would cover recognizably similar content. Some subjects are more territorially specific, though often in a way that still transcends national boundaries, such as music, literature, religion, architecture and art. They are often the signifiers of larger cultural associations, sometimes referred to as 'civilizations'. But there are a few subjects which are very different in content from one nation to another, of which history is the most potent. To be sure, the history of the world is (or ought to be) the same whichever part of it you happen to be in; and the outlines of the history of the United States or the United Kingdom ought to be the same whether you inhabit either of those countries or live elsewhere. But since the nineteenth century, history has also been important in the creation of particular national identities, which means that what is taught in a classroom in Hong Kong or Melbourne or Accra or Berlin or Washington DC may be completely different: the history of a particular nation, of great interest to its citizenry and their sense of shared identity, but of less interest to others, who have their own national history and their own national consciousness instead.[2]

Thus regarded, history is simultaneously a global academic discipline, but also the avatar of many distinct national identities, and these two endeavours, and the people who seek to promote them, rarely align or agree. Many academics see the purpose of history as subverting rather than supporting national myths; many public figures see history as an essentially engaged education in citizenship – and many teachers occupy a position somewhere in between. Perhaps this helps explain why the teaching of history in schools has, during the last two or three decades, become so contested and controversial around the world; for as the power and autonomy of the nation state seems increasingly undermined, by everything from the ICT revolution to global warming, and as nations become ever more conscious of their ethnic variety and diversity, it becomes harder to agree on a single, shared national narrative. And since a single, shared national narrative is thought to be one of the major constituents of national identity, the decline in the attraction and conviction of such accounts is both a cause and consequence of the weakening of the hold of the nation state itself. Although specific to separate countries, these are also global phenomena, by which few nations have recently been unaffected; and any discussion of the place of history in the classrooms of English schools must recognize that this is our local version of something going on the world over.

Government, Politics, Education and History

Within that broader global framework, our first observation regarding the teaching of history in English state schools across the century-and-more from 1900 is that very few governments have been especially interested in education, let alone in the subject which is our particular concern. Most administrations before the Second World War did not seriously expect to be interested, and did not claim that they were; but many since then have claimed that they were, yet in practice demonstrated only limited concern or commitment. Many prime ministers have regarded Education as a low-priority cabinet post, and ambitious politicians have either not wanted to do the job at all, or sought to move on from it to something bigger and more important, as soon as they possibly could. This explains why, since the Board of Education was first established, there have been 49 Presidents, Ministers and Secretaries of State in charge of Education, and the majority of them have held office for two years or less.[3] In such a brief span of time, it is scarcely possible for a minister to get to know his or her civil servants, let alone embark on any major policy initiatives, and it is difficult to imagine any serious organization, in business, industry or academe, where so rapid a turnover in the senior position over so long a span of time would seriously be tolerated.

Across the twentieth century, only five ministers out of these 49 stand out as being exceptionally creative and commanding figures at Education, seeing the potential in the post, appreciating the importance of schools and universities, and being determined to do something about them: the eighth Duke of Devonshire, who initially established the Board of Education; H.A.L. Fisher who passed the reforming measure that bears his name; R.A. Butler who carried his own transformative legislation a generation later; Sir Keith Joseph, who invented Thatcherism and brought it to Education; and Kenneth Baker who steered through another Education Reform Act. But while these were unusually powerful and dominant ministers, there were significant limits in each case to what they were able to accomplish: Devonshire was at the end of his career and did not stay long; most of the provisions of Fisher's Act fell victim to the inter-war spending cuts; Butler's Act never brought about a genuinely tripartite secondary system with 'parity of esteem' between different types of school; Joseph alienated the teachers and did not carry a major piece of reforming legislation; and while Baker undeniably did, the truncating of the National Curriculum in history after he had left office is a vivid reminder of the considerable gap between what ministers want to happen, and what may actually happen.

Significantly, only three of these five held office for longer than average: being in power for several years rather than just one or two helped them to make an impact, but a long tenure of office was not absolutely essential (Lord Eustace Percy was in office for more than four years, but the combination of tight finance and his own lack of political weight meant he made virtually no impact). Below these few front-ranking ministers has been a second serious tier: those figures who were less politically imaginative or creative, but who were especially good at getting more resources out of the government to spend on schools, teachers, equipment and programmes. There have been four of them: George Tomlinson, David Eccles, Margaret Thatcher and David Blunkett. All of them held the top job at Education for longer than average, which gave them the chance to oversee the spending of the increased funds they had fought for and won. Unlike the top five, this second four were not so much interested in fundamentally reforming or changing the system, but in making it work better by ensuring that it was more generously financed and supported, and as a result, some of them made more impact at the level of individual schools and classrooms than those few visionary ministers who were unable fully to deliver on their more broad-ranging programmes of reform.

These were the nine ministers who mattered most at Education, either as creative reformers or as successful fighters of their departmental corner in cabinet; the remaining 40, who made little impact, and who generally held office for brief duration, divide into two categories. There were those who were able, ambitious and determined on a major career, such as Augustine Birrell, Lord Halifax, Quintin Hogg, Michael Stewart, Anthony Crosland, Kenneth Clarke and Charles Clarke, who had their eye to the main chance and were eager to move on (and were happy to be moved on) to bigger and better things, and who in consequence made their most significant political impact after they had left Education rather than while they were there. The second category were those politicians of limited ability and aspiration, for whom running the Board or Ministry or Department of Education was either the summit of what they had hoped for, or of what they were allowed to achieve by their leader. In this category come figures such as Lord Eustace Percy, Sir Charles Trevelyan, Sir Edward Boyle, Mark Carlisle and John Patten: in every case, their political career culminated (or foundered) at Education, and fizzled out soon afterwards.

By comparison with the rest of Whitehall, a disproportionately large number of women have held the senior post at Education, amounting to seven in all since the Second World War. For Prime Ministers who felt the obligation to appoint a woman to their cabinet, Education was for a long time seen as the only place to put them. It was a 'domestic' portfolio, which seemed right for a woman, and in any case, a majority of teachers were women, too; whereas the other home departments were less appropriate. In the case of health, women were the nurses but the doctors who ran things were mostly men; and housing was about doing business with representatives of the male and macho construction industry. So these were no place for a female minister. Yet with only one extraordinary exception, and like many of the men who made little impact, the careers of the women who went to Education invariably fizzled out: Ellen Wilkinson, Florence Horsbrugh, Shirley Williams and Gillian Shephard never held office again, while Estelle Morris and Ruth Kelly did so only briefly.[4] The great exception (though Heath clearly did not expect her to be) was Margaret Thatcher: the only female education minister to hold major office thereafter, the only education minister of either gender to go on to be prime minister (though Halifax and Butler could probably have done so had they exerted their claims), and the only education minister of either gender to have had a degree in science.

Across the twentieth century, and taking the men and the women together, the sociological trajectory of those in charge of Education is familiar: from aristocracy, via the middle class, to a more varied social mix, including some from working class backgrounds. But during the whole of the time the Board and Ministry and Department have existed, the majority of those in charge of Education have had no first-hand experience of the schools over which they presided, and only a minority (Wilkinson, Stewart, Short, Shephard, Blunkett and Morris) had any direct experience of being trained or employed as a teacher (though only one of *them* appears in the top nine in charge of Education, so knowing the subject first-hand does not necessarily result in enhanced performance). Twelve of those in charge of Education had studied history at university: more than any other subject. Two more, H.A.L. Fisher and Lord Stanhope, were respectively a distinguished and a devoted practitioner of the subject. But only two of them tried to do anything special for history in schools, and in neither case did they succeed: Fisher was eager to improve and promote history teaching, but his initiative did not survive the post-war cuts in government spending and his own departure from office; Kenneth Baker wanted history to be included in the National Curriculum as a compulsory subject up to the age of 16, but that did not in the end happen.

A further reason why most ministers in charge of Education have come and gone with bewildering and excessive rapidity, is that for the most part, the pace of change in educational matters has itself been very slow (which is also why ministers should be prepared to stay in post for a long time, but why they generally do not wish to do so). It took from 1918 to 1947 to raise the school leaving age from 14 to 15, and from 1947 to 1973 to raise it again to 16, since when there has been no change whatsoever. In the same way, long periods of retrenchment have been interspersed with long periods of growing expenditure: inter-war economy, then more money in the 1950s and 1960s, followed by severe cuts in the 1970s and 1980s, and then by more money again during the 1990s and 2000s. And there have been conventional wisdoms and shared assumptions which have also defined and united successive (and overlapping) generations of educationalists and policy makers: from the 1900s to the 1930s, the primacy of elementary education; from the mid 1930s to the mid 1960s the importance of a tripartite secondary system; from the early 1960s to the mid 1980s the belief in comprehensive schools; from the mid 1980s to the mid 2000s a concern for standards, targets, performance and accountability; and since then a concern with the creation of academies and the freeing of schools from local authority control.

One reason why the dynamic of educational reform is so slow is that it proceeds by a gradual (and often unacknowledged) pattern of inter-generational evolution and broad political consensus. To be sure, education has on occasions been a source of bitter, significant and lasting controversy, from the debates on the Balfour Bill in the early 1900s to those on the National Curriculum in the 1980s. But in general, educational reform in the twentieth century has proceeded with some measure of agreement, co-operation and common ground. Both the Fisher and the Butler Education Acts were passed at times of coalition governments when party warfare was largely in abeyance. The comprehensive school revolution of the 1960s and 1970s required no major piece of legislation, and it was supported or passively acquiesced in by Labour and Conservative governments alike. The push towards a national curriculum was initiated by a Labour Prime Minister, but it was subsequently carried into law by a Conservative government. And today, there is probably a greater degree of agreement between the coalition and Labour front benches on educational policy, at least regarding schools, than either would publicly be prepared to admit.

Taking the long view, those in charge of education have reflected opinion much more often than they have tried to lead it, many have simply wanted to keep the show on the road, and even those who had higher ambitions rarely achieved all that they set out to do. Time and again, there was, and there still is a big discrepancy between what ministers ideally want to achieve, and what they can realistically accomplish, between intention and realization. And despite a few outstanding exceptions, too many of those in charge of Education have had no strong personal interest in the subject, and the average calibre of ministers has not been high. Estelle Morris (who did know something about the subject) resigned because she did not think she was up to the job. She was far from being unusual in not being up to the job; where she was both unique and admirable was in having the courage and the self-knowledge to own up to it.

During the first half of the twentieth century, some mandarins at the Board or Ministry or Department, such as Sir Robert Morant, or Sir Maurice Holmes, were major players across Whitehall: 'statesmen in disguise', supporting and sometimes dominating their minister, and driving policy forward under the guise of civil service impartiality. And just occasionally, the whole department has been engaged in and energized for reform, as was certainly the case in 1944 and again in the mid 1960s. But since the Second World War, the senior civil servants have tended to be closer to the educational professionals, the HMIs and local authorities, and have been less engaged with, and wielded less influence across, Whitehall more generally. One indication of this tendency towards marginalized departmental introversion is that just as many ministers have failed to go on from Education to higher things in government, few senior civil servants have gone on from Education to wield power at the very heart of government, in the Treasury, the Cabinet Office or the Home Office. Nowadays, Education is a big department, but it also remains in some ways a curiously isolated one.

Such has been the structure of power and authority in education in England across the twentieth century. Successive governments provided funding, often at levels deemed inadequate, and occasionally sought to restructure a system that was so varied and localized that it scarcely deserved to be called a 'system' at all. Moreover, until the 1980s, governments of all political persuasions believed it was not their job or responsibility to interfere in local decisions about what should be taught in schools, or how it should be taught; and even though this changed in 1988, with the establishment of the National Curriculum, this still left heads and teachers with considerable freedom as to what they could teach. It is in this broader political and administrative context that history as a taught subject in the classrooms of English schools needs to be set and understood, for it is this context which in many ways sets the limits to what was educationally possible in history or in any other subject, and that is why we have devoted such attention to it in the foregoing pages.

Continuity and Change in History Teaching

In the aftermath of the First World War, when the school leaving age had just been raised to 14, the advice given by the Board of Education was that history in schools should begin with the telling of stories to infants, and should gradually develop into something more rigorous and substantial; and that in so doing it should provide an outline history of the nation across the centuries, but it should also be concerned with Europe and the wider world. In the aftermath of the establishment (and revision) of the National Curriculum in the early 1990s, the compulsory study of history in the classroom still ended at 14, and the declared aim was that history in schools should begin with the telling of stories to infants, and should gradually develop into something more rigorous and substantial; and that in so doing it should provide an outline history of the nation across the centuries, but it should also be concerned with Europe and the wider world. Here is one measure of how little has changed in the history that has been taught in English schools, and the pupils to whom it has been taught. For most of them, across the twentieth century, the history education they have received has terminated at 14 – or earlier. To be sure, more pupils than ever since the Second World War have studied history beyond the age of 14 and taken examinations in it, but this has not been – and is not – true of the majority.

Here is another significant continuity. Across the whole of the twentieth century, there is abundant evidence that history has been badly taught by bad teachers in bad schools (and on occasions badly taught in good schools, too), which might be elementary, primary, grammar, secondary modern or comprehensives. Across the decades, the reports of HMIs often deplore uninspired teaching, unengaged pupils, out-of-date textbooks, and a lack of library and other resources. And these depressing revelations are corroborated by the many unhappy recollections of former pupils: the teachers were boring and uninspiring, 'chalk-and-talk' meant the excruciating tedium of rote learning; the same period was taught again and again with no sense of progression; 'progressive' history was vague and disjointed; such history as was learned in school was immediately forgotten thereafter; and having left school, there was no incentive to reconnect with the subject in later life. At the tenth annual meeting of the Historical Association, held in London in January 1916, Miss Spalding noted that there was 'a grave tendency amongst grown up people to be shocked that children did not know all that the grown ups thought they ought to know', and little has changed in the intervening decades.[5]

Yet across the whole of the twentieth century, there is also abundant evidence that history has been well taught by good teachers in good schools (and on occasions well taught in bad schools, too), which might be elementary, primary, grammar, secondary modern or comprehensives. Across the decades, the reports of HMIs often acclaim inspired teaching, engaged pupils, excellent text books, and an abundance of library and other resources. And these encouraging revelations are corroborated by the many happy recollections of former pupils: the teachers were engaging and inspiring; 'chalk-and-talk' meant the telling of enthralling stories; there was a real sense of chronological and intellectual progression across the school years; 'progressive' history was liberating and exciting; such history as was learned in school was long remembered thereafter; and having left school, there was every incentive to stay with the subject as a lifelong interest. The number and proportion of those who were excited by history at school, and who remained captivated by it thereafter, is no easier to quantify than the number who were positively repelled or merely indifferent. But they, too, have always been there.

It is easy and also important to make the point that history has always been well taught and has always been badly taught in English schools (and no doubt the same may be said of other countries, too); but it is less easy to agree on what the criteria of evaluation are, or on which of them are the most important, or even on how some of them can be assessed. An HMI report might applaud the history teaching in a certain school, yet also regret that the examinations results were not good enough. A teacher might feel he or she was doing an excellent job, instructing pupils in some of the essential names and dates in the national story; but the class might be bored, inattentive and unappreciative. Pupils might recall that they had greatly enjoyed their history lessons, but this could have been because they had had a good time in the classroom, yet didn't learn (or remember) much about the past. At schools as at universities, the connection between a high level of student satisfaction and getting a good education, in history or any other subject, is not straightforward. Being well taught might mean getting a good basis of factual knowledge, or acquiring certain skills and sensibilities, or being good at passing examinations. And does someone who has recently obtained an A grade at A Level today know as much history as someone who was awarded an A grade 30 years ago? That is an easy question to ask, but it is exceptionally difficult to answer.

These continuities and contrasts in the practices of teaching history and the experiences of being taught history have been replicated in other ways. There have been those who stress the importance of dates and monarchs, and those who dismiss this as a meaningless accumulation of numbers and names. There have been those who advocate the importance of political and constitutional history, and those who urge the competing claims of economic or social history. There have been those who favoured national history, and those who have stressed the alternative claims of local history, or of imperial or European or global history. There have been those who have urged the need to take the long view, to get a sense of the historical process unfolding across the centuries, and those who insist on the need to focus in depth on short periods, using documents and original sources. There have been those who lament that the same period is studied too often, and those who urge that this concentration and focus leads to greater knowledge and understanding. There have been those who stress that history is about acquiring specific knowledge of the past, and those who insist that it is about cultivating sensibilities and acquiring skills that are independent of particular detail. There are those who believe that young people learn most of their history in school, and those who believe that they get more of it from what they do and see and learn and experience outside.

In the same way, there are those who believe that the purpose of teaching history is to inculcate a love of country, and those who believe that it cannot do that, and/or that it should not even try to do that. In 1830, S.T. Coleridge called for a system of national education which would 'form and train up the people of the country to be obedient, free, useful and organizable subjects, citizens and patriots, living to the benefit of the state and prepared to die in its defence'.[6] That was also the belief of Stalin in Russia 100 years later, and it is clearly shared by his successors in the Kremlin today. Yet such a view almost certainly exaggerates the importance and impact of school teaching in forming adult attitudes to political issues, and in this country it has generally been frowned upon by most politicians and civil servants. To be sure, Lord Meath, King George V and Winston Churchill lamented that the history taught in schools was insufficiently rousing, uplifting, patriotic and imperial. But for the most part, the official view has been that school was a place for teaching national history but *not* for teaching national propaganda. On the whole, it 'wasn't pushed' in the classroom.[7] That was what Communists and Fascists did, and other dictatorial regimes; but it was not done, and it should not be done, here. That is why, and like their colleagues in all other subjects, history teachers are employed by schools, and are not agents of the state.

As the foregoing paragraphs make plain, the discussion of history teaching in schools has always been, and is still now, often over-dichotomized and polarized – between (for example) national or global history, the recent or the more distant past, dates and facts or ideas and concepts, content versus skills, knowledge versus empathy. This adversarial way of looking at history in the classroom reflects both the partisan manner in which politicians so often present their policies, and also the disputatious approach that many university-based historians take to their subject – debating whether it is an art or a science, concerned with analysis or narrative, stressing continuity or change, focusing on the general or the particular, or written for a professional or lay audience.[8] Yet much of this polarization is at the level of polemic, theory and pedagogy, and there is rather less of it in the classroom and in practice, where most teachers would probably agree that history should be both national and global, concerned with the recent and the distant past, about dates and facts as well as ideas and concepts, teaching content and skills, and imparting knowledge and cultivating empathy. As our own surveys repeatedly make plain, there is more common ground among many history teachers than the debates in their professional journals sometimes suggests.

Of course, it is very encouraging that there is so much professional and public engagement in current debates about history in schools – and the fact that there is no equivalently engaged debate for any other subject is a further sign of the particular resonance of history (and, it bears repeating, not just in this country but in many others, too). All the participants share the view that history is important, that we need to know about the past both for its own sake and for the perspective it affords on the present. Yet it is ironic that much of the discussion about the teaching of history in schools is itself extraordinarily a-historical. In two recent issues of the *London Review of Books*, some distinguished historians (inconclusively) debated skills versus knowledge, apparently unaware that such matters have been (inconclusively) debated for over 80 years. Another distinguished historian recently published an article in the *Guardian*, claiming that 'history has never been so unpopular in British schools'.[9] But it is difficult to see what evidence could be mobilized to support this tendentious and alarmist claim. Indeed, too much of the current discussion of history in schools assumes that there was once a golden age from which we have recently fallen perilously away. But as we have sought to show, no such golden age in history teaching or in history learning has ever in fact existed.[10]

One of the purposes of history is to provide perspective, and this book has sought to offer just such a perspective on the current discussions on the teaching of history in English state schools. But history also enjoins us to keep a sense of proportion, and that, too, has often been lacking, especially in much of the mainstream media, which delights in scare stories, and stray facts with no context, and prefers to intensify disagreement rather than to explore common ground. Yet it cannot be too often repeated that debate and anxiety and hope about teaching history in schools is not confined to these shores. It is also important to remember that there has never been a time when parents have not deplored the fact that their children do not know enough history, especially of their own country. Nor has such ignorance been confined to history. How many people can name ten plays that Shakespeare wrote, or ten novels that Dickens authored? Or locate the Falkland Islands on a map, or remember the height of Mount Everest? Or recite the second law of thermodynamics, or tell their femur from their tibia? There is a great deal of human knowledge than most of us do not know, and part of that unknown knowledge is inescapably about the past. Of course we should never cease to teach and learn and know more history, but let us keep the perspective and proportion that history constantly enjoins.

There is, then, more continuity to many of the issues surrounding the teaching of history in English schools than is often known or readily recognized. But two massively significant changes also merit attention, not least because their consequences for history in the classroom are still not yet fully worked out. The first is that it has only been in the second half of the twentieth century that the issue arose of what sort of schools, what sort of education, and what sort of examinations should be provided for all those boys and girls now staying on for longer than ever before – initially to the age of 15, and subsequently to the age of 16. The decision by the state to assume responsibility for the compulsory mass education of adolescents after the Second World War was something wholly without precedent, as was the undertaking to provide a tripartite system of secondary education and, when that was deemed not to have worked, a comprehensive system. The extended debates and discussions concerning the type of history to be taught in these schools, and to those greater numbers who chose to study it at 15 and above, which became so important from the 1960s onwards, need to be understood in the context of these broader developments.

This country has only had a mass system of education for those aged 15–16 for the last half a century, which means it is still in its early stages and surely has not yet reached a fixed or settled form. Even more recent, more transformative, and more incomplete has been the impact across the last 30 years of the revolution in ICT. As with the advent of mass education for adolescents, this is not a development confined to the teaching of history in schools, and nor is it restricted to this country. But there can be no doubt that as a result, both inside the classroom and beyond, children today engage with history, and apprehend the past by a range of virtual, digital, visual and electronic means that were simply unimaginable a generation ago. Taking the long view, this is bound to have a greater impact in the classroom than the imposition of a National Curriculum – in history or indeed in any other subject. But it is too soon to know whether it will do away with teachers telling stories about the past, or whether it will make the telling of such stories seem more necessary and more important, not less. All that can be hazarded by way of prediction is that there are more transformative times ahead, and the impact of the next generation of innovative technology on history teaching will once again be massive – and in ways that cannot yet be foreseen.

History, the Curriculum and the Classroom Future

One of the purposes of this book has been to make plain the astonishing array of different forces and circumstances which help determine the sort of history and the quality of history that a particular teacher will actually teach to a group of pupils in an individual classroom. These include, in varying combinations, the policies and resources emanating from central government, the degree of support from the local authority, the location and quality of the school, the amount of time available in the timetable, the skill and commitment of the teacher, the background and interest of the pupils, the extent to which they engage with history outside the classroom as well as inside, and the availability of textbooks, worksheets and ICT. One conclusion to be drawn is that the best way to ensure that history (or, indeed, any other subject) is well taught is to ensure that it is taught in schools that are well funded, well resourced, well managed, and well led. A second, which is abundantly supported by the majority of those whom we have interviewed and who have filled in our forms, is that it is the teacher above all who makes the difference. The more encouragement and support teachers can be given, in history or any other subject, to get on with their job, the better.

Where, then, does the National Curriculum for history fit into this? The answer to that question is not as straightforward as it might seem: for whatever the problems that history in schools is currently facing, it is not clear that the solution is to redesign the National Curriculum yet again, even though there seems a strong temptation in some quarters to believe that the National Curriculum is both the problem and the solution, and successive governments seem unable to resist the temptation to keep tinkering with it. In recent years, distinguished historians have come up with their own appropriately enthralling versions of what a National Curriculum in history might look like.[11] But in fact the current version covers a long, sequential span of the nation's history from early times to the present, and there is ample provision for European history across a similarly broad span and of the history of the world beyond, which seems appropriate for the multi-cultural and globally connected society that our nation now is. Perhaps too much attention is given to the bleaker side of history (the slave trade and the Holocaust), and insufficient to the triumphs of the human spirit; but on the whole it is a well-meant and well-balanced outline.

The main problems – and they are real – lie elsewhere. First, and as successive Ofsted reports have revealed, the coherence of the curriculum on paper often fails to translate into coherence in the classroom, as too many unconnected topics are taught, sometimes not even in chronological sequence, and often with no sense of how they relate to each other. This in turn arises from the relentless pressure on the timetable: as new subjects are embraced or imposed, and as the time allocated to history becomes correspondingly less, the temptation to abandon broad chronology and the big picture in favour of discrete and unrelated topics grows ever stronger. A second difficulty is that the National Curriculum in history ends at age 14, which means that too much is crammed in to Key Stage 3, and that there is no connection with, or input into, the syllabuses that are taught for GCSE, which may merely repeat what has already been taught. A third issue is the secretive and unaccountable nature of the examining boards for GCSE and at A Level, and their close connection with publishers, as in the case of Pearson and Edexcel, along with the stress on league tables of results, which discourage some schools from entering their pupils for examinations such as history which are perceived to be 'difficult'.[12]

In the light of these concerns, our recommendations are few and straightforward. To begin with, and as was originally intended when the National Curriculum was created, we urge that history should be made a compulsory subject in all state schools until the age of 16. This would place our nation for the first time on an equal footing with most others in Europe, and it should also help ensure that history is studied for an appropriate amount of time in schools where it is at present hard-pressed, and it would then be taught in schools which at present do not teach it because it might depress their performance in the examination league tables. Making history compulsory to the age of 16 would also ensure that a fully integrated curriculum could be devised across Key Stages 3 and 4, which would lessen the likelihood of repetition, uncrowd the syllabus, and ensure all boys and girls were able to study history at a relatively advanced age, when they might benefit most from doing so. It would also, and for the first time, establish a close connection between the National Curriculum in history and the GCSE examinations in the subject, and this should be made the occasion for an inquiry into the functioning and regulation of the examination boards: how much are they profit-making businesses, and how much are they disinterested agencies of evaluation and accreditation?

The lack of official interest in the workings of GCSE and A Level examinations in history is one of the regrettable consequences of the fact that the National Curriculum in history currently ends at age 14. For it is not just that the GCSE needs to be integrated into the National Curriculum and that the financial and assessment activities of examining bodies need to be investigated: there should also be serious scrutiny of the papers the examining boards offer, and more effort made to ensure that schools do not repeat the same topics or periods at A Level that have already been studied and sat for GCSE. If the GCSE became the final two years' work in the National Curriculum, then most of the examinations would be some aspects of modern British, European and world history. It ought then to be made impossible to repeat these courses at A Level, except in very exceptional circumstances, and boards and schools should be encouraged to offer a broader chronological range of papers and courses than many at present do. And at both GCSE and A Level, greater attention should be given to the balance between course work and examinations, and the extent to which modularization has undermined coherent and continuous learning, and essay-writing skills. Here are important areas needing official investigation.

Nor is the position of history in primary schools all that satisfactory – especially bearing in mind that under the present arrangements, most pupils may spend more time learning history as infants and juniors at Key Stages 1 and 2 than they do at secondary school in Key Stage 3. But in recent times, history in primary school seems to have slipped back from its improved position in the years immediately after the introduction of the National Curriculum, and this needs investigation; as does what appears to be the inadequate level of support given to primary teachers who are no experts in the subject, but who would like to do more and do it better. Here, as often, the two recent Ofsted reports contain much good sense and give much wise advice. All they lack is a broader temporal perspective than the three-year cycles on which they operate. The earlier *Suggestions* and *Recommendations* about history in the classroom emanating from the Board or Ministry of Education often began with a historical survey. It might be too much to ask Ofsted to incorporate such perspectives today. But all those at Ofsted and, more generally at the Department of Education, who are concerned about history in schools would do well to read the earlier official publications, and also as many of the HMIs' reports from earlier decades, as they can.

For anyone who cares about the teaching of history in schools, be they ministers or civil servants, inspectors or educationalists, teachers or parents, the main concern must be to do more to ensure that there is sufficient time in the classroom, and the necessary continuity across the years from five to sixteen, to make it possible to convey not only the excitement and allure of the subject, but also to establish some broad chronology and to outline at least some part of the big picture. That may be the aim of the National Curriculum in history, but much more needs to be done than is being done (and can be done) at present to ensure that it is fully and properly realized. Now that it is possible to look up the names and dates of all the country's kings and queens on Google or Wikipedia, and more generally to access information about the past in unprecedented quantities and overwhelming abundance, the need to provide boys and girls with some sort of broad framework and long perspective on the past is more urgent than ever. Insofar as they relate to the study of history in the classroom, all timetabling, all teaching, all curricula, all examining should be devoted to fulfilling that overriding purpose.

Beyond that, we offer suggestions relating to the broader contexts and constraints for history or any other taught subject in schools, beginning with Westminster and Whitehall. We cannot urge too strongly that those politicians in charge of Education should be kept in post for much longer than the pitifully inadequate average time of two years, so that they can master their portfolio, get to know their civil servants, engage with the broader educational community, and ensure their department has a serious agenda on which they mean to deliver, in terms both of resources and initiatives. But there is no point in ministers staying longer if they are not up to the job, and so we also urge that in future, more serious attention should be given than has too often been the case in the past to the qualifications and appropriateness and experience of those who are appointed to be in charge. There also needs to be a broader appreciation, in Whitehall and Westminster, and in the world beyond, of the limits to what can be achieved, even by the most energetic, creative, resourceful and long-serving minister in charge of Education. We also suggest that the civil servants in the Department of Education need to be less bunkered and blinkered, and become more integrated with their colleagues elsewhere in Whitehall.

Our second broad recommendation (which must, perforce, be no more than a wish) is the need to raise the standard of public discussion about education in general, and about history in schools in particular. There can be no more important subject in any country than the education of the next generation, but the current discussion rarely rises to an appropriate level of well-informed or responsible seriousness. Moreover, there is something peculiarly sad and unhelpful about an older generation denouncing the alleged educational shortcomings of a younger generation, when it is the very older generation which is itself responsible for these alleged shortcomings. To be sure, there are serious matters of concern, and in the case of history teaching we have sought to identify them and to suggest ways of dealing with them. But across much of the media, there is too much talk of crisis, too much irresponsible scare mongering, too much adversarial polarization of views, insufficient awareness of what is happening elsewhere in the world, and a reprehensible lack of the sort of historical perspective we have sought to provide in this book for the teaching of history, and which urgently needs to be provided for other subjects, too.

We end with words about history from the people who matter most, namely teachers and pupils, and they are, appropriately and by turn encouraging, cautionary and exhilarating. Here is an upbeat view of the status of the subject in the classroom today: 'History is quite good at adapting; it has had to ... In many schools, history remains the most popular optional subject, despite everything that is thrown at it. It is resilient in that sense.'[13] Here is a second opinion, confident and committed, yet also expressing serious and well-justified anxiety:

History's a popular and successful subject in my school ... because the department is well qualified, bright, hard working, stable and innovative ... It's the most popular option at GCSE ... However, such is the hold of exam league tables that the pressure is now on to not let students who would get below a [grade] C do it. Unless the league table madness diminishes soon, I can see a whole category of child being disenfranchised from history.[14]

And here, finally, is a recollection of a former pupil who, encountering one sinister and significant survival from the past in tangible, physical form, suddenly remembered the history she had been taught in class, and understood why it mattered:

> We went to Germany on holiday, and we visited Dachau Concentration Camp ... And I think it, in some ways, brought to life my history ... That was after I'd done O level and had given up history ... we'd been told about the gas chambers and all this. And then to see them, you think, 'Ah yes ... that's what she was telling us about'; so that was good.[15]

Appendixes

A. Names of Interviewees
B. Names of Lenders and Donors
C. School Certificate Examinations in History in 1923
D. History Syllabuses from the 1970s Onwards
E. History Examination Candidates and Results, 1919–2010
F. Principal Education Ministers, 1900–2010
G. The History in Education Website

Appendix A: Names of Interviewees[*]

Secretaries of State:
Kenneth Baker, Lord Baker of Dorking
David Blunkett, MP
Kenneth Clarke, MP
John MacGregor, Lord MacGregor of Pulham Market
Estelle Morris, Baroness Morris of Yardley
Gillian Shephard, Baroness Shephard of Northwold

Her Majesty's Inspectors of Schools:
John Hamer
Scott Harrison
Roger Hennessey (also key HMI for the National Curriculum Working
    Group)
Michael Maddison

Local Authority Advisers:
Ian Coulson
Tim Lomas
Andy Reid (also former member of the National Curriculum Council)

Higher Education:
Ros Ashby (teacher training)
David Burrell (teacher training)
Eric Evans (examinations)
Alan Farmer (teacher training)
Penelope Harnett (teacher training)
Peter Lee (teacher training)
Jon Nichol (teacher training)

National Curriculum History Working Group (1989–90):
Chris Culpin (also text book author and former Director of SHP)
Gareth Elwyn Jones (teacher trainer, also on Welsh History Committee)
Peter Marshall (academic)
Ann Low-Beer (teacher training)

Schools History Project:
Ian Dawson
Michael Riley
Denis Shemilt
David Sylvester

[*]   Some interviews were conducted with pairs or groups of interviewees.

Extra-curricular history:
David Anderson (museum education)
Nick Whines (broadcasting)

Teachers:
Doug Belshaw
Simon Bishop
John D. Clare (also text book author)
Patricia A. Dawson
John Edgar
John Heffernan
Evelyn Hinde
Chris Hinton
Michael Hinton
John Hite
Eric Houlder
Darren Hughff
Diana Laffin
Katy Main
Chris McGovern
John Simkin (also text book and website developer)
Rob Snow
Linda Turner
Maggie Wilson
Roberta Wood

Trainee teachers:
Ruth Blower
Candice Brockwell
Daniel Burke
Steve Loman
Charlotte Newton
Ben Turner
Katherine Tunnadine
Ben Wells

Pupils:
Marian Clarke
Pat Dawson
Enid Deeble
Ernie Dodd
Irene Eaton

Sarah Ensor
Bill Endersby
Rosa Friend
John Geddes
D.B. Gordon
Kenneth Kelsey
Kathryn Ingram
Christine Jackson
Sheila Kotak
Ceril Little
Derek Little
Rosa Major
David Newham
Bridget Phillipson, MP
Norman Roper
Annie Whitehead
Anon.

Appendix B: Names of Lenders and Donors

Of educational resources and materials:
Ian Colwill
Ian Fell
Robert Guyver
Val Gwynn
Roy Lewis
Terry Marston
Andy Reid
John T. Smith
Nick Whines

Of school work or other school materials:
Jillian Andrews
Michael Andrews
Ray Andrews
Audrey Brown
David Cannadine
Marian Clarke
Ian Colwill
Charlotte Crow
Enid Deeble
Ernie Dodd
Irene Eaton
Bill Endersby
Sarah Ensor
Rosa Friend
John Geddes
Sue Hardiman
John Hite
Kathryn Ingham
Julie Johnson
Kenneth Kelsey
Kirran Klein
Muriel Longhurst
Holly Mulvihill
Bridget Phillipson
Norman Roper
Monica Wafford
Annie Whitehead
John Yapp
Joan Young

Appendix C: School Certificate Examinations in History in 1923*

The following examination boards offered these history periods:

Oxford and Cambridge Joint Board
English   878–(1154–1216)–1485
               1461–(1529–1563)–1714
               1714–(1816–1854)–1901
The period in brackets is in each case a 'Special Period' within the corresponding longer periods.
A period of European History is allowed in place of a Special Period.

Oxford Locals
English   BC 55–1880
British Empire   1492–1784–1904
General   410–1215
                       1803–1880
France   1789–1914
USA   1783–1917
Greek History   BC 445–323
Roman History   BC 146–14

Cambridge Locals
English   1066–1485 ⎫
                       1485–1688 ⎬ any two
                       1688–1815 ⎪
                       1815–1914 ⎭
British Empire   1492–1914
European   1789–(1815–1878)–1910
Greek History
Roman History

Bristol
English   BC 55–1485 ⎫
                       1485–1714 ⎬ one or more
                       1688–1910 ⎭
Greek   up to BC 323
Roman   BC 753–AD 14

---

*   Board of Education, *Report on the Teaching of History* (London, 1923), Appendix II, p. 55. Compiled by SSEC Investigators in History in the First and Second Examinations.

Durham

English	BC 55–1603
	1453–1815
	1763–1919
English and European	1100–1500
	1600–1815
	1789–1919
Greek History	BC 594–404
Roman History	BC 264–49

Greek [527–431] together with Roman [133–49].

London

English   1066–1485 ⎫
                     1485–1685 ⎬ any two
                     1688–1901 ⎭

European   1789–1910

Ancient – General Course of Greek and Roman History and an outline of the earlier Monarchies.

Northern Joint Board

English   BC 55–1485 ⎫
                     1485–1714 ⎬ any two
                     1714–1902 ⎭

European   1756–1904

Ancient History of Greece and Rome

Appendix D: History Syllabuses from the 1970s Onwards

A Typical History Syllabus 11–16 in the 1970s

Age	Content Covered
11–12	Ancient World History to Norman Conquest
12–13	British, European and World History, 1066–1485
13–14	British, European and World History, 1485 to 17th, 18th or 19th century
14–16	*Either* Modern British History 1815–1945
	Or Modern British and European History 1789–1939
	Or British Social and Economic History 1700–1945
	Or Modern World History 1870–1945

Source: SCHP, *A New Look at History* (Holmes McDougall, 1976), p. 26.

The Schools Council History 13–16 Project Syllabus 1976

Framework of Syllabus	Example of Content for Trial Schools
Study in Development A study of the factors affecting the development of a topic through time.	Medicine
Enquiry in Depth A study of aspects of a period of the past involving imaginative reconstruction and contrast with the present.	*One of the following:* Elizabethan England 1558–1603 Britain 1815–1851 The American West 1840–1890
Studies in Modern World History Three studies on modern issues viewed historically.	*Three of the following:* The Rise of Communist China The Move to European Unity Arab-Israeli Conflict The Irish Question

Framework of Syllabus	Example of Content for Trial Schools
History Around Us A study of the history around us, using the visible evidence as the starting point. This will involve visits to sites.	One of the following: Prehistoric Britain Roman Britain Castles and fortified houses 1066–1550 Country houses 1550–1800 Church buildings and furnishings 1066–1900 Studies in the making of the rural landscape Town development and domestic architecture 1700 to the present Industrial Archaeology Aspects of the historical development of the locality

Source: SCHP, A New Look at History (Holmes McDougall, 1976), p. 20.

The National Curriculum for History March 1991 (Key Stages 1–3 only)*

Age	Core Study Units	Supplementary or Extension Units
Key Stage 1 (ages 5–7)	'Everyday life' in the past with a focus on changes in their own lives and their families', changes in British life since World War II and the way of life in a period beyond living memory; the lives of famous men and women; past and commemorated events, such as the Gunpowder Plot and the Olympic Games.	

Age	Core Study Units	Supplementary or Extension Units
Key Stage 2 (ages 7–11)	Invaders and Settlers (Romans, Anglo-Saxons & Vikings); Tudor and Stuart times; *either* Victorian Britain *or* Britain since 1930; Ancient Greece; Exploration and Encounters 1450–1550	A study of a topic over a long period (e.g. transport, houses & places of worship); A local history topic; A past non-European society (e.g. Ancient Egypt, the Indus Valley, the Aztecs, Benin)
Key Stage 3 (ages 11–14)	The Roman Empire; Medieval Realms: Britain 1066–1500; The Making of the United Kingdom: Crowns, Parliaments and Peoples 1500–1750; Expansion, Trade and Industry: Britain 1750–1900; The Era of the Second World War.	A depth or thematic study in British history (e.g. Castles & Cathedrals, the British Empire and its impact in late 19thC, Britain & the Great War 1914–1918); A turning point in European History (e.g. the Crusades, the French Revolution); A past non-European society (e.g. Imperial China, India under the Mughal Empire; indigenous peoples of North America; Black peoples of the Americas 16th–early 20thC).

Note: All of the mandatory study units and compulsory content are included, but some of the text has been summarized and some of the exemplar topics have been omitted.

Source: DES, *History in the National Curriculum (England)* (London, March 1991).

The National Curriculum for History 1995 (Dearing Review)*

Age	Study Units
Key Stage 1 (ages 5–7)	Everyday life in the past with a focus on changes in their own lives and their families' and the way of life in Britain in a period beyond living memory; the lives of famous men and women; past and commemorated events, such as the Gunpowder Plot and the Olympic Games.

Key Stage 2 (ages 7–11)	Romans, Anglo-Saxons & Vikings in Britain; Life in Tudor times; *either* Victorian Britain *or* Britain since 1930; Ancient Greece; A local history topic; A past non-European society (e.g. Ancient Egypt, the Indus Valley, the Aztecs, Benin).
Key Stage 3 (ages 11–14)	Medieval Realms: Britain 1066–1500; The Making of the United Kingdom: Crowns, Parliaments and Peoples 1500–1750; Britain 1750–circa 1900; The Twentieth-century World; An era or turning point in European History (e.g. the Crusades, the French Revolution); A past non-European society (e.g. Imperial China, India under the Mughal Empire; indigenous peoples of North America; Black peoples of the Americas 16th–early 20thC).

Note: All of the mandatory study units and compulsory content are included, but some of the text has been summarized and some of the exemplar topics have been omitted.

Source: DfES, *History in the National Curriculum: England* (London, 1995).

The National Curriculum for History 1999*

Age	Study Units
Key Stage 1 (ages 5–7)	Changes in their own lives and the way of life of their family or others around them; the way of life of people in the more distant past who lived in the local area or elsewhere in Britain; the lives of significant men, women and children from the history of Britain and the wider world; past and commemorated events, such as the Gunpowder Plot and the Olympic Games.
Key Stage 2 (ages 7–11)	Local history study; British history – Romans, Anglo-Saxons & Vikings in Britain; Britain and the wider world in Tudor times; *either* Victorian Britain *or* Britain since 1930; A European history study – Ancient Greece; A world history study (e.g. Ancient Egypt, the Indus Valley, the Aztecs, Benin).

Age	Study Units
Key Stage 3 (ages 11–14)	Britain 1066-1500; Britain 1500–1750; Britain 1750–1900; A European study before 1914 (a significant period or event); A world study before 1900 (a study of cultures, beliefs and achievements of an African, American, Asian or Australasian society); A world study after 1900 (twentieth-century world, including the two World Wars).

*Note: All of the mandatory study units and compulsory content are included, but some of the text has been summarized and some of the exemplar topics have been omitted.
Source: DfES/QCA History: The National Curriculum for England (London, 1999).

The 2007 National Curriculum for History Revision to Key Stage 3*

Key Stage 3 (ages 11–14)	British History: The development of political power from the Middle Ages to the twentieth century; the different histories and changing relationships of the peoples of England, Ireland, Scotland and Wales; The impact of the movement and settlement to, from and within the British Isles; Changes in lives, beliefs, ideas and attitudes of people in Britain and factors which have driven changes (e.g. technology, economic development, war, religion and culture; Trade, colonisation, industrialisation and technology, the British Empire and its impact in Britain and overseas, the slave trade, resistance and decolonisation. European and World History: The impact of significant political, social, cultural, religious, technological and/or economic developments and events on past European and world societies; The changing nature of conflict and cooperation between countries and peoples and its lasting impact on national, ethnic, racial, cultural and religious issues, including the two world wars and the Holocaust and the role of European and international institutions in resolving conflicts.

*Note: All of the mandatory study units and compulsory content are included, but some of the text has been summarized and some of the exemplar topics have been omitted.

Source: QCA, History: Programme of Study for Key Stage 3 and Attainment Target (London, 2007).

Appendix E: History Examination Candidates and Results, 1919–2010

History Examination Results 1919–1950

First Examination (School Certificate)

Year	Total Entries	% offering history	% passes with credit
1919	25,539	88.8	57.0
1922	37,911	87.8	48.1
1924	45,797	92.8	49.2
1926	48,084	89.8	44.5
1927	48,366	88.0	42.3
1928	49,377	87.8	48.3
1929	52,024	87.3	48.6
1930	55,148	87.4	48.1
1931	58,217	87.0	49.4
1932	60,298	87.0	47.6
1933	58,465	85.5	48.5
1934	56,179	84.6	49.6
1935	58,568	83.5	49.1
1936	64,553	84.0	49.2
1937	63,397	82.0	49.7
1938	62,690	81.4	49.6
NB No results statistics relating to subjects appear to have been published for the war years and immediately after			
1947	87,113	81.1	46.7
1948	91,729	81.0	47.2
1949	92,441	80.5	47.1
1950	79,697	79.8	46.5

Notes:

1. These statistics relate to schools in England and Wales.
2. These statistics cover all schools, state and independent.
3. The passes given are for those who passed 'with credit' – a higher level than a pass. The Board of Education did not issue figures for individual subject pass rates without credit.

Sources: Reports of the Board of Education from 1925–26 up to 1950.

History Examination Results 1951-2010

Year	O level History Total Entries	% pass rate			Year	GCSE History Total Entries	% pass rate (A*-C grade)
1951	66,250	57.2					
1952	69,160	57.9			1988	217,300	45.2
1953	81,770	58.4			1989	218,380	47.6
1954	82,417	58.4			1990	195,680	49.2
1955	84,538	60.4			1991	190,680	52.0
1956	86,547	59.3			1992	188,008	52.4
1957	85,631	57.8			1993	195,737	53.7
1958	95,133	57.4			1994	207,350	54.2
1959	108,604	58.1			1995	223,357	53.5
1960	118,671	57.2			1996	212,407	55.7
1961	120,413	58.4	CSE History Total Entries	% Grade 1	1997	207,486	56.8
1962	134,086	58.6			1998	189,070	58.3
1963	159,844	57.8			1999	188,934	60.2
1964	157,795	55.5			2000	190,300	61.3
1965	145,633	56.5	16,743	9.0	2001	195,200	61.3
1966	140,915	56.9	35,704	12.0	2002	194,000	62.1
1967	139,113	55.7	48,471	12.8	2003	194,800	63.5
1968	138,785	55.5	58,665	13.8	2004	205,500	64.2
1969	129,247	57.5	67,941	14.2	2005	204,200	66.0
1970	128,548	57.5	73,832	14.9	2006	208,100	66.1
1971	128,190	57.8	79,150	14.7	2007	204,300	67.2
1972	130,061	58.8	90,081	15.5	2008	204,000	67.9
1973	131,594	58.4	94,329	15.3	2009	197,800	69.1
1974	138,581	57.4	132,772	13.3	2010	198,800	70.2
1975	142,511	58.1	140,246	14.0			
1976	149,242	57.0	144,486	14.8			
1977	143,327	57.4	156,846	13.8			
1978	135,181	57.2	159,476	13.6			
1979	135,458	58.0	164,038	13.3			
1980	No data		No data				
1981	129,991	58.8	174,511	13.5			
1982	132,404	58.4	174,703	12.7			
1983	125,932	59.9	176,821	13.5			
1984	124,053	59.4	173,727	13.8			
1985	126,609	57.0	163,058	15.3			
1986/87	No data		No data				

Notes on CSE/O level/GCSE data:

1. Many schools entered candidates for both CSE and O level.

2. Web-based data from 2000 onwards.

3. These statistics cover England & Wales until 1977; from 1978, England only.

4. These statistics cover all schools, state and independent.

Sources:

CSE/O level

Reports of the Ministry of Education and the Statistics of Public Education for England and Wales, 1951–1960.

Statistics of Education 1961–79 (England & Wales 1961–77, England only 1978 onwards) and Statistics of School Leavers CSE and GCE England 1980–96.

GCSE

Statistics of Education School Examinations GCSE and GCE 1991.

Statistics of Education Public Examinations GCSE and GCE 1992–2000.

Web data for 2000–09 at http://www.education.gov.uk/rsgateway/DB/SFR (accessed 24–26.02.1020).

History Examination Results 1919–1950

Second Examination (Higher School Certificate)

Year	Total Entries	% offering history	% pass rate
1920	472	14.8	85.0
1926	2,673	34.4	77.9
1927	2,819	34.5	78.1
1928	3,067	35.4	79.7
1929	2,981	32.8	79.1
1930	3,187	33.2	77.5
1931	3,524	32.0	76.5
1932	4,015	32.5	75.0
1933	4,291	33.1	75.3
1934	4,023	32.4	74.4
1935	3,645	32.0	75.3
1936	3,443	30.6	75.5
1937	3,579	29.9	75.2
1938	3,880	29.4	79.5
NB No results statistics relating to subjects appear to have been published			
for the war years and immediately after			
1947	7,442	28.3	79.5
1948	8,775	29.5	77.6
1949	9,278	28.4	77.2
1950	9,833	28.6	77.6

Notes:

1. These statistics relate to schools in England and Wales.

2. These statistics cover all schools, state and independent.

Sources: Reports of the Board of Education from 1925–26 up to 1950.

History Examination Results 1951–2010

A level History

Year	Total Entries	% pass rate	Year	Total Entries	% pass rate
1951	10,230	77.2	1981	36,060	69.5
1952	9,299	76.9	1982	37,768	69.8
1953	9,926	75.7	1983	38,145	69.6
1954	10,200	75.9	1984	36,870	69.9
1955	11,217	76.3	1985	35,075	69.8
1956	11,997	75.1	1986	27,050	77.0
1957	12,931	74.7	1987	28,670	78.8
1958	13,549	74.0	1988	27,190	81.9
1959	13,766	72.2	1989	29,570	81.7
1960	15,685	71.8	1990	31,040	84.6
1961	17,831	73.8	1991	30,160	85.7
1962	20,177	71.7	1992	32,643	83.7
1963	21,768	73.1	1993	32,811	84.5
1964	25,159	71.0	1994	31,954	85.4
1965	30,580	71.4	1995	32,129	87.1
1966	31,043	71.6	1996	32,867	87.2
1967	32,691	72.4	1997	33,035	87.6
1968	34,377	72.7	1998	31,627	88.5
1969	35,146	71.4	1999	33,420	88.4
1970	34,956	70.6	2000	33,140	89.2
1971	35,992	72.5	2001	34,001	89.2
1972	36,439	71.6	2002	35,132	97.5
1973	36,271	71.5	2003	36,513	98.3
1974	36,374	71.3	2004	38,150	98.2
1975	36,290	71.4	2005	39,199	98.2
1976	37,891	70.9	2006	40,673	98.2
1977	39,166	71.7	2007	40,542	98.5
1978	35,765	70.6	2008	42,107	98.9
1979	35,228	68.9	2009	42,842	99.2
1980	No Data		2010	45,146	99.2

Notes:
1. 1951–77 for England and Wales. 2. 1978 onwards England only. 3. 1986–91 data for 'school leavers' all ages. 4. 1991–9 cover 17 year olds in English schools, sixth form and FE colleges. 5. 1999–2010 cover 16–18 year olds in all schools and colleges in England. 6. Figures for 2002 onwards relate to A2 pass rates only. Under Curriculum 2000, candidates with weak grades at AS tend not to continue to A2, thus boosting the pass rate of the latter. 7. These statistics cover all schools, state and independent.

Sources:
Reports of the Ministry of Education and the Statistics of Public Education for England and Wales, 1951–1960. Statistics of Education 1961–79 (England & Wales 1966–77, England only 1978 onwards) and Statistics of School Leavers CSE and GCE England 1980–93. Statistics of Education School/Public Examinations GCSE and GCE in England: Statistical Volume 1991–2000 (Government Statistical Service 1994–8, Office of National Statistics 1999–2000). Data for A level 199902009 taken from www.education.gov.uk/rsgateway/DB/SFR (accessed 24-16.02.2010).

Appendix F: Principal Education Ministers, 1900–2010

Name	School	University	Date of Appointment	Party of Government
President of the Board of Education				
Duke of Devonshire	Eton	Cambridge	1 April 1900	Conservative
Marquis of Londonderry	Eton	Oxford	8 August 1902	Conservative
Augustine Birrell	Amersham Hall	Cambridge	10 December 1905	Liberal
Reginald McKenna	King's College	London	23 January 1907	Liberal
Walter Runciman	South Shields HS	Cambridge (history)	12 April 1908	Liberal
Joseph Pease	Tottenham	Cambridge	23 October 1911	Liberal
Arthur Henderson	Elementary		25 May 1915	Coalition (Labour)
Marquis of Crewe	Harrow	Cambridge	18 August 1916	Coalition (Liberal)
H.A.L. Fisher	Winchester	Oxford	10 December 1916	Coalition (Liberal)
Edward Wood (later Lord Irwin)	Eton	Oxford (history)	24 October 1922	Conservative
Charles Trevelyan	Harrow	Cambridge (history)	22 January 1924	Labour
Lord Eustace Percy	Eton	Oxford (history)	6 November 1924	Conservative
Sir Charles Trevelyan	See above	See above	7 June 1929	Labour
Hastings Lees-Smith	Aldenham	Oxford (history)	2 March 1931	Labour
Sir Donald Maclean	Haverford West GS		25 August 1931	National (Liberal)
Lord Irwin (Viscount Halifax)	See above	See above	15 June 1932	National (Conservative)
Oliver Stanley	Eton		7 June 1935	National
Earl Stanhope	Eton	Oxford	28 May 1937	National
Earl De La Warr	Eton	Oxford	27 October 1938	National
Herwald Ramsbotham	Uppingham	Oxford	3 April 1940	National (Conservative)
R.A. Butler	Marlborough	Cambridge (history)	20 July 1941	National (Conservative)
Minister of Education				
R.A. Butler	See above	See above	3 August 1944	National (Conservative)
R. Law	Shrewsbury	Oxford (history)	25 May 1945	Caretaker (Conservative)
Ellen Wilkinson	Stretford Road	Manchester (history)	3 August 1945	Labour
George Tomlinson	Rishton Wesleyan		10 February 1947	Labour
Florence Horsbrugh	St Hilda's Folkestone		2 November 1951	Conservative
Sir David Eccles	Winchester	Oxford	14 October 1954	Conservative
Viscount Hailsham (later Quintin Hogg)	Eton	Oxford	13 January 1957	Conservative
Geoffrey Lloyd	Harrow	Cambridge	17 September 1957	Conservative

Name	School	University	Date of Appointment	Party of Government
Sir David Eccles	See above	See above	14 October 1959	Conservative
Sir Edward Boyle	Eton	Oxford (history)	13 July 1962	Conservative
Secretary of State for Education and Science				
Quintin Hogg	See above	See above	1 April 1964	Conservative
Michael Stewart	Christ's Hospital	Oxford	18 October 1964	Labour
Anthony Crosland	Highgate	Oxford	22 January 1965	Labour
Patrick Gordon Walker	Wellington	Oxford (history)	29 August 1967	Labour
Edward Short	Secondary	Durham	6 April 1968	Labour
Margaret Thatcher	Kesteven & Grantham Girls	Oxford	20 June 1970	Conservative
Reginald Prentice	Whitgift	London School of Economics	5 March 1974	Labour
Fred Mulley	Warwick	Oxford	10 June 1975	Labour
Shirley Williams	St Paul's Girls	Oxford	10 September 1976	Labour
Mark Carlisle	Radley	Manchester	5 May 1979	Conservative
Sir Keith Joseph	Harrow	Oxford	14 September 1981	Conservative
Kenneth Baker	St Paul's Boys	Oxford	21 May 1986	Conservative
John MacGregor	Merchiston Castle	St Andrews (econ/ history)	24 July 1989	Conservative
Kenneth Clarke	Nottingham High	Cambridge	2 November 1990	Conservative
Secretary of State for Education				
John Patten	Wimbledon	Cambridge (history)	10 April 1992	Conservative
Gillian Shephard	North Walsham Girls	Oxford	20 July 1994	Conservative
Secretary of State for Education and Employment				
Gillian Shephard	See above	See above	5 July 1995	Conservative
David Blunkett	Royal National College for the Blind, Shrewsbury	Sheffield	2 May 1997	Labour
Secretary of State for Education and Skills				
Estelle Morris	Whalley Range Grammar (Girls)	Coventry Coll. of Ed.	8 June 2001	Labour
Charles Clarke	Highgate	Cambridge	24 October 2002	Labour
Ruth Kelly	Sutton High/ Westminster	Oxford	15 December 2004	Labour
Alan Johnson	Sloane Grammar		5 May 2006	Labour
Secretary of State for Children, Schools and Families				
Ed Balls	Nottingham High	Oxford	28 June 2007	Labour
Secretary of State for Education				
Michael Gove	Robert Gordon's College	Oxford	11 May 2010	Conservative

Appendix G: The History in Education Website

Many of the resources gathered by the Project are accessible on the History in Education website at: http://www.history.ac.uk/history-in-education

The site includes:

1. Audio recordings – 68 recorded interviews between half an hour and two hours long, which include former secretaries of state, HMIs, members of the National Curriculum Working Group, curriculum innovators, teacher trainers, a museum educator, a schools broadcaster, teachers (both past and present) and former pupils. These will also be available via the British Library Sound Archive at www.bl.uk/nsa

2. Transcripts of all our interviews in word files which are fully searchable.

3. Digests of quotations from our interviewees' comments on particular themes, such as 'learning to teach history', Britishness and national identity', 'chronology and the National Curriculum' and 'the moral role of history in schools'.

4. Summaries of the 335 survey responses we received, using quotations from the forms, in themes and by the decade (from the 1920s to the 1980s) in which the respondents were born. The themes include teachers' memories of their career and curriculum change, their approach to teaching and the status of history in school over the years, and pupils' memories of history in the primary school, how they were taught and teaching aids and other school activities supporting history.

5. A photographic archive featuring a selection of the school work sent to us by respondents covering the period 1930–2002.

6. A collection of papers and accompanying PowerPoint presentations on topics and themes which Jenny Keating and Nicola Sheldon have written during the Project. These cover the 'story of school history' from 1900–2010 in more detail and using more of the oral history evidence than could be contained in the published book. There are also sundry papers dealing with specialist topics related to history teaching, such as schools broadcasting, teacher training, textbooks, inspection, examinations and technology in the classroom.

List of Abbreviations

Departments, Institutions and Organisations

BoE	Board of Education
DoE	Department of Education
DES	Department of Education and Science
ED	Education Department
HA	Historical Association
HiEP	History in Education Project
LCC	London County Council
LMA	London Metropolitan Archives
MoE	Ministry of Education
Ofsted	Office for Standards in Education
SCHP	Schools Council History 13–16 Project
SHP	Schools History Project
TNA	The National Archives

Journals and Periodicals

BJES	*British Journal of Educational Studies*
H	*History*
HoE	*History of Education*
HoEQ	*History of Education Quarterly*
HoESB	*History of Education Society Bulletin*
HJ	*Historical Journal*
HWJ	*History Workshop Journal*
JCH	*Journal of Contemporary History*
JCS	*Journal of Curriculum Studies*
JEAH	*Journal of Educational Administration and History*
JEPTCR	*Journal of Experimental Pedagogy and Training College Record*
JIH	*Journal of Interdisciplinary History*
PA	*Public Administration*
PBA	*Proceedings of the British Academy*
PH	*Primary History*
P&P	*Past & Present*
TCBH	*Twentieth Century British History*
TCJ	*The Curriculum Journal*
TH	*Teaching History*

A Note on Sources

The following manuscript collections have been consulted in the preparation of this book:

AEB, SEG examination papers and associated reports at the Assessment and Qualifications Alliance (AQA) Archives (University of Surrey, Guildford).

Archive of British Publishing and Printing (University of Reading, Reading).

Archives re the Geffrye museum's educational activities (Geffrye Museum, London).

BBC files (BBC Written Archives, Caversham, Reading).

Board of Education, LCC & ILEA files (London Metropolitan Archives, London).

Examiners' reports and papers (Cambridge Assessment Archives, Cambridge).

Governmental files on education – mainly 'ED' files (The National Archives, Kew).

Historical Association records in the Manuscripts and Special Collections (University of Nottingham, Nottingham).

London History Teachers' Association records (Institute of Education, London).

Mass Observation Archive in the Special Collections (University of Sussex, Falmer, Brighton).

Multicultural education materials (Birmingham City Library Archives, Birmingham).

Newspaper cuttings about the Priory School dispute (East Sussex Record Office, Lewes, East Sussex).

Original school material (British Schools Museum, Hitchin, Herts).

Original school material (Museum of the History of Education University of Leeds, Leeds).

Outdated Textbook Collection (History of Education Project, Durham).

Recent Historical Association material (Historical Association, Kennington, London).

SHP archive at the Brotherton Library Special Collections (University of Leeds, Leeds).

University of London examiners' reports and papers (Senate House Library, London).

Notes

Introduction

1. *Guardian*, 17 June 2010. See also J. Zajda, 'Transforming Images of Nation-Building: Ideology and Nationalism in History School Textbooks in Putin's Russia', in R. Guyver and T. Taylor (eds), *History Wars and the Classroom: Global Perspectives* (London, 2011), pp. 125–43.
2. D. Brandenberger, *National Bolshevism: Stalinist Mass Culture and the Formation of Modern Russian National Identity, 1931–1956* (Cambridge, MA, 2002), p. 24; D. Priestland, *The Red Flag: Communism and the Making of the Modern World* (London, 2009), pp. 160–1.
3. T. Taylor, 'Under Siege from Right and Left: A Tale of the Australian School History Wars', in Guyver and Taylor, *History Wars in the Classroom*, pp. 25–50; S. Macintyre and A. Clark, *The History Wars* (Melbourne, 2003).
4. R. Shorto, 'Founding Father', *New York Times Magazine*, 14 February 2010, pp. 32–9, 46–7. See also S.J. Foster, 'Politics, Parallels and Perennial Curriculum Questions: The Battle Over School History in England and the United States', *TCJ*, ix (1998), pp. 15–64; K. Barton, 'Wars and Rumours of War: The Rhetoric and Reality of History Education in the United States', in Guyver and Taylor, *History Wars in the Classroom*, pp. 189–204.
5. M.P. Gonzalez, 'Legacies, Ruptures and Inertias: History in the Argentine School System', in Guyver and Taylor, *History Wars in the Classroom*, pp. 1–23; R. Sieborger, 'Dealing with a Reign of Virtue: the Post Apartheid South African School History Curriculum', in Guyver and Taylor, *History Wars in the Classroom*, pp. 145–60.
6. R. Tharpar, 'The History Debate and School Textbooks in India: A Personal Memoir', *HWJ*, no. 67 (2009), pp. 87–98; N. Bhattacharya, 'Teaching History in Schools: The Politics of Textbooks in India', *HWJ*, no. 67 (2009), pp. 99–110.
7. A. Clark, 'Teaching the Nation's Story: Comparing Public Debates and Classroom Perspectives on History Education in Australia and Canada', *JCS*, xli (2009), pp. 745–62; M. de Vos, 'The Return of the Canon: Transforming Dutch History Teaching', *HWJ*, no. 67 (2009), pp. 111–24; S. Lassig and K.H. Pohl, 'History Textbooks and Historical Scholarship in Germany', *HWJ*, no. 67 (2009), pp. 124–39; Y.N. Soysal and S. Szakacs, 'Reconceptualizing the Republic: Incorporating "Diversity" in Citizenship Teaching in France', *JIH*, xli (2010), pp. 97–115; T. Taylor, 'Denial in the Classroom: Political Origins of the Japanese Textbook Controversy', in Guyver and Taylor, *History Wars in the Classroom*, pp. 89–106.

8. D. Cannadine, *National Portrait Gallery: A Brief History* (London, 2007), p. 9; C. Geertz, *The Interpretation of Cultures* (London, 1975), pp. 7, 14; B. Bailyn, *Education in the Forming of American Society* (New York, 1960), p. 14.

9. For a pioneering study, see R. Phillips, P. Goalen, A. McCully and S. Wood, 'Four Histories, One Nation? History Teaching, Nationhood and a British Identity', *Compare*, xxix (1999), pp. 153–69.

10. L.W. Evans, 'The Evolution of Welsh Educational Structure and Administration, 1881–1921', in History of Education Society (ed.), *Studies in the Government and Control of Education since 1860* (London, 1970), pp. 43–68; K.O. Morgan, *Rebirth of a Nation: Wales, 1880–1980* (Oxford, 1981), pp. 22–4, 105–6, 178–9; G.E. Jones, 'Which Nation's Curriculum? – The Case of Wales', *TCJ*, v (1994), pp. 5–16.

11. P.L.M. Hillis, 'Scottish History in the School Curriculum', *Journal of Scottish Historical Studies*, xxvii (2007), pp. 191–208; E.A.Cameron, *Impaled Upon a Thistle: Scotland since 1880* (Edinburgh, 2010), pp. 28–34, 146–49; J. Fulton, *The Tragedy of Belief: Division, Politics and Religion in Ireland* (Oxford, 1991), pp. 176–80; M. Elliott, *The Catholics of Ulster: A History* (London, 2000), pp. 458–60.

12. G. Sutherland, 'Administrators in Education after 1870: Patronage, Professionalism and Expertise', in G. Sutherland (ed.), *Studies in the Growth of Nineteenth-Century Government* (London, 1972), pp. 263–85.

13. We have interviewed every Secretary of State for Education (or equivalent) from Kenneth Baker to Charles Clarke. Only John Patten declined to be interviewed, while Ruth Kelly and Alan Johnson had only recently held office, and Ed Balls was still in post.

14. B. Harrison, *Seeking a Role: The United Kingdom, 1951–1970* (Oxford, 2009), pp. 348–9.

15. Harrison, *Seeking a Role*, p. 357.

16. R.I. McKibbin, *Classes and Cultures: England, 1918–1951* (Oxford, 1998), p. 206.

17. DoE, *Education in 1951, being the Report of the Ministry of Education and the Statistics of Public Education in England and Wales* (London, 1952), pp. 87–9, 94–5.

18. B. Pimlott, *Harold Wilson* (London, 1992), p. 24; Harrison, *Seeking a Role*, pp. 50–1.

19. K. Robbins, '*History*, the Historical Association, and the "National Past"', *H*, lxvi (1981), pp. 413–25.

20. D. Cannadine, *Making History Now and Then: Discoveries, Controversies and Explorations* (London, 2008), p. 25.

21. P. Readman, 'The Place of the Past in English Culture, c. 1890–1914', *P&P*, no. 186 (2005), pp. 147–99; P. Mandler, *History and National Life* (London, 2002).

22. G. Strauss, 'The State of Pedagogical Theory, c1530: What Protestant Reformers Knew About Education', in L. Stone (ed.), *Schooling and Society* (Baltimore, 1976), pp. 72–84.

23. A. Zilversmit, 'The Failure of Progressive Education, 1920–1940', in Stone, *Schooling and Society*, pp. 252–61.
24. V.E. Chancellor, *History for their Masters: Opinion in the English History Textbook, 1800–1914* (Bath, 1970). For broader comparisons, see V.R. Berghahn and H. Schissler (eds), *Perceptions of History: International Textbook Research on Britain, Germany and the United States* (Oxford, 1987); B. Vanhulle, 'The Path of History: Narrative Analysis of History Textbooks – A Case Study of Belgian History Textbooks (1945–2004)', *HoE*, xxxviii (2009), pp. 263–82.
25. Cannadine, *National Portrait Gallery*, pp. 27–8.
26. G. Searle, *A New England? Peace and War, 1885–1918* (Oxford, 2004), p. 50.
27. P. Thompson, *The Edwardians: The Re-Making of British Society* (London, 1975), pp. 16–18; J. Rose, *The Intellectual Life of the British Working Classes* (London, 2001), pp. 156–8.
28. L. Stone, 'Literacy and Education in England, 1640–1900', *P&P*, no. 42 (1969), pp. 83–92; C.F. Kaestle, '"Between the Scylla of Brutal Ignorance and the Charybdis of a Literary Education": Elite Attitudes toward Mass Schooling in Early Industrial England and America', in Stone, *Schooling and Society*, pp. 177–91; E. Weber, *Peasants into Frenchmen: The Modernization of Rural France, 1870–1914* (Stanford, CA, 1976), pp. 332–6.
29. J.O. Springhall, 'Lord Meath, Youth and Empire', *JCH*, v (1970), pp. 97–111; P. Horn, 'English Elementary Education and the Growth of the Imperial Ideal, 1880–1914', in J.A. Mangan (ed.), *Benefits Bestowed?: Education and British Imperialism* (Manchester, 1988), pp. 39–55; J. English, 'Empire Day in Britain, 1904–1958', *HJ*, xlix (2006), pp. 247–76.

Chapter 1   History Goes to School, 1900–18

1. HA Archive: Acc 1435 Box 9, *Report of Conference of Teachers, 1906*, p. 35.
2. F.M.L. Thompson, *The Rise of Respectable Society: A Social History of Victorian Britain, 1830–1900* (London, 1988), pp. 135–51; G. Sutherland, 'Education', in F.M.L. Thompson (ed.), *The Cambridge Social History of Britain, 1750–1950* (3 vols, Cambridge, 1990), vol. iii, *Social Agencies and Institutions*, pp. 141–54.
3. K.T. Hoppen, *The Mid-Victorian Generation, 1846-1886* (Oxford, 1998), pp. 597–600.
4. BoE, *Report of the Board of Education, 1899–1900*, vol. i, *The Report* (London, 1900), p. 102.
5. ED, *Code of Regulations for Day Schools* (London, 1900), p. 4; G.R. Batho, 'Sources for the History of History Teaching in Elermentary Schools, 1833–1914', in T.G. Cook (ed.), *Local Studies and the History of Education* (London, 1972), pp. 139–40.

6. BoE, *Report of the Board of Education for the Year 1902–03* (London, 1903), p. 27; B. Porter, *The Absent-Minded Imperialists: Empire, Society and Culture in Britain* (Oxford, 2004), pp. 180–1.
7. E.J. Hobsbawm, *The Age of Empire, 1875–1914* (London, 1987), pp. 149–50, 262–4.
8. E. Weber, *Peasants into Frenchmen: The Modernization of Rural France, 1870–1914* (Stanford, CA, 1976), p. 333.
9. J.E.B. Musson, 'The Unionist Coalition and Education, 1895–1902', *HJ*, xx (1977), pp. 607–45; G.R. Searle, *A New England? Peace and War, 1886–1918* (Oxford, 2004), pp. 329–34.
10. See Appendix F.
11. P. Jackson, *The Last of the Whigs: A Political Biography of Lord Hartington, Later Eighth Duke of Devonshire (1833–1908)* (London, 1994), pp. 309–19.
12. G.W. Kekewich, *The Education Department and After* (London, 1920), is a highly personal account.
13. M.I. Cole (ed.), *Beatrice Webb's Diaries, 1912–1924* (London, 1952), p. 98; F.R. Bryant (ed.), *The Coalition Diaries and Letters of H.A.L. Fisher: The Historian in Lloyd George's Cabinet* (4 vols, Lewiston, NY, 2006), vol. ii, p. 450.
14. G. Sherington, *English Education, Social Change and War, 1911–1920* (London, 1981), p. 179.
15. D.N. Chester, 'Robert Morant and Michael Sadler', *PA*, xxviii (1950), pp. 109–16; N. Middleton and S. Weitzman, *A Place for Everyone: A History of State Education from the End of the Eighteenth Century to the 1970s* (London, 1976), p. 122; R. Lowe, 'Personalities and Policy: Sadler, Morant and the Structure of Education in England', in R. Aldrich (ed.), *In History and In Education: Essays Presented to Peter Gordon* (London, 1996), pp. 98–115; T. Taylor, 'An Early Example of the Fascist Mentality: Robert Morant's Rise to Power', *JEAH*, xvii (1985), pp. 48–62.
16. P.H.J.H. Gosden, *The Development of Educational Administration in England and Wales* (Oxford, 1966), pp. 100–5; Sir L.A. Selby-Bigge, *The Board of Education* (London, 1927), preface.
17. ED, *Code of Regulations for Day Schools* (London, 1900), pp. 34–9.
18. ED, *Revised Instructions Issued to Her Majesty's Inspectors and Applicable to the Code of 1900* (London, 1900), pp. 6, 17, 18.
19. BoE, *Suggestions for the Consideration of Teachers and Others Concerned with the Work of Public Elementary Schools* (London, 1905), pp. 5, 8–9, 61.
20. BoE, *Suggestions* (1905), pp. 9, 62.
21. BoE, *Suggestions* (1905), pp. 62–3.
22. BoE, *Suggestions* (1905), pp. 122–4.
23. BoE, *Suggestions for the Consideration of Teachers and Others Concerned in the Work of Public Elementary Schools, Revised Edition Installment no 6, Suggestions for the Teaching of History* (London, 1914).
24. BoE, *Suggestions* (1905), p. 122.
25. *The Times*, 14 December 1908.

26. BoE, *Report of the Board of Education for the Year 1901–02* (London, 1902), p. 20.
27. BoE, *Teaching of History in Secondary Schools* (Circular 599, London, 1908), p. 2.
28. Circular 599, pp. 2–3.
29. Circular 599, pp. 5–7.
30. Circular 599, pp. 6–8.
31. TNA: ED 22/36, BoE, *Memorandum in Explanation and Expansion of the Board's Circular on the Teaching of History in Secondary Schools* (London, 1908), p. 1.
32. *Memorandum*, pp. 3–5.
33. TNA: ED 12/48, Memo to Inspectors from W.N. Bruce, 25 November 1908.
34. TNA: ED 12/48, Handwritten notes by R.L. Morant, 17 October 1908.
35. Circular 599 and the accompanying *Memorandum* were reprinted as BoE, *Memoranda on Teaching and Organization in Secondary Schools: History* (London, 1912).
36. A. Watts, 'Cambridge Local Examinations 1858–1945' in S. Raban (ed.), *Examining the World: A History of the University of Cambridge Local Examinations Syndicate* (Cambridge, 2008), p. 42.
37. BoE, *Report of the Consultative Committee on Examinations in Secondary Schools* (London, 1911).
38. Circular 849, *Examinations in Secondary Schools* (July 1914), p. 2.
39. *Report of the Consultative Committee*, p. 28.
40. Searle, *A New England?*, pp. 650–5.
41. D. Cannadine, *Making History Now and Then: Discoveries, Controversies and Explorations* (London, 2008), pp. 22–3.
42. HA, *The Historical Association, 1906–1956* (London, 1957), pp. 7–8.
43. *Report of Conference of Teachers, 1906*, pp. 39–40.
44. HA, *Historical Association*, pp. 8–10.
45. C.J. Wrigley, 'The Branches of the Historical Association, 1906–2006', *The Historian*, no. 91 (2006), pp. 45–7.
46. HA, *Historical Association*, pp. 14–22.
47. *Report of Conference of Teachers, 1906*, pp. 35–9.
48. Cannadine, *Making History Now and Then*, pp. 19–20; J. Bryce, 'Presidential Address', *PBA*, vi (1913–14), pp. 121–2; J. Bryce, 'World History', *PBA*, ix (1919–20), pp. 189–92; S. Martin, *The Order of Merit: One Hundred Years of Matchless Honour* (London, 1907), pp. 312–13.
49. J. Bryce, *On The Teaching of History in Schools* (London, 1907), p. 1.
50. Bryce, *On The Teaching of History*, pp. 3–9.
51. Bryce, *On The Teaching of History*, pp. 1, 9; J.T. Seaman, *A Citizen of the World: The Life of James Bryce* (London, 2006), pp. 119–32.
52. HA, *Historical Association*, p. 15.
53. F.J.C. Hearnshaw, 'The Place of History in Education', *H*, i–ii (1912–13), p. 34; C.H.K. Marten, 'Some General Reflections on the Teaching of History', *H*, i–ii (1912–13), p. 87.

54. *Report of the Proceedings of the Seventh Annual Meeting of the Historical Association, held on January 10 and 11 1913* (HA leaflet no. 31, London, 1913), p. 12; Marten, 'General Reflections', p. 86.

55. Searle, *A New England?*, pp. 46–9; H. Hendrick, *Children, Childhood and English Society, 1880–1990* (Cambridge, 1997), pp. 88–9; S. Shuttleworth, *The Mind of the Child: Child Development in Literature, Science and Medicine, 1840–1900* (Oxford, 2010), pp. 267–89, 353–63.

56. H. Hendrick, 'Child Labour, Medical Capital, and the School Medical Service', in R.Cooter (ed.), *In the Name of the Child: Health and Welfare, 1880–1940* (London, 1992), p. 47.

57. H. Finlay-Johnson, *The Dramatic Method of Teaching* (London, 1912), pp. 16–19.

58. Finlay-Johnson, *Dramatic Method*, pp. 53–4, 69.

59. HA, *Source-Books* (HA leaflet no. 1, London, 1907).

60. M.W. Keatinge, *Studies in the Teaching of History* (London, 1910), pp. 101–2.

61. M. Lightfoot Eastwood, 'Review of *Studies in the Teaching of History* by M.W. Keatinge', *International Journal of Ethics*, xxi (1911), pp. 241–2.

62. E. Holmes, *What Is and What Might Be* (London, 1911); R.J.W. Selleck, *English Primary Education and the Progressives, 1914–1939* (London, 1972), p. 26; P. Gordon, 'The Writings of Edmond Holmes: A Reassessment and Bibliography', *HoE*, xii (1983), p. 20.

63. *Report of the Proceedings of the Sixth Annual Meeting of the Historical Association, held on January 13th 1912* (HA leaflet no. 30, London, 1912), pp. 24–7.

64. G.E. Hodgson, 'The Use of Historical Drama', *JEPTCR*, iii (1915), pp. 162–72; K. Osborne, 'M.W. Keatinge: A British Approach to Teaching History Through Sources', *Canadian Social Studies*, xxxviii (2004), p. 4.

65. Hobsbawm, *Age of Empire*, p. 150.

66. Thompson, *Respectable Society*, pp. 149–51; P. Thompson, *The Edwardians: The Remaking of British Society* (London, 1975), pp. 73–4; H.C. Dent, *1870–1970: Century of Growth in English Education* (London, 1970), pp. 18–19; P. Horn, *Education in Rural England* (Dublin, 1978), pp. 252–73.

67. Searle, *A New England?*, p. 49; L. Rose, *The Erosion of Childhood: Child Oppression in Britain, 1860–1918* (London, 1991), ch. 17; S. Humphries, *Hooligans or Rebels? An Oral History of Working-Class Childhood and Youth, 1889–1939* (Oxford, 1981), p. 92.

68. J. Rose, *The Intellectual Life of the British Working Classes* (London, 2001), pp. 146–9.

69. Rose, *Intellectual Life of the British Working Classes*, pp. 165–8.

70. Searle, *A New England?*, pp. 50–1; Thompson, *Rise of Respectable Society*, pp. 134–42; D. Rubinstein, *School Attendance in London, 1870–1914: A Social History* (Hull, 1969), pp. 49, 114–16.

71. Hendrick, 'Child Labour', p. 51; M.J. Childs, 'Boy Labour in Late Victorian and Edwardian England, and the Remaking of the Working Class', *Journal of Social History*, xxiii (1987), pp. 790–2.

72. BoE, *Report of the Board of Education for the Year 1913–1914* (London, 1914), p. 68; M. Vlaeminke, *The English Higher Grade Schools: A Lost Opportunity* (London, 2000), pp. 130–78.

73. O. Banks, 'Morant and the Secondary School Regulations of 1904', *BJES*, iii (1954), pp. 33–41; O. Banks, *Parity and Prestige in English Secondary Education: A Study in Educational Sociology* (London, 1955), pp. 31–49; R. Lowe, 'Robert Morant and the Secondary Regulations of 1904', *JEAH*, xvi (1984), pp. 37–46; N. Whitbread, 'The Early Twentieth-Century Secondary Curriculum Debate in England', *HoE*, xiii (1984), pp. 221–33; N.D. Daglish, 'The Politics of Educational Change: The Case of the English Higher Grade Schools', *JEAH*, xix (1987), pp. 36–50.

74. H. Hendrick, *Children, Childhood and English Society, 1880–1990* (Cambridge, 1997), p. 66; M. Daunton, *Wealth and Welfare: An Economic and Social History of Britain, 1851–1951* (Oxford, 2007), p. 505; BoE, *Regulations for Secondary Schools (from 1st August 1904 to 31st July 1905)* (London, 1904), p. 552; Circular 599, p. 2.

75. Thompson, *Rise of Respectable Society*, pp. 149–50; T.R. Gourvish, 'The Rise of the Professions', in T.R. Gourvish and A. O'Day (eds), *Later Victorian Britain, 1870–1900* (London,1988), pp. 21–2, 28.

76. Hoppen, *Mid-Victorian Generation*, p. 47; A. Tropp, *The School Teachers: The Growth of the Teaching Profession in England and Wales* (London, 1957), pp. 18–40; A.M. Carr-Saunders and P.A. Wilson, *The Professions* (Oxford, 1933), p. 252; Searle, *A New England?*, pp. 96–7.

77. H.C. Dent, *The Training of Teachers in England and Wales, 1800–1975* (London, 1977), pp. 47–54; BoE, *Report of the Board of Education for the Year 1907–1908* (London, 1909), pp. 62–4.

78. Dent, *Training of Teachers*, pp. 55–6; P.H.J.H. Gosden, *The Evolution of a Profession: A Study of the Contribution of Teachers' Associations to the Development of School Teaching as a Professional Occupation* (Oxford, 1972), p. 209.

79. R. Aldrich, 'The Training of Teachers and Educational Studies: The London Day Training College, 1902–1932', *Paedagogica Historica*, xl (2004), pp. 617–31.

80. S.J. Colledge, 'The Study of History in the Teacher Training College, 1888–1914', *HoESB*, xxxvi (1985), pp. 45–6; BoE, *Report of the Board of Education for the Year 1905–06* (London, 1906), p. 42.

81. TNA: ED 24/479, O. Airy, 'Suggestions on the Teaching of History in Training Colleges', 4 December 1905, pp. 1–9; *Report of the Board of Education for the Year 1907–1908*, p. 72; Dent, *Training of Teachers*, p. 73; Gosden, *Evolution of a Profession*, p. 214; F. Widdowson, '"Educating Teacher": Women and Elementary Teaching in London, 1900–1914', in

L. Davidoff and B. Westover (eds), *Our Work, Our Lives, our Worlds: Women's History and Women's Work* (Basingstoke, 1986), pp. 99–123.

82. R.H. Soltau, 'The Piers Plowman Histories', *H*, i–ii (1912–13), pp. 223–4.

83. LCC, Education Committee, *Report of a Conference on the Teaching of History in London Elementary Schools* (London, 1911), pp. 39–40.

84. V.E. Chancellor, *History for their Masters: Opinion in the English History Textbook, 1800–1914* (Bath, 1970), pp. 12, 112–38.

85. *Journal of Education* (August, 1902), p. 527.

86. BoE, *Memoranda on Teaching and Organization in Secondary Schools* (1912), pp. 11–13; LCC, *Report*, pp. 39–40; *Journal of Education* (November, 1907), p. 752.

87. G.F. Bridge, 'Text-books of History and Literature', *JEPTCR*, ii (1914), p. 447; *Journal of Education* (May 1907), p. 329; Chancellor, *History for their Masters*, p. 114; LMA: LCC/EO/PS/02/007: Education Committee, Memorandum by Sir Robert Blair on the Teaching of History in the Highest Classes of Elementary Schools, February 1918; LCC, *Report*, p. 40.

88. Anon., 'The History Teaching Exhibition', *H*, iii–iv (1914–15), p. 140.

89. *Report of Conference of Teachers, 1906*, pp. 40–5; HA, *Illustrations, Portraits and Lantern Slides, Chiefly for British and Modern History* (HA leaflet, no. 12, London, 1908); LMA: LCC/EO/DIV6/SHE/LB/1, Logbook of Sherington Road School; Berkshire Record Office: R. Coles, 'Methods Employed within History Teaching and Attitudes towards the Past Evident in Berkshire Elementary School Log Books, 1901–1919: Report of Findings' (unpublished paper, August 2009), p. 4.

90. Anon., 'Wanted, Historical Plays', *H*, i–ii (1912–13), p. 110; X., 'Historical Plays for Village Children', *H*, i–ii (1912–13), pp. 212–16; B.O., 'Clothing the Dry Bones of History', *H*, iii–iv (1914–15), pp. 39–41; R.D. Bramwell, *Elementary School Work, 1900–1925* (Durham, 1961), pp. 45–6; *Report of the Board of Education for the Year 1910–11* (London, 1911), p. 35.

91. LCC, *Report*, p. 40; LMA: LCC/EO/PS/02/007: R. Blair, 'Report on the Teaching of History in London', LCC, Education Committee, 12 July 1917, p. 6; G. Batho, 'History Textbooks, 1870–1914: A Note on the Historical Association Collection at Durham', *History of Education Society Bulletin*, no. 33 (spring 1984), p. 16.

92. P. Brindle, 'Past Histories: History and the Elementary School Classroom in Early Twentieth-Century England' (unpublished PhD thesis, University of Cambridge, 1998), p. 106.

93. Gosden, *Educational Administration in England and Wales*, pp. 106–8; G. Sutherland, 'Administrators in Education After 1870: Patronage, Professionalism and Expertise', in G. Sutherland (ed.), *Studies in the Growth of Nineteenth-Century Government* (London, 1972), pp. 263–86.

94. R. Betts, 'Robert Morant and the Purging of H.M.Inspectorate, 1903', *JEAH*, xx (1988), pp. 54–9; R.T.F. Goodings and J.E. Dunford, 'Her Majesty's Inspectorate of Schools, 1839–1989: The Question of Independence', *JEAH*, xxii (1990), p. 3; P. Gordon, 'Policy Formation and the Work of His

Majesty's Inspectorate, 1918–1945', in D. Crook and G. McCulloch (eds), *History, Politics and Policy-Making in Education: A Festschrift Presented to Richard Aldrich* (London, 2007), p. 89.

95. J. Rose, 'Willingly to School: The Working Class Response to Elementary Education in Britain, 1875–1918', *Journal of British Studies*, xxxii (1993), p. 115.

96. Rose, *Intellectual Life of the British Working Classes*, p. 146; E. Holmes, *In Quest of An Ideal: An Autobiography* (London, 1920), pp. 63–4.

97. BoE, *West Central Division, General Report for the Year 1899* (London, 1900), pp. 12–13.

98. BoE, *West Central Division*, pp. 12–13.

99. *Report of the Board of Education, 1900–1901*, vol. i, *The Report* (London, 1900), pp. 85, 135.

100. BoE, *General Reports of HM Inspectors on Elementary Schools and Training Colleges for the Year 1902* (London, 1903), pp. 20, 74.

101. *General Reports ... for the Year 1902*, pp. 77, 81.

102. *General Reports ... for the Year 1902*, pp. 74–5, 77, 85, 91, 115.

103. *General Reports ... for the Year 1902*, pp. 20, 81, 139.

104. C.H. Rolph, *London Particulars* (Oxford, 1980), p. 29.

105. J. Common, *Kiddar's Luck* (London, 1951), pp. 89–90.

106. Quoted in Rose, *Intellectual Life of the British Working Classes*, p. 163.

107. F. Collie, 'The "Problem Method" in the History Courses of the Elementary School', *JEPTCR*, i (1912), p. 236.

108. TNA: ED 77/209, BoE, 'An Experiment in Teaching English and History' (London, 1912), pp. 1, 16–19.

109. BoE, *General Reports on Higher Education with Appendices for the Year 1902* (London, 1903), p. 65.

110. TNA: ED 109/3708, Report of First Inspection of the Roan School (Boys), Greenwich, held on the 6th, 7th and 8th May 1907, p. 10.

111. TNA: ED 109/3986, Report of First Inspection of the County Secondary School, Kentish Town, St Pancras, held on the 1st, 2nd, 3rd and 4th February 1910, p. 9.

112. TNA: ED 35/1656A, Report of First Inspection of the County Secondary School, Fulham, London, held on the 4th, 5th, 6th and 7th May, 1909, p. 13.

113. R. Roberts, *The Classic Slum: Salford Life in the First Quarter of the Century* (Manchester, 1971), p. 112; Horn, *Education in Rural England*, pp. 254–5. See also: J.A. Mangan (ed.), *Benefits Bestowed? Education and British Imperialism* (Manchester, 1988); K. Castle, *Britannia's Children: Reading Colonialism Through Children's Books and Magazines* (Manchester, 1996); S. Heathorn, *For Home, Country and Race: Constructing Gender, Class and Englishness in the Elementary School, 1880–1914* (Toronto, 2000); W. Marsden, '"Poisoned History": A Comparative Study of Nationalism, Propaganda and the Treatment of War and Peace in the Late Nineteenth- and Early Twentieth-Century School Curriculum', *HoE*, xxix (2000), pp. 29–48.

114. F. Willis, *101 Jubilee Road: A Book of London Yesterdays* (London, 1948), pp. 74–7.

115. Porter, *Absent-Minded Imperialists*, pp. 67–72; Chancellor, *History for their Masters*, pp. 136–8.

116. Porter, *Absent-Minded Imperialists*, pp. 201–3; W.R. Lawson, *John Bull and His Schools* (Edinburgh, 1908), pp. 217–18.

117. *Report of the Imperial Education Conference 1911* (London, 1911), pp. 51, 70; C.P. Lucas, 'On the Teaching of Imperial History', *H*, i (1916–17), pp. 5–11; J.O. Springhall, 'Lord Meath, Youth and Empire', *JCH*, v (1970), pp. 97–111; R. Betts, 'A Campaign for Patriotism in the Elementary School Curriculum: Lord Meath, 1892–1916', *HoESB*, xxxxvi (1990), pp. 38–45; J.G. Greenlee, *Education and Imperial Unity, 1901–26* (London, 1987), p. 103.

118. BoE, *Suggestions* (1914), p. 1.

119. C.H. Firth, 'The Study of Modern History in Great Britain', *PBA*, vi (1913–14), p. 139; *Report of the Imperial Education Conference, 1911*, p. 70.

120. E.O. Lewis, 'Popular and Unpopular School-Subjects', *JEPTCR*, ii (1913), pp. 89–98.

121. A. Newton, *Years of Change: Autobiography of a Hackney Shoemaker* (London, 1974), p. 47; Hobsbawm, *Age of Empire*, pp. 326–6.

122. Weber, *Peasants into Frenchmen*, p. 110; K.A. Schleunes, *Schooling and Society: The Politics of Education in Prussia and Bavaria, 1750–1900* (New York, 1989), pp. 7, 50–98; S.L. Harp, *Learning to be Loyal: Primary Schooling as Nation Building in Alsace and Lorraine, 1850–1940* (DeKab, IL, 1998), pp. 10, 106.

123. J.W. Headlam, 'The Effect of the War on the Teaching of History', *H*, iii (1918–19), p. 12; L. Simpson, 'Imperialism, National Efficiency and Education, 1900–1905', *JEAH*, xvi (1984), p. 34.

124. Thompson, *Rise of Respectable Society*, pp. 145–51; J.M.G. Holdstrom, 'The Content of Education and the Socialization of the Working-Class Child, 1830–1860', in P. McCann (ed.), *Popular Education and Socialization in the Nineteenth Century* (London, 1985), p. 106.

125. BoE, *Memoranda on Teaching and Organization in Secondary Schools* (Circular 869, London, 1914), p. 2.

126. Circular 869, pp. 3–4.

127. TNA: ED 12/218, Minute by J.W. Headlam, 19 September, 1917.

128. TNA: ED 29/1680, Minute by J.W. Headlam-Morley, 4 September 1918; Minute by T.W. Phillips, 11 October 1918.

129. BoE, *Suggestions for the Consideration of Teachers and Others Concerned in the Work of Public Elementary Schools* (London, 1918), p. 90.

130. BoE, *Suggestions* (1918), pp. 93–4.

131. BoE, *Humanism in the Continuation School* (Educational Pamphlet no. 43, London, 1921), p. 54. The pamphlet had been prepared by J. Dover Wilson, an HMI, in 1918.

132. A. Marwick, *The Deluge: British Society and the First World War* (London, 1978 edn), pp. 116–19.

133. M.M. Allan, 'The Teacher as Social Worker', *JEPTCR*, iii (1916), p. 210; Dent, *Training of Teachers*, pp. 89–94.

134. Marwick, *Deluge*, p. 243.

135. Headlam, 'Effect of the War on the Teaching of History', pp. 11–12; P. Mantoux, 'The Effect of the War on the Teaching of History', *H*, iii (1918–19), pp. 13–18; C.P. Lucas, 'On the Teaching of Imperial History', *H*, i (1916–17), pp. 5–11; J. Corbett and W.H. Hodges, 'The Teaching of Naval and Military History', *H*, i (1916–17), pp. 12–24; A.M. Bayly, *The Value of History as a Factor in Moral Education* (HA leaflet no. 37, London, 1915).

136. H.A.L. Fisher to Mrs Green, 7 June 1917, printed in *H*, ii (1917–18), pp. 65–6.

Chapter 2 History in Peace and War, 1918–44

1. Fisher's life is well covered in H.A.L. Fisher, *An Unfinished Autobiography* (London, 1940); D. Ogg, *Herbert Fisher, 1865–1940: A Short Biography* (London, 1947); and, most recently, in the introduction to F.R. Bryant (ed.), *The Coalition Diaries and Letters of H.A.L. Fisher: The Historian in Lloyd George's Cabinet* (4 vols, Lewiston, NY, 2006), vol. i, pp. 1–52, and in A. Ryan, 'Fisher, Herbert Albert Laurens (1865–1940)', *Oxford Dictionary of National Biography* (Oxford, 2004) online edn, May 2010 [http://0-www.oxforddnb.com.catalogue.ulrls.lon.ac.uk/view/article/33141, accessed 28 July 2011].

2. H.A.L. Fisher, *The Medieval Empire* (2 vols, London, 1898); H.A.L. Fisher, *Studies in Napoleonic Statesmanship: Germany* (London, 1903); H.A.L. Fisher, *The History of England from the Accession of Henry VII to the death of Henry VIII (1485–1547)* (London, 1906); H.A.L. Fisher, *Bonapartism* (Oxford, 1908); H.A.L. Fisher, *The Republican Tradition in Europe* (London, 1911); idem, *Napoleon* (London, 1913).

3. N. Annan, 'The Intellectual Aristocracy', in J.H. Plumb (ed.), *Studies in Social History: A Tribute to G.M. Trevelyan* (London, 1955), pp. 242–87; H.A.L. Fisher (ed.), *The Constitutional History of England: A Course of Lectures Delivered by F.W. Maitland* (Cambridge, 1908); H.A.L. Fisher, *The Collected Papers of Frederic William Maitland* (3 vols, Cambridge, 1911); H.A.L. Fisher, *James Bryce* (2 vols, London, 1927); H.A.L. Fisher, *A History of Europe* (3 vols, London, 1935–36); H.A.L. Fisher, *Pages from the Past* (Oxford, 1939); D. Cannadine, *G.M. Trevelyan: A Life in History* (London, 1993), pp. 9, 22, 25.

4. Ogg, *Fisher*, p. 21; Bryant, *Coalition Diaries*, vol. i, pp. 20–2; vol. iii, p. 698; vol. iv, pp. 1096, 1252.

5. H.A.L. Fisher, *Studies in History and Politics* (Oxford, 1920); Bryant, *Coalition Diaries*, vol. ii, pp. 399, 443, 632.

6. M. Thomson, *David Lloyd George: The Official Biography* (London, 1948), pp. 49–51; F. Owen, *Tempestuous Journey: Lloyd George His Life and*

Times (London, 1954), pp. 19–25; J. Grigg, *The Young Lloyd George* (London, 1973), pp. 32–3; B.B. Gilbert, *David Lloyd George: A Political Life*, vol. i, *The Architect of Change, 1863–1912* (London, 1987), pp. 28–9.

7. J. Grigg, *Lloyd George: From Peace to War, 1912–1916* (London, 1985), pp. 495–6; D. Lloyd George, *War Memoirs* (6 vols, Boston, 1936–37), vol. vi, *1918*, pp. 295–305; Bryant, *Coalition Diaries*, vol. i, pp. 11, 24–8; vol. iii, pp. 1027–8.

8. D.W. Dean, 'H.A.L. Fisher, Reconstruction and the Development of the 1918 Education Act', *BJES*, xviii (1970), esp. p. 261; D.H. Akenson, 'Patterns of English Educational Change: The Fisher and the Butler Acts', *HoEQ*, xi (1971), pp. 143–54; G.E. Sherington, 'The 1918 Education Act: Origins, Aims and Development', *BJES*, xxiv (1976), pp. 66–85.

9. Bryant, *Coalition Diaries*, vol. i, p. 271; A. Marwick, *The Deluge: British Society and the First World War* (London, 1978 edn), pp. 116–19, 242–6.

10. R. McKibbin, *Classes and Cultures: England, 1918–1951* (Oxford, 1998), pp. 206–7.

11. Bryant, *Coalition Diaries*, vol. i, pp. 18–19.

12. Bryant, *Coalition Diaries*, vol. i, p. 22.

13. Bryant, *Coalition Diaries*, vol. i, pp. 39, 41, 104; vol. iii, p. 724; McKibbin, *Classes and Cultures*, pp. 207–8.

14. Bryant, *Coalition Diaries*, vol. i, pp. 39–42; vol. iii, pp. 881–4, 909, 930–1; Lord Eustace Percy, *Some Memories* (London, 1958), p. 93; McKibbin, *Classes and Cultures*, p. 208.

15. R. Jenkins, *Nine Men of Power* (London, 1974), pp. 139–40; A. Roberts, *'The Holy Fox': A Biography of Lord Halifax* (London, 1991), pp. 15–16.

16. A.J.A. Morris, *C.P. Trevelyan, 1870–1958: Portrait of a Radical* (Belfast, 1977), pp. 155–62.

17. Lord Eustace Percy, *The Privy Council Under the Tudors* (Oxford, 1907); Lord Eustace Percy, *The Study of History* (London, 1935).

18. Percy, *Some Memories*, pp. 92–123.

19. Morris, *Trevelyan*, pp. 174–83; D.W. Dean, 'Difficulties of a Labour Educational Policy: The Failure of the Trevelyan Bill, 1929–1931', *BJES*, xvii (1969), pp. 293–8.

20. The Earl of Birkenhead, *Halifax: The Life of Lord Halifax* (London, 1965), pp. 147–53, 323–37.

21. McKibbin, *Classes and Cultures*, pp. 213–14.

22. A. Newman, *The Stanhopes of Chevening: A Family Biography* (London, 1969), pp. 348–9.

23. McKibbin, *Classes and Cultures*, p. 221.

24. Percy, *Some Memories*, p. 123; Sir L. Selby-Bigge, *The Board of Education* (London, 1927), pp. 22–8.

25. P.H.J.H. Gosden, *The Development of Educational Administration in England and Wales* (Oxford, 1966), pp. 105–12; R. Aldrich and P. Gordon, *Dictionary of British Educationists* (London, 1989), pp. 121, 194, 220, 241; Selby-Bigge, *Board of Education*, p. 78.

26. BoE, *Report of the Consultative Committee on Psychological Tests of Educable Capacity and Their Possible Use in the Public System of Education* (London, 1924), pp. 108–19.

27. BoE, *Report of the Consultative Committee on the Education of the Adolescent* (London, 1927), pp. 34, 44, 173–6.

28. BoE, *The New Prospect in Education* (London, 1928).

29. Sir P. Nunn, 'The "Break at Eleven" and the Senior School', in Lord Eustace Percy (ed.), *The Year Book of Education 1932* (London, 1932), pp. 151–2; Lord Eustace Percy, Sir P. Nunn and Professor D. Wilson (eds), *The Year Book of Education 1935* (1935), p. 13.

30. BoE, *Report of the Consultative Committee on Secondary Education with Special Reference to Grammar Schools and Technical High Schools* (London, 1938), pp. 357–8, 380.

31. For one example, see G.T. Rimmington, 'The Development of Senior Elementary Schools in Leicester before 1944', *HoESB*, lx (1997), pp. 24–32.

32. McKibbin, *Classes and Cultures*, pp. 208–9.

33. A.P. Jephcott, *Girls Growing Up* (London, 1942), p. 43; E. Slater and M. Woodside, *Patterns of Marriage: A Study of Marriage Relationships in the Urban Working Classes* (London, 1951), p. 65.

34. BoE, *Suggestions for the Consideration of Teachers and Others Concerned with the Work of Public Elementary Schools* (London, 1918), p. 90; O.E. Shropshire, *The Teaching of History in English Schools* (New York, 1936), p. 21.

35. BoE, *Suggestions* (1918), pp. 92, 99.

36. BoE, *Suggestions* (1918), pp. 93–4.

37. BoE, *Suggestions* (1918), pp. 98–9.

38. BoE, *Handbook of Suggestions for the Consideration of Teachers and others Concerned in the Work of Public Elementary Schools* (London, 1927), pp. 135–8.

39. BoE, *Handbook*, pp. 122–3.

40. BoE, *Handbook*, pp. 124–6.

41. BoE, *Report of the Consultative Committee on The Primary School* (London, 1931), pp. 93, 99, 139, 170–1.

42. BoE, *Handbook of Suggestions for the Consideration of Teachers and others Concerned in the Work of Public Elementary Schools* (London, 1937), p. 402.

43. TNA: ED 12/218, T.W. Phillips to J.W. Headlam, 26 January 1918; TNA ED 24/1680, Memorials from WEA and HA [undated] and from Cambridge teachers, 6 March 1919; 'Discussion at the Annual Meeting', *H*, iii (1918), pp. 19–24.

44. TNA: ED 24/1680: C.H. Firth to H.A.L. Fisher, 13 May 1919, 15 June 1919; Report of the Conference on the Teaching of History (and Geography) held at the offices of the Board of Education on Thursday and Friday, 24th and 25th April, 1919, pp. 11–12. Despite the intention to give equal attention

to history and geography, few geographers attended and the emphasis was almost entirely on history.

45. TNA: ED 23/116 20/97/Y: Fisher memorandum [January 1920].
46. TNA: ED 12/219, Reports of History Committees 'A' and 'B' Appointed by the President, January 1920, pp. 3–6.
47. TNA: ED 12/219: Memorandum to Mr Chambers, 4 December 1922; note, 9 May 1923.
48. BoE, *Report on the Teaching of History* (Educational Pamphlet, no. 37, London, 1923), pp. iii–iv.
49. Bryant, *Coalition Diary*, vol. ii, p. 436; BoE, *Report on the Teaching of History*, pp. 15, 19.
50. BoE, *Report on the Teaching of History*, pp. 28, 33.
51. BoE, *Report of the Consultative Committee on The Education of the Adolescent* (London, 1927), pp. 200–3.
52. BoE, *Education of the Adolescent*, pp. 199–201.
53. W.C. Sellar and R.J.Yeatman, *1066 and All That* (London, 1930), p. 5.
54. BoE, *A Review of Junior Technical Schools in England* (London, 1937), p. 17; BoE, *Suggestions in Regard to Teaching in Junior Technical Schools* (London, 1937), p. 68.
55. BoE, *Report ... with Special Reference to Grammar Schools and Technical High Schools*, p. 174.
56. Secondary School Examinations Council, *The School Certificate Examination – Being the Report of the Panel of Investigators appointed by the Secondary School Examinations Council to enquire into the Eight Approved School Certificate Examinations held in the Summer of 1931* (London, 1932), p. 79. For specimen examination syllabuses, see Appendix C.
57. T.W. Phillips, 'The System of School Examinations, with Special Reference to the Position of History in the Higher Certificate Examinations', *H*, xvii (1933), p. 328.
58. C.H.K. Marten, 'The First School Examination and the Teaching of History', *H*, xiii (1928), pp. 21–2; Secondary School Examinations Council, *The School Certificate*, pp. 81–4.
59. BoE, *Report ... with Special Reference to Grammar Schools and Technical High Schools*, p. 256; J. Roach, 'Examinations and the Secondary Schools, 1900–1945', *HoE*, viii (1979), p. 56.
60. Bryant, *Coalition Diaries*, vol. i, p. 49; vol. iii, p. 1027.
61. J. Stevenson, *British Society, 1914–45* (Harmondsworth, 1984), pp. 122, 129, 185.
62. BoE, *Education in England and Wales, being the Report of the Board of Education for the School Year 1924–25* (London, 1926), p. 102; BoE, *Education in England and Wales, being the Report of the Board of Education for the School Year 1925–26* (London, 1927), p. 158.
63. TNA: ED 12/219, Report of the Committee appointed by the President of the Board of Education to inquire into the training of teachers of History [June 1920], pp. 5–7, 15–16.

64. H.C. Dent, *The Training of Teachers in England and Wales, 1800–1975* (London, 1977), pp. 98–110; R. Aldrich, 'The Training of Teachers and Educational Studies: The London Day Training College, 1902–1932', *Pedagogica Historica*, xl (2004), p. 627.

65. HA, *The Historical Association, 1906–1956* (London, 1957), pp. 27–47; K. Robbins, '*History*, the Historical Association and the "National Past"', *H*, lxvi (1981), p. 423.

66. HA, *The Historical Association*, pp. 36–37; Marten, 'First School Examination', pp. 21–9.

67. The findings are published in *H*, xix (1929), pp. 51–4; *H*, xxiv (1939), pp. 50–2.

68. R.J.W. Selleck, *English Primary Education and the Progressives, 1914–1939* (London, 1972), pp. 23–47; *The Times*, 16 October 1936.

69. H.M. Madeley, *History as a School of Citizenship* (London, 1920), p. 10; L. Fox Lee, 'The Dalton Plan, and the Loyal, Capable, Intelligent Citizen', *HoE*, xxix (2000), p. 131.

70. F. Crossfield Happold, *The Study of History in Schools as a Training in the Art of Thought* (HA leaflet no. 69, London, 1927), pp. 3–5; F. Crossfield Happold, *The Approach to History* (London, 1928), pp. 38–40; M.V.C. Jeffreys, 'The Subject-Matter of History in Schools: A Case for a New Principle of Selection', *H*, xx (1935), pp. 235–41; M.V.C. Jeffreys, 'The Teaching of History by Means of "Lines of Development": Some Practical Experiments and Their Results', *H*, xxi (1936), pp. 232–8.

71. BoE, *Report of the Consultative Committee on Books in Public Elementary Schools* (London, 1928), p. 34.

72. F.C. Moore, 'England', in Working Committee of a Special Commission on Education, *Report on Nationalism in History Textbooks* (Stockholm, 1928), p. 95.

73. F.H. Johnson, 'History Courses and Textbooks', *H*, xiii (1928), pp. 243–6.

74. HA, *A List of Illustrations for Use in History Teaching in Schools* (HA leaflet no. 82, London, 1930), p. 5; *The Times*, 5 November 1938.

75. Sir H.A. Miers, 'Museums and Education', *Journal of the Royal Society of Arts* (February 1929), pp. 370–1; B. Winstanley, 'The Use and Development of Museum Services for Schools', in G.Z.F. Bereday and J.A. Lauwerys (eds), *The Year Book of Education 1960: Communication, Media and the School* (London, 1960), pp. 296–7; S. Thompson, 'Museum Services for Schools', in ibid., p. 300.

76. B.J. Elliott, 'Genesis of the History Teaching Film', *TH* (October 1977), p. 3; G.T. Hankin, 'The Cinematograph in the Classroom: Scenario of a Film Dealing with the Industrial Revolution', *H*, viii (1924), pp. 275–83; A.F. Pollard quoted in *H*, xi (1926), p. 38.

77. *The Times*, 29 October 1930; Elliott, 'Cinematograph in the Classroom', pp. 4–5.

78. A. Briggs, *The History of Broadcasting in the United Kingdom*, vol. ii, *The Golden Age of Wireless* (Oxford, 1965), p. 189; Carnegie United Kingdom

Trustees, *Educational Broadcasting: Report of a Special Investigation in the County of Kent during the Year 1927* (Dunfermline, 1928).

79. M. Somerville, 'How School Broadcasting Grew Up', in R. Palmer (ed.), *School Broadcasting in Britain* (London, 1952), pp. 11–12; B.J. Elliott, 'B.B.C. History Talks for Schools: The Early Years', *TH*, iv (1976), pp. 350–8.

80. Briggs, *Golden Age of Wireless*, pp. 198, 206.

81. HiEP: interview, M. Clarke, 12 May 2010, p. 6.

82. HiEP: interviews, N. Roper, 5 August 2010, p. 4; K. Kelsey, 24 March 2010, p. 4.

83. HiEP: interview, R. Major, 5 August 2010, p. 7; survey, RM/P20/HiE4.

84. McKibbin, *Classes and Cultures*, pp. 218–19.

85. Stevenson, *British Society, 1914–45*, p. 258.

86. Selby-Bigge, *Board of Education*, pp. 154–8; P. Gordon, 'Policy Formation and the Work of His Majesty's Inspectorate, 1918–45', in D. Cook and G. McCulloch (eds), *History, Politics and Policy-Making in Education: A Festschrift presented to Richard Aldrich* (London, 2007), pp. 89–100.

87. Selby-Bigge, *Board of Education*, pp. 123, 147–50.

88. BoE, *General Report on the Teaching of History in London Elementary Schools, 1927* (London, 1927), pp. 8, 12, 15–16.

89. BoE, *General Report on the Teaching of History in London Elementary Schools, 1927*, p. 7.

90. BoE, *Report on the Instruction of the Young in the Aims and Achievements of the League of Nations* (London, 1932), p. 7; B.J. Elliott, 'The League of Nations and History Teaching in England: A Study in Benevolent Bias', *HoE*, vi (1977), pp. 131–41; H. McCarthy, 'The League of Nations, Public Ritual and National Identity in Britain, c. 1919–56', *HWJ*, no. 70 (2010), pp. 109–33.

91. HiEP: surveys, EF/P27/HiE11; MC/P28/HiE14; WL/P29/HiE19.

92. HiEP: surveys, BE/P19/HiE55; RM/P20/HiE4.

93. HiEP: surveys, JC/P24/HiE9; AW/P27/HiE3.

94. HiEP: surveys, SK/P29/HiE6; ED/P29/HiE189.

95. HiEP: surveys, JW/P29/HiE13; SK/P29/HiE6.

96. HiEP: survey, AW/P27/HiE3.

97. HiEP: survey, ED/P29/HiE189.

98. TNA: ED 109/4077, Wandsworth Technical Institute Secondary School: Supplementary Inspection, 26th and 27th June, 1923, pp. 1–3.

99. LMA: EO/PS/12/P10/1-2, Report of Inspection of Parliament Hill County School, St Pancras, London, held on 8th, 9th, 10th and 11th June 1926, p. 7.

100. TNA: ED 109/3712, Report of Inspection of Roan School for Boys, Greenwich, London, held on 15th, 16th, 17th and 18th November, 1938, pp. 2–3, 6–7.

101. HiEP: interview, J. Geddes, 21 July 2010, p. 6.

102. HiEP: survey, BE/P19/HiE55.

103. HiEP: survey, NR/P23/HiE186.

104. HiEP: survey, JC/P24/HiE9.

105. HiEP: survey, KK/P23/HiE8.

106. Secondary School Examination Council, *The School Certificate*, p. 84.

107. Secondary School Examination Council, *The Higher School Certificate Examination – Being the report of the Panel of Investigators appointed by the Secondary Schools Examination Council to enquire into the Eight Approved Higher School Certificate Examinations held in the Summer of 1937* (London, 1938), p. 65.

108. Marten, 'First School Examination', p. 23.

109. See Appendix E.

110. Quoted in P. Brindle, 'Past Histories: History and the Elementary School Classroom in Early Twentieth Century England' (unpublished PhD thesis, University of Cambridge, 1998), p. 55.

111. B. Porter, *The Absent-Minded Imperialists: Empire, Society and Culture in Britain* (Oxford, 2004), pp. 263–4; H.M. Burton, *The Education of the Countryman* (London, 1943), pp. 24–8; McKibbin, *Classes and Cultures*, pp. 208–9.

112. Bryant, *Coalition Diaries*, vol. i, p. 214; vol. ii, p. 566; Percy, *Some Memories*, pp.106–9. For a similar anti-League view, see T.F. Tout, 'The Middle Ages in the Teaching of History', *H*, viii (1923), pp. 3–4.

113. BoE, *Education in 1938: Being the Report of the Board of Education and the Statistics of Public Education for England and Wales* (London, 1939), pp. 93, 129.

114. B. Simon, *Education and the Social Order, 1940–1990* (New York, 1991), p. 25; P. Gordon, R. Aldrich and D. Dean, *Education and Policy in England in the Twentieth Century* (London, 1991), pp. 59–60.

115. McKibbin, *Classes and Cultures*, pp. 220–1.

116. P.H.J.H. Gosden, *Education in the Second World War: A Study in Policy and Administration* (London, 1976), p. 72; B.J. Elliott, 'The Impact of the Second World War Upon History Teaching in Britain', *JEAH*, xxvi (1994), p. 154.

117. Correspondence, *H*, xxv (1940), p. 6.

118. HiEP: interviews, E. Deeble, 10 August 2010, p. 6; D.B. Gordon, 4 August 2010, pp. 1–2; survey, DG/P33/HiE20.

119. HiEP: surveys, MC/P33/HiE33; PJ/P35/HiE46.

120. HiEP: survey, AW/P27/HiE3.

121. HiEP: survey, JW/P29/HiE13.

122. M.V.C. Jeffreys, 'The Study of History in Schools', *The New Era*, xxi (1940), pp. 162–3.

123. J.D. Mackie, 'The Teaching of History and the War', *H*, xxv (1940), pp. 138–40; Robbins, '*History*, the Historical Association and the "National Past"', p. 424.

124. Correspondence, *H*, xxx (1945), pp. 177–8.

125. BoE, 'The schools in wartime', memoranda nos 26, 28, 33, 36, 39, 40; Gosden, *Education in the Second World War*, pp. 86–7; Elliott, 'Impact of the Second World War upon History Teaching', p. 156.

126. BoE, *Curriculum and Examinations in Secondary Schools: Report of the Committee of the Secondary School Examinations Council appointed by the President of the Board of Education in 1941* (London, 1943), pp. 99–101.

127. S.M. Toyne, 'History and the Norwood Report', *H*, xxix (1944), pp. 68–70.

128. R.R. Reid and S.M. Toyne, *The Planning of a History Syllabus for Schools* (HA pamphlet no. 128, London, 1944).

129. Elliott, 'Impact of the Second World War upon History Teaching in Britain', p. 158.

Chapter 3   History and the Welfare State, 1944–64

1. R.A. Butler, *The Art of the Possible* (London, 1971), p. 17.

2. P. Stafford, 'Political Autobiography and the Art of the Possible: R.A. Butler at the Foreign Office, 1938–1939', *HJ*, xxviii (1985), pp. 901–22.

3. Lord Eustace Percy, *Some Memories* (London, 1958), pp. 96–7.

4. Butler, *Art of the Possible*, pp. 90, 108.

5. P. Hennessy, *Never Again: Britain, 1945–51* (London, 1992), p. 145.

6. P. Addison, *The Road to 1945: British Politics and the Second World War* (London, 1975), pp. 171–2.

7. G. Bernbaum, *Social Change and the Schools, 1918–1944* (London, 1967), p. 105; R. McKibbin, *Classes and Cultures: England, 1918–1951* (Oxford, 1998), p. 221.

8. H.C. Dent, *Education in Transition* (London, 1944), pp. 204–15; P. Addison, *Now the War is Over: A Social History of Britain, 1945–51* (London, 1985), p. 145; Butler, *Art of the Possible*, p. 94.

9. Hennessy, *Never Again*, p. 156; K. Jeffereys, 'R.A. Butler, the Board of Education and the 1944 Education Act', *H*, lxix (1984), pp. 315–31; J. Harris, 'Political Ideas and the Debate on State Welfare', in H.L. Smith (ed.), *War and Social Change: British Society in the Second World War* (Manchester, 1986), pp. 239–46; M. Barber, *The Making of the 1944 Education Act* (London, 1994), esp. pp. 107–22.

10. BoE, *On Educational Reconstruction* (London, 1943), p. 19; Addison, *Road to 1945*, p. 238.

11. B. Simon, *Education and the Social Order, 1940–1990* (New York, 1991), p. 61; D. Kynaston, *Austerity Britain, 1945–51* (London, 2007), pp. 27–9; BoE, *Curriculum and Examinations in Secondary Schools: Report of the Committee of the Secondary School Examinations Council appointed by the President of the Board of Education in 1941* (hereafter Norwood Report) (London, 1943), p. 4.

12. Norwood Report, pp. 2–3.

13. McKibbin, *Classes and Cultures*, p. 224.

14. P.H.J.H. Gosden, *Education in the Second World War: A Study in Policy and Administration* (London, 1976), pp. 321–31.

15. Education Act 1944, Sec 1(1) and Sec 8(1): see D. Gillard, *The History of Education in England*, at www.educationengland.org.uk/documents/pdfs/1944-education-act.pdf (accessed 4 August 2011).

16. B. Harrison, *Seeking a Role: The United Kingdom, 1951–70* (Oxford, 2009), pp. 49–50.

17. Hennessy, *Never Again*, pp. 158–62.

18. McKibbin, *Classes and Cultures*, p. 233.

19. Simon, *Education and the Social Order*, p. 106.

20. Hennessy, *Never Again*, p. 160.

21. McKibbin, *Classes and Cultures*, pp. 226–7; Harrison, *Seeking a Role*, p. 50; P. Hennessy, *Having It So Good: Britain in the Fifties* (London, 2006), pp. 72–4; P. Addison, *No Turning Back: The Peacetime Revolutions of Post-War Britain* (Oxford, 2010), pp. 38–41.

22. *The Times Educational Supplement*, 3 December 1954; P. Addison, *Churchill on the Home Front, 1900–1945* (London, 1992), pp. 416–17.

23. Hennessy, *Having It So Good*, pp. 217–18.

24. Addison, *No Turning Back*, p. 47; N. Annan, *Our Age: English Intellectuals Between the World Wars – A Group Portrait* (New York, 1990), p. 407; R. Lowe, *Education in the Post-War Years* (London, 1988), pp. 89–91.

25. D. Sandbrook, *Never Had It So Good: A History of Britain from Suez to the Beatles* (London, 2005), p. 395.

26. D. Dean, 'Preservation or Renovation? The Dilemmas of Conservative Education Policy 1955–1960', *TCBH*, iii (1992), pp. 14–15; D. Kynaston, *Family Britain, 1951–57* (London, 2009), pp. 411–12.

27. MoE, *Secondary Education for All: A New Drive* (London 1958), pp. 4–6.

28. MoE, *Half Our Future: A Report of the Central Advisory Council for Education (England)*, (London 1963) (hereafter Newsom Report), pp. xiii–xiv.

29. Simon, *Education and the Social Order*, pp. 214, 273; Addison, *No Turning Back*, p. 158. From April to October 1964, Boyle was demoted to being Minister of State (although still with a seat in the cabinet) in the new Department of Education and Science, of which Quintin Hogg was Secretary of State, and in overall charge of education for a second brief time.

30. Newsom Report, p iv; Addison, *No Turning Back*, pp. 157–8; C. Cook and D. McKie (eds), *Decade of Disillusion: Britain in the Sixties* (London, 1972), p. 172.

31. Addison, *No Turning Back*, p. 157.

32. Harrison, *Seeking a Role*, p. 349; Addison, *No Turning Back*, pp. 39, 47, 156.

33. BoE, *On Educational Reconstruction*, p. 11.

34. Harrison, *Seeking a Role*, p. 349; C. Chitty, 'Central Control of the School Curriculum, 1944–87', *HoE*, xvii (1988), p. 322.

35. MoE, *Teaching History* (pamphlet no. 23, London, 1952, 4th impression, 1960), p. 7.

36. MoE, *Teaching History*, pp. 10–11.

37. MoE, *Teaching History*, pp. 21–6.

38. MoE, *Primary Education: Suggestions for the Consideration of Teachers and Others Concerned with the work of Primary Schools* (London 1959), p. v.
39. MoE, *Teaching History*, p. 11.
40. MoE, *Teaching History*, pp. 31–6.
41. MoE, *Teaching History*, p. 11.
42. MoE, *Teaching History*, p. 31.
43. MoE, *Teaching History*, p. 12.
44. MoE, *Teaching History*, pp. 13–20.
45. Norwood Report, pp. 140–1.
46. Gosden, *Education in the Second World War*, pp. 380–7; Simon, *Education and the Social Order*, pp. 111–12.
47. J.A. Petch, *Fifty Years of Examining: The Joint Examination Board, 1903–1953* (London, 1953), pp. 92–3.
48. Simon, *Education and the Social Order*, pp. 113–14.
49. P. Fisher, *External Examinations in Secondary Schools in England and Wales, 1944–1964* (Leeds, 1982), pp. 32–3.
50. MoE, *Secondary School Examinations other than the GCE: Report of a Committee appointed by the Secondary Schools Examinations Council in July 1958* (London 1960), Table 3, p. 60; V. Brooks, 'The Role of External Examinations in the Making of Secondary Modern Schools in England, 1945–65', *HoE*, xxxvii (2008), p. 454.
51. A.C.F. Beales, 'Fifty Years of Historical Teaching', in HA, *The Historical Association 1906–1956* (London, 1957), p. 100.
52. Beales, 'Fifty Years', p. 102.
53. Gosden, *Education in the Second World War*, pp. 109–15.
54. Gosden, *Education in the Second World War*, pp. 388–410; H.C. Dent, *The Training of Teachers in England and Wales, 1800–1975* (London, 1977), pp. 111–15.
55. Dent, *Training of Teachers*, pp. 121–8.
56. A. Tropp, *The School Teachers: The Growth of the Teaching Profession in England and Wales from 1800 to the Present Day* (London, 1957), pp. 248–70; Dent, *Training of Teachers*, pp. 134–42.
57. Harrison, *Seeking a Role*, pp. 33–4, 350.
58. MoE, *Teaching History*, pp. 17, 18.
59. M. Reeves, *Why History?* (London, 1980), p. 53.
60. MoE, *Teaching History*, pp. 23–6.
61. MoE, *Teaching History*, pp. 41–51.
62. S. Purkis, 'The Unacceptable Face of History?', *TH*, no. 26 (1980), pp. 34–6; but cf. S. Lang, '"Mr History": The Achievement of R.J. Unstead Reconsidered', *TH*, no. 58 (1990), pp. 24–6.
63. For example, M. Reeves, *The Medieval Village* (London, 1954); M. Reeves, *The Medieval Castle* (London, 1960); M. Reeves, *The Elizabethan Country House* (London, 1984).
64. Reeves, *Why History?*, pp. 61–72.

65. HiEP: interview, M. Hinton, 25 January 2010, pp. 4, 11; surveys, RL/T27/HiE5; ED/T31/HiE11; EJ/T32/HiE8; HS/T33/HiE10; AE/T34/HiE19.

66. HiEP: survey, AW/P27/HiE3.

67. *The Times*, 4 June 1945.

68. J.A. Harrison, 'Films and Filmstrips', in G.Z.F. Bereday, J.A. Lauwerys (eds), *The Year Book of Education 1960: Communication, Media and the School* (London 1960), pp. 296–7.

69. K. Fawdry, *Everything but Alf Garnett: A Personal View of School Broadcasting*, (London, 1974), p. 49.

70. A. Briggs, *The History of Broadcasting in the United Kingdom*, vol. v, *Competition* (Oxford, 1995), p. 468.

71. MoE, *Teaching History*, p. 44.

72. A. Briggs, *The History of Broadcasting in the United Kingdom*, vol. iv, *Sound and Vision* (Oxford, 1979), pp. 831–8.

73. Briggs, *Competition*, p. 181; *BBC Annual Report, 1961–62* (London, 1962), p. 34.

74. HiEP: interview, C. Little, 13 May 2010, p. 6.

75. HiEP: survey, MP/T24/HiE1.

76. Briggs, *Sound and Vision*, p. 189.

77. Harrison, *Seeking a Role*, pp. 350–2; M. Croft, *Spare the Rod* (London, 1954), pp. 11, 79; E. Blishen, *Roaring Boys: A Schoolmaster's Agony* (London, 1955), pp. 104, 230; Kynaston, *Austerity Britain*, pp. 564–78; Kynaston, *Family Britain*, pp. 160–2, 408–14.

78. P. Gordon, 'Policy Formation and the Work of His Majesty's Inspectorate, 1918–45', in D. Crook and G. McCulloch (eds), *History, Politics and Policy-Making in Education: A Festschrift presented to Richard Aldrich* (London, 2007), pp. 100–5; E.L. Edmonds, *The School Inspector* (London, 1962), pp. 148–53.

79. O.A. Hartley, 'Inspectorates in the British Central Government', *PA*, 1 (1972), p. 451; R.F. Goodings and J.E. Dunford, 'Her Majesty's Inspectorate of Schools, 1839–1989: The Question of Independence', *JEAH*, xxii (1990), pp. 4–5.

80. BBC Written Archives Centre: R16/757/1, The School Broadcasting Council for the United Kingdom, 'Report on a Survey of History Teaching and Listening to World History and History I in Primary and All Age Schools', May 1955.

81. HiEP: surveys, KI/P52/HiE92; RT/P53/HiE90.

82. TNA: ED 109/9123, Report by HM Inspectors on Reigate Grammar School, Surrey, inspected on 22nd, 23rd, 24th and 25th November 1949, pp. 3–7; ED 109/9200, Report by HM Inspectors on the Joseph Rowntree Secondary School, New Earswick, Yorkshire (North Riding), inspected on 10th, 11th and 12th May 1949, p. 6.

83. TNA: ED 109/9138, Report by HM Inspectors on Hastings High School for Girls, Hastings, inspected on 26th, 27th, 28th and 29th February 1952, p. 9; ED 109/9200, Report by HM Inspectors on Lady Lumley's Grammar School, Pickering, Yorkshire (North Riding), inspected on 16th, 17th and

18th March 1954, pp. 3, 4, 6; ED 109/9200, Report by HM Inspectors on Northallerton Grammar School, Yorkshire (North Riding), inspected on 4th, 5th, 6th and 7th May 1954, p. 6.

84. HiEP: survey, RH/P42/HiE71.
85. SCHP, *A New Look at History* (Edinburgh, 1976), p. 26.
86. HiEP: interview, C. Little, 13 May 2010, pp. 10–11; survey, CL/P38/HiE23.
87. HiEP: survey, DS/P44/HiE58.
88. HiEP: survey, SW/P43/HiE65.
89. HiEP: interview, S. Ensor, 15 June 2010, p. 6; surveys, JI/P52/HiE132; AF/P54/HiE103; SE/P55/HiE97.
90. HiEP: survey, IS/P45/HiE72.
91. HiEP: survey, PW/P40/HiE76.
92. HiEP: survey, SC/P45/HiE190.
93. HiEP: surveys, IS/P45/HiE72; JL/P46/HiE198; RL/P48/HiE75.
94. HiEP: surveys, RT/P53/HiE90; JS/P54/HiE89.
95. TNA: ED 109/2011, Report by HM Inspectors on Stanley Technical Trade School, Croydon, inspected on 29th February, 1st and 2nd March 1956, p. 6; ED 109/9399, Report by HM Inspectors on Walton County Secondary Technical School, Liverpool, inspected on 5th, 6th, 7th and 8th February 1957, p. 6.
96. K.J.R. Robson and H.H. Briscoe, 'History in the Secondary School', *The Vocational Aspect of Secondary and Further Education*, no. 15, (1955), pp. 128–34.
97. HiEP: interview, S. Kotak, 6 August 2010; survey, SK/P29/HiEP6.
98. G. Rudé, 'The Common History Syllabus in the Comprehensive School', in B. Simon (ed.), *New Trends in English Education: A Symposium* (London, 1957), p. 152.
99. Rudé, 'Common History Syllabus', p. 157.
100. B.D. Vernon, *Ellen Wilkinson, 1891–1947* (London, 1982), pp. 222–3; Hennessy, *Never Again*, p. 159. Our italics.
101. MoE, *Teaching History*, p. 13.
102. MoE, *Teaching History*, pp. 37–9.
103. C. Cannon, 'Social Studies in Secondary Schools', *Educational Review*, xvii (1964), p. 21.
104. TNA: ED 109/9379, Report by HM Inspectors on Norbury Manor County Secondary Girls' School, Croydon, inspected on 25th, 26th and 27th January 1956, pp. 2, 5; ED 109/9363, Report by HM Inspectors on Nechelles County Modern School, Birmingham, inspected on 9th, 10th, 11th and 12th June 1958, p. 5; ED 109/9363, Report by HM Inspectors on Harborne Hill County Modern School, Birmingham, inspected on 23rd, 24th, 25th and 26th February 1959, p. 8.
105. HiEP: survey, RL/T27/HiE5.
106. HiEP: interviews, E. Hinde, 25 January 2010, p. 6; E. Houlder, 2 July 2010, p. 7.
107. E. Blishen, *The School That I'd Like* (Harmondsworth, 1969), p. 66; HiEP: survey, DC/P60/HiE138.
108. HiEP: interview, D.Newham, 12 May 2010, p. 9; survey, DN/P38/HiE29.

109. HiEP: survey, JL/P49/HiE66.
110. M. Booth, *History Betrayed?* (London, 1969), p. 66.
111. For this paragraph, see Appendix E.
112. *Hansard, Lords*, vol. 132, 20 June, col. 276; 11 July, col. 796.
113. *Hansard, Commons*, vol. 460, 27 January 1949, cols. 1075–76.
114. Quoted in A. Low-Beer, 'Books and the Teaching of History in School', *H*, lxix (1979), p. 394.
115. A. Syriatou, 'Teaching European History in English Secondary Schools, 1947–75', in B. Brivati and H. Jones (eds), *From Reconstruction to Integration: Britain and Europe since 1945* (London, 1993), p. 174; R. Weight, *Patriots: National Identity in Britain, 1940–2000* (London, 2002), p. 354; N. Joicey, 'A Paperback Guide to Progress: Penguin Books, 1935–c.1951', *TCBH*, iv (1993), pp. 44–56.
116. D. Cannadine, *Making History Now and Then: Discoveries, Controversies and Explorations* (London, 2008), pp. 149–59.

Chapter 4   History for a Nation 'In Decline', 1964–79

1. B. Harrison, *Finding a Role? The United Kingdom, 1970–1990* (Oxford, 2010), pp. 410–11.
2. J.E. Alt, *The Politics of Economic Decline: Economic Management and Political Behaviour in Britain since 1964* (Cambridge, 1979); B.R. Tomlinson, 'The Contraction of England: National Decline and the Loss of Empire', *Journal of Imperial and Commonwealth History*, ix (1982), pp. 58–72; P. Warwick, 'Did Britain Change? An Inquiry into the Causes of National Decline', *JCH*, xx (1985), pp. 99–133; D.A. Low, *The Contraction of England* (Cambridge, 1985).
3. M. Kogan (ed.), *The Politics of Education: Conversations with Edward Boyle and Anthony Crosland* (Harmondsworth, 1971), catches many of these shared presumptions.
4. For one attempt to define and address these issues, see J.H. Plumb, 'The Historian's Dilemma', in J.H. Plumb (ed.), *Crisis in the Humanities* (Harmondsworth, 1964), pp. 24–44.
5. B. Pimlott, *Harold Wilson* (London, 1992), pp. 511–12; J. Callaghan, *Time and Chance* (London, 1987), p. 409; K.O. Morgan, *Callaghan: A Life* (Oxford, 1997), pp. 117–18.
6. DES, 'Circular 10/65: the organisation of secondary education', 12 July 1965: see D. Gillard, *The History of Education in England*, at www.educationengland.org.uk/documents/des/circular10-65html (accessed 4 August 2011).
7. S. Crosland, *Tony Crosland* (London, 1982), pp. 141–8.
8. For a vivid and appreciative picture of Crosland from a junior minister's perspective, see S. Williams, *Climbing the Bookshelves* (London, 2009), pp. 169–79.

9. P.C. Gordon Walker, *The Sixteenth and Seventeenth Centuries: The Rise of the Nations* (London, 1935); P.C. Gordon Walker, *An Outline of Man's History* (London, 1939); P.C. Gordon Walker, 'Capitalism and the Reformation', *Economic History Review*, viii (1937), pp. 1–19.

10. E. Short, *Education in a Changing World* (London, 1971), pp. 77–81.

11. P. Addison, *No Turning Back: The Peacetime Revolutions of Post-War Britain* (Oxford, 2010), p. 158. (As Crosland had recognized, Scotland was outside the remit of the Secretary of State, while Northern Ireland opted out, and retained the eleven plus and its grammar schools until 2008.)

12. M. Thatcher, *The Path to Power* (London, 1995), pp. 17–18.

13. Pimlott, *Harold Wilson*, p. 512.

14. J. Campbell, *Margaret Thatcher*, vol. i, *The Grocer's Daughter* (London, 2000), pp. 221–4.

15. J. Campbell, *Edward Heath: A Biography* (London, 1993), p. 387; H. Young, *The Iron Lady: A Biography of Margaret Thatcher* (New York, 1989), p. 69.

16. Campbell, *The Grocer's Daughter*, pp. 228–9.

17. Campbell, *Heath*, pp. 388–9; Young, *Iron Lady*, p. 71.

18. Campbell, *The Grocer's Daughter*, pp. 211–14.

19. Young, *Iron Lady*, pp. 67, 78.

20. Thatcher, *Path to Power*, p. 166; Young, *Iron Lady*, p. 68; Addison, *No Turning Back*, p. 159; G. Smith, 'Schools', in A.H. Halsey and J. Webb (eds), *Twentieth Century British Social Trends* (3rd edn, Basingstoke, 2000), p. 199.

21. Williams, *Climbing the Bookshelves*, pp. 233–9.

22. Smith, 'Schools', in Halsey and Webb (eds), *Twentieth-Century British Social Trends*, p. 199

23. Central Advisory Council for Education (England), *Children and their Primary Schools* (hereafter Plowden Report) (London, 1967), vol. i, pp. 189–91.

24. Plowden Report, vol. i, pp. 225–6.

25. Plowden Report, vol. i, pp. 228–9.

26. Plowden Report, vol. i, p. 227.

27. Plowden Report, vol. i, pp. 226–30.

28. Plowden Report, vol. i, p. 226.

29. Central Advisory Council for Education (England), *Half Our Future* (hereafter Newsom Report) (London, 1963), pp. 124, 163.

30. Newsom Report, pp. 164–5.

31. Newsom Report, p. 166.

32. Newsom Report, pp. 166–7.

33. DES, *Towards World History* (education pamphlet no. 52, London, 1967), pp. 3–5, 10, 16–17.

34. DES, *Towards World History*, pp. 16–17.

35. DES, *Towards World History*, pp. 18–20.

36. DES, *Towards World History*, pp. 22–6.

37. Plowden Report, vol. i, p. 226; DES, *Towards World History*, p. 7.

38. J.W. Docking, 'History and the CSE', *TH*, i, no. 3 (1970), pp. 292–3.

39. G. Partington, *Teacher Education in England and Wales* (London, 1999), p. 25.

40. M. Honeybone, 'The Development of Formal Historical Thought in Schoolchildren', *TH*, ii, no. 6 (1971), p. 148; HiEP: interview, D. Burrell, 21 May 2009, pp. 18–19.

41. J. Fines and R. Verrier, *The Drama of History: An Experiment in Co-operative Teaching* (London, 1974).

42. J. West, 'Primary School Children's Perception of Authenticity and Time in Historical Narrative Pictures', *TH*, no. 29 (1981), pp. 8–10.

43. R.N. Hallam, 'Piaget and Thinking in History', in M. Ballard (ed.), *New Movements in the Study and Teaching of History* (London, 1970), pp. 162–78.

44. M. Price, 'History in Danger', *H*, liii (1968), pp. 342–7.

45. P.M. Giles, 'History in the Secondary Schools: A Survey', *JCS*, v (1973), p. 139.

46. W.M. Lamont, 'Teaching History, A *Black Paper* Reconsidered', *TH*, i, no. 1 (1969), pp. 144–7; R. Wake, 'Where Have We Got To?', *TH*, ii, no. 6 (1971), pp. 169–71.

47. Schools Council, *Humanities for the Young School Leaver: An Approach Through History* (London, 1969), p. 10.

48. J.B. Coltham and J. Fines, *Educational Objectives for the Study of History* (HA pamphlet no. 35, Oxford, 1971), pp. 10–16.

49. J. Coltham, 'Educational Objectives and the Teaching of History', *TH*, ii, no. 7 (1972), pp. 278–9; M. Roberts, 'Educational Objectives for the Study of History: The Relevance of Dr Coltham's and Dr Fines' Framework to "O" Level Courses', *TH*, ii, no. 8 (1977), pp. 347–50.

50. Sylvester, 'Change and Continuity', pp. 15–16; P.H.J.H. Gosden and D.W. Sylvester, *History for the Average Child* (Oxford, 1968); HiEP interview: D. Sylvester, 7 July 2009, pp. 1, 5.

51. There is a full description of the Project in D. Shemilt, *History 13–16 Evaluation Study* (Edinburgh, 1980), pp. 1–9.

52. SCHP, *What is History?* (Edinburgh, 1976); SCHP, *A New Look at History* (Edinburgh, 1976).

53. SCHP, *New Look*, p. 13; see also Appendix C.

54. SCHP, *New Look*, pp. 47–8.

55. SCHP, *New Look*, p. 21; Gosden and Sylvester, *Average Child*, p. 48; HiEP interview: D. Sylvester, 7 July 2009, pp. 1–4.

56. SCHP, *New Look*, pp. 40–1.

57. G.R. Elton, 'What Sort of History Should We Teach?', in Ballard, *New Movements*, pp. 221–30; Shemilt, *History 13–16*, p. v; HiEP interview: D. Sylvester, 7 July 2009, p. 19.

58. HiEP: interviews, A. Farmer, 9 July 2009, p. 6; C. Culpin, 22 September 2009, p. 11.

59. HiEP: interviews, J.D. Clare, 7 April 2010, pp. 9–10; S. Harrison, 6 May 2009, p. 6; C. Culpin, 22 September 2009, p. 9; D. Shemilt, 3 July 2009, p. 9; I. Dawson, 9 June 2009, pp. 12–13.

60. SCHP, *New Look*, p. 21; R. Wolfson, 'Schools Council History 13–16 Project: An Upper Schools' Experience', *TH*, no. 27 (1980), pp. 25–30; B. Swinnerton and I. Jenkins, *Secondary School History Teaching in England and Wales: A Review of Empirical Research, 1960–1998* (Leeds, 1998), p. 24.

61. The six-volume series is as follows: R.E.C. Burrell, *The Invaders* (Oxford, 1980); R.E.C. Burrell, *The Middle Ages* (Oxford, 1980); R.E.C. Burrell, *Tudors and Stuarts* (Oxford, 1981); P.F. and M. Speed, *Britain Becomes a World Power* (Oxford, 1979); P.F. and M. Speed, *The Modern Age* (Oxford, 1979); P.F. and M. Speed, *Twentieth Century World* (Oxford, 1982).

62. E.g. P. Moss, *History Alive: Introductory Book* (St Albans, 1970); P. Moss , *Modern World History* (St Albans, 1978); R.J. Cootes and L.E. Snellgrove, *The Ancient World* (Harlow, 2nd edn, 1991); R.J. Cootes and L.E. Snellgrove, *The Middle Ages* (Harlow, 2nd edn, 1989).

63. For instance, the Documentary History series of 29 titles available by 1979, such as A. Kendall, *Medieval Pilgrims* (London, 1970); M. Gibson, *The Vikings* (London, 1972); J. Dorner, *People of Elizabethan England* (London, 1973).

64. HiEP: interview, A. Reid, 4 September 2009, p. 3.

65. D. Warnes, 'The Home-Brewed Textbook: How to Produce Your Own History Classroom Texts', *TH*, no. 31 (1981), pp. 26–7.

66. HiEP: interview, J. Simkin, 4 June 2009, p. 21; e.g. J. Simkin, *Contemporary Accounts of the Second World War* (Brighton, 1984); J. Simkin, *Contemporary Accounts of the Industrial Revolution* (Brighton, 1984).

67. B.J. Elliott, 'BBC History Talks for Schools: The Early Years', *TH*, iv, no. 16 (1976), p. 358.

68. HiEP interview: N. Whines, 19 January 2010, p. 23. From 1972 to 2002, Whines worked as a BBC radio and TV producer specializing in history programmes.

69. K. Fawdry, 'Television for Schools' in *A Lecture by Kenneth Fawdry, Head of School Broadcasting, Television* (London, 1967), pp. 6–10; HiEP interview: N. Whines, 19 January 2010, pp. 6–7.

70. HiEP: interview, N. Whines, 19 January 2010, pp. 22–3.

71. HiEP: interview, N. Whines, 19 January 2010, p. 11; information recorded in informal interview with I. Fell, 18 January 2010.

72. HiEP: interview, P.A. Dawson, 12 April 2010, p. 11.

73. HiEP: information recorded in informal interview with K. Moorse, 21 June 2010.

74. HiEP: interview, D. Anderson, 15 June 2009, pp. 7–9; J. Duckworth, 'Imagination in Teaching History', *TH*, ii (1971), pp. 49–52.

75. M.B. Booth, *History Betrayed?* (London, 1969), pp. 1–32.

76. J. Nichol, 'The Teaching of History, 11–18: A Consistent Approach', *TH*, no. 25 (1979), pp. 9–14.

77. R.E. Aldrich, 'New History: An Historical Perspective', in A.K. Dickinson, P.J. Lee and P.J. Rogers (eds), *Learning History* (London, 1984), pp. 210–24.

78. HiEP: interview, A. Reid, 4 September 2009, p. 5; P.J. Rogers, *The New History: Theory into Practice* (HA pamphlet, Teaching of History Series, no. 44, London, 1980).

79. DES, *Primary Education in England: A Survey by H.M. Inspectors of Schools* (London, 1978), pp. 72–3.

80. HiEP: interview, P. Harnett, 9 September 2009, pp. 13–15. For a contemporary debate on the effects of child-centred learning on history teaching in primary schools see: C. Steedman, 'Battlegrounds: History in Primary Schools', *HWJ*, no. 17 (1984), pp. 102–12; W.M. Lamont, 'History in Primary Schools: A Comment', *HWJ*, no. 19 (1985), pp. 144–7.

81. HiEP: interview, P. Harnett, 9 September 2009, pp. 2–3, 20.

82. HiEP: surveys, GA/P56/HiE199, AS/P60/HiE137, EH/P63/HiE106.

83. HiEP: surveys, AG/P61/HiE152, NF/P62/HiE142, AS/P63/HiE167.

84. A. Low-Beer and J. Blyth, *Teaching History to Younger Children* (HA pamphlet, no. 52, London, 1983), pp. 5, 8, 14–17.

85. TNA: ED 109/9596, Report by HM Inspectors on Eastfield County Grammar School, Wolverhampton, inspected on 4th and 5th February and 13th March, 1964, pp. 2, 6–8.

86. TNA: ED 109/9680, Report by HM Inspectors on Luton Secondary Technical School, Luton, inspected on 1st to 4th June 1965 and other dates, pp. 2, 10–11.

87. TNA: ED 109/9596, Report by HM Inspectors on St Chad's College, Wolverhampton, inspected on 1st to 5th June 1964, p. 4.

88. TNA: ED 109/9619, Report by HM Inspectors on Manor Secondary School for Girls, Cambridgeshire, inspected on 3rd to 6th May, 1965 pp. 5–6; ED 109/9688, Report by HM Inspectors on St Edmund's Roman Catholic Secondary Modern School, Portsmouth, inspected on 8th to 11th February 1966, p. 9.

89. TNA: ED 109/9619, Report by HM Inspectors on Burwell County Secondary School, Cambridgeshire, inspected on the 19th and 20th May 1965, p. 3; ED 109/9688, Report by HM Inspectors on Eastney County Secondary School for Boys, Portsmouth, inspected on the 12th to 15th October 1965, pp. 6, 8–9.

90. TNA: ED 109/9807, Report by HM Inspectors on Wallington High School for Girls, London Borough of Sutton, inspected 10–14 November 1980, p. 2: 'Wallington High School for Girls is one of the four maintained single-sex grammar schools in the London Borough of Sutton.'

91. See for instance, these articles from the early 1970s: M.C. Atkinson, 'The Secondary School History Syllabus', *TH* i, no. 4 (1970), pp. 288–91; C. Newcombe, 'Wargames in the Classroom', *TH*, i, no. 4 (1970), pp. 300–2; R.G.E. Wood, 'Archive Units for Teaching', *TH* ii, no. 6 (1971), pp. 158–65; E. Rayner, 'American History in Schools', *TH* ii, no. 7 (1972), pp. 261–4.

92. TNA: ED 109/9807, Report by HM Inspectors on Featherstone High School, London Borough of Ealing, inspected 14–18 June 1976, pp. 1–3, 5–7.

93. TNA: ED 109/9807, Report by HM Inspectors on Ravenscroft Comprehensive School, Barnet, inspected 29 September–3 October 1980, pp. 2, 20–1.
94. TNA: ED 109/9807, Report by HM Inspectors on Townfield School, Hayes, London Borough of Willingdon, inspected 24–28 March 1980, pp. 20–22.
95. HiEP: interview, J.D. Clare, 7 April 2010, p. 4.
96. HiEP: surveys, GD/P50/HiE91; SE/P55/HiE97.
97. HiEP: surveys, MM/P52/HiE95; DC/P60/HiE138.
98. HiEP: interview, D. Burrell, 21 May 2009, p. 11; survey, SS/T45/HiE34.
99. HiEP: interviews, E. Houlder, 2 July 2010, p. 6; P.A. Dawson, 12 April 2010, p. 11.
100. HiEP: surveys, MJ/P51/HiE94; HP/P53/HiE98.
101. HiEP: survey, JD/P61/HiE156.
102. HiEP: interviews, C. Hinton, 11 January 2010, p. 6; J. Edgar, 15 June 2010, p. 9; J.D. Clare, 7 April 2010, p. 21.
103. HiEP interview, J. Edgar, 15 June 2010, p. 8.
104. HiEP: surveys, CH/P67/HiE169; KM/P70/HiE160.
105. HiEP: surveys, ZB/P71/HiE115;FM/P65/HiE139/CH/P66/HiE157; JD/P71/HiE116.
106. HiEP: survey, SH/P67/HiE170.
107. HiEP: survey, FK/P69/HiE107.
108. HiEP: surveys, MS/P58/HiE196; JB/P62/HiE149.
109. HiEP: surveys, DC/P60/HiE137; HM/P54/HiE202.
110. HiEP: surveys, JB/P66/HiE104; SH/P66/HiE181.
111. For this and the next paragraph, see Appendix E.
112. B. Davies and P. Pritchard, 'History Still in Danger?', *TH*, iv, no. 14 (1975), pp. 113–16; R.F. Moore, 'History and Integrated Studies: Surrender or Survival?', *TH*, iv, no. 14 (1975), pp. 109–12; B. Parker, 'History Abandoned?', *TH*, no. 30 (1981), pp. 3–5; T.L. Fisher, 'Can History Survive?', *TH*, no. 32 (1982), pp. 8–10; R.F. Moore, 'History Abandoned? The Need for a Continuing Debate', *TH*, no. 32 (1982), pp. 26–8; M. Parker, 'History in Danger', *TH*, no. 35 (1983), pp. 3–5.
113. HiEP: interiew, E. Evans, 29 June 2009, p. 18.
114. HiEP: interview, P.A. Dawson, 12 April 2010, p. 20.
115. H. and J. Patrick, 'Home Examinations after 1945', in S. Raban (ed.), *Examining the World: A History of the University of Cambridge Local Examinations Syndicate* (Cambridge, 2008), p. 94.
116. C.F. Strong, *History in the Secondary School* (London, 1964), pp. 74–9.
117. HiEP: interviews, S. Ensor, 15 June 2010, p. 20; A. Whitehead, 13 April 2010, p. 27; C1371-60 (anonymised interview), 2 July 2010, pp. 25–6.
118. J. Terraine, *The Great War* (London, 1963); M. Arnold-Forster, *The World at War* (London, 1974).
119. K. Clark, *Civilisation: A Personal View* (London, 1969); A. Cooke, *America: A Personal History* (New York, 1973).

120. D. Cannadine, *In Churchill's Shadow: Confronting the Past in Modern Britain* (London, 2003), pp. 237–40; R. Strong (ed.), *The Destruction of the Country House, 1875–1975* (London, 1975).

121. R. Boyson, *The Ashworth Cotton Enterprise: The Rise and Fall of a Family Firm, 1818–1880* (Oxford, 1970).

122. Harrison, *Finding a Role?*, p. 383; *Black Paper 1975: The Fight for Education* (London, 1975), p. 1.

123. Harrison, *Finding a Role?*, pp. 384–5.

124. Morgan, *Callaghan*, pp. 502–3, 540–1.

125. Williams, *Climbing the Bookshelves*, pp. 233–4.

126. DES, *School Examinations: The Report of the Steering Committee Established to Consider Proposals for Replacing the General Certificate of Education Ordinary Level and Certificate of Secondary Education Examinations by a Common System of Examining* (London, 1978).

127. DES, *Curriculum 11–16: Working Papers by Her Majesty's Inspectorate: A Contribution to Current Debate* (London, 1978), pp. 3–4, 60.

128. Callaghan, *Time and Chance*, pp. 409–12; Harrison, *Finding a Role?*, p. 385; Morgan, *Callaghan*, p. 541.

Chapter 5   History in the National Curriculum, 1979–2010

1. B. Harrison, 'Mrs Thatcher and the Intellectuals', *TCBH*, v (1994), pp. 206–45.

2. D. Cannadine, *In Churchill's Shadow: Confronting the Past in Modern Britain* (London, 2003), pp. 37–41; C. Barnett, *The Collapse of British Power* (London, 1972); C. Barnett, *The Audit of War: The Illusion and Reality of Britain as a Great Nation* (London, 1986); M.J. Wiener, *English Culture and the Decline of the Industrial Spirit, 1850–1980* (Cambridge, 1981).

3. J. Campbell, *Margaret Thatcher*, vol. i, *The Grocer's Daughter* (London, 2000), p. 214.

4. M. Thatcher, *The Downing Street Years* (London, 1993), pp. 595–6; B. Porter, '"Though Not an Historian Myself …": Margaret Thatcher and the Historians', *TCBH*, v (1994), pp. 246–56.

5. P. Addison, *No Turning Back: The Peacetime Revolutions of Post-War Britain* (Oxford, 2010), p. 302.

6. Harrison, 'Thatcher and the Intellectuals', pp. 211–12.

7. A. Denham and M. Garnett, *Keith Joseph* (London, 2001), pp. 30–3, 46–8.

8. M. Thatcher, *The Path to Power* (London, 1995), p. v.

9. Denham and Garnett, *Keith Joseph*, p. 368.

10. Harrison, 'Thatcher and the Intellectuals', p. 236; Denham and Garnett, *Keith Joseph*, p. 367; M. Wilkinson, *Lessons from Europe: A Comparison of British and West European Schooling* (London, 1977).

11. Denham and Garnett, *Keith Joseph*, pp. 375–8, 396.

12. P.J. Rooke, *Bulmershe: The Life of a College, 1964–89* (Reading, 1992), pp. 83–4.
13. D. Jones, *School of Education, 1946–1996* (Leicester, 2001), p. 50; Brooke, *Bulmershe*, p. 142.
14. DES, *A Framework for the School Curriculum* (London, 1980); DES, *The School Curriculum* (London, 1981); Campbell, *Grocer's Daughter*, p. 240.
15. DES, *Better Schools – A Summary* (London, 1985); DES, *Better Schools: Evaluation and Appraisal Conference, Birmingham, 14–15 November 1985* (London, 1986), p. 178.
16. Denham and Garnett, *Keith Joseph*, pp. 399–400; B. Harrison, *Finding a Role? The United Kingdom, 1970–1990* (Oxford, 2010), p. 385.
17. Denham and Garnett, *Keith Joseph*, pp. 386–7.
18. K. Baker (ed.), *The Faber Book of English History in Verse* (London, 1988); K. Baker, *The Prime Ministers: An Irreverent Political History in Cartoons* (London, 1995); K. Baker, *The Kings and Queens: An Irreverent Cartoon History of the British Monarchy* (London, 1996); K. Baker (ed.), *A Children's English History in Verse* (London, 2000); K. Baker, *George IV: A Life in Caricature* (London, 2005); K. Baker, *George III: A Life in Caricature* (London, 2007).
19. K. Baker, *The Turbulent Years: My Life in Politics* (London, 1993), pp. 167–8; R. Weight, *Patriots: National Identity in Britain, 1940–2000* (London, 2002), pp. 575–6; Addison, *No Turning Back*, pp. 301–3.
20. Harrison, *Finding a Role?*, pp. 386–7.
21. Baker, *Turbulent Years*, pp. 192–3.
22. HiEP: interview, J. Hamer, 1 June 2009, pp. 35–9.
23. HiEP: interview, M. Maddison, 21 September 2009, pp. 18–22.
24. J. Patten, *English Towns, 1500–1700* (London, 1978); J. Patten (ed.), *Pre-Industrial England* (London, 1979); J. Patten (ed.), *The Expanding City* (London, 1983).
25. G. Shephard, *Shephard's Watch: Illusions of Power in British Politics* (London, 2000).
26. G. Partington, *Teacher Education in England and Wales* (London, 1999), p. 77.
27. C. Mullin, *Decline and Fall: Diaries, 2005–2010* (London, 2010), p. 453.
28. T. Blair, Speech to US Congress, 17 July 2003, full text available at http://news.bbc.co.uk/go/pr/fr/-/1/hi/uk politics/3076253.stm (accessed 8 August 2011).
29. *Independent on Sunday*, 29 May 2011; *Daily Telegraph*, 16 June 2011.
30. Mullin, *Decline and Fall*, pp. 3, 63, 257, 451.
31. Sir Keith Joseph, 'Why Teach History in School', in *Historical Association Conference* (London, 1984), pp. 2–3; Weight, *Patriots*, p. 575.
32. DES, *GCSE the National Criteria* (London, 1985), p. 1, assessment objective 3.
33. G.R. Batho, M. Booth and R. Brown, *Teaching GCSE History* (rev. edn., London, 1987), pp. 42–3; N.Tate, *GCSE Coursework: A Teacher's Guide to Organisation and Assessment* (Basingstoke, 1987), p. 79; H. and J. Patrick,

'Home Examinations after 1945', in S. Raban (ed.), *Examining the World: A History of the University of Cambridge Local Examinations Syndicate* (Cambridge, 2008), p. 98.

34. R. Phillips, *History Teaching, Nationhood and the State: A Study in Educational Politics* (London, 1998), pp. 18–21.

35. Phillips, *History Teaching*, p. 4.

36. Baker, *Turbulent Years*, pp. 196–7; HiEP: interview, K. Baker, 22 October 2009, p. 6.

37. M.Thatcher, *The Downing Street Years* (London, 1993), p. 596; HiEP: interview, R. Hennessey, 11 November 2009, p. 11.

38. HiEP: interview, T. Lomas, 30 March 2009, p. 8.

39. HiEP: interviews, R. Hennessey, 11 November 2009, pp. 13–14; information recorded in informal interview with A. Prochaska, 24 August 2010; A. Prochaska, 'The History Working Group: Reflections and Diary', *HWJ*, no. 30 (2990), p. 83.

40. Thatcher, *Downing Street Years*, p. 596.

41. Thatcher, *Downing Street Years*, p. 597.

42. Phillips, *History Teaching*, p. 68; HiEP: interviews, T. Lomas, 30 March 2009, p. 10; R. Hennessey, 11 November 2009, p. 15; J. MacGregor, 3 November 2009, pp. 6–7.

43. DES, *National Curriculum History Working Group, Final Report* (London, 1990), pp. 7–8, 13–14, 116.

44. D. Graham with D. Tytler, *A Lesson for Us All: The Making of the National Curriculum* (London, 1993), p. 67.

45. Phillips, *History Teaching*, p. 69; copies of letters responding to consultation, September–October 1989, courtesy of R. Guyver.

46. G. Elwyn Jones, 'The Debate over the National Curriculum for History in England and Wales, 1989–90: The Role of the Press', *TCJ*, xi (2000), pp. 299–322; *The Times*, 2 April 1990.

47. *The Times*, 19 March 1990, 4 April 1990; *Independent*, 19 March 1990.

48. R. Samuel, 'History, the Nation and the Schools', *HWJ*, no. 30 (1990), pp. 75–80.

49. Jones, 'Debate over the National Curriculum', p. 319; *Times Educational Supplement*, 25 May 1990, 8 June 1990.

50. Phillips, *History Teaching*, pp. 83–9, 94–6.

51. HiEP: interview, A. Reid, 4 September 2009, pp. 20–1.

52. HiEP: interview, K. Clarke, 28 January 2010, p. 17.

53. HiEP: interview, K. Clarke, 28 January 2010, p. 11.

54. Phillips, *History Teaching*, pp. 104–8.

55. See Appendix D.

56. Phillips, *History Teaching*, p. 115.

57. HiEP: interview, T. Lomas, 30 March 2009, p. 11.

58. Phillips, *History Teaching*, p. 118.

59. Sir R. Dearing, *The National Curriculum and its Assessment: Final Report* (hereafter Dearing Report) (London, 1994), p. 46.

60. Phillips, *History Teaching*, pp. 120–1.

61. S. Lawlor (ed.), *The Dearing Debate: Assessment and the National Curriculum* (London, 1993); C.J.M. McGovern, *The SCAA Review of National Curriculum History: A Minority Report* (York, 1994), p. 3; HiEP: interview, C. McGovern, 28 August 2009, pp. 32–3.

62. Dearing Report, pp. i–v, 2–15; Department for Education and Employment, *History in the National Curriculum: England* (London, 1995), pp. 2–17, gives the statutory requirements.

63. K. Crawford, 'History in the Primary Curriculum: Back to the Basic Past?', *TH*, no. 75 (1974), pp. 15–19; Phillips, *History Teaching*, p. 126.

64. Department for Education and Employment, *Education for Citizenship and the Teaching of Democracy* (London, 1998).

65. www.dcsf.gov.uk/everychildmatters/ (accessed 12 June 2009).

66. HiEP: interview, D. Blunkett, 3 November 2009, pp. 1–2.

67. See Appendix D.

68. Sir K. Ajegbo, *Diversity and Citizenship* (London, 2007), pp. 8, 41–2; Qualifications and Curriculum Authority, *History: Programme of Study for Key Stage 3 and Attainment Target (Extract from the National Curriculum 2007)* (London, 2007), paragraph 1.2 under 'Key Concepts'; paragraph 3f under 'Range and Content'.

69. HA, *T.E.A.C.H.: Teaching Emotive and Controversial History* (London, 2007), p. 15.

70. www.healthyschools.gov.uk/Themes/Default.aspx (accessed 12 June 2009); www.teachernet.gov.uk/wholeschool/Communitycohesion/ (accessed 12 June 2009) – introduced in the Education and Inspections Act 2006.

71. HiEP: interview, L. Turner/R. Snow, 1 July 2010, p. 34.

72. DES, *Aspects of Primary Education: The Teaching and Learning of History and Geography* (London, 1989), pp. 8–10.

73. HiEP: interviews: A. Farmer, 9 July 2009, p. 13; P. Harnett, 9 September 2009, pp. 12–14.

74. HiEP: interview, P. Harnett, 9 September 2009, pp. 15–18; S. Purkis, 'Support for the Supplementaries', *PH*, no. 4 (1993), p. 8.

75. HiEP: surveys, AW/P80/HiE200; AH/P82/HiE193; AG/P90/HiE140.

76. J. Fines, 'No Nonsense!', *PH*, no. 6 (1994), pp. 4–6.

77. HiEP: interview, J. Nichol, 3 August 2009, p. 11; J. Fines and J. Nichol, *Teaching Primary History* (London, 1997) p. viii.

78. P. Noble, 'Editorial', *PH*, no. 2 (1992), p. 4; C.F. O'Neill, 'A Good Start?' *PH*, no. 3 (1993), pp. 8–9.

79. HiEP: interview, A. Reid, 4 September 2009, p. 24.

80. D. Sylvester, 'Change and Continuity in History Teaching, 1900–93', in H. Bourdillon (ed.), *Teaching History* (London, 1994), p. 19; F.M. Connelly, 'What is the Future for the History National Curriculum?', *TH*, no. 74 (1994), p. 23; Ofsted, *A Review of Primary Schools in England, 1994–1998* (London, 1998), paragraph 12.7, n.p., available at www.archjive.official-documents.co.uk/document/ofsted/ped/ped.htm (accessed 8 August 2011).

81. HiEP: interview, R. Hennessey, 11 November 2009, p. 18.

82. HiEP: interview, C. Culpin, 22 September 2009, p. 18.

83. HiEP: interviews: L. Turner/R. Snow, 1 July 2010, p. 26; D. Hughff, 8 April 2010, p. 11.

84. HiEP: surveys, RB/T48/HiE35; AF/T54/HiE67.

85. HiEP: surveys, JTS/T52/HiE40; BH/T57/HiE50; interview, C. Hinton, 11 January 2010, pp. 15–16.

86. R.J. Cootes, *Medieval Realms: Key Stage 3* (Walton-on-Thames, 1992); I. Dawson and P. Watson, *Medieval Realms, 1066–1500* (Oxford, 1991).

87. C. Culpin, *Making History: World History from 1914 to the Present Day* (Glasgow, 1984); J.D. Clare, *Agricultural Change since 1750* (Basingstoke, 1988); P. Harnett, *Ginn History, Key Stage 2, Teachers Handbook* (Aylesbury, 1991); I. Dawson, *Oxford History Study Units, Teachers Resource Books* (Oxford, 1992–95).

88. HiEP: interview, E. Evans, 29 June 2009, p. 7.

89. F. Blow and A.K. Dickinson, *New History and New Technology* (London, 1986), p. 9.

90. A. Ross, 'Microcomputers and Local History Work in a Primary School', *TH*, no. 36 (1983), pp. 10–14; *Times Educational Supplement*, 3 December 1993.

91. Ofsted, *ICT in Schools: Effect of Government Initiatives: Secondary History* (London, 2002), pp. 4–6; e.g. source materials on the First World War available at www.nationalarchives.gov.uk/pathways/firstworldwar/index. htm (accessed 25 March 2011).

92. See www.schoolhistory.co.uk/forum/index.php?showtopic=12998 for tributes to the 'virtual' support given by John D. Clare to other history teachers (accessed 31 March 2011).

93. HiEP: interview, C. Hinton, 11 January 2010, p. 25.

94. T. Haydn, 'Computers and History: Rhetoric, Reality and the Lessons of the Past', in T. Haydn and C. Counsell (eds), *History, ICT and Learning in the Secondary School* (London, 2003), p. 12; T. Haydn, 'History Teaching and ICT', in I. Davies (ed.), *Debates in History Teaching* (Abingdon, 2011), p. 237; Ofsted, *History for All: History in English Schools, 2007–10* (London, 2011), p. 52.

95. HiEP: information recorded in informal interview with J. Belbin, 19 November 2009.

96. N. Smith, *The History Teacher's Handbook* (London, 2010), p. 103.

97. D. Cannadine (ed.), *History and the Media* (Basingstoke, 2004); S. Schama, *A History of Britain*, vol. i, *At the Edge of the World?, 3000 BC–AD 1603* (London, 2000); vol. ii, *The British Wars, 1603–1776* (London, 2001); vol. iii, *The Fate of Empire, 1776–2000* (London, 2002).

98. HiEP: surveys, CG/T80/HiE111; FB/T81/HiE115; RB/T81/HiE125; RW/ T82/HiE116; JW/T83/HiE108.

99. HiEP: interview, J.D. Clare, 7 April 2010, p. 10.

100. HiEP: survey, ZB/P71/HiE115.

101. HiEP: surveys, ZB/P71/HiE115; RW/P73/HiE172.

102. HiEP: surveys, AL/P77/HiE183; KC/P79/HiE143; JH/P67/HiE185.

103. HiEP: surveys, EAC/P75/HiE176; AL/P77/HiE183; RW/P73/HiE172.

104. HiEP: surveys, MP/P79/Hie119; RW/P79/HiE117.

105. HiEP: surveys, AL/P77/HiE183; RW/P73/HiE172; EAC/P75/HiE176.
106. HiEP: survey, LB/P78/HiE150.
107. HiEP: surveys, GM/P70/HiE158; JD/P71/HiE116.
108. HiEP: information from informal interview with I. Colwill, 17 June 2010.
109. Phillips, *History Teaching*, pp. 22–3.
110. A. Low-Beer, 'Empathy in History', *TH*, no. 55 (1989), pp. 8–12; Southern Regional History Examinations Board Working Paper, *Empathy in History: From Definition to Assessment* (Eastleigh, 1986); C. Portal, 'Empathy as an Objective for History Teaching', in C. Portal (ed.), *The History Curriculum for Teachers* (Lewes, 1987), pp. 93–4; HiEP: surveys, MP/P79/HiE119; MP/P79/HiE119.
111. HiEP: interview, C. McGovern, 28 August 2009, p. 5; Phillips, *History Teaching*, p. 44.
112. See Appendix E for this and subsequent paragraphs.
113. Baker, *Turbulent Years*, pp. 220–1.
114. C. White, 'The Dearing Final Report – Threat or Opportunity?', *TH*, no. 75 (1994), p. 5; Fines, 'No Nonsense!', p. 4.
115. HiEP: interview, C. Culpin, 2 September 2009, pp. 14–15.
116. Ofsted, *History in the Balance: History in English Schools, 2003–07* (London, 2007), pp. 7, 11; Ofsted, *History for All*, p. 4.
117. Ofsted, *History For All*, pp. 5, 13–15, 22.
118. HA, *Primary History Survey (England): 3–11* (London, 2011), p. 5; Ofsted, *History for All*, p. 5.
119. www.qca.org.uk/qca_10325.aspx (accessed 16 June 2009); R. Harris and T. Haydn, '30% Is Not Bad Considering ...', *TH*, no 134, (2009), pp. 27–34.
120. Ofsted, *History for All*, pp. 48–9; HiEP: interview: D. Hughff, 8 April 2010, p. 17.
121. C. Culpin, 'What Kind of History Should School History Be?', *The Historian*, xcv (2007), p. 9.
122. Ofsted, *History in the Balance*, p. 14.
123. Ofsted, *History for All*, pp. 40, 45.
124. Ofsted, *History in the Balance*, pp. 22–4; HiEP: survey, JW/T83/HiE108.
125. HiEP: interview, P. Lee/R. Ashby, 3 September 2009, p. 45.
126. Ofsted, *History in the Balance*, p. 4.
127. Ofsted, *History in the Balance*, p. 4.
128. Ofsted, *History for All*, p. 6; HA, *Findings from the Historical Association Survey of Secondary History Teachers* (London, 2010), available at www.history.org.uk/resources/secondary_resource_3754_8.html (accessed 9 August 2011).
129. Ofsted, *History in the Balance*, p. 7; Ofsted, *History for All*, p. 8.

Conclusion

1. B. Bailyn, *Education in the Forming of American Society* (New York, 1960), p. 14.

2. For one recent example, see F.L. Kan, *Hong Kong's Chinese History Curriculum from 1945: Politics and Identity* (Hong Kong, 2007).

3. The full list is printed as Appendix F. There is a discrepancy between the number of names (49) and the number of terms of office (55). This is accounted for by the fact that Wood/Irwin, Trevelyan, Eccles and Hailsham/Hogg held the office twice, and that the title was changed during the tenure of R.A. Butler and Gillian Shephard.

4. To be sure, Wilkinson died in office, and Williams and Shephard were unlucky in that the governments of which they were members were defeated at the polls and were out of power for many years. Nevertheless, the general pattern is both clear and suggestive.

5. *Report of the Proceedings of the Tenth Annual Meeting Held at University College, London, on Friday 7th January, and Saturday 8th January 1916* (HA, leaflet no. 41, London, 1916), p. 14.

6. S.T. Coleridge, *Constitution of Church and State* (London, 1830), p. 65.

7. HiEP: interview, K. Ingham, 24 March 2010, p. 9.

8. D. Cannadine, *Making History Now and Then: Discoveries, Controversies and Explorations* (London, 2008), pp. 27–32.

9. R.J. Evans, 'The Wonderfulness of Us (the Tory Interpretation of History)', *London Review of Books*, 17 March 2011, pp. 9–12; Letters, *London Review of Books*, 14 April 2011, pp. 5–6; N. Ferguson, 'History has Never Been so Unpopular', *Guardian*, 29 March 2011.

10. A. Elliott, *State Schools since the 1950s: The Good News* (Stoke on Trent, 2007), pp. vii, 59, 135.

11. S. Schama, 'My Vision for History in Schools', *Guardian*, 9 November 2010; N. Ferguson, 'Too Much Hitler and the Henrys', *Financial Times*, 9 April 2010.

12. K. Crawford and S. Foster, 'The Political Economy of History Textbook Publishing in England', in J. Nicholls (ed.), *School History Textbooks Across Cultures* (Oxford, 2006), pp. 93–104.

13. HiEP: interview, T. Lomas, 30 March, 2009, p. 29.

14. HiEP: interview, C. Hinton, 11 January 2010, p. 27.

15. HiEP: interview, S. Ensor, 15 June 2010, pp. 16–17.

Index

Compiled by Sue Carlton

Page numbers in **bold** refer to photographs

1066 and All That (Sellar and
    Yeatman) 75, 99, 115

A Level exams 16, 116, 156, 214–15,
    234–5, 254
  increasing pass rate 215, 216
  see also examinations; General
    Certificate of Education
A Level/Sixth Form courses 136, 154,
    165, 170, 175–7, 202
  quality of teaching 212–13
  repetition 171, 197, 235
  textbooks 122
  virtual learning environments
    209–10
academies 191, 218, 225
Acton, John Dalberg, Lord 30
Addison, Christopher 137
Ajegbo report on citizenship 201
America (BBC series-Cooke) 178
*Annual Bulletin of Historical
    Literature* 33
Asquith, H.H. 21
'assisted places' scheme 182
Associated Examining Board 116,
    155–6, 192, 214–15
Associated-Rediffusion 124
atlases 49, 52, 75, 86, 90, 120, 169
Australia
  and aborigines 2
  national narrative 1–2

baby-boomers 108, 121, 157, 184
Bachelor of Education degree 157
Baker, Kenneth 186–7, 189, 193–4,
    202, 215, 222
  and history as compulsory subject
    to age 16 197, 224
Baldwin, Stanley 65, 66, 103

Balfour Education Act *see* Education
    Act (1902)
Balls, Ed 191
Barnett, Correlli 181
Barrie, James 37
Barrow, R.H. 125
Baynes, N.H. 78
BBC 82–3, 123–4, 126, 134, 163–4
Beales, A.C.F. 117–18
Bell, Vanessa 61
Belloc, Hilaire 95
Beloe Report (1960) 117
Bermondsey Central Technical School
    91
Better Schools (White Paper) 185, 186
Bevin, Ernest 104
Bindoff, S.T. 138
biographies 24, 44, 48, 71, 73, 120–1
Birrell, Augustine 20, 21, 223
birth rate 108, 184
Black Papers 178–9
blackboard 130
  see also chalk-and-talk
Blair, Tony 189–90
Bledisloe, Charles Bathurst, Viscount
    137
Blishen, Edward 125
'block grant' scheme 18, 19, 23, 49
Blunkett, David 102, 190–1, 201,
    222, 224
Blyth, Joan 168
Board of Education 4, 18, 20–3, 68
  Consultative Committee 61, 68–70,
    80
  during First World War 57–8, 59
  during Second World War 97, 100
  and film and broadcasting 82, 83
  guidance to teachers and inspectors
    23–8, 36, 45, 54, 58, 70–3, 79

Board of Education *continued*
  and inspectorate 47, 85
  permanent secretaries 21–2, 63, 68
  Presidents 20–1, 22, 61–8, 102–4, 221, 222
  and propaganda 57–8, 95–6
  and School Certificate 29, 76
Board of Education recommendations 24, 26, 45–6
Bonar Law, Andrew 65
Booth, Martin 136
Boyle, Sir Edward 109–10, 117, 223
Boyson, Rhodes 178
Bridge, G.F. 45
Briggs, Asa 125
Britain
  national decline 140–1, 147–8, 154
  national narrative 3
British Empire 8, 152
  school broadcasting and 83
  teaching about 14, 24, 54, 55–6, 58, 76, 86, 95–6, 137
  textbooks and 54
British Film Institute 82
British history 24, 36, 58, 71–3, 90, 126, 182
  in international context 72, 152, 154
  and National Curriculum 194, 196, 206, 217
Brown, George 142
Brown, Gordon 190, 191
Bruce, William N. 28, 61–2
Bryce, James 1, 34–6, 38, 61
Bulmershe College of Education (Reading) 157
Burnham scale 64
Burt, Cyril 79–80, 108
Burwell County Secondary School (Cambridgeshire) 169
Bury, J.B. 30
Butler, R.A. 4, 67, 102–6, 110, 118, 222
  see also Education Act (1944)

Callaghan, James 141, 142, 146, 147, 179–80, 184
Carlisle, Mark 182, 183, 185, 223
Carlyle, Thomas 30

Carnegie Trust 82
Central Advisory Council for Education 109, 148
Central Council for School Broadcasting 83
Centre for Policy Studies 183
Century of Change – 1860–1960, A (BBC series) 124
Certificate of Secondary Education (CSE) 117, 139, 155, 156, 170–1
  abolition of 185, 213
  and coursework 161, 164, 192
  examination results 252
  experimental 160
  influence on GCSE 192, 193
  marking standards 177
  and new history 173
  and world history 154, 165, 170
  see also examinations
chalk-and-talk 117, 129–30, 160, 165, 171, 177, 211, 212, 227, 228
  see also oral methods; stories; teachers, inspirational
Chamberlain, Neville 66, 67, 103
child psychology 10, 37, 158–9
Child Study Society 37
'child-centred' education 10, 78, 79, 119, 149, 157, 166, 177
  criticism of 179, 182
children's magazines 37, 138
chronological approach 50, 74–5, 126, 127–8, 132, 134, 150, 168
  Board of Education guidance 23, 24–5, 26, 71, 112
  and HA guidance 33, 34
  and National Curriculum 194, 197, 217, 236
  neglect of 58–9, 157, 165, 217, 234
  schools broadcasting 164
  and textbooks 120
  see also dates; kings and queens; time charts/timelines
Churchill, Winston 67, 98, 102–3, 105, 107–8, 110, 230
Chuter Ede, James 104
Circular 10/65 (DES) 143, 144–5
Circular 849 (Board of Education) 29, 76

citizenship 80, 90, 111, 190, 221, 229
  Ajegbo report on 201
  Board of Education guidance 24,
    25, 59–60, 75
  and HA guidance 34, 36
  National Curriculum and 200, 216
civil servants 5–6, 181–2, 226, 236
Civilisation (BBC series-Clark) 178
civilization, development of 26, 62, 72
Clare, John D. 208
Clark, Kenneth 178
Clarke, Charles 191, 223
Clarke, Kenneth 187–8, 189, 197,
  200, 202, 206, 223
class size 65, 85, 106, 190
Code of Regulations for Day Schools
  23, 49
Coleridge, S.T. 229
colleges of education 9, 157, 189,
  203, 205
Collie, Frances 51
Collingwood, R.G. 78
Coltham, Jeanette B. 159–60
Common, Jack 50
Common Market 140, 141
Commonwealth history 72, 73, 101,
  113, 155
comprehensive schooling 70, 97, 105,
  106, 109–11, 141, 181–2
  comprehensive revolution 142–8,
    154–5, 156, 173, 180, 202, 225
  concerns about standards 178–80
  and GCSE 192
  and history teaching 7, 131–2, 142,
    148–66, 168, 170, 173, 175
  HMIs and 169–71
  Labour Party and 97, 106, 108, 139
  and new subjects 176–7
computers 209
continuous assessment 186
Cooke, Alastair 178
Cootes, R.J. 162, 208
Core Study Units 197–8, 200
corporal punishment 40
Coulton, C.G. 36–7
counter-revolution in education
    (Thatcher government) 180, 182,
    184–9, 202–3
coursework 155, 161, 164, 192, 209

Cowie, Rev. Leonard W. 122
Cox, Brian 178
Crewe, Robert Crewe-Milnes,
  Marquis of 21
Crick, Bernard 190
Croft, Michael 125
Crosland, Anthony 142, 143, 146–7,
  223
Crossman, Richard 142
curiosity 10, 25, 39, 43–4, 79, 112,
  129
Curriculum Study Group 138

Dalton Plan 80
dates 26, 35, 48, 71–2, 75, 81, 95,
  229, 236
  access through internet 210, 236
  memorizing 14–15, 33, 51, 72, 94,
    129, 130
  reaction against 58–9, 72, 80, 161,
    171
  see also chronological approach;
    time charts/timelines,
    rote-learning
Dawson, Ian 208
De la Mare, Walter 37
De la Warr, Herbrand Sackville, ninth
  Earl 67
Dearing, Sir Ron 199–200
denominational schools 18, 20, 104
Dent, H.C. 40
Department of Education and Science
  145, 179, 181–2, 185
Department of Innovation,
  Universities and Skills 191
Devonshire, Spencer Cavendish,
  eighth Duke of 20, 21, 22, 222
Dewey, John 79
Dictionary of National Biography 31
Docking, J.W. 155
drama 71, 88, 120, 150, 157, 161,
  164, 173–5, 204
'dramatic' method 37–8, 46
Dudley College of Education 157
duplicating machines 122
Dyson, A.E. 178

Eastfield County Secondary School for
  Boys (Wolverhampton) 168

Eastney County Secondary School for Boys (Portsmouth) 169
Eccles, David 102, 108–9, 110, 138, 222
Edexcel 234
Education Act (1870) (Forster's) 18, 42, 64
Education Act (1902) (Balfour) 5, 20–1, 22, 59, 63, 103, 141
Education Act (1918) (Fisher's) 64, 104, 222, 225
Education Act (1936) 66, 67
Education Act (1944) (Butler's) 5, 104–6, 107, 110, 126, 222, 225
Education Act (1976) 146–7, 182
Education of the Adolescent, The (Hadow Report 1927) 61, 68, 74–5
Education Reform Act (1988) 5, 186–7, 222
education spending 108, 110, 145, 146, 190–2, 224–5
    cuts 64, 65, 66, 77, 182–3, 222, 225
education system
    administration of 4–6
    see also Board of Education; ministers of education; Ministry of Education
Educational Foundation for Visual Aids 123
Educational Objectives for the Study of History (HA pamphlet) 159–60
Edwards, O.M.E. 44
elementary schools 18–25, 40–3, 48–52, 54–5, 56, 87–8
    see also elementary/secondary system; primary schools
elementary/secondary system 18–101
    during First World War 55–60
    during Second World War 97–101
    inter-war years 61–96
    pre-First World War 18–55
eleven-plus 106, 108, 109, 147
    phasing out of 143, 146, 148, 154, 157, 166
    see also selection; tripartite system
Elton, G.R. 122, 138

empathy 15, 161, 162, 192, 193, 202, 213–14, 230
Empire Day 15, 53, 54, 56, 96, **96**
Employment of Children Act (1903) 41
English Historical Review 30, 32
English history 23, 26, 45, 74, 76, 127–8
ethnic diversity 171, 192, 196, 200, 201, 221
European history 53, 90, 94, 140
    A level syllabus 156, 165, 170, 214–15
    Board of Education recommendations 24, 26, 36, 57, 74
    and examinations 76, 112
    HA and 33, 101
    and National Curriculum 198, 233
    O level syllabus 127–8, 155
    textbooks 121–2
European Union 181
Evans, David 62
Evans, Eric 177, 208
Every Child Matters 200–1
examinations 16, 28–30, 76–7, 112, 244–5
    boards 28–9, 234
    impact on history teaching 77, 78–9, 94–5, 100, 127–8, 137, 168–9
    and internal assessment 115–16
    numbers choosing O Level, A Level and CSE courses 136–7, 175–7, 215, 216
    problems of parallel systems of GCE and CSE 177
    results 251–4
    standardization 29, 35, 193
    and world history 154
    see also Certificate of Secondary Education; General Certificate of Education; General Certificate of Secondary Education; Higher School Certificate; School Certificate

Featherstone High School (Ealing) 170

Ferguson, Niall 210
film 82, 83, 122–3, 208–9
    projectors 82, 123, 134
filmstrips 122
Fines, John 157, 159–60, 204
Finlay-Johnson, Harriet 37–8, 39, 46
First Churchills, The (BBC drama)
    178
First World War 29, 55–60, 63, 74
    BBC documentaries on 178
Firth, C.B. 80
Firth, C.H. 30, 32, 54–5, 73
Fisher, H.A.L. 21, 61–5, 67, 96, 102,
    183, 222
    interest in history 61, 62, 68, 73–4,
    224
    opinion of Morant 22
    and school broadcasting 83
    and teacher training 77–8
    and teachers pay and conditions 77
    see also Education Act (1918)
Fletcher, C.R.L. 45
Forster, W.E. 18, 42, 64
Forsyte Saga, The (BBC drama) 178
Fourth Reform Act (1918) 59–60
Framework for Expansion 145
France 19–20, 31, 56
free school milk 106
Freeman, Anthony 213
Freeman, Edward Augustus 30
Froude, J.A. 30
Fulham County Secondary School 53,
    54

Gardiner, S.R. 30, 44
Geddes Axe (1922) 64, 65, 67
General Certificate of Education
    (GCE) 116–17, 154, 155–6, 165
    see also A Levels; examinations; O
    Levels
General Certificate of Secondary
    Education (GCSE) 16, 185–6,
    192–3, 202, 213–14
    history syllabuses 192
    and National Curriculum 197, 200,
    206, 213, 234–5
    pass rates 216
    see also examinations
George V, King 96, 230

Germany 31, 67, 102–3
Gomm, Amy 50–1
Google 210, 236
Gordon Walker, Patrick 142, 143
governors/governing bodies 185, 186
Grahame, Kenneth 37
grammar schools 7, 69–70, 107,
    108–9, 141, 179
    and comprehensive revolution
    142–3, 145, 146, 147, 169, 182,
    187
    and external examinations 116
    and extra-curricular activities 125
    and history teaching 90, 112–13,
    127–31, 171–3
    see also selection; tripartite system
Great War, The (BBC documentary-
    Terraine) 178
Green Book 104, 125
Green, J.R. 30, 44
Green, V.H.H. 122

Hadow, Sir William 68–9, 70, 72,
    74–5, 79
Hailsham, Viscount (*later* Quintin
    Hogg) 108, 109, 110, 223
Haldane, Richard, Lord 22, 63
Halifax, Edward Wood, Lord *see*
    Wood, Edward
Hankin, G.T. 83
Hanson, Alfred 100
Happold, F. Crossfield 80
Harborne Hill County Modern School
    (Birmingham) 134
Harnett, Penelope 208
Hastings High School for Girls 127
Headlam (*later* Headlam-Morley),
    James Wycliffe 25–8, 56, 57–8,
    74
Hearnshaw, F.J.C. 36
Heath, Edward 140, 141, 144, 145,
    146, 182, 224
Henderson, Arthur 21
heritage 31, 115, 178, 196, 204
Heritage Foundation (US) 2
higher education 191
    expansion 9, 139, 141, 157
    see also universities

Higher School Certificate 16, 29, 76, 89, 94, 95, 116
Historical Association (HA) 8, 31–9, 54, 73, 78–9
 50th anniversary exhibition 117–18
 and film 82
 and First World War 59
 and illustrations 33, 46, 81
 and National Curriculum 195
 and Norwood Report 101
 Teaching History journal 159
History Alive series 162–3
History in Education website 257
History (HA journal) 33, 79, 98, 99, 100
History Long Ago (BBC series) 163, 164
History Not So Long Ago (BBC series) 163, 164
History and Social Sciences Teachers' Centre (Clapham) 164–5
history teaching
 and academic fashions 9–10, 16
 co-ordinated with allied subjects 27, 35, 133, 159
 continuity and change 227–32
 and cultural differences 220–1
 early views on 30–9
 and government 221–6
 inadequacy of 31–2, 33–4, 35, 42, 48–55, 227–8
 selective approach 27–8
 syllabuses after 1970 246–50
 and timetable pressures 13, 200–1, 202, 216–17, 219, 234, 236
History Working Group 194–6
HMIs (Inspectors of Schools) 5, 16, 47–9, 149, 166, 179, 184, 228
 during Second World War 125–6
 encouraging school visits 23
 and end of tripartite system 168–71, 180
 inter-war years 85–6, 88–9
 post-Second World war era 126, 127, 131
 replaced by Ofsted 187–8, 202
 see also Office for Standards in Education (Ofsted)
Hogg, Quintin *see* Hailsham, Viscount

Holland Park Comprehensive School 110
Holloway Comprehensive School 131, 132
Holmes, E.G.A. 38–9, 47–8, 79
Holmes, Sir Maurice 68, 226
Horsbrugh, Florence 107–8, 110, 144, 224
How Things Began (radio series) 123
How We Used to Live (Yorkshire Television) 164
Howard, John 2
Howard, Miss M.A. 31–2, 33–4, 36
Hughes, Bettany 210
humanities 159
Humanities for the Young School Leaver (Schools Council) 159

ICT revolution 210, 211, 232
 see also computers; internet
illustrations 33, 46, 52, 74, 81
 in textbooks 44, 80–1, 162–3
imagination 15, 25, 34, 37–8, 43, 45, 71, 112, 121
 sympathetic understanding 115, 160, 195, 214
 see also empathy
 see also drama; stories; teachers, inspirational; visual aids
Inner London Education Authority, abolition of 186, 202
Institute of Education 43
Institute of Historical Research 62
institutes of education 118
Instructions for Inspectors 23
intelligence
 fixed levels of 110
 testing 80, 105, 108
interactive whiteboard 210
internet 209–10
Iraq, invasion of 190
Isaacs, Jeremy 178
Islington Green School, written work **158, 174**
ITV 124, 163–4

Jackdaw series 163, 172
Jarvis, Charles 58
Jay, Douglas 142

Jeffreys, M.V.C. 80, 99, 100
Johnson, Alan 191
Johnson, F.H. 81
Joseph Rowntree Secondary School (New Earswick) 127
Joseph, Sir Keith 102, 145, 182–7, 189, 192, 193, 202, 214, 222
Junior History series (OUP) 162, 163

Keatinge, M.W. 38, 39
Kekewich, Sir George 21–2
Kelly, Ruth 191, 224
Kentish Town County Secondary School 52–3
Kesteven and Grantham Girls' school 144
Key Stage tests 193
  see also Standard Assessment Tests
kings and queens 45, 48, 56, 74, 172, 194
  accessing information on internet 236
  memorizing 15, 41, 51, 120, 130, 149
Kipling, Rudyard 45, 53

Lady Lumley's Grammar School (Pickering) 127
Ladybird books 120–1, 162
Lancaster Pamphlet series 208
Lane, Allen 138
Lavender Hill School, written work 84
Law, Richard 105, 110
League of Nations 60, 72, 75, 86–7, 97, 98, 100
Lee-Smith, Hastings 66, 67
Lessons from Europe: A Comparison of British and West European Schooling (Centre for Policy Studies) 183
Lewis, E.O. 55
libraries
  school 34, 52, 86, 169
  training colleges 43, 78
life-long learning 25
'lines of development' method 80, 90, 99, 198
Linklater Thompson, Miss C. 45, 81

literacy 151, 191, 201, 218
literacy hours 200
Littlehampton Comprehensive School, written work 153
Liverpool Girls' School 51
Lloyd, Geoffrey 108, 109, 110
Lloyd George, David 21, 61, 62, 64, 73, 77
Lodge, Richard 54
London Day Training College 43
London Review of Books 231
London schools, 1927 report on history teaching 86
Londonderry, Charles Vane-Tempest-Stewart, Marquis of 20, 21, 22, 47
Longford, Frank Pakenham, Lord 142
Low-Beer, Ann 168
Lucas, C.P. 54
Luton Secondary Technical School 168–9

Macaulay, Thomas Babington 24, 30
MacDonald, Ramsay 66
McGovern, Chris 213
MacGregor, John 187, 194, 195
McKenna, Reginald 20–1
Mackie, J.D. 99–100
Mackinder, Halford 54
Maclean, Sir Donald 66, 67
Macmillan, Harold 107, 108
McMillan, Margaret and Rachel 79
McNair, Sir Arnold 118
Madeley, Helen 80
magic lanterns/lantern-slides 45–6, 81–2, 86, 88, 122
Maitland, F.W. 30, 61
Major, John 187
Manor Secondary Modern School for Girls (Cambridgeshire) 169
maps 53, 71, 75, 89, 90, 122, 129
Marten, C.H.K. 36, 78–9, 81
Maud, Sir John 106–7
Maude, Francis S. 62
Mauldeth Road Primary School (Manchester), written work 97
Mayflower Histories 80
Meath, Lord 54, 230
Meccano 37

medical inspections 22
Men of the Past – From the Remotest Past to Roman times (BBC series) 124
Minchinden Grammar School (North London), written work **114**
ministers of education 5, 221–4, 225–6, 236, 255–6
see also Board of Education, Presidents; Secretaries of State
Ministry of Education 4, 110, 111, 116, 119–20, 123–4, 137, 235
Montessori, Maria 79
Morant, Sir Robert 22, 28, 42–3, 47, 68, 226
Morecambe Grammar School, written work **133**
Morris, Estelle 191, 224, 226
Moss, Peter 163
Mowat, R.B. 81, 83, 121
Muir, Ramsay 55
Mulley, Fred 146, 147
Mullin, Chris 191–2
multiple choice questions 193
Myers, J.N.L. 78

National Curriculum 185, 192, 193–202, 225, 233–4
additional subjects imposed under Labour 200–1, 202, 216–17
assessment stages and targets 199, 200, 203, 206
and controversial topics 201, 202
developments towards 178–80
and GCSE and A Level courses 213, 234–5
impact on history teaching 203–9, 216–18, 226
review and revision of 199–200
and teacher training standards 189
truncated at age 14 197, 200, 206, 218, 222, 227, 234
National Curriculum Council 196
History Task Group 199, 204
national identity 1, 14–15, 19–20, 56, 137, 220–1
national narrative 1–3, 10, 128, 141–2, 165, 177–8, 194, 221
National Rifle Association (US) 2

National Society for the Prevention of Cruelty to Children 37
National Trust 31, 124, 138, 178, 210
National Union of Teachers 42
Nechells County Modern School (Birmingham) 134
Nelson's Highways of History 44
Nesbit, Edith 37
New Education Fellowship 39, 79
New Era, The 39
'new history' 165–6, 173, **174**, 194
new schools 106, 107
Newsom, John 81
Newsom Report 81, 110, 151–2, 154
Newton, Arthur 55–6
Nichol, Jon 204
Norbury Manor County Secondary Girls' School (Croydon) 134
Northallerton Grammar School 127
Northern Ireland 4
Norwood Report (1943) 105, 115–16, 125–6
Norwood, Sir Cyril 100–1, 105
Nuffield Primary History Project 204–5
numeracy 151, 191, 201, 218
numeracy hours 200
nursery schools 79
free places 190

O Level courses and exams 16, 116–17, 159, 160
abolition of 185
experimental 160
history syllabus 127–8, 155–6, 165, 170–1, 175
and SCHP course 161, 162
see also examinations
Office for Standards in Education (Ofsted) 188–9, 202, 235
reports 205, 216–18, 219, 233
and use of technology 209
see also HMIs (Inspectors of Schools)
Olivier, Laurence 178
oral methods 49, 53, 117, 120, 169
see also chalk-and-talk; teachers, inspirational

Oxford and Cambridge Examination Board 28
Oxford and Cambridge Universities, and history degree courses 30–1

pageants 30, 46, 88, 124–5
Parkhurst, Helen 80
Parliament Hill County School for Girls 89
'patch method' 119, 134, 165
patriotism 2, 20, 34, 53, 56, 97, 103, 137–8, 197, 229–30
Patten, John 188, 199, 223
'payment by results' 18, 19
Peach, Lawrence du Garde 120–1
Pearson 234
Pease, Joseph Albert 21
pedagogy 7, 13, 37, 103, 219
    and culture 219
    traditional 171, 182, 187
Pelham, Sir Edward 68
Percy, Lord Eustace 65–6, 67, 68, 83, 97, 102, 103, 222, 223
photocopiers 163
physical education 67, 151
Piaget, Jean 158–9
Piers Plowman Histories 44, 81, 83
Plowden Report 148–50, 154
Pollard, A.F. 30, 31–2, 33, 44, 45, 82
Potter, Beatrix 37
Power, Eileen and Rhoda 80, 83
Prentice, Reg 146, 147
Price, Mary 159
Primary History Association 203
Primary History (journal) 205
Primary School The (Hadow Report 1931) 72, 79
primary schools 106, 107, 112, 120–1, 126–7, 235
    after comprehensive revolution 148–50, 165–6, 168
    building programme 145
    and National Curriculum 200–1, 203–6, 216, 218
    see also elementary schools; Plowden Report
Priory School (Lewes) 213
progressive education 79–80, 119, 169, 171, 177, 193, 202

progressive history 227–8
projectors 81, 210
    ceiling-mounted data projectors 209
    film 82, 123, 134
    filmstrip 122
projects/topics 126, 150, 166–8, 172
pupil-teachers 42–3, 63, 117
pupils
    experiences of history teaching 11–15, 48–55, 83–5
    medical inspections 22
    recollections 87–8, 90–4, 126–31, 135–6, 166–8, 171–6, 204, 211–13, 228–9, 238
    strikes 40
Putin, Vladimir 1

Raine's Foundation School for Boys, (East London) **93**
Ramsbotham, Herwald 67
Ransome, Mrs 44
Ravenscroft Comprehensive School (Barnet) 170
Rayner, Brigadier 137
readers 44–5, 49, 54
    see also textbooks and readers
Reagan, Ronald 2
Redgrave, Michael 178
Reed Brett, Sidney 121–2
Reeves, Marjorie 119, 121
Reid, Dr Rachel 31, 32, 101
Reigate Grammar School (Surrey) 127
religious instruction 151, 159
Report on the Teaching of History (1923) 74, 78
resources 10–11, 16
    see also libraries; school visits; textbooks; visual aids
Riley, Michael 208
Roan Boys School (Greenwich) 52, 89
Robbins Report 138–9, 157
Roberts, Robert 53
Rolph, C.H. 50
Rose, Jonathan 40, 48
rote learning 40, 41, 51, 87, 88, 120, 227
    see also dates, memorizing; kings and queens, memorizing

Royal Commission on Historical Monuments 31
Royal Historical Society 30, 32
Rudé, George 131–2
Runciman, Walter 21
Russia 1

Sadler, Sir Michael 22
St Chad's College (Wolverhampton) 169
St Edmund's Roman Catholic Secondary Modern School (Portsmouth) 169
Samuel, Raphael 196
Schama, Simon 210, 211
scholarship scheme 22
school boards 18
    abolition of 20, 22
School Broadcasting Council 163
school broadcasts
    radio 82–3, 120, 123, 163, 164
    television 123–4, 163–4
school buildings 40, 63, 84, **84**, 85, 110, 191
    improving 191
    school-building programme 84, 106, 108, 145
School Certificate 16, 29, 76, 78–9, 94–5, 96, 100, 115–17, 136
school leaving age 18, 41, 63, 68, 107
    raising to 11 12
    raising to 14 12, 64, 227
    raising to 15 12, 65, 66, 67, 69, 106, 116, 118, 224
    raising to 16 70, 97, 104, 106, 109, 143, 145, 154–5
school meals 22, 40, 106
Schools Council for the Curriculum and Examinations 138, 145, 149, 159, 160, 177, 184, 193
    abolition of 193, 202
Schools Council History Project (SCHP) (*later* Schools History Project (SHP)) 160–2, 165, 193, 194, 213
Schools Curriculum Assessment Authority (SCAA) 199–200

Schools History Project (SHP) 194, 213
    see also Schools Council History Project (SCHP)
Scotland 4, 194
Scott, Sir Walter 38
Second World War 67, 97–101, 118
secondary modern schools 7, 69, 107, 108–9, 125
    and examinations 116–17
    and history teaching 113, 115, 118, 132, 134–5, 169, 171–2
secondary schools 25–30, 41–4, 52–5, 69–70, 73–7, 88
    see also comprehensive schooling; grammar schools; secondary modern schools; technical high schools; tripartite system
Secondary Schools Examinations Council 76, 94, 116, 117
Secretaries of State 147
Seeley, J.R. 30, 53
Selby-Bigge, Sir Lewis 22–3, 61, 63, 68, 85
selection 70, 79–80, 108, 149
    ending 143, 144, 146, 147
    see also eleven-plus
Sellar, W.C. 75
Shephard, Gillian 181, 188, 189, 224
Short, Edward 143–4, 147, 224
Simkin, John 163
Skidelsky, Robert 195–6, 214
skills versus content debate 195–6, 230–1
Snellgrove, L.E. 162
social engineering 180, 190
social history 74, 75, 90, 101, 124, 131, 162, 209, 213, 229
social studies 132–3, 159, 169, 170
Southern Universities Board 162
Spens, Will 69–70, 75, 76–7, 97, 102
Stalin, Joseph 1, 229
Standard Assessment Tests (SATs) 199–200
    see also Key Stage tests
Stanhope, Earl 66–7, 68, 224
Stanley, Oliver 66, 67
Stanley Technical Trade School (Croydon) 131